Berghahn Books
NEW YORK · OXFORD

Croatian Film Association

First edition published in 2012 by Hrvatski filmski savez (Croatian Film Association) www.hfs.hr

In association with Berghahn Books www.berghahnbooks.com

© 2012 by the Croatian Film Association (Hrvatski filmski savez)

All rights reserved. Except for the quotation of short passages for the purposes of criticism and review, no part of this book may be reproduced in any form or by any means, electronic or mechanical, including photocopying, recording, or any information storage and retrieval system now known or to be invented, without written permission of the publisher.

British Library Cataloguing in Publication Data
A catalogue record for this book is available from the British Library

Berghahn books ISBN 978-0-85745-894-0 (paperback)

For the publisher:
Vera Robić

Editor of the Croatian Film Association's Publication Series (Naklada Hrvatskog filmskog saveza): Diana Nenadić

Design: Mileusnić+Serdarević
Printed by: Intergrafika
Zagreb, May 2012

Publication of this book has been made possible by the financial support of the Croatian Audiovisual Centre, and the American Councils for International Education (ACTR/ ACCELS) with funding through the National Endowment for the Humanities.

Cataloging-in-Publication Data Available in the computer catalogue of the National and University Library in Zagreb under number 805006

Croatian Film Association ISBN 978-953-7033-38-5

Library of Congress Cataloging-in-Publication Data

In contrast : Croatian film today / edited by Aida Vidan & Gordana P. Crnković -- 1st ed.
  p. cm.
  Includes filmography.
  Includes bibliographical references and index.
  ISBN 978-0-85745-894-0 (pbk. : alk. paper)
1. Motion pictures--Croatia--History--21st century. 2. Motion pictures--Croatia--History--20th century. 3. Motion pictures--Croatia--Reviews. I. Vidan, Aida. II. Crnković, Gordana P., 1963-
  PN1993.5.C87I53 2012
  791.43094972--dc23
                  2012020414

In Contrast:
Croatian Film Today

Edited by Aida Vidan & Gordana P. Crnković

Contents

10	**In Contrast: Croatian Film Today** by Aida Vidan
	Essays
21	**Croatian Film in the Yugoslav Context in the Second Half of the Twentieth Century** by Ivo Škrabalo
41	**Institutions, Infrastructure, Industry: Croatian Film or a Battle for Survival** by Tomislav Kurelec
49	**From a Cinema of Hatred to a Cinema of Consciousness: Croatian Film after Yugoslavia** by Jurica Pavičić
59	**The New Croatian Documentary: Between the Political and the Personal** by Diana Nenadić
76	**Croatian Animation, Then and Now: Creating Sparks or Just a Little Bit of Smoke?** by Sanja Bahun
89	**Gender in Contemporary Croatian Film** by Mima Simić
	Conversations
100	**A Conversation with Rajko Grlić:** *Films Are Stories About People, Not About Ideas* by Aida Vidan and Gordana P. Crnković
116	**A Conversation with Vinko Brešan:** *No Aesthetics without Ethics* by Aida Vidan and Gordana P. Crnković
129	**A Conversation with Joško Marušić:** *Sending Messages to Unknown Friends* by Sanja Bahun
136	**A Conversation with Nenad Puhovski:** *Documentarism as a Personal and Social Mission* by Diana Nenadić

Reviews

152   Dalibor Matanić: *Fine Dead Girls*
(*Fine mrtve djevojke*, 2002)
reviewed by Marko Dumančić

158   Kristijan Milić: *The Living and the Dead*
(*Živi i mrtvi*, 2007)
reviewed by Nikica Gilić

162   Rajko Grlić: *Border Post*
(*Karaula*, 2006)
reviewed by Vida Johnson

169   Ognjen Sviličić: *Sorry for Kung Fu*
(*Oprosti za kung fu*, 2004); *Armin* (2007)
reviewed by Hana Jušić

176   Antonio Nuić: *Sex, Drink and Bloodshed*
(*Seks, piće i krvoproliće*, 2004); *All for Free*
(*Sve džaba*, 2006); *Donkey* (*Kenjac*, 2009)
reviewed by Mario Kozina

183   Lukas Nola: *Celestial Body*
(*Nebo, sateliti*, 2000);
Alone (*Sami*, 2001)
reviewed by Bruno Kragić

188   Snježana Tribuson: *The Three Men
of Melita Žganjer*
(*Tri muškarca Melite Žganjer*, 1998)
reviewed by Karla Lončar

192   Arsen Anton Ostojić:
A Wonderful Night in Split
(*Ta divna splitska noć*, 2003)
reviewed by Inna Mattei

196   Vinko Brešan: *How the War Started
on My Island* (*Kako je počeo rat na mom otoku*, 1996);
Witnesses (*Svjedoci*, 2003);
Will Not End Here (*Nije kraj*, 2008)
reviewed by Katarina Mihailović

202   Goran Rušinović:
Buick Riviera, 2008
reviewed by Nataša Milas

206	**Goran Dević and Zvonimir Jurić:** *The Blacks* (*Crnci*, 2009) reviewed by Lorraine Mortimer
211	**Krsto Papić:** *When the Dead Start Singing* (*Kad mrtvi zapjevaju*, 1998) reviewed by Boško Picula
216	**Goran Dukić:** *Wristcutters: A Love Story*, 2006 reviewed by Maxim Pozdorovkin
220	**Hrvoje Hribar:** *What is a Man Without a Moustache?* (*Što je muškarac bez brkova?*, 2005) reviewed by Mima Simić
225	**Zrinko Ogresta:** *Fragments: Chronicle of a Vanishing* (*Krhotine — Kronika jednog nestajanja*, 1991); *Washed Out* (*Isprani*, 1995); *Red Dust* (*Crvena prašina*, 1999); *Here* (*Tu*, 2003); *Behind the Glass* (*Iza stakla*, 2008) reviewed by Tomislav Šakić
232	**Tomislav Radić:** *What Iva Recorded* (*Što je Iva snimila 21. listopada 2003*, 2005) reviewed by Petra Belković Taylor
236	**Branko Schmidt:** *The Melon Route* (*Put lubenica*, 2006); *Metastases* (*Metastaze*, 2009) reviewed by Zhen Zhang
241	**A Note on Contributors**
247	**General Biliography**
253	**Filmography**
259	**Index**

Acknowledgements

This project has benefited from the support of many individuals and institutions. First and foremost, we would like to express our gratitude to an inspiring team of contributors, in particular to Diana Nenadić, who helped at every step of the process. We are indebted to the Croatian Film Association (*Hrvatski filmski savez*) and its Director Vera Robić, and the Croatian Audiovisual Centre (*Hrvatski audiovizualni centar*), our principal associates on the Croatian shore. Both institutions went out of their way to provide practical and financial help in order to make the publication of this book possible.

We are thankful to Hrvoje Turković of the Academy of Dramatic Art in Zagreb (*Akademija dramskih umjetnosti*) and to Nikica Gilić of the School of Humanities and Social Sciences, University of Zagreb (*Filozofski fakultet*) for providing contacts and suggestions in the early phase of the project, as well as to Jurica Pavičić of the University of Split for informal conversations and exchanges on film which significantly broadened our perspectives. Since the inception of this project, we have lost two important scholars and filmmakers who both contributed immensely to Croatian film and a general knowledge about it, Ante Peterlić and Ivo Škrabalo. Ante Peterlić, premier film theorist and ardent supporter of the idea that the Croatian film institutions should be free of the government's control or oversight, instilled a profound love for film in many generations of his students (the editors included) at University of Zagreb's Department of Comparative Literature and the Academy of Dramatic Art. His enthusiasm and captivating lectures resonate throughout this collection. Ivo Škrabalo's pioneering role in identifying and preserving of the Croatian national film corpus is visible in any bibliography dealing with the film from this part of the world. We were fortunate to have him as a contributor to this collection of essays; we witnessed history in our crash-course conversations with him on film and politics in summers of 2010/11 and were touched by the extent of his hospitality and support. They will be deeply missed by both scholarly and film communities.

We wish we could share with our readers more of the atmosphere and spirit in which the interviews presented here took place, and we would like to thank the directors — Vinko Brešan, Rajko Grlić, Joško Marušić, and Nenad Puhovski — for exciting conversations and for allowing us glimpses into their world. We could not have produced this book without the help of our graphic designer Željko Serdarević and the Croatian Film Archive (*Hrvatska kinoteka*) and its Director Carmen Lhotka, who were instrumental in supplying the visual materials.

Very special thanks go to Caryl Emerson of Princeton University and Svetlana Boym of Harvard University for their unwavering support of this project, as well as to our language editor Ellen Elias Bursać, who has navigated tirelessly and elegantly between the two languages.

We are indebted to Birgit Beumers and *KinoKultura* for backing and facilitating the electronic publication of these essays which first appeared as a special issue of the online journal *KinoKultura* in May 2011. It was a real pleasure to work with Marion Berghahn and Mark Stanton of Berghahn Books who welcomed and helped launch this volume in its final phase.

This project has received assistance from the American Councils for International Education: ACTR/ACCELS, with funding through the National Endowment for the Humanities. We express our appreciation to these institutions and especially to Sarah Krueger, who helped us with many practical aspects of the grant. Both the Pula and Motovun film festivals made their screenings and forums open to us in the summer of 2010, for which we offer our deep thanks.

Aida Vidan & Gordana P. Crnković

In Contrast:
Croatian Film Today
by Aida Vidan

Despite decades of rich and diverse production and broad international recognition, general knowledge about Croatian film remains rather limited, in particular in the West. This seeming contradiction is not the only paradox related to Croatian cinema. Thus when my co-editor, Gordana P. Crnković, and I set out to produce a book on Croatian film, we faced a simple yet challenging question: which year to begin with and how to explain this complex situation? To speak of Croatian film as starting only with 1991, when Croatia seceded from Yugoslavia, would mean disregarding the directors who both laid the foundations for a nascent cinema and created some of the basic orientations visible in the works of younger Croatian filmmakers. Entirely disregarding the Yugoslav polycentric film industry would provide only a partial picture since despite distinct local flavors, the regional film centers shared resources, studios, actors, film professionals, and audiences, and cooperated much more efficiently than the political structures ever did. It was necessary therefore to include this early stage in the picture.

The reality is different now, however, and despite continuous collaboration within the region (immediately apparent if one checks the lists of co-producers for most films), there are many points of differentiation and these had to be explored as well. One Croatian director of the younger generation, Ognjen Sviličić, has recently said: "Today the living conditions of people in Croatia, Serbia, and Slovenia are quite dissimilar. The consequence of this situation is that a Croat does not perceive a Slovenian film as a reflection of his own life." (quoted from Anja Šošić, *Film i rat u Hrvatskoj*, in *Zapis* 64-65, 2009). In addition to the clear need for a determination of idiosyncratic features that characterize different film schools in the Balkans (in this case, the one which stemmed from the Zagreb film circle), and with an eye to the earlier socialist period and a re-evaluation of film in the early stages of Croatian statehood, we also need to consider the current state of affairs. As indicated by Sviličić, the picture has changed and is continuing to change. The face of Croatian film is significantly different now compared to the early or late 1990s. With the departure of Franjo Tuđman, the first Croatian president, who held a relatively tight grip on the film industry, and with the subsequent disassociation of political and cultural structures, a stage has opened for a new group of filmmakers who have engaged both domestic and foreign audiences in ways that were previously unthinkable.

Some topics dealt with both in films of the 1990s and again in the last few years have received quite a different treatment. The recurrence of certain subjects, such as war and its broader consequences for society, could even serve as a barometer of change in the young democracy as it resulted in achievements that have transformed the landscape of Croatian film. The inclination of Croatian filmmakers toward introspective, psychological probing as a way of commenting on more general processes taking place in society was already there in the 1960s and 1970s, and in the last decade has particularly come to the fore. This orientation is, for instance, quite different from that of neighboring Serbia and even Bosnia and Herzegovina, whose film schools have thus far been more notable for their carnivalistic approach and exploitation of dark humor. This is not to say, of course, that psychological inquisitiveness is exclusive to Croatian filmmakers, or that comedy remains the principal interest of Serbian or Bosnian directors (a case in point is the recent Serbian film *Huddersfield*, 2007, by Ivan Živković, which turns the carnivalistic into deep psychological probing), but one can recognize these tendencies and make an attempt to look at the underlying causes that have shaped certain stylistic choices.

A statement by another young Croatian filmmaker, Lukas Nola, that he "belong[s] to the generation from which the war was stolen" (Škrabalo, *Hrvatska filmska povijest ukratko 1896-2006*, pp. 182-3) is equally telling. During the period when Croatia was being established as an independent state, several recognized members of the older generation of filmmakers, owing to their ties to the new political elite, depicted the creation of the new state with an accent on ideological rather than artistic components. Film was employed as an instrument of nation-building narrative. On the other hand, filmmakers of the younger generation, a number of whom actually served at the front and witnessed the war first-hand, did not have access to the funds necessary to translate their life experiences and their visions of a new society into celluloid form. It was only in the early 2000s, when Croatia began striding towards a more secure democracy, that some of these filmmakers received an opportunity to share their stories. New options for funding were additionally increased when Croatia became eligible, a few years ago, for Eurimage funding (the European Cinema Support Fund operating under the umbrella of the Council of Europe).

The syntagm "Young Croatian Film" was coined in the nineties by Petar Krelja, a renowned Croatian filmmaker and theoretician. It was further popularized by Ivo Škrabalo, one of our contributors, as "New Croatian Film" to include a generation that was then just graduating from the Zagreb Academy of Dramatic Art and establishing itself in contrast to (one could even say despite) the older practitioners of film. This new group of directors was unified not by common artistic orientation, but rather by a negative definition, since their principal shared ground was their resistance to the political pragmatism of the moment and a search for new artistic avenues with which to portray Croatian everyday life. Stylistically, however, they could not be placed in a single compartment, and their works still await an in-depth analysis for English-speaking audiences (we have included reviews of some of their works here). Such diversity of cinematic expression in the new and upcoming generation is a promising phenomenon, and most certainly one that deserves to be investigated in greater detail.

Considering this situation and the general scarcity of available information, we decided to use this opportunity to present Croatian film from both a diachronic and a synchronic perspective, leaning towards the latter. The purpose of this project is thus two-fold: to explain some of the complexities in the development of this national cinema by providing a much needed albeit succinct historical overview of the Yugoslav and post-Yugoslav periods, and to offer insight into a selection of the more interesting films of the last two decades since Croatia became an independent country. In the sparse body of contributions on South Slavic cinema, several book-length studies in English address the Croatian film industry to a degree and for this reason should be mentioned here: Daniel J. Goulding's *Liberated Cinema: The Yugoslav Experience* (1985), Dina Iordanova's *Cinema of Flames: Balkan Film, Culture and the Media* (2001), Pavle Levi's *Disintegration in Frames: Aesthetics and Ideology in the Yugoslav and Post-Yugoslav Cinema* (2007), and a collection edited by Andrew James Horton, *The Celluloid Tinderbox: Yugoslav Screen Reflections of a Turbulent Decade* (2000; <http://www.ce-review.org/>). While all of these volumes are outstanding contributions to a hitherto insufficiently researched area, they all share a focus on Partisan and Yugoslav-disintegration films, i.e., the war genre more than any other category, with the exception perhaps of the Serbian "black wave." Given the political situation of the region, this is not surprising at all, but at the same time it leaves a large segment of the regional film industry unexplored, including many Croatian produced and co-produced films.

Until the wars of the 1990s tore the Balkans apart, film production in this part of the world was commonly discussed under the umbrella term "Yugoslav film," and it may seem that this trend has continued to an extent even nearly twenty years after the demise of the country. As long as Croatia was a part of Yugoslavia, trying to define the scope of its contribution in an amalgam production of the six republics would have been perceived as a political act, and would have been condemned. In fact, it was only at the zenith of Yugoslav communism that the first attempts to chronicle Croatian cinematography surfaced, most notably in a volume by Ivo Škrabalo entitled *Between the Audience and the State* (*Između publike i države*, 1985), followed by his *101 Years of Film in Croatia* (*101 godina filma u Hrvatskoj*, 1998). Neither volume is yet available in English. This book is thus meant to bridge the gap and provide much-needed information in English about Croatian film, while keeping both its development within the Yugoslav era in perspective and focusing on those elements that are idiosyncratic and unique to it.

As is the case with many aspects of Croatian culture, the country's film industry is in fact older than the state itself. Although its roots were planted before World War II, it started taking big strides in the early Yugoslav period, to be crowned with a series of fine achievements in the period between the 1960s and the dissolution of the country. Each of the six republics had its own film production centers (which often collaborated on more involved projects), but the final output appeared always, as Ivo Škrabalo puts it, as "the Yugoslav brand" (see his article in this volume). Internally, however, despite multiple tangential points, these productions each had their own physiognomy. During the socialist era costlier projects, in particular Partisan spectacles which had huge backing from the Communist Party, were often co-produced by studios from different republics and included artists from various localities, which made individual republics' participation less distinct. Many other smaller budget films relied on common resources, often using actors or services from other regional centers. Still, this is not to say that each republic did not have its own full-fledged film industry and profile. Although the list of masterpieces is much longer, Croatian hallmark titles from the older period include Nikola Tanhofer's modernist *H-8* (1958), Zvonimir Berković's dramaturgically complex *Rondo* (1966), Ante Babaja's visually intricate *Breza* (*The Birch Tree*, 1967), Rajko Grlić's politically provocative *Samo jednom se ljubi* (*The Melody Haunts My Reverie*, 1981), and Zoran Tadić's metaphysical *Ritam zločina* (*Rhythm of the Crime*, 1981). Each of these films left an imprint not only in the region but has also been recognized as a major contribution to world cinema.

For a film industry that had originated in a different political system — and under the "Yugoslav" heading that encapsulated a variety of approaches, several very active studios, and a number of orientations — it was risky if not impossible to insist on national identity. The establishment of Croatia in 1991 brought about a different set of political circumstances, and during this difficult period it was often filmmakers who through their work provided a healthy and humane perspective on what was happening in the war-torn country. They were frequently highly critical of official politics and this, in turn, made their work quite challenging, sometimes impossible to produce. As already mentioned, it was not easy to obtain financial support for younger filmmakers since funding was firmly controlled by the state. It was only in 2003, after the renowned film scholar Ante Peterlić became the head of the special committee dealing with national film production, that the new generation of directors saw a significant change. The situation improved further with the establishment of the Croatian Audiovisual Centre in 2008, with clearer protocols for competitions for new projects and a better strategy — albeit still in development — for the course of the national film industry. Croatian Radiotelevision has played a major part as a producer from early on, but big credit should also be given to several small independent producers who were instrumental in bringing us some of the best films from this period. In general, scarcity of independent producers (owing to the transitional economy) remains one of the big obstacles for this film industry. Having survived the swings of the political pendulum and generated, for a small film industry, a number of interesting films, and finally, having reached a mature stage at which film can exist both as an engaged and de-politicized entity, Croatia is now facing a new type of hurdle: a dire economic situation that leaves meager resources for the arts in general, including film. Whether the directors and institutions will be able to navigate successfully the Scylla and Charybdis of monetary fluctuations, poor distribution, and competition with Hollywood blockbusters, remains to be seen, but if anything has been learned from the rocky history of the region, it is that interesting ideas are sometimes brought to fruition despite harsh conditions.

For a number of reasons we have entitled this introduction and, by extension, this collection of essays "In Contrast: Croatian Film Today." Although the articles presented here were not commissioned with the primary goal of defining Croatian cinema, our hope was nonetheless to create a more nuanced picture of a film industry that existed as a part of a larger whole and which, in the last twenty years, despite incessant practical and political obstacles, has been moving on in important ways. There are indeed multiple possible answers to the question "in contrast — to what?": in contrast to the earlier Yugoslav film production, to the regional film industries of the post-Yugoslav period, to other East-Central European cinemas, to the multimillion-dollar Hollywood blockbusters, to the Croatian political mainstream, to capitalist-style film production, to its own various generational and gender trends, and, finally, to different stylistic choices representing directors' diverse *Weltanschauungen* and preoccupations. Visual in nature, the word "contrast" also points to a variety of cinematic approaches that have yielded movies as diverse as Arsen Ostojić's *A Wonderful Night in Split* (*Ta divna splitska noć*, 2004), Lukas Nola's *Celestial Body* (*Nebo sateliti*, 2001), Kristijan Milić's *The Living and the Dead* (*Živi i mrtvi*, 2007), Goran Rušinović's *Buick Riviera* (2008), Antonio Nuić's *Donkey* (*Kenjac*, 2009), and Goran Dević and Zvonimir Jurić's *The Blacks* (*Crnci*, 2009). Be it for political, artistic, or other reasons, the concept of contrast thus permeates the entire history of Croatian film, and we wish to think about and explore this particular cinema as a series of developments that reflect on and generate one another, rather than as a series of isolated phenomena.

To answer in depth all the "contrasting" questions posed here would be too ambitious a goal for this collection. As the range of articles suggests, however, we have worked towards uncovering at least some of the most salient issues. We were lucky to have on board some of the best specialists in the area of South Slavic film, from whose knowledge and enthusiasm we have benefited tremendously. In addition, we decided to include several prominent film practitioners, who provided a unique "insider look" at Croatian film. History looms large in just about every aspect of the arts in recent years, film included. The six longer articles are meant to offer both a historical perspective and a closer look into the development of different film categories in Croatia (feature, documentary, animated film). Ivo Škrabalo, a veteran of film historiography, situates Croatian cinema within Yugoslav frameworks and provides the basic periodization with an analysis of genre trends, while keeping the political background very much on the radar. Jurica Pavičić concentrates on the period since Croatia became an independent country, devoting considerable attention to the interpretation of political and historical circumstances and their effects on individual films. In addition, he discusses the general impact film itself has had on its audiences in conveying particular interpretations of history and observes a parallel process of maturation that unfolds in film and society. Tomislav Kurelec considers the problems facing the industry and investigates the devastating consequences that the combination of war and a transitional economy have had on film. These two factors caused Croatia's film infrastructure to collapse, only to be rebuilt and restructured in a relatively short period of time. The process is still ongoing.

Diana Nenadić writes about the enormous role documentary film played as a social corrective in the country during the last twenty years. In the war-riddled economy and on the volatile political scene it was still possible to make documentaries, and during this period many filmmakers of different generations used the camera in a true Vertovian sense. They captured the faces of a rapidly changing society, including the positive, the negative, the hidden, and the forbidden. Some of them lost their lives at the front, others had to live with threats and discrimination because the camera-eye spoke at times of unpleasant truths. Their persistence was crowned by one of the most interesting festivals in this part of the world, ZagrebDox: International Documentary Film Festival, which just completed its seventh year. In addition, Nenadić speaks with the festival's founder and artistic director, Nenad Puhovski, who in 1996 also founded Factum: Documentary Film Project, the largest and most influential independent documentary production in the region, which has financed a number of excellent projects.

Sanja Bahun explores the area of animation, an extremely important area of Croatian film, and its renowned Zagreb School, which in 1961 brought home an Academy Award for Dušan Vukotić's *Ersatz*, a work that fifty years after its creation is if anything even more poignant today in its commentary on modern life. Since 1972 Zagreb has been home to the second oldest European international festival of animated film, Animafest. Although not always equally visible, the Zagreb School has remained a creative hub which is now bustling with a new generation of film-makers exploring their ideas in the context of the latest technological possibilities. Bahun also brings us a conversation with one of the most prominent figures from the Croatian animation scene, director Joško Marušić. The fact that Croatian cinema is sparsely populated with women (except when it comes to acting) made us consider the possibility of including an article that addresses this area. We reached the conclusion, however, that the situation merits closer investigation. Even when they do not sit in the director's chair (and every now and then some do!), women have been an important driving force in many projects. A good example is the complex editing of Vinko Brešan's award-winning film *Witnesses*, for which credit goes to Sandra Botica Brešan. From a sociological perspective, the depiction of women in film in what is a traditional, patriarchal, and Catholic society raises an assortment of issues that Mima Simić tackles with spirit.

Our interviews with Rajko Grlić and Vinko Brešan, two directors who belong to a more mature generation and who have been widely recognized outside Croatia, offer perspective on their own very interesting oeuvres, and cast light on the practical side of filmmaking in Croatia, as well as the development of the medium in its socio-historical context. It is our regret that we could not include more conversations with directors in this collection, but for those who read Croatian a series of interesting interviews can be found in Anja Šošić's excellent study *Film i rat u Hrvatskoj* (*Zapis* 64-65, 2009, <http://www.hfs.hr/hfs/zapis_clanak_detail.asp?sif=32527>).

The seventeen reviews included in this collection are specific inasmuch as they often provide a glimpse into the most relevant aspects of a director's oeuvre (often more than one film). Although this selection had to leave out many titles worthy of mention, it does represent the core of Croatian cinema today. Reviewers coming from diverse film backgrounds have ensured a multiplicity of perspectives on the works they investigate. With the eruption of the wars of Yugoslav disintegration in the 1990s, the world was captivated by films focusing on the ongoing conflict. As Jurica Pavičić points out in his contribution to this book, this period remains marked in particular by the films of Serbian directors such as Srđan Dragojević and (Bosnian-born) Emir Kusturica, as well as the Macedonian-American Milčo Mančevski, all of whom depicted the Balkans as the epitome of inexorable and vicious cycles of hatred. In the chaos of war that engulfed the region this is how the Balkans were perceived, and this is the perception to which the region itself catered. Discussing the general cultural ramifications of Balkan-Western relations, Slavoj Žižek calls this phenomenon "falsification by a foreign gaze" (Žižek, *The Parallax View*, 377). While the films were deservedly praised for their artistic accomplishments, they also generated heated debate concerning a reductionist perception of history (a theory of perpetual tribal violence that cannot be stopped) which removes any ethical and/or political responsibility for what was going on. Despite these issues (and it should also be noted that there are different interpretations, see for instance, Gordana P. Crnković's "Milcho Manchevski's *Before the Rain* and the Ethics of Listening," *Slavic Review* 70, no.1, 2011), it is important that such artistic visions of the 1990s exist. What is not good, however, is that very few other voices reverberated quite so loudly partially because the Balkans no longer draw the type of political attention they did in the 1990s. The films coming from this corner of the world may be as good or even better, but they do not have the political propeller pushing them to the fore. And to say that politics does not matter would be an equally reductive view.

Our attempt here was to convey at least a part of the very diverse palette of topics that occupies Croatian filmmakers, and to weaken, if not entirely erase, the aura of "otherness." Even when it comes to the war, the films reviewed here provide a different vision from those that captivated the world in the 1990s and reflect a variety of styles by filmmakers as dissimilar as Krsto Papić, Rajko Grlić, Vinko Brešan, Lukas Nola, Kristijan Milić, Goran Dević, and Zvonimir Jurić. Many other topics, however, loom large on Croatian screens: the possibility of a gay relationship in a conservative environment (Dalibor Matanić), a woman's position in a provincial patriarchal milieu, the westernizing of transitional societies and exploitation of war trauma (Ognjen Sviličić), the destabilization of basic units of society — family, community, friendship networks (Antonio Nuić), the relativization of gender roles through the spectacles of irony (Snježana Tribuson), a lost generation refracted — albeit in contrasting ways — through the problems of drugs and suicide (Arsen Anton Ostojić, Goran Dukić), the past as agony transposed (Goran Rušinović), the misplaced values of a society in transition (Zrinko Ogresta, Tomislav Radić, Branko Schmidt) — to give just a quick glimpse of the thematic range of the films selected for review here. What becomes immediately apparent is how many of these themes are pertinent in other European film industries, and, with the possible exception of narratives of a war-traumatized society, how little "otherness" there is in them. We can monitor exactly what is conveyed by the title of Jurica Pavičić's article: a process moving "from a cinema of hatred to a cinema of consciousness." The variety of wonderfully different films attests not only to enviable artistic capabilities despite abysmal financial circumstances, but also to the fact that this corner of the world has been much richer and more complex — even in terms of its cinema — than the general perception of it has allowed. What we are seeing in the last few years is a gradual orientation away from war topics and towards themes of the everyday. The fate of those on the margins dominates the narratives at times, but more and more frequently directors are reaching for "the next-door" type of story (Sviličić's *Sorry for Kung Fu* and his most recent *Two Sunny Days*, Nuić's *Donkey*, Hribar's *What is a Man Without a Moustache*, Ogresta's *Behind the Glass*, Radić's *What Iva Recorded*, and Grlić's *Just Between Us*). Such narratives of the ordinary have yielded some of the best movies of recent years in the non-commercial segment of European production, and my prediction is that Croatian cinema too will be increasingly looking in this direction.

At the end of an introduction for a collection of this profile, the somewhat subversive question arises of whether the notion of national cinema is needed at all. In an age when small film industries rely heavily on co-producing as sometimes the only possible *modus operandi*, why do we need relative denominations such as Croatian, Bosnian, Romanian, Turkish, or, for that matter, any other cinema? Even during the process of editing this issue, we have (not surprisingly) run into a situation so well captured in Adela Peeva's documentary *Whose is This Song?* (Чия е тази песен?, 2003): one song — or in our case one film — belonging to several countries. This is becoming more the rule than the exception, especially for countries operating under the umbrella of Eurimage. The most recent example of such cooperation is a project entitled *Love Island* (*Otok ljubavi*) by Bosnian director Jasmila Žbanić, which received the bulk of its funding from Croatia, where the story takes place and the film will be shot. It is interesting that on the list of Croatian co-productions this year we also find the name of Peter Greenaway, whose film *Goltzius and the Pelican* was shot in the northern part of the country. For the film industry of a country with extraordinarily filmic landscapes, strong studios (we need only recall how many foreign films used the services of Jadran Film during the socialist era), and a lower cost of living than in the West, there may be — for once — some advantages. Providing partial funding and services for foreign filmmakers is a creative way to boost the country's film industry, but whether a given film should be regarded as belonging to this or that category depends more on the world depicted in the film, its language, who the director is, etc. and far less on the financing. For a region which has its differences but also many things in common, the trend of co-productions is likely to continue.

There is the question of audience as well which, despite being divided by borders and some linguistic differences, remains far more interested in a good film than in its origin. It is indicative that just days prior to the NATO bombing of Yugoslavia (consisting then of Serbia and Montenegro) in 1999, one of the most prominent Serbian directors, Srđan Dragojević, was invited to be a guest at Zagreb's Kinoteka (the principal Croatian cinephile institution) for a screening of his provocative film *The Wounds* (*Rane*, 1998). Croatian-produced films can thus count on wider regional audiences, just as can those from the other ex-Yugoslav republics. Even the two most renowned festivals in the country, the national film festival in Pula and the international Motovun Film Festival, both taking place in July on the northern Croatian peninsula of Istria, have a contrasting component in the sense that the former is the festival of Croatian national cinema and the latter an alternative stage open to Croatian, regional, and world film. The Pula festival was established in 1954 as the festival of Yugoslav film, and as of 1991 continued as a festival of Croatian film with a European dimension. Motovun is younger, established in 1999, and was conceived in the first decade of Croatian statehood when an insistence on political uniformity precluded many interesting regional films from being shown on the principal stage in Pula. Although Motovun maintains the true spirit of a teenage rebel showing innovative, provocative, and artistically charged titles from around the world, Pula too is beginning to depart from the narrowly defined concept of a national film forum and seems inclined to open its doors to more versatile programs. For a small country to have two major film festivals in such close temporal and geographic proximity may seem superfluous, but whoever has visited both will quickly come to the conclusion that they complement one another in effective ways.

As we can see from this brief analysis of production and audiences, the question of a national cinema is a loaded one, as has been underscored in Andrew Higson's much quoted article "The Concept of National Cinema" (*Screen* 30, no 4, 1989) published just as Eastern Europe was beginning to redraw its borders. This concept has been made even more relevant with regard to Southeastern Europe, but also to other countries, such as Germany and Turkey, which in recent years have yielded a number of co-productions (largely owing to the considerable Turkish immigrant population in Germany) and successfully created a cinematic bridge between the two cultures. Why then should we continue insisting on the concept of national cinema in a time of transnational productions? There is no simple answer to this question, as a now hefty literature on the subject would suggest. However a quote from the interview with Rajko Grlić in this book helps put things in perspective: "Cinemas have disappeared and we have multiplexes and one hundred American films which hold on tight to 95% of the world screens. There is only 5% of the cinematic space in the world for you to enter with a non-studio film. There are about 2000 films competing for 5% of the space."

Although at times national cinemas have been used (and abused) as an apparatus for establishing national narratives, in more democratic environments they are needed as an inoculation against commercial networks — in much the same way that festivals are turning into venues for showing non-commercial films that cannot be seen anywhere else. Small national cinemas thus operate as a counterforce to uniformity and often reject the notion of entertainment as their primary *raison d'être*. From this there follow aesthetic idiosyncrasies, but also a type of political and social engagement with their local cultures which questions (or at times supports) prevalent discourses in society, a dimension largely absent from commercial and globalizing productions such as Hollywood. It is beyond any doubt that Croatian cinema has served exactly this function over the past twenty years. It has also brought local flavors and stories with ethical dimensions about ordinary people, and it is such stories, to quote Vinko Brešan and Rajko Grlić once again, that are essential for films with universal appeal. If Croatian cinema continues to move in this direction, we should eagerly anticipate its new titles.

Essays

Croatian Film in the Yugoslav Context in the Second Half of the Twentieth Century
by Ivo Škrabalo

Croatian film entered the twenty first century with an array of awards and favorable reactions from numerous international film festivals. Let us mention only the most relevant. Vinko Brešan's *Witnesses* (*Svjedoci*), a psychological drama about dark aspects of the Croatian Independence War, was featured in 2004 on the official program of the Berlin film festival where it took two awards. In addition, it received the highest recognition at festivals in Jerusalem, Karlovy Váry and Motovun. Awards were also taken home by other filmmakers from festivals with a focus on Eastern European cinema. Particularly noted were directors belonging to what is called *young Croatian film* (Ogresta, Sviličić, Matanić, Nuić, Hribar), but also veterans who had appeared first on the Yugoslav scene (Grlić, Radić, Schmidt, Šorak).

In the festival season 2009/2010 the psychological war drama *The Blacks* (*Crnci*, 2009) by directorial tandem Zvonimir Jurić and Goran Dević resonated widely in international circles, receiving awards at Cottbus and Linz as well as at Belgrade and Ljubljana. At the Sarajevo Film Festival, which in recent years has become the most important regional forum for authors and works of post-Yugoslav cinema, but also for films from the broader field of Southeastern Europe, Croatian actors have been particularly praised (Leon Lučev, Rakan Rushaidat, Marija Škaričić, and Zrinka Cvitešić). "The Heart of Sarajevo" — as the principal award in the regional competition is called — was given in 2008 to *Buick Riviera* by young Croatian director Goran Rušinović.

In addition to regular invitations to an increasing number of international festivals catering to art film, broad recognition of Croatian films suggests that this country's cinema is acquiring its own identity which is distinct from that of the other post-Yugoslav and similar "small" film industries. Although Croatian production is recognized in its own right, it has nonetheless not yet launched world-renowned works such as the recent Romanian films (and earlier, the Czech, Hungarian, and Polish films), nor has it taken home awards from the so-called "A" festivals.

Croatian film goes back further, however, than the newly founded state. It is generally unknown that more than half a century ago, in the late 1950s and early 1960s, two Croatian films were granted the highest forms of recognition. *The Year-Long Road* (*Cesta duga godinu dana*, 1958) by visiting Italian director Giuseppe De Santis, filmed and made in Croatian

Francé Štiglic: *The Ninth Circle* (*Deveti krug*), 1960

production, won a Golden Globe and was nominated for an Academy Award among five foreign-language nominees. Two years later *The Ninth Circle* (*Deveti krug*, 1960) by Francé Štiglic, a tragic love story about the efforts of residents of Zagreb to rescue several Jewish citizens from persecution by the criminal Ustasha/Fascist regime, received the same nomination. These were, in fact, the first successes of the nascent Yugoslav film industry and, as a result, little note was made of these movies as Croatian films, produced at Zagreb's Jadran Film. Namely, in Tito's Yugoslavia there was only one brand: Yugoslav film. At the moment when the first state institution for film production was established by political decree in 1944, the rising Yugoslav film industry was not shackled by tradition. Not one of the six republics of the newly pronounced federal state — with the relative exception of Croatia — had inherited an organized film industry. One should say, however, that since the early days of the twentieth century they had all shared an ambition to get a domestic film industry going. These film enthusiasts, operating mostly in isolation, lived to see the undoing of their dreams as a shared fate.

Development of an organized film industry in Yugoslavia was in fact accomplished by the victorious communist government and, as a result, film was treated exclusively as the domain of so-called socialist (rather than nation-specific) culture. First and foremost, diligent party ideologists followed Lenin's famous statement from 1922 that "film, for us, is the most important of all art forms." This justified their need for film production, but also gave them reasons for increased vigilance in terms of its ideological control.

Film Production in the Independent State of Croatia

In April 1941 when Hitler's *Blitzkrieg* collapsed the military and state structures of the Kingdom of Yugoslavia (which, following Hitler's plans, the occupiers divided into as many as nine districts with different forms of governance), the Independent State of Croatia was established. This provisional quisling creation was ruled by the Ustasha regime with an extreme fascist/Nazi orientation. For all practical purposes the political and military domination of the Third Reich and Mussolini's Italy turned this totalitarian

Oktavian Miletić: *Lisinski*, 1944

quasi-state (comprising also of today's Bosnia and Herzegovina) into a protectorate. Already in the first months of its governance, the Ustasha regime commenced with film production for the purposes of war propaganda, and it soon founded a film production company called *Croatian Motion Pictures* (*Hrvatski slikopis*). A film journal (as a form of war propaganda) was regularly put together and showed there, a practice which lasted until the Axis powers capitulated in May 1945. It was within the context of this production that the first Croatian sound feature was made, *Lisinski* (1944), directed by one of the most renowned film pioneers, Oktavijan Miletić (1902-1987). The film focused on the biography of Vatroslav Lisinski, composer of the first Croatian opera during the nineteenth-century National-Revival period. Despite its overly emotional depiction of Revivalist ideas and focus on patriotic fervor, the production quality of *Lisinski*, evident in the cinematography, set design, music, and sound testified to the professional level of expertise of Zagreb film enthusiasts.

Paradoxically, it was during the Ustasha regime that the material and technical infrastructure for film production was created. As propaganda was the principal function of film during this time, much of the modern equipment was obtained from Germany. At the end of the war, despite the plans to have the equipment transferred back to Germany, all of it was salvaged. In order to make this possible, the employees of *Hrvatski slikopis*, working subversively with the Partisan movement, secretly filmed the retreat of the defeated armies and the Partisans entering Zagreb. From these materials Branko Marjanović made his documentary film *Liberation of Zagreb* (*Oslobođenje Zagreba*, 1945), which was also known as *Film News No. 1* (*Filmske novosti broj 1*) since it marked the beginning of regular production of a film journal in new Yugoslavia. This unique cinematic gaze witnessing the collapse of the Ustasha regime can be taken as both a real and a symbolic juncture in the continuity of Croatian cinema. It also meant a new beginning for professional development within the communist Yugoslav context in which Croatia was one of six federal units.

In the Beginning: The Soviet Model

Hindsight sometimes lets us see history as full of unexpected paradoxes. The existence of the criminal Ustasha-Nazi regime (for four years), followed by the oppression of the Partisan-Communist era (for forty-five years), brought about both fortune and misfortune in terms of the formation and development of Croatian as well as Yugoslav cinema.

Without the political and propaganda needs generated by the totalitarian regime, the state would not have secured funds for the film industry, and without monetary support the film pioneers would not have enjoyed the opportunity for continuous work. On the other hand, technical prosperity was, needless to say, paid for in spades by constraints on artistic freedom and a servicing of the antidemocratic and inhumane regimes. The choice of topics was dependent on the political tides, and there were times when the filmmakers did not even have a say as to style. Nonetheless, the most important task in this first period was to master the craft of making movies, even if this was to be done at a cost and while abiding to the prescribed ideological strictures.

"We voluntarily castrated ourselves," said director Branko Belan when explaining in retrospect why the first filmmakers did not even question the ideological premises to which they had to hold if they were to remain artistically active. After these first enthusiasts came new ones, inheriting the accrued knowledge and supplementing it with new skills. So it was that the film profession in Croatia was begun. One should keep in mind, however, that the creation, development, and survival of Croatian and Yugoslav institutionalized cinema with a continuous production of feature films as well as other genres was at its core bound to politics, its historical permutations, and pragmatic metamorphoses.

Even before the end of the war, in the fall of 1944, the Partisans organized the Yugoslav State Film Company (*Državno filmsko preduzeće Jugoslavije*) with branch offices in each of the federal units. Its principal purpose was to seize from the occupiers the film equipment, supplies of raw materials, and archives found at each of the film centers. The private movie theaters (approximately 180 in Croatia) were gradually appropriated or nationalized in the course of the first postwar year.

The Yugoslav cinema was organized on the basis of the Soviet model (this was true, after all, for almost all other aspects of life immediately after World War II), and the movies focused on the Partisan heroic victories that ended the war. Because it now owned the technology, Croatia was able to make the first documentaries. Among these, special attention was given to *Jasenovac* (1945), showing the notorious concentration camp for Jews, Serbs, Roma, and Croatian anti-fascists, and filmed immediately after the liberation of the camp in the spring of 1945. As Zagreb had inherited more or less fully equipped studios that were taken over undamaged after the Partisan liberation, they provided technical services for the other film centers in Yugoslavia in those first years.

Despite strong centrist tendencies present in all spheres of social life, the film production of new Yugoslavia was not all concentrated in one lo-

President Josip Broz Tito
A model of the Jadran film complex

cation, but instead was organized on federal principles from its very inception. Thus it never yielded to a Yugoslav Hollywood, Babelsberg, or Cinecittá. One could say that even the ideological monism of the winning Communist Party was not absolute, since film life in each national center developed at a different pace, allowing for the distinct traditions, mindsets and cultural interests of each community. Still, for the survival and development of both Croatian and Yugoslav film it was decisive that the state took the industry under its wing.

A Brief Phase of Socialist Realism

Croatian (as well as Serbian and Slovenian) films of the 1940s and early 1950s followed Soviet models. This aesthetic and ideological approach known as *socialist realism* was a requirement for any form of creative activity. The term was never elaborated further in Yugoslavia so its interpretation relied on the Soviet definition as proclaimed at the First All-Union Congress of Soviet Writers as early as 1934 when one of Stalin's favorite collaborators, A. A. Zhdanov, announced in his introductory speech that artists were "engineers of people's souls" and used this expression for the recommended aesthetic orientation in literature and the arts in general (the term had actually first been used in *Literaturnaja Gazeta* in 1932). Although never formulated precisely as an obligatory political directive in Yugoslavia, it was still imposed as a strong suggestion, which requested that art "depict life in a realist manner," and foregrounded the struggle of the masses for a better future in communism when ideas of justice and equality would prevail and the collective would be superior to the individual.

Not many Partisan films were made in Croatia during the period of *socrealism*. For a full seven years (from 1949 to 1956) not a single war movie was made, but rather the beginner-directors were learning the ropes of the filmmaking process. They were also broadening their interest to include a range of topics and genres while not departing from the canon of the official aesthetics. Within a rather modest scope (typically one, or exceptionally two, films per year), Croatian film production may have been tainted ideologically, but it was diverse in terms of themes and genre: the film industry probed the interests of the audiences and, at the same time,

Krešo Golik: *The Blue 9* (*Plavi 9*), 1950

it chalked up experience. The first film of a "lighter genre," *The Blue 9* (*Plavi 9*, 1950) by Krešo Golik (1922-1996) had, for that time, a phenomenal audience reception. This was a didactic sport comedy which explored the affirmation of a new type of socialist ethics in the realm of physical fitness.

Bakonja fra Brne (1951) is considered to be the most mature film of the early period, directed in a proficient yet static manner by Fedor Hanžeković (1913-1997), a director favored by the regime. This screen version of a wry novel on monastery life by Simo Matavulj (standard reading in every school curriculum) became, in the era when the communist government was settling accounts with the church, an anti-religious pamphlet populated with caricatures of Franciscan monks. The film unravels at a slow pace, spells out too much, and never hides its political slant. From first to last take it represents a true example of *socrealism* in Croatian film, never overstepping the boundaries set by the socio-political times during which and owing to which it was made.

The first Croatian film which had the honor of being censored, *Ciguli Miguli* (1952) by Branko Marjanović, was also shot around the same time. This harsh and bizarre ban imposed by the Party was directed at Joža Horvat, scriptwriter, author of popular theater comedies much in the spirit of the new regime who had hitherto never been criticized. What is more, he was a veteran of the Partisan resistance and an influential member of Agitprop, the Party council which kept a vigilant eye on ideological suitability. The director, Branko Marjanović (1909-1996), was the most experienced and best-educated collaborator of *Hrvatski slikopis* whose previous film on Partisan battles against the Ustasha, *The Flag* (*Zastava*, 1949), was even honored with an award by the government. The degree to which this banned film was harmless in mocking the ineptitude of the local bureaucracy could be judged only a quarter century later when the ban was finally lifted in 1977. Allegedly Tito himself had insisted on the censorship. The film had to wait until 1989 and the eve of the fall of socialism to be shown in regular movie theaters.

Branko Belan: *The Concert* (*Koncert*), 1954
Vatroslav Mimica: *Mr. Ikl's Jubilee* (*Jubilej gospodina Ikla*), 1955

The Fifties: A Time of Easing

Stalin's condemnation of Tito and expulsion of Yugoslavia from the communist bloc in 1948 did not immediately change cultural politics, but control gradually abated and the Soviet model was no longer obligatory. Artists sensed a greater freedom in the realm of style although an ideological commitment was still expected of them. There followed a period of relative liberation in the cultural sphere and this brought about significant new strides, especially in the visual arts. Film directors could now turn to other models. This, of course, did not automatically ensure spectacular results, but it did widen their horizons.

A dozen films were produced at this stage (some of which were made by future big names of Croatian cinema), and in them one can recognize an effort to examine and absorb the achievements of world and European film. In his first feature, *In the Storm* (*U oluji*, 1952), Vatroslav Mimica (1923) relies on the principles of the American thriller set on a Dalmatian island, while in his comedy *Mr. Ikl's Jubilee* (*Jubilej gospodina Ikla*, 1955) he follows *slapstick* patterns. A prewar social story, *Stone Horizons* (*Kameni horizonti*, 1953), by Šime Šimatović (1919) relies on elements of Italian neo-Realism, while the poetic parable *A Girl and an Oak* (*Djevojka i hrast*, 1955) by Krešo Golik is characterized by the influence of Mexican cameraman Gabriel Figuero's black-and-white photographic expression. Branko Belan's (1912-1986) *The Concert* (*Koncert*, 1954) evokes associations with the French prewar *film noir* and is the best-directed film of this period although its qualities were not recognized at the time. It was re-evaluated only by the new generation of film critics two decades later to be pronounced the most accomplished Croatian film of the early years.

Croatian films of the fifties were the most interesting and mature within Yugoslav production thanks to their narrative structure, compelling directorial solutions based on a solid knowledge of world trends, and minimal concessions to the ruling ideology. One of the most productive and competent directors, Branko Bauer (1921-2002), started his career with two youth-adventure films *Blue Seagull* (*Sinji galeb*, 1953) and *Millions on the Island* (*Milioni na otoku*, 1955), neither of which was burdened with socialist didactic themes. He became fully established with the exceptionally well-directed urban war film *My Son Don't Turn Round* (*Ne okreći se*

Branko Bauer: *My Son Don't Turn Round* (*Ne okreći se sine*), 1956
Fedor Hanžeković: *Master of His Own Body* (*Svoga tela gospodar*), 1957

sine, 1956), a psychological drama which stood apart from the clichéd coverage of Partisan subject matter in other film centers. To everyone's surprise, the film triumphed at the country's principal film festival in Pula. His subsequent movie, a Macedonian production, *Three Girls Named Anna* (*Tri Ane*, 1959), anticipated in part the critical treatment of social themes which became a focus of the so-called "black wave" (particularly in Serbian cinematography) in the coming decade.

In July of 1954 a film festival was begun in Pula: it was at first a modest screening of domestic films in the imposing ancient arena, but it soon grew to be the main Yugoslav feature film festival. As a hybrid that included audience screenings, critical evaluation of the gamut of Yugoslav film production, and a competition among the national cinemas within the multinational federation, the Pula festival gradually acquired the status of an event where criteria were defined and new values launched. Large audiences and open-air shows gave the event a special feel. Interaction between the audience's populism and the critics' elitism (and the unavoidable supervision by the political overseers) gave this exceptional "international festival of Yugoslav film" momentum, allowing it to have a real impact on the thematic and stylistic orientation of all Yugoslav cinema centers for more than three decades. The fact that Yugoslav President Tito had a summer residence on the nearby Brioni islands was yet another twist. As a movie lover he regularly watched most of the films at private screenings, and on occasion he joined the public screenings in Pula in a special seating area in the sold-out Roman amphitheater.

The unquestionable preeminence of Croatian films in the fifties was confirmed through a series of awards: starting with 1956 and Bauer's *My Son Don't Turn Round*, films in Croatian production took the top awards nearly every year and also drew large audiences in all the republics. One of the most-viewed Croatian films of the fifties was *Master of His Own Body* (*Svoga tela gospodar*, 1957), the last of Fedor Hanžeković's three films, popular all over the country. It was an entertaining although rather conventional screen version of the eponymous play by Slavko Kolar, a sentimental tale interwoven with humor in the *kajkavian* (north Croatian) setting and dialect, depicting the grinding poverty of rural life.

The following year brought Nikola Tanhofer's (1926-1998) *H-8* (1958), a tense story about a collision between a bus and a truck, a movie that

Nikola Tanhofer: *H8*, 1958
Giuseppe De Santis: *The Year-Long Road* (*Cesta duga godinu dana*), 1958

launched this excellent director known for his modern, lapidary expression. The polyphonic script by Zvonimir Berković and Tomislav Butorac allowed Tanhofer to display his directorial skills, opening the film with the announcement of the tragedy yet not revealing until the very end who the casualties would be. Among the passengers on the bus one recognizes people from all walks of life. Anticipating in a sense the future "catastrophe genre," this classic of Croatian cinema truthfully tackles everyday themes as elegantly as any of the most recognized European film of the day, its well-deserved award at the Pula festival further reinforcing the impression of the preeminence of Croatian film within the Yugoslav film industry of the fifties.

From the start the Zagreb film center was open to directors from elsewhere. However, a visit by Giuseppe De Santis (1917-1997), a great figure of Italian neo-Realism who directed the expensive production *The Year-Long Road* (*Cesta duga godinu dana*, 1958) had no lasting impact. This socially engaged story, though not altogether convincing, about a local initiative to build a rural road in the rugged setting of the Dalmatian hinterland featured several Italian stars (Massimo Girotti, Silvana Pampanini, Eleonora Rossi Drago) and a number of prominent domestic actors. The film was characterized by elements of a late and somewhat stylized neo-Realism. The local producer may have been disappointed with it, but the lengthy film did win a prestigious Golden Globe and was the first Croatian film (under the Yugoslav umbrella) to be nominated for an Oscar for best foreign film. It also received a Golden Gate for acting (Girotti).

Soon another debut film was making ripples on the Croatian film scene: Veljko Bulajić's (1928) *Train Without a Timetable* (*Vlak bez voznog reda*, 1959). The author made bold with the influences of the American classical western as well as with resonances from Italian neo-Realism in this epic evocation of postwar colonization in which entire villages of people from the southern rugged combat zones are transported by train to the fertile northern plains. Unfortunately, he never hints at the fact that these new colonizers are appropriating land hitherto owned by members of the German minority (known as the *Donauschwaben*), who have been forcefully relocated by state decree to the western part of wartorn Germany. Because of its innovative subject matter and mosaic-like dramaturgy this film became a turning point in the development of both Croatian and Yugoslav film.

The formative period of knowledge and acquisition of the craft was drawing to a close. At this time the central Zagreb production company, Jadran Film, was a target of outraged criticism, especially by aspiring directors who resented the fact that visiting artists were brought in from other centers with no selection process. Indeed, a number of films of questionable quality was shot in Zagreb by minor directors from other parts of the country. Still, one positive exception justifies, at least to a degree, all the failures. Using a script by Croatian author Zora Dirnbach, the leading Slovenian director, Francé Štiglic (1919-1993), shot a tragic love story, *The Ninth Circle* (*Deveti krug*, 1960), about Zagreb inhabitants who saved Jews from deportation to concentration camps. This work brought Jadran Film (and the Yugoslav/Croatian film industry) another Academy Award nomination in the category of foreign film. Even after half a century, this film remains at the very top in all the surveys, one of the finest Croatian films of all times.

The Sixties: Auteur Cinema

Auteur Cinema, as Croatian film in the nineteen sixties is customarily labeled, was the result of filmgoers' dissatisfaction with the spiritual sterility and creative stagnation in the system controlled by the production companies. The idea that a decisive role in the complex process of filmmaking should be in the hands of those who made the films — the authors — seemed logical enough. The financial crisis of the federal fund (for which there was ever less funding for a growing number of films) accelerated its decentralization (1962). In a few years (starting in 1967) the system of financing was modified so support was not provided to production companies for their annual production programs, but rather to individual projects submitted directly by the authors via public competitions. In this way the authors partly assumed the role of producer, i.e. they moved into a stronger position in relation to dominant Jadran Film. Successful dissemination of the concept of auteur cinema (in Truffaut's sense of *cinéma d'auteur*) was directly influenced by the Parisian publication *Cahiers du Cinéma*, which served as a theoretical source for the French New Wave. Works such as those by Bergman, Fellini and Antonioni furnished the arguments for a different understanding of film, while a political agreement reached by Tito and Khrushchev opened the door to films from the post-Stalin era, but also for those by Polish, Hungarian, Czech and Slovak directors. In addition, there were Yugoslav films that departed from the usual conventions — the Slovenian *Dancing in the Rain* (*Ples v dežju / Ples na kiši*, 1961) and *The Sand City* (*Peščeni grad / Pješčani grad*, 1962) by Boštjan Hladnik (1929-2006), as well as the Serbian *And Love Has Vanished* (*Dvoje*, 1961) and *Days* (*Dani*, 1963) by Aleksandar Petrović (1929-1994) — inspiring others to shoot different types of films and to entertain greater creative ambitions.

In Croatia, opposition to conventional film was most visible in the circle of Zagreb amateur filmmakers, especially at festivals which erased the division between amateur and professional film. These forums, called

Vatroslav Mimica: *Kaya* (*Kaja, ubit ću te!*), 1967
Prometheus from the Island of Viševica (*Prometej s otoka Viševice*), 1964

GEFF (*Genre-film festival*), were held as of 1963 in Zagreb every other year and included dissident filmmakers from all the Yugoslav centers. However, the closest source of inspiration for auterism was the Zagreb School of Animated Film. Its creative success, acknowledged worldwide, can be attributed to a more liberal creative climate as there was far less political supervision in animation than in feature film. In the late fifties and early sixties, international affirmation came with a series of important awards: in 1962 the first Oscar ever given to a non-American animated film went to *Surrogate* (*Ersatz / Surogat*) by Dušan Vukotić, and the Golden Lion in Venice was awarded to Vatroslav Mimica's *The Loner* (*Samac*).

After a decade of working on animated film, where his hermetic style brought him international recognition, Vatroslav Mimica (1923) created the first auteur film in Croatia and among the first in Yugoslavia, *Prometheus from the Island of Viševica* (*Prometej s otoka Viševice*, 1964). Thematically the film remained within the context of the ruling ideology, but the main character's personal settling of accounts broaches the sensitive issue of moral responsibility for revolutionary deeds that harmed other people. Its complex dramaturgy, cinematography, and editing, have made this film the hallmark of modern Yugoslav cinema. Mimica worked to bring his future films into sync with concurrent European tendencies (especially with the types of films shown at European festivals), which some critics ridiculed, labeling this approach *socialist aestheticism* (as opposed to *socialist realism*) whose purpose was allegedly to mask the sterility of the content with beauty of form. The general audience did not show much understanding for Mimica's modernist orientation, and, not surprisingly, some ten thousand spectators in Pula's ancient amphitheater booed one of his more suggestive films *Kaya* (*Kaja, ubit ću te!*, 1967).

The creative climate of the 1960s also propelled several debutants who had to wait a long time to present their films. These supreme achievements departed in many ways from the ruling conventions, especially in terms of ideas and style, as evident already in Zvonimir Berković's (1928-2009) *Rondo* (1966). This urban film about an unusual marital triangle received many awards and was one of the few Croatian films shown in movie theaters across Europe. Structurally evoking a complex piece of music, with stunning dramaturgy and refined camera work (Tomislav Pinter was director of photography), Berković's thought-provoking film was essential

Ante Babaja: *The Birch Tree* (*Breza*), 1967
The King's New Clothes (*Carevo novo ruho*), 1961

for defining some of the dominant narrative patterns in Croatian film. Prompted by this film, critics recognized a general tendency to organize the plot in a circular manner and referred to this narrative pattern as "Rondo-style dramaturgy."

There are many good reasons to assert that the best Croatian films of the Yugoslav period came to life in the sixties, during the more inspired period of auteurism. These films were made by authors who were aesthetically isolated and were looking, each in his own way, for adequate expressive vehicles. They were not connected in any way by programmatic or generational commonalities. Another lone voice from this group belonged to Ante Babaja (1927-2010), an author for whom the medium of film was always in the service of an artistic *Weltanschauung* and who did not hesitate to experiment with unconventional expressive means. After several interesting short and documentary films, Babaja's first feature, *The King's New Clothes* (*Carevo novo ruho*, 1961) — a carefully stylized reworking of Andersen's fairy tale — contained recognizable allusions to the cult of (Tito's) personality. The supreme visual aspect owes a lot to the *high-key* technique[1] of the veteran Oktavijan Miletić and colorful effects achieved by Jagoda Buić's vivid costumes. Thoughtfully stylized but insufficiently polished, the film occasionally stumbles in its pacing as it was expanded from a medium-length to a full-length feature. This flaw simplified the job of the ideological censors and, though it was not formally banned, the film never made it to the festivals or wider audiences, while the critics had a reserved response. It took Babaja a full six years to make another film, *The Birch Tree* (*Breza*, 1967), which showed the full range, however, of his creative skills. Based on a lyrical short story by Slavko Kolar about the fate of a gentle peasant girl who differs from village women as a birch does from the beech tree, Babaja painted a complex picture of both an ambiance and a mindset in which harshness and tenderness weave together. In collaboration with the masterful camera of Tomislav Pinter he enriched the visual aspect of the film in the spirit of the Croatian naïve painters and created a classic of the Croatian cultural heritage.

1] *High-key* technique yields a picture in bright diffused light with no shadows. The costumes and the elements on the set appear as a refined stylization with the effect of a dream or something surreal.

Krešo Golik: *I Have Two Mothers and Two Fathers* (*Imam 2 mame i 2 tate*), 1968
One Song a Day Takes Mischief Away (*Tko pjeva zlo ne misli*), 1970

Liberalization in all spheres of Yugoslav society in the second half of the sixties was evident after Aleksandar Ranković was removed from his long-time position as head of the police and the secret service in July 1966. This atmosphere of decreased ideological control allowed Krešo Golik, one of the most respected pioneer directors, to return to feature film with great success after a ten-year hiatus imposed for political reasons. During a period of competing authorial idiosyncrasies, Golik bravely filmed his come-back piece *I Have Two Mothers and Two Fathers* (*Imam 2 mame i 2 tate*, 1968). This is a great exemplar of an ostensibly conventional narrative film, which, however, through its gentle and positive humor, focuses with sensitivity on the problems of children whose parents have divorced.

Golik's next film was the musical comedy *One Song a Day Takes Mischief Away* (*Tko pjeva zlo ne misli*, 1970), a refined populist film on interwar Zagreb which achieved cult status with the viewers, while critics twice pronounced it the best Croatian film ever. These two films defined Golik as one of the most creative individuals in Croatian film. He also inspired a shift that had to happen after the ascent and then exhaustion of modernist auteur film: a return to an organized narrative.

Partisan Film

Very few Croatian films of the sixties occupied themselves with the anti-fascist war. For this reason newcomer Antun Vrdoljak (1931) surprised everyone with his Partisan feature *When You Hear the Bells* (*Kad čuješ zvona*, 1969). Equally avoiding ideological rhetoric and modernist challenges, he adhered to a recognizable but spirited narration (following the diary of hero Ivan Šibl) and depicted the experiences of a political commissar from Zagreb in the first days of the anti-fascist uprising in 1941. He also painted a vital picture of sensitive inter-ethnic relations and clashes between villages peopled with a religiously and ethnically mixed population. The film was well received by the audience as well as at festivals (a silver medal in Moscow). Vrdoljak soon shot the sequel *The Pine Tree in the Mountain* (*U gori raste zelen bor*, 1971) which had some 300,000 viewers in Croatia alone! By using an exceptional group of actors he was able to tease open the psychology and mindsets in the early stages of the uprising. Although

Veljko Bulajić: *The Battle of Neretva* (*Bitka na Neretvi*), 1969
Spanish poster for *The Battle of Neretva*

Vrdoljak shot many other films (and left a negative mark as Tuđman's trusted person and key player in film and media during the period of autocratic nationalism of the 1990s), these two films are generally considered to be a specific Croatian contribution to the genre of Partisan film (jokingly called *easterns*), one of the most authentic genres that emerged from the Yugoslav cinema.

Super-productions intended to enhance Tito's personality cult drew particularly large audiences. *The Battle of Neretva* (*Bitka na Neretvi*, 1969) by Veljko Bulajić, sponsored by Marshal Tito himself, enjoyed considerable international recognition and was even nominated for an Academy award as best foreign film. Although directed by an author who resided in Croatia, in terms of production and ideology this is largely a Yugoslav film. All film centers as well as distributors from several republics worked together on its creation and marketing. It is remembered as the prototype of an extremely expensive project supported by the state well beyond what regular film funds allowed. The film included a team of nearly sixty domestic and world stars (among them Orson Welles, Yul Brynner, Hardy Krüger, Sylva Koscina, Franco Nero, Sergei Bondarchuk, as well as recognized local names such as Boris Dvornik and Bata Živojinović). The pompous premiere was a celebration of the Tito cult and it was held in Sarajevo on the most important state holiday in the presence of celebrated foreign guests flown in from Rome and Paris. The grandiosity of this project drew the audiences (an unbelievable three million viewers in Yugoslavia!), but it also attracted foreign distributors who showed the film in more than seventy countries. At a recent festival in Moscow it was pronounced one of the ten most important films about World War II.

In almost all the Yugoslav republics many similarly ambitious but less successful spectacles were made and they were all characterized by a combination of megalomania and mythomania. Among such films — ironically labeled the "red wave" as opposed to the negative and subversive "black wave" — the most well known is *The Battle of Sutjeska* (*Sutjeska*, 1973), by Croatian director Stipe Delić (1925-1999) who tried to repeat Bulajić's production and dramaturgical formula, with Richard Burton playing Tito.

Social Criticism and Black Wave

Croatian films from the period of auteurism did not show much interest for dealing critically with contemporary issues in society, but rather focused on individual psychological states, with particular attention to style and means of expression. At the same time, the creators of what is known as the "black wave" in Serbian cinematography perceived the auteur approach as a chance to delve into the most sensitive political and social issues. Still, the Croatian film *Face to Face* (*Licem u lice*, 1963) by Branko Bauer may have been one of the first titles to open the door to a more daring exploration of contemporary societal problems. Even in his earlier film *Three Girls Named Anna* (*Tri Ane*, 1959) this recognized master of the traditional narrative structure pointed to both the possibility and the need of addressing reality critically. Bauer was an exceptional director, but his orientation meant that he was not an aesthetic innovator. Still, his contribution is vast in terms of development of cinematic literacy, an articulation of film language, and an understanding of the potential that moving pictures could have in this part of the world. His constructively critical *Face to Face* treats a conflict between a worker and the omnipotent Party structures, and owing to its topic, it made quite a stir. It was also significant for the rise and spread of the socially critical film in Yugoslavia, which, as stated earlier, took particularly deep roots in Serbia.

The sixties yielded a corpus of important films capped under the somewhat simplifying term "black wave" (Croatian: *crni val*; Serbian: *crni talas*), a dangerous label launched by the re-activated overseers of ideology with the principal purpose of persecution. This period in Yugoslav cinema is not dominated by ideologically subtle films from Zagreb, but rather by spirited Serbian achievements from authors such as Živojin Pavlović, Dušan Makavejev, Želimir Žilnik and others. One Belgrade critic elegantly said that the Croatian films in these years were smart while the Serbian films were razor-sharp.

In Croatia Krsto Papić (1933) was among the first to join the trend of a critical examination of reality with his suggestive *Handcuffs* (*Lisice*, 1969). If judged from the social and critical perspective, this is to date the most incisive Croatian film. Focusing on the taboo-topic of the 1948 rupture and the purging of Stalin's followers using his selfsame methods, the film won the Golden Arena in Pula, but the authorities banned its screening at the Cannes festival where it was supposed to appear in the official program.

Papić's next film *Acting Hamlet in the Village of Mrduša Donja* (*Predstava Hamleta u selu Mrduša Donja*, 1973) is a heavily politicized screen version of a play by Croatian playwright Ivo Brešan, in which backward and self-serving local political figures insist on their vulgar interpretation of Shakespeare's play at an amateur performance venue. Needless to say, the film received its share of ideological criticism and obstacles at festival showings. Papić had to wait a full fifteen years to shoot *My Uncle's Legacy* (*Život sa stricem*, 1988), the third part of his trilogy on the ruthless relationship between government officials and the individual. Again Papić had to fight harsh political criticism and interference even as he was shooting the film.

The Seventies: A Collective Self-Censorship

A fundamental change in the political and social climate swept Yugoslavia in late 1971. With a single stroke Tito and Party removed a group of leading politicians and suppressed the Croatian national-liberal movement known as the Croatian Spring. For all practical purposes this ended a five-year phase of relative liberalism in politics and culture. The following year liberal party circles in Serbia met the same fate. The ideological supervision of all segments of culture tightened soon thereafter. Many artists and intellectuals found their names on (never made public) black lists and were removed from public life. This often meant that it was impossible for them to pursue their profession. The most notorious case was the prison sentence served by Serbian director Lazar Stojanović for his film *Plastic Jesus* (*Plastični Isus*, 1971).

In Croatia several leading intellectuals and writers received prison sentences in 1972 which were several years in length, mostly for the "crime of reasoning" (*delikt mišljenja*). This was the most severe form of repression after World War II. Many cultural publications were shut down or disciplined. Although only one documentary was officially banned, a number of others were removed from the public eye without a formal ban. The atmosphere in Croatia during the seventies was marked by omnipresent repression and trauma, resulting in creative sterility in the realm of film. Ideological rigidity forced some filmmakers to remain silent (either by decree or voluntarily), while those who continued to shoot exercised self-censorship.

As far as the subject matter is concerned, the seventies in Croatia saw a number of fairly well made social essays, some of them distinctive in terms of visuals and editing, which dealt with marginal contemporary phenomena. They carried a dose of mild criticism which passed fairly unnoticed and presented reality in a truthful manner. The most relevant work from this lukewarm selection is *Journalist* (*Novinar*, 1979) by Fadil Hadžić (1922-2011).This is probably the most mature of Hadžić's many films in which, with much bitterness, he depicts negative experiences in the area of journalism, his long-time profession.

Bogdan Žižić (1934) in his film *Don't Lean Out the Window* (*Ne naginji se van*, 1977) was among the first to address the disheartening subject of the *gastarbeiters* (Croatian immigrants working temporarily abroad in Western countries, especially Germany) in a mode similar to the acerbic style of his documentaries, while Nikola Babić (1935), another great documentary maker, based the feature *Crazy Days* (*Ludi dani*, 1977) on the same theme, laced with bitter humor. The first feature by theater and TV director Tomislav Radić (1940), entitled *The Living Truth* (*Živa istina*, 1972), aroused great interest among filmgoers (and political suspicions). In this film Radić applies the *cinéma direct* approach ingeniously to realize a stunningly convincing portrait of a popular actress. It is easy to see that politically less risky genres were being favored as a result of the political circumstances.

Two children's films made in the seventies stood apart and reached beyond Croatia: *Lone Wolf* (*Vuk samotnjak*, 1972) by Obrad Gluščević (1913-

Zvonimir Berković: *The Scene of a Crash* (*Putovanje na mjesto nesreće*), 1971
Ante Babaja: *Gold, Frankincense and Myrrh* (*Mirisi, zlato, tamjan*), 1971

1980) is considered one of the most mature and emotional films to have emerged from this part of the world. It was seen by a large domestic and foreign audience and received five prestigious awards from several specialized international festivals. Similar praise could be given to *Train in the Snow* (*Vlak u snijegu*, 1976) by Mato Relja (1922-2006), a brilliant film based on the eponymous cult juvenile novel by Mato Lovrak. As some of the most memorable films from this period one should mention Golik's *Violet* (*Ljubica*, 1978), a compassionate reflection on the position and psychological situation of a single mother, as well as two impressive screen versions of Slobodan Novak's novels: Ante Babaja's *Gold, Frankincense and Myrrh* (*Mirisi, zlato, tamjan* 1971) and The *Lost Homeland* (*Izgubljeni zavičaj*, 1980). After his brilliant first feature Berković shot only one more film in this decade, a complex psychological melodrama *The Scene of a Crash* (*Putovanje na mjesto nesreće*, 1971) which was appreciated by the critics far more than by the author himself.

The film that marked the entire seventies both in terms of the number of festival awards and the huge controversies it sparked was a war feature by Lordan Zafranović (1944) entitled *Occupation in 26 Pictures* (*Okupacija u 26 slika*, 1978). Along with his colleagues from Zagreb, Belgrade, and Sarajevo who all studied film directing at the renowned Prague Academy of Film, Zafranović belongs the so-called "Prague school" characterized by an unstaged approach to reality and bitter humor and cynicism. *Occupation in 26 Pictures* is a provocative film which structures the events that took place in Dubrovnik in the first days of World War II into an epic frame-work. It is especially remembered for a chilling episode lasting approximately seven minutes in which the Ustashas slaughter and bash the passengers they have captured on a bus that moves through the backdrop of the glorious ancient city. This scene of brutal bloodshed as contrasted with the utmost beauty is handled with such unrelenting naturalism that it can be justifiably catalogued among the most cruel and effective scenes of political horror in domestic and world film in general. Drawn by the explicit images of violence and sex, audiences flocked to the Yugoslav movie theaters. The recognition which this film achieved at festivals, combined with the fact that it emphasized the criminal nature of the Ustasha regime, made Zafranović a poster boy of the Yugoslav communist *establishment*. In the revived atmosphere of iron-hand rule after

Lordan Zafranović: *Occupation in 26 Pictures (Okupacija u 26 slika)*, 1978
The Fall of Italy (Pad Italije), 1982

the repression of the Croatian Spring, this film went hand in hand with the Party conviction that treated any attempt by Croats to forge an identity of their own as tantamount to the Ustasha program. Having been sensitized by the crackdown on the Croatian Spring, the unofficial public stance in Croatia was that *Occupation in 26 Pictures* was a malicious pamphlet intended to stoke anti-Croatian sentiment. For this reason there was a refusal to recognize certain stylistic merits which this cunningly conceptualized and beautifully shot film does have. During the period of creative repression Zafranović's film became a paradigm for ideologically desirable substance in elitist modernist packaging, and it was thus officially imposed as a model for others.

The Weary Eighties

After the political success of *Occupation in 26 Pictures*, Zafranović made two more films about revolutionaries' fates (*The Fall of Italy / Pad Italije*, 1982; and *Evening Bells / Večernja zvona*, 1986), combining them into a trilogy that was supposed to depict the dramatic history of the Yugoslav revolution through personal fates. The films, however, rapidly faded from the collective memory.

Rajko Grlić (1947) is another member of the Prague school who made some of his most important films in this decade with record box office sales, among them *The Melody Haunts My Reverie* (*Samo jednom se ljubi*, 1981). This is an unconventional postwar melodrama about a victorious revolutionary who is brought down professionally and personally by his love for a woman from the bourgeoisie. Owing to its thematic and stylistic complexity, Grlić's next film, *In the Jaws of Life* (*U raljama života*, 1984), might be the most suitable for identifying the attributes of the Prague school. Based on a popular novel by Dubravka Ugrešić with a simple story line, it branches its subject matter in an ironic direction and organizes the narrative into two parallel plots. These postmodernist stylistic interventions shape the film into a complex and somewhat stylized grotesque in which the life and kitsch-philosophy of a young secretary on the one hand and the sophisticated intellectual media elite on the other are treated with a hefty dose of sarcasm.

In the course of Yugoslavia's final decade, Croatian cinema reached a point of stability: competitions for funding were announced at regular intervals, sources of financing were determined by law, and production oscillated between five and eight films per year. A generational change was clearly on its way: some of the veterans made listless movies, and new names started cropping up. The authors coming from the Croatian segment of the Prague school were already established (Zafranović and Grlić), while for the budding *new-genre* film this was a particularly productive decade with directors such as Tadić, Ivanda, Tomić, and Šorak.

Shot with a low budget, outside the regular financing system, Zoran Tadić's (1941-2007) black and white *Rhythm of the Crime* (*Ritam zločina*, 1981) has been pronounced the best Croatian film of the eighties and it has become a classic that has opened a new chapter in the history of aesthetic and stylistic orientations here. Tadić created a tense detective feature with elements of a fantastic mystery; he is thought of as the founder of new-genre film. This orientation is based on a return to established genre determinants in terms of style, in line with what was advocated by an influential group of critics, the so-called "Hitchcockians." As they positioned themselves counter to ideologically colored conventions, this faction reached for traditional genres from the standard Hollywood production of the forties and fifties which had been rediscovered by the French New Wave in the sixties and the new Hollywood directors in the late seventies. With minimal funds but with the vast support of both critics and colleagues, Tadić shot six low-budget films in ten years. They resonated more within film circles than with the general audience. Nonetheless they introduced stylistic innovations not only in Croatia, but also in other film communities of the region. This refreshing take on the narrative film, following genre determinants, had an impact on many other directors, among them Dejan Šorak (1954) whose melodrama *An Officer with a Rose* (*Oficir s ružom*, 1987) was a major success in all the Yugoslav republics.

After a successful beginning with Partisan films Antun Vrdoljak turned his attention entirely to Croatian literature. His polished screen versions of two important contemporary prose and drama works — *Cyclops* (*Kiklop*, 1982) by Ranko Marinković and *The Glembays* (*Glembajevi*, 1988) by Miroslav Krleža — were received surprisingly well across the country. Well received was also a debut film by Branko Schmidt (1957) entitled *Sokol Did Not Love Him* (*Sokol ga nije volio*, 1988). This was the first Croatian film which dared to show a column of exhausted soldiers and civilians on a forced march after the generals of the vanquished army of the Independent State of Croatia surrendered to the western allies near the city of Bleiburg in southern Austria only to be handed over to and executed by Tito's victorious troops. The principal character of this war drama is a patriarchal peasant who tries to save his property and family during the war years, something that is only possible by astutely evading engagement by either the Ustasha or the Partisan armies. Poetic realism and a brutal truthfulness saved the film from the political censure that was expected but surprisingly never materialized. In the eighties even the censors were growing weary.

A New Beginning

Although film appeared as a new visual attraction in Croatia at the end of the nineteenth century — quite early and almost concurrent to other middle European countries — it took nearly half a century for the domestic film industry to take root as a sustainable system. Film production in Croatia has become not only continuous and more or less systematic since the 1940s, but other branches of the film industry (distribution, screening technologies, technical equipment, criticism, professional education) have been gradually building into a network. The most relevant perhaps is the fact that film as a medium of communication and artistic expression has become firmly rooted in Croatian culture and society in the course of the second half of the twentieth century.

Throughout this time Croatian film has been saddled, however, with an identity crisis. Namely, the cinema in Yugoslavia was regularly treated as a single whole and as a product of socialism, which implied that film art was an unquestionable outgrowth of Yugoslavism (understood as an ideology) and as such should favor a supra-national determination. It was not advisable to emphasize the national background of any film since this could easily have been qualified as nationalism. For this reason Croatian authors and their works inevitably appeared on the world scene under the Yugoslav umbrella.

The changing reality in the politics and society of the new state (Croatia was internationally recognized in January 1992) allowed its cinema to finally acquire a national identity. This has not proven to be an obstacle for a productive collaboration with colleagues from the neighboring countries with which Croatia has shared a great deal of common history in the twentieth century. Thus Croatian film found itself at the beginning again. Fortunately, this time the starting point was not zero. Most important of all is that its development has left us with a significant film heritage including a large number of fine films in a variety of genres and that these creations occupy central positions on the scale of cultural values in Croatia.

The new beginning has put forth an entirely new generation of young filmmakers, mostly educated at Zagreb's Academy of Dramatic Art. In the first years of the country's independence, film was an art that still had to find its way. There was nothing new coming out, but two of the older masters were finalizing work they had begun in the old system. For this reason the films *Stone Gate* (*Kamenita vrata*, 1991) by Ante Babaja and *Countess Dora* (*Kontesa Dora*, 1993) by Zvonimir Berković, both professors to a new generation of directors at the Academy, almost symbolically signify another link in the continuous chain of development. The future of Croatian film belongs to their students.

Translated by Aida Vidan

Institutions, Infrastructure, Industry: Croatian Film or a Battle for Survival
by Tomislav Kurelec

The First Steps: Jadran film

It has become customary to link the violent disintegration of Yugoslavia with the demise of a film industry that was known, at least occasionally, to draw considerable international attention. Its successes delighted not only film-makers and film enthusiasts, but also the government, given that it further underscored the cooperation between the different nationalities and showed the strength of the socialist model that had been created. Even before the end of World War II, on 9 February 1945, the State Film Company (*Državno filmsko preduzeće*) was established and relatively soon (15 July 1946) separate republic film companies were funded and employed filmmakers. Many of them had only modest film experience and some had none — having to learn their job "hands on." Croatia's production company was called Jadran Film, but in the first years after World War II the existence of six film companies (one in each republic) did not result in distinct profiles for each of them. Most projects, in fact, were cooperative efforts, such as the first feature of the new country, *Slavica* (1947), which was naïve and oversaturated with revolutionary élan. It was produced by Serbian Avala Film from Belgrade, but the director, Vjekoslav Afrić, and most of the actors were from Croatia. Similarly, *This Nation Will Live* (*Živjeće ovaj narod*, 1947), an anti-fascist epic and the first film made by Zagreb's Jadran Film, was directed by Nikola Popović who, along with the majority of the actors, was from Serbia.

A substantial change in production came about in the 1950s. After the rupture of relations with the Soviet Union the demand to adhere to socialist-realist themes relaxed, and, equally importantly, filmmakers were no longer "workers" employed in production companies but could enjoy "independent status." Both of these components contributed to a gradual profiling of the film production of each republic, although filmmakers in the former Yugoslavia often worked in other republics over the years. This was particularly true for the popular actors, as well as for some big ticket items such as Veljko Bulajić's *The Battle of Neretva* (*Bitka na Neretvi*, 1969), which had to be made jointly in order to depict the Partisan antifascist movement in spectacular terms which impressed not only domestic audiences but viewers worldwide.

Do You Miss Censorship?

After the fall of socialism, the disappearance of ideological censorship gave Croatian authors as well as those from the other transitional countries an opportunity to express their views more freely and to address the situation in society from a more critical perspective regardless of whether they focused on topics from the past, or from the latest wave of changes. It may seem a paradox that the greater freedom initially brought about weaker films in most of the transitional states, including Croatia. Most of the authors could not resist the temptation to convey more bluntly what they had previously masked with metaphors, and this overabundance of candor diminished the value of many movies that ended up lacking in sophistication and subtlety at the symbolic level.

This problem was particularly glaring in Croatia during the aggression of pro-Serbian forces after it first declared independence in 1991. With the goal of showing the horrors of war and identifying the real aggressors, the first Croatian films about these tragic events left the impression of propaganda. In addition, they had a major problem with domestic filmgoers who did not wish to face once again the traumas they had experienced in real life, while foreign audiences were simply not interested in films with such a salient political agenda. It was only Vinko Brešan's humorous and layered *How the War Started on My Island* (*Kako je rat počeo na mom otoku*, 1996), reminiscent, in structure, of Czech comedies, which represented the war — without pathetic overtones or propaganda — as a clash between a Mediterranean civilization and a repressive government. This drew over three hundred thousand viewers to the movie theaters, a greater number than for some of the Hollywood blockbusters, and tenfold more than many other Croatian films, marking thus a gradual change in attitude among Croatians toward their own film industry.

Distribution: From Popular Entertainment to Elitism

The disintegration of Yugoslavia and the beginning of Croatian independence significantly influenced the viewer's stance not only toward Croatian film, but to film in general. In a short period of time the number of the movie theaters dropped drastically — from one hundred eighty-eight to eighty-four — only to be further cut in the subsequent ten years to barely over fifty.

Many movie theaters were physically destroyed during the war, others became non-profitable partly because people avoided congregating in areas where bombardments could be expected, and partly because of the general impoverishment of the population caused by the war. Although in the first years after independence the cost of a movie ticket was halved and amounted to about $1, even this was not low enough for the majority of the population whose average monthly salary was at that time about $75.

Nonetheless, the first national festival Days of Croatian Film (*Dani hrvatskog filma*) organized at Zagreb's Student center in early 1992 in the midst of Serbian hostilities and accompanied by air-raid sirens filled for the entire eight days the city's biggest movie theater that seats over one thousand people. However, this shining moment of Croatian film was rooted not as much in the love for domestic celluloid art as it was a show of patriotism. The inhabitants of Zagreb wanted to give a festive screening to the films made during and despite the hostilities, demonstrating that they, just like the film artists, were not frightened by threats and air-raids. That this event was an exception was proven in the coming years. The end of the war and a return to normal living conditions did not bring larger numbers of people back to the movie theaters. Even now, the number of box-office tickets does not exceed two and a half million per year, which is on average somewhat more than half a ticket per person. By contrast, sales were nine times bigger in the early 1980s, over twenty million. This indicates that a large segment of the population simply does not go to the movies, while the rest go irregularly (once in several months) and pick five to six of the most popular titles. Since tastes and genre preferences differ, some films do draw satisfactory attendance, but it is interesting to observe that one third of the premieres of foreign films (including those coming from Hollywood) do not yield significantly better results when compared to Croatian films.

A certain amount of sensationalism in the media treatment of Croatian film and insistence on a general lack of interest for it created an extremely negative effect — dissuading even those who have never seen a single Croatian film to give it a chance. Thus after the lengthy initial period when the media looked favorably on domestic film, a negative image started to take hold based at times on judgments of those who had little or nothing to do with film. And yet, even those Croatian films which sold a mere several thousand tickets at the box-office were seen by hundreds of thousands of people when shown on television. Considering these statistics, it is not surprising that Croatian Radiotelevision appears as a co-producer for most of the domestic titles. As a rule, daily media in Croatia avoid deeper probing into these kinds of issues since a systematic investigation does not carry the flavor of sensation. It is clear, though, that a more serious analysis is overdue.

Movies are no longer the favorite (and least expensive) popular entertainment, and the reason for this is not solely the increase in the price of the ticket. Although the average Croatian sees fewer films in the movie theater than before, it is likely that outside the theater s/he sees more films than ever. Fifteen years ago one could watch no more than ten films a week in translation on Croatian television while now, at least in theory, one can see that many every day. In the same period the number of videos (VHS) and, subsequently, DVDs has gone shooting up and many decide to enjoy the comfort of their own home and free or much cheaper entertainment. They also have at their disposal a greater selection of television films. In addition, they are not bothered by the recommendation that film can be truly experienced only on a big screen since a large number of

Croatian movie theaters have not been renovated for years and are not only uncomfortable, but the video and audio reproduction is inferior to what could be had at home for a modest investment.

Still, at least some theaters make an attempt to support variety through specialized programs, catering to the audiences who follow European film festivals in particular (for the screening of which there is financial incentive from European funds). It is a paradox, though, that the leading experts at national and commercial TV companies do not register this discrepancy between the interests that the audiences exhibit in their capacity as moviegoers and TV spectators. While the former segment is mostly younger individuals, the latter includes all segments of the population — including those who never go to movie theaters. Also, among those who see films on the big screen, the viewers often opt for foreign films guessing (correctly) that they will be able to see the domestic titles on television anyway. A relevant question is therefore whether the interest for domestic titles that non-moviegoers exhibit could be put to good use in some way to persuade them to attend movie theaters at least from time to time. As the infrastructure, including movie venues, is beginning to improve, this may serve in the future as an incentive for some parts of the population to enjoy film events outside their homes. A part of the problem is not exclusive to Croatia since on the one hand artistic films are shown rarely, as a rule, and in specialized theaters having to compete with blockbusters, while on the other, they compete (especially when it comes to the younger viewers) with the Internet both as alternative entertainment and as a source of free downloads. All this attests to the fact that the decrease of ninety percent (even a bit more for Croatian films) in box-office sales over the last thirty or so years is not as much a reflection of the merits or quality of domestic films as it is a consequence of technological advancement (in which Croatia is no different from other countries). In addition, this negative effect was augmented by war destruction in Croatia. Even if it is difficult to assess whether films are watched less nowadays than they used to be (here we take into consideration all forms of viewing), film showings in movie theaters seem to have stopped being popular entertainment and have started turning into an elitism of sorts.

Production: Between Socialist Habits and Challenges of Market Economy

Although the position of the film industry in Croatia as well as the audience's view of it have changed in the course of the last decades, its organization and the manner in which films are produced (in particular the distribution of production funds) have adjusted far less than one would expect, especially given the transformation that society as a whole underwent after the war. At first glance it even appears that many modifications are superficial and that only individual people have been replaced (though not always!) while the structure has remained nearly intact. Although many of these individuals (operating mostly as part of various multi-member film committees) could not be denied their expertise, it could be noted that at least some were more concerned with the state's interests than the quality of the films, which might seem logical in a system where the state secures the production money. This kind of situation in which national film is dependent on government support is not unusual in smaller industries that cannot ensure survival based solely on box-office sales. In Croatia, however, the roots of the system were planted in socialism and the failure to introduce changes in the 1990s has been costly.

Once again, we have to look at the historical context to understand the full ramifications of the problem. In socialism the government, as the peoples' representative, concerned itself primarily with the functioning of social mechanisms. It presented ideological control as a way to ensure the rule of the working class over material production and the workers' rights to live from their work. These clichéed phrases were then used occasionally as a threat to those who did not subscribe to them. In cases of such disobedience in the area of film, the money for a given project did not come from the budget for culture but was secured from the percentage of box-office sales, including foreign sales. At the moment when the numbers of moviegoers started decreasing in the 1980s, Croatia was the only republic in Federal Yugoslavia in which a substantial amount of money, 1.5% of the obligatory TV monthly subscription to Radiotelevision Zagreb for TV set owners (now Croatian Radiotelevision), went directly into the film industry fund. In other words, the film industry was not financed directly through the Ministry of Culture, but rather it was managed, just like many other areas outside the arts, by a body known as the Self-Managed Community Services (*Samoupravna interesna zajednica* — SIZ). The greatest part of SIZ income went towards financing feature films (although a portion also went to documentaries, short features, experimental, and animated films). A fraction of the resources was used for quality improvement since a special committee evaluated the achievements of each individual film which, in turn, generated additional funding. Furthermore, in some periods there were special incentives for bringing audiences to movie theaters and for this reason the film would be given additional funding that would match its earnings at the box-office. One could say that such a system was quite productive for Croatian filmmakers since, just as their counterparts in other socialist countries, they mastered a complex stylistic vocabulary in order to avoid political censorship. Due to a number of successful co-productions, Zagreb's Jadran Film became a reputable production company with a world-wide reputation.

Unfortunately, these positive elements were overshadowed by numerous obstacles. Behind this shiny surface the fact remains that in the 1980s feature-film production was modest and amounted, for instance, in 1983 to only one film, while in 1986 it was increased by only one more coproduction supported by another Yugoslav republic. There are multiple reasons why this seemingly promising situation did not yield a greater number of films. One of them is the need to have the entire financing in place before the shooting began. By contrast, in Serbia many more films were made, mostly in the production of working communities (*radne zajednice*) which were formed for individual projects and in which film artists invested their own money with the risk that they might lose it if the film were a flop. In Croatia, the expectation was that not only the funds for film itself, but also the profit margin for the producer (most often Jadran Film) needed to be secured before shooting began. This approach turned out to be both advantageous and disadvantageous. While the leading names in Croatian film industry at the time claimed that it was precisely this industry that was most professional in the Yugoslav context, others saw this as a hindrance. The very fact that Jadran Film and, in rare instances, other producers were guaranteed profit at the outset and that the profit was later increased by the film's earnings at the box office destroyed the premises on which professional production is based — accepting both risk and responsibility for a film's success to insure the producer's full engagement in the process of making and placing the film, i.e. its production and distribution.

This situation demonstrates particularly well the downside of socialist self-management. Jadran Film is a company which was established first and foremost through the involvement of diverse filmmakers, their efforts and products, and even partly owing to income generated by them which was plowed back into the company and was supposed to serve as a foundation for future work. However, the funds were diverted to profitable co-productions which made Jadran Film a sizeable producer on a world scale — not only in terms of investments, but also profits. This capital, which, according to the then ruling ideology of socialist self-management, was supposed to belong to the workers (in this case filmmakers), never made it into their hands. Rather, it was held by the company and probably ended up in the pockets of its leading managers. In addition, the company would appropriate almost a quarter of the funds allocated to the film to start with since it charged exorbitant rates for its services. In cases when a foreign agent offered a contract to a Croatian actor in a co-productions, Jadran Film appropriated an extremely high percentage (usually 85%) of the fee paid to the actor by the foreign producer. If the actor challenged this system, he or she would lose even the remaining 15% of the original fee — and 15% was still much more than what would have been paid for a similar role in a Croatian film.

After the collapse of Yugoslavia and the end of the Croatian Homeland War, there were radical changes in all segments of society so it was reasonable to expect that the model of financing in the film industry would be entirely transformed as well. But the only part of the system that changed initially was the segment that was the most reminiscent of socialism: the self-managed community services were cut and, as a result, there was no money from the box-office tickets (which was minimal anyway because of the turbulence of war as explained above). Furthermore, no percentage was coming from subscriptions to national radiotelevision which the state shielded less as a public service and far more as a propaganda machine of the new regime under the authoritarian leadership of the first president, Franjo Tuđman. Film fell under the auspices of the Ministry of Culture and was financed directly from the state budget. To make things more complicated, Croatian Radiotelevision consented to a tacit agreement to become a co-producer of every Croatian film though it would not have the right to decide which films were going to be made. For this purpose it had to earmark funds equal to those secured by the Ministry with the relief being that a part of the support need not be in money but could be rendered in services (technical assistance, editing, etc.).

In effect, nothing changed in the mechanism through which the projects were selected. Special committees consisting now not of five but of three members continued to do the job, and for several years the decision was made by only one commissioner. Although at times one is tempted to wonder about the competence of some of the committee members, the bulk of the problem seems to lie elsewhere. The principal issue remains that, with the rare exception, the only films made are those financed by the Ministry of Culture along with Croatian Radiotelevision in a way which not only covers all expenses but also secures profit for the producers. Consequently, the producers continue to be free of any risk or responsibility for their product and often ask for additional funds in order to send the film to foreign festivals or for English subtitling. Abolishing the small percentage of funds awarded on the basis of the film's success (according to various film juries and box-office results) has visibly de-incentivized the producers in their efforts (or lack thereof!) for the quality of the films or their launching on both domestic and foreign markets. And without producers' responsibility for the films in whose credits they appear and assuming at least a part of the financial risk, it is difficult to expect healthy developments in the film industry.

Any suggestion that producers might invest own funds in film has to face a justified argument that Croatian film — just as with the films of other small countries — simply cannot return the invested funds. Still, one wonders whether a possible solution to the problem could be to give the winning projects approximately 80% of the funds, and to award the remaining 20% to finished products based on the previously agreed criteria for success: yield at domestic box-offices, visibility at international festivals, foreign sales, etc. This model would allow non-commercial and small national film industries such as Croatia's to make (but also to lose!) some money. Unfortunately, there has been no serious move in the direction of a more productive model for financing in the film industry (especially by the Ministry of Culture), and, as a result, Croatian film still does not have the infrastructure that most of Europe has.

With the exception of allocating funds from the state budget, not much has been done to protect the film industry. After socialist Yugoslavia's dedication to film because of its significant propaganda potential, and after the initial period of Croatian independence when film was unfortunately also used at times for non-cinematic purposes, a more democratic Croatia stopped caring as much about this area of art at the institutional level. Sure enough, film has remained relevant as a segment of culture, however, it was not given the kind of priority as those areas which could attest to the existence of the nation for many centuries. As it would have been awkward for the state to allow Croatian film to fade into the background of successful Yugoslav titles, help was provided but the infrastructure was not reshuffled. It is therefore surprising that this kind of climate with a general lack of enthusiasm produced not the same, but even better results in terms of the number of feature films. Instead of barely four films in the past, the last decade has been yielding six to eight titles annually. It is difficult to say whether this unquestionable success has been the result of measures by the Ministry of Culture that are invisible to the public or of efforts by filmmakers themselves, especially the younger generation which has not had a chance to rely on socialist habits. One thing, however, is sure: after fifteen years of trying to persuade the Ministry of Culture to consider a bill to regulate the film industry, it was the filmmakers who played the decisive role in 2007 when a comprehensive law on audiovisual activities was finally passed. Although even this did not prove sufficient in terms of protecting the film industry through certain mechanisms that are customary in other parts of Europe (such as obligatory quotas or an incentive for showing domestic films, tax breaks for sponsors, or bank loans with special rates), it did make the Croatian Audiovisual Centre (Hrvatski audiovizualni centar — HAVC) possible with its role as a film institute much like those in Scandinavian countries or Greece.

For the time being the impression is that the Audiovisual Centre will have a difficult time bringing to fruition concepts which are, for the most part, quite good but not easily realizable with the modest staff that the Centre has at its disposal. Significant steps forward were made during the brief period when Albert Kapović (1957–2008) was at its head, in particular in the area of international co-productions. One of the significant changes in the law obligates the Audiovisual Centre to rely on several new sources of financing such as a percentage of the brutto revenue from audiovisual producers and distributors, national commercial television, regional television, cable distributors, etc. If this is realized, it will provide a way for the Croatian film industry to survive despite many problems that still need to be addressed and a serious economic crisis in the country.

Translated by Aida Vidan

From a Cinema of Hatred to a Cinema of Consciousness: Croatian Film after Yugoslavia
by Jurica Pavičić

In the last week of July 1991, the Croatian coastal city of Pula seemed to be an absolutely peaceful place. The city at the tip of the Istrian Peninsula was ready — as it always was at that time of year — for the annual Yugoslav film festival to begin. As every year in July, the city was plastered with film posters, the press center was already open, the catalogues printed, and the whole city was ready to welcome the most famous of the festival guests: Hollywood actor of Croatian origin, John Malkovich. Pula looked perfectly normal and calm.

But, circumstances that summer in Yugoslavia were far from normal and calm. In June, Slovenia, the northernmost Yugoslav federal unit, had proclaimed its independence, and the federal army had responded with a brief, six-day military campaign. Conflict in Croatia between the pro-independence government and parts of the Serbian minority had slowly progressed from local skirmishes to a full-scale war. On the very day the festival opened, six men died in an exchange of gunfire near the eastern Croatian town, Erdut, several cities were shelled by the federal army, Yugoslav People's Army troops cut off the electricity supply for the southern Croatian cities, and nationalist extremists blew up shops of local merchants of the Serbian nationality in Osijek and Vinkovci. Under these circumstances, the very idea of a Yugoslav film festival seemed obviously bizarre. The festival board of directors was run at the time by two future political opponents: liberal film historian Ivo Škrabalo, and nationalist film director Antun Vrdoljak, already politically active in Franjo Tuđman's Croatian Democratic Union (Hrvatska demokratska zajednica — HDZ). On the very first day of the festival, after the morning press screening, the board of the festival shut Pula 1991 down for good.

That day in July was not just the end of the Yugoslav film festival in Pula — the key event of film life in communist Yugoslavia — but in a certain way it was also a symbolic end of Yugoslavia itself. If federal communist Yugoslavia was largely the conceptual invention of *bon vivant* dictator Josip Broz Tito, cinema had always been Tito's favorite toy and a privileged demonstration of his cultural prowess. Within Yugoslav communism, cinema and (especially) the partisan war epics played a role similar to the role of cathedrals in medieval Christianity. Cinema was considered the absolute essence of the Titoist spirit, and the Pula festival — geographically situated near Tito's summer residence at Brioni islands — was the key social event

Nedeljko Dragić: *Pula film festival*, caricature, 1967

in a Yugoslav, glittery and glamorous version of communist totalitarianism. That July 1991, the Yugoslav cinema finally died. After 45 years of successful history and 890 feature films, after five foreign film Oscar nominations, the first non-American Oscar for an animation short, after several awards in Berlin, Cannes, Venice, Oberhausen and Annecy, one of the most prestigious national cinemas in Eastern Europe dissolved overnight.

The post-Yugoslav secessions continued for the next decade, and in place of the former federal state we now have six or seven independent countries (the number depends on whether we count *de facto* independent Kosovo). Each of these countries meanwhile started its own national cinema. Some of the film historians — such as Slovak-American Nataša Durovicová or Bulgarian-British Dina Iordanova — are rather suspicious of the "proliferation of the new film historiographic entities to match the various, continuously redrawn state boundaries," (Iordanova 2005: 235). Durovicová mocks the publication of the book *One Hundred Years of Slovakian Film History*, claiming that none of that continuity existed "apart from Czechoslovakia" (Iordanova 2005: 235). In the specific Yugoslav case, the dilemma is hardly a dilemma. Due to the specific, Yugoslav form of federalism, each of the eight federal units had its own film studio and government film fund. Each of the local studios had an obligation to shoot films in the local language (including in Albanian in Kosovo), and build a local pool of skilled professionals. The Pula festival — as the central annual film event — always had included an element of competition between the federal states, and the distribution of prizes was always politically tricky and nationally sensitive. At the same time, the national studios were trying to hire the best directors and the most popular stars, wherever they came from, hoping for commercial success.

That kind of Yugoslav cinema — based on a meticulously polished balance between local/national and all-Yugoslav — died in July '91. Instead, new national cinemas emerged, each of them in their own specific cultural, ideological and economic circumstances. One of these was Croatian.

Nineties: Being the Victim, Playing the Victim

During the 90s, Croatian cinema started its new life in quite an unfavorable environment. From '91 to '95, Croatia was at war, and its central and eastern regions were occupied by Serbian/Yugoslav military forces. The young state was firmly controlled by Tuđman's HDZ party and dominated by exaggerated nationalism, the overblown influence of the Catholic church and the personal cult of President Tuđman himself. During the 90s, Croatia was a good example of the process typical for Eastern Europe, almost to the degree of caricature, described by Ravetto Biagoli as an "enormous amount of historical revisionism" where the "return to a nation state is more a product of imagination and dreams than a historical fact" (Ravetto Biagoli 2005: 182). The massive revisionism and renewed clerical conservatism in the Croatian case had been mixed with a justified feeling of helplessness and anger, typical for every community faced with outside aggression. Croats felt they were victims not only of Yugo-Serbian army attack, but also of western passivity and ignorance.

Such a mixture of feelings had its own cinematic expression in a specific type of cinema. During the nineties, this was ironically dubbed by its opponents "državotvorni film" (state-building cinema), but a more descriptive name for it could be the "cinema of self-victimization." The first and most typical example of this model was *A Time For...* (*Vrijeme za...*, 1993), a war epic directed by Oja Kodar, painter and wife of many years of director Orson Welles. In that film — as in most films of self-victimization — the Croatian war was described as a simplified binary showcase in which naïve, well-intentioned Croats were stabbed in the back by their Serbian neighbors. Characters are black and white to the point of caricature, and divided almost exclusively along ethnic lines. In films of self-victimization, even if a Croat displays moral weaknesses, he redeems these failings through a noble deed; if any Serb seems friendly and honest at the beginning, he will most probably turn out to be treacherous and wicked. Films of self-victimization often imitate classic war epics, because they include scenes of mass destruction, movements of the masses, battles, and pompous scenes with music and slow motion. Therefore, some critics and historians — including Ivo Škrabalo (1998: 441) — have compared these films with Tito's partisan war epics, disregarding the vast difference between them. Tito's communist partisan epics were the product of an ideology which considered itself historically victorious, successful and self-assured, so — analogously — the main characters of these films are active heroes who confront obstacles and fight back a mighty enemy. This is why the partisan genre could merge so smoothly with Hollywood, and many popular partisan films indeed recycled dramatic devices of Hollywood classics, particularly westerns (such as *My Darling Clementine* in Žika Mitrović's *Captain Leshi* / *Kapetan Leši*, or *Rio Bravo* in Nikola Tanhofer's *Double Circle* / *Dvostruki obruč*; see, Pavičić 2008). Unlike partisan films, films of self-victimization refrain from dramatic use of an active hero, and any kind of violent response, revenge, or counterattack is either totally omitted or deferred with an open ending, which often includes a final freeze frame (as in Neven Hitrec's film *Madonna / Bogorodica*, 1999).

Such a weird dramaturgical choice is no accident. As political philosopher Boris Buden writes, during the early 90s the previously dominant political message from Croatia to the West (*"we are Europeans…we are like you"*) shifted to a simple message: *"we are victims"*: "The identity of Croatia formed through a process of recognition was the identity of pure victimhood… Croatia was recognized after becoming a victim," (Buden 1999: 81). In the Croatia of the 90s, being a victim had become too valuable a source of political capital to be compromised by the simple pleasure of action cinema. By introducing lame, passive and helpless anti-heroes, the films of self-victimization implicitly sent a political message to undifferentiated, abstract "Westerners": *we aren't doing anything at all, we are just victims*. These films, therefore, not only represent the predominant chauvinism of the period, they are also symptomatic of colonial, submissive passivity typical for the Croatian political tradition. This is probably the reason why these films were loathed by both sides in the ideological confrontation. The film community, critics, and intellectuals criticized them as trivial, nationalistic and shallow. War veterans, on the other hand, despised these same films because they felt that, instead of depicting them as heroes, the films showed them as mere sheep for the slaughter. In an ironic twist, the war veterans of the city of Dubrovnik organized a boycott in 1999 of the film *Dubrovnik Twilight* (*Dubrovački suton*, Željko Senečić, 1999) — produced by Tuđman's son Stjepan (!) — because they felt it represented them as helpless cowards!

Comical Subversion

The pretension, ceremonialism and pomposity of Tuđman's official culture were an easy target for derision: it is therefore no wonder that the most popular cultural product of the Croatian 90s was the political satire of the newspaper *Feral Tribune*, which ridiculed Tuđman and caricatured aspects of his ideology on a weekly basis. Hence it is hardly surprising that the most representative films of the Croatian 90s were comedies. The best and most popular examples are two late 90s comedies by director Vinko Brešan, *How the War Started on My Island* (*Kako je počeo rat na mom otoku*, 1997), and *Marshal* (*Maršal*, or: *Marshal Tito's Spirit* 1999). Both of them were huge successes, and the first — *How the War Started on My Island* — is still unsurpassed as a hit in the history of Croatia, seen by 346,000 moviegoers, one twelfth of the entire population. Both films enjoyed a solid international reception, winning prizes in the Forum sidebar program of the Berlinale. But, these lightweight comedies make sense primarily within Croatia's social context, since Brešan's comediographic model clearly and intentionally subverts nationalist political jargon and highbrow pretension.

How the War Started on My Island tells the story of the first days of the 1991 war on a small Dalmatian island. Local civilians demonstrate and march back and forth in front of the gate to a small military barracks to

Vinko Brešan: *Marshal (Maršal)*, 1999

convince soldiers to surrender and leave the island. The commander at the barracks, Aleksa (Ljubomir Kerekeš), is a stubborn fanatic who has rigged the ammunition warehouse with a fuse and threatens to blow up the whole town. Self-appointed leaders of the local "crisis task force" send for Aleksa's wife *and* mistress — both of whom are locals — believing they might be able to change his mind. The main "ingredients" in Brešan's comedy appear to come straight out of nationalist propaganda: we have charming, genuine local Croats, their peaceful "resistance through culture" vs. a fanatic Serbian officer. But Brešan takes these ingredients and undermines them one by one. The local political leaders are funny, childishly shrewd, and totally incompetent. Both of them try to conceal their communist biographies and repeat new political slogans like parrots. Aleksa is presented as a menace, yet at the same time as sympathetic, since he is probably the only one in this charade who truly believes in anything. On a stage out in front of the barracks locals organize a program replete with crass music and pompous political speeches which regularly crosses over into mockery due to technical problems or comic incidents (such as a fight between Aleksa's two women). Brešan stages the political discourse of the era only to undermine it as a mere charade and mockery. Instead of official propaganda depicting Serbs and Croats as longtime, essential enemies, Brešan's films shows their lives as intertwined through friendship, marriage, sports, sex and food (in the most quoted line, Aleksa's wife offers to make the dish of *pasta sciutta* for him if he will come out).

Released immediately after the war, *How the War Started on My Island* served as mass collective therapy for Croats, still traumatized by the war. At the same time, by showing imperfect, yet human and sympathetic Aleksa, Brešan humanized the figure of the enemy: by laughing at Aleksa, the Croatian audience stopped hating him. Brešan achieved a similar effect of forging a new political consensus in his next comedy, *Marshal* (1999). Again set on a Dalmatian island, the film tells a story about a small town where the locals regularly see the ghost of Josip Broz Tito. Initially reluctant, the locals — run by an unscrupulous mayor and hotel owner — see this as an opportunity for "nostalgia tourism" and spread gossip about paranormal events. *Marshal* was an obvious comment on the "ostalgie" trend all over Eastern Europe, which seems on the surface to be a political counterattack against capitalism, but at its core is just the opening of a new consumer niche within the market economy. By showing the satirical "invasion" of the old partisans on the islands, Brešan was preparing the audience emotionally for the coming political events. Tuđman died only a couple of weeks after the film's release, ex-communists (the Social Democratic Party — SDP) won the election and for the first time overthrew the right-wing party, HDZ. Brešan's *Marshal* was again a therapeutic exercise, a drama that prepared society for an "unnatural," "incestuous" situation: the electoral victory of former communists in the new Croatian state.

The New Century: New Heroes for a New Society

That election victory — on January 3, 2000 — changed Croatia completely, and for the better. Although HDZ returned to power at 2004, and although nationalist feelings and the Catholic church still have a vast impact on Croatian society, Croatia has never slipped back into the grotesque socio-political model of the 90s. During the next decade, Croatian society started its own, delayed version of the transition, fighting with the "regular" obstacles typical for Central and Eastern Europe, from corruption to painful reforms, unemployment, ridiculous consumerism, the trivialization of the media. In the new social context, Croatian cinema for the first time in its history had no normative ideology or prescribed political pattern to follow, at least not one imposed domestically. On the other hand, there was also no audience to please. Interest for local films in Croatia has never been high. During the 90s, what interest was there diminished radically due to the devastating effect of the bad propaganda films. Croatian cinema entered the new century with no Central Committee listening, no godfather in a white uniform to please, but also with no audience to address. As has been the case in other East European countries (i.e. Romania), international festivals, and foreign specialty art houses became the main (if not only) target market for future films.

The new decade changed the landscape not only of Croatian cinema, but of post-Yugoslav cinema in general. During the 90s, the type of post-Yugoslav cinema that dominated festival and art circuits was films like those of Emir Kusturica, Srđan Dragojević (*Pretty Village Pretty Flame / Lepa sela lepo gore*), or Milčo Mančevski (*Before the Rain / Pred doždot*). Films of this poetic group usually represent the Balkans and ethnic conflict as a never-ending circle, an eternal chain of violence rooted deeply in local culture, beyond repair, and incomprehensible for outsiders. Besides, these films were representing the Balkans as an exotic, violent and picturesque Ruritania, an object of western fear and loathing, but were also attractive to the western gaze for "untamed" negative passions and alleged "authenticity." Such a stylistic model therefore became very popular in the West, but at the same time it was criticized locally as politically regressive and colonial. Films of this group — especially those of Emir Kusturica — provoked a long theoretical and critical debate, since their opponents claimed that they culturalize (and, therefore, de-politicize) war, and send an isolationist message (more in Žižek 1996, Krasztev 2000, Jameson 2004).

Ognjen Sviličić: *Armin*, 2007
Sorry for Kung Fu (*Oprosti za kung fu*), 2004

With the new decade, the cards have been reshuffled. After the fall of the old war leaders, all the post-Yugoslav societies started the process of democratic consolidation, they all poised to "join Europe" and no one wanted to be "authentic" and/or "incomprehensible" any more. In such a political landscape, the old "Kusturica school" became unfashionable and locally unwelcome, opening a path to an entirely new type of post-Yugoslav cinema. This type, which emerged after 2000, is clearly represented by Bosnian Golden Bear winner *Grbavica* (2006) by Jasmila Žbanić. The Balkan screen was suddenly full of sober, minimalistic dramas set in unexotic urban settings, dealing with active, western-like heroes who actively seek to change their destiny and fight against the heritage of war. This new model of cinema — which might be called the "cinema of normalization," or "cinema of consolidation" (see Pavičić, 2010) — was strongest in Bosnia and Herzegovina and Croatia, where it dominated in the first years of the new decade. In Croatian cinema, this new poetic model does not have a single obvious representative standing out as globally visible, in contrast to the situation in Bosnia. But most of the most successful Croatian films from the early 2000s could be interpreted through this stylistic change.

One of them is *Here* (*Tu*, 2003, Zrinko Ogresta), a mosaic drama which won the Karlovy Vary prize in 2004. This sad, elegantly subtle film follows five stories about five former war comrades who are coping with mundane lives in the banality of postwar Zagreb. Their present lives are totally unremarkable, but there is something invisible yet crucial about them: the war experience afflicted them, and inflicted deep, sad wounds. In *Fine Dead Girls* (*Fine mrtve djevojke* 2002, Dalibor Matanić) postwar urbanity is again depicted as the gloomy space of everyday struggle: in this film, two young lesbians struggle to cope with their hostile, intolerant neighborhood. In *Melon Route* (*Put lubenica*, 2006, Branko Schmidt) an impoverished war veteran and drug addict saves a young Chinese woman, an illegal immigrant, and — in a bloody finale resembling Cronenberg's *History of Violence* — wipes out the local smugglers and their rich boss. In *Sorry for Kung Fu* (*Oprosti za kung fu* (2004) by Ognjen Sviličić, a young village girl and returnee from Germany forces her patriarchal parents to accept her pregnancy without marriage, and her newborn Asian baby.

Probably the most typical example of this poetic model is *Armin* (2007), a film made by Ognjen Sviličić again, which premiered at the Berlinale 2007. The heroes of *Armin* are a father and son (Emir Hadžihafizbegović, Armin Omerović) who travel from Bosnia to Zagreb where young Armin is supposed to audition for a German movie coproduction. The father believes that Armin will be cast for the film because he plays the accordion so well. Once they get to Zagreb, they realize that the fine, decent German filmmakers have no interest in Armin's accordion, but are all too interested in his epilepsy, a disease they believe (since they automatically apply a media pattern) to have been caused by war trauma. They talk to Armin and his father about making a documentary about them, but the Bosnians decline. They don't want to be accepted through victimhood, if they can't be accepted through their culture. By staging within the film the dilemma of the colonial gaze, Sviličić in *Armin* is implicitly criticizing the previous model of Balkan cinema, always ready to please the West by representing "Balkan freaks." Or — as Sviličić said in an interview — the characters in *Armin* "refuse to be accepted only through war, and therefore refuse colonisation" (Šošić, 67).

Armin clearly represents the core of the new trend in Croatian (and regional) cinema. Instead of self-exoticizing, "films of normalization" offer sober realism, a minimalism, a return to classic narrative style, and heroes who actively search for their place within the new society, which is wide open for opportunity but offers no security. Such films implicitly comment on the new economic reality of the young capitalist society, in which their heroes depend on themselves and their problem-solving attitude.

Reflecting the Past

The reality of the young capitalist society, however, is not the only topic crucial for Croatian film in a new decade. A second, equally important topic was (and still is) the bleak heritage of recent history. While most of the cinema in the 90s gave comfort to society by offering to Croatian moviegoers an easily digestible representation of Croatia as a plain and simple victim (and the aggressor as a cartoonish, cardboard villain), the films of the new decade see history as something far more complex.

This process started in the 90s, primarily in literature. During late 90s, previously dominant postmodernist fiction was replaced by a new wave of "*stvarnosna proza*" (reality fiction) which treats social reality — including war, war crimes, drugs, domestic violence — with striking, rough naturalism. The new generation of writers — among them many journalists — offer an entirely different, unflattering representation of (post)war reality. The new literature has been criticized from two opposite directions: the postmodernists have attacked it as conservative, resorting to realist, non-experimental writing. Conservatives have been irritated by the "tabloid" topics of the new fiction and have criticized it for being negativistic, sensationalist and self-promoting. Nevertheless, the literature of reality fiction has gained in popularity which was initially far greater than the popularity of the filmmakers and films of those years. As a consequence, the filmmakers addressed this literature as its source. Dalibor Matanić made a screen adaptation of a grotesque, humorous, dark short story collection about the rural Croatian heartland *Lika Cinema* (*Kino Lika*) by Damir Karakaš. Kristijan Milić made a film based on a Bosnian war novel *The Living and the Dead* (*Živi i mrtvi* by Josip Mlakić). Rajko Grlić's film *Borderpost* (*Karaula*) — the first to be co-produced by all the post-Yugoslav countries — was based on a humorist bestseller by writer Ante Tomić. Another novel of Tomić's — *What Is a Man Without a Moustache* — was filmed by director Hrvoje Hribar, and that film became the biggest local hit of the decade (over 150,000 tickets sold). Goran Rušinović shot a screen version of the novel *Buick Riviera* by Miljenko Jergović. This film, shot in Fargo, North Dakota, tells the story of two men from Bosnia — a Muslim and a Serb — who meet in a small town in the American Midwest many years after the war, reviving the passive-aggressive relations between the two ethnic groups once again, far from home. This film won first prize at Sarajevo Film Festival in 2008.

The dark subterranean reality of the previously idealized Homeland War became what was probably the central topic of Croatian national life after 2000. During this decade, faced with many war crimes trials, many real or alleged heroes of Croatian society turned out to be murderers or responsible for mass destruction, and the society as a whole had to face a painful dilemma: either to dig deep into this shameful undercurrent, or live in comfortable denial. Dealing with the recent past had become a central topic of Croatian journalism, literature and film. And — after a long, bitter decade of debates and polemics — Croatian cinema produced a film which offers an original cinematic visualization of this moral struggle. The title of this film is *The Blacks* (*Crnci*, 2009), it was directed in the peripheral Eastern Slavonian city of Osijek by two newcomers, Goran Dević and Zvonimir Jurić.

The Blacks begins at dawn of an autumn day in the first year of war. The first part of the film follows a group of Croatian soldiers in black uniforms who are secretly traversing swamps on the Slavonian plains. Shot mainly in green and black, the film has a bucolic beauty, and shows taciturn, grim fathers, sons and brothers on a risky war mission. The visual approach of the film immediately stirs memories for the Croatian moviegoers, reminding viewers of wartime jingles on Croatian television, shots of a young but serious soldier hiding in bushes with Mark Knopfler's *Brothers in Arms* as the music cover. In terms of atmosphere, the first act of *The Blacks* reminds us of southern Gothic thrillers such as *Deliverance* or *Southern Comfort*. This first act — elliptical, enigmatic, shot in long shots — ends abruptly when the Blacks (the name of the squad) end up stranded in a minefield.

At that moment, *The Blacks* unexpectedly changes setting and time. The rest of the film happens 24 hours earlier, when all the soldiers who later die are still alive, and instead of pastoral, beautiful exteriors, the film is isolated in the interior of an abandoned office building. The hero of the film, Novi (Krešimir Mikić), is a newcomer who has joined the Blacks. While waiting for equipment and weapons, he listens, watches, and learns the secrets of the isolated brotherhood. The Blacks defy the commands of their superiors, pillage abandoned shops, and arrest and torture townspeople in an underground basement. In the scene at the emotional climax of the film, Novi opens the basement doors, and one of the Blacks (himself a junkie, acted by Franjo Dijak) switches on the light: the brief panoramic shot shows piles of bloody clothes and bloodstains on the wall, visual signs of the executions which had taken place there. That brief shot is the visual climax of new Croatian cinema, it is a crystal reflection of a bitter past.

By changing the chronological sequence in the story, Jurić and Dević turn the cinematic machine against the viewer. The dramaturgy of the film represents the Homeland War first through its official version (bright, pastoral, heroic), and then, afterwards, through its underground version, claustrophobic, dark, Gothic and suffocating. In that way, the audience of *The Blacks* passes through the same process of rude awakening that all of Croatian society passed between 2000 and 2010. The cinematic device in Dević's and Jurić's film re-enacts mutations of the national conscience.

Introducing a retrospective of classic Yugoslav cinema in Zagreb in 2010, Italian film critic and expert on (post)Yugoslav cinema Sergio Germani wrote that "[*The*] *Blacks* by Dević and Jurić is the most important film produced in the new cinemas on the territories that used to be Yugoslav... That's the film that from today's point of view understands the greatness of the (black wave) films, whose bleakness was previously despised by the bureaucrats, and later by the fanatic nationalists. After two decades over determined by the recent war... The film *The Blacks* with its utter blackness gives the final verdict" (Germani 2010: 33). We can only add: *The Blacks* presents a final verdict not only for the whole grim historical era, but also for a marvelous decade, a decade in which Croatian cinema was resurrected from political mire and moral sleaze to reach the maturity of a modern European national cinema.

Works Cited

- Buden, Boris. 1999. "Europa je kurva." In *Mediji i rat*. Belgrade: Agencija argument.
- Germani Grmek, Sergio. 2010. "Let mrtve ptice." In *Subversive film festival — retrospektiva jugoslavenskog filma 1955-1990*. Zagreb: Subversive Film festival, Bijeli val.
- Iordanova, Dina. 2005. "The Cinema of Eastern Europe, Strained Loyalties, Elusive Clusters." In Aniko Emre, ed. *Eastern European Cinemas*. New York-London: Routledge.
- Jameson, Fredric. 2004. "Thoughts on Balkan Cinema." In Atom Egoyan & Ian Balfour, eds. *Subtitles*. Massachusets Institute of Technology.
- Krasztev, Peter. 2000. "Who Will Take the Blame? — How to Make an Audience Grateful for a Family Massacre." In Andrew James Horton, ed. *The Celluloid Tinderbox, Yugoslav Screen Reflections of a Turbulent Decade. Central European Review* 2000, June 2009.

The New Croatian Documentary: Between the Political and the Personal
by Diana Nenadić

The "new age" formally began in Croatia in May 1990. The first multi-party elections since World War II rejected the single-party communist system and, not long thereafter, in a republic-wide referendum, the groundwork was laid for withdrawing Croatia from the multi-national Yugoslav federation, a country which failed to become a "melting pot," infringing instead on the freedom of its peoples and national cultures. As with intellectuals and other artists, filmmakers, particularly documentarians — in the closest contact with reality — believed they had finally gotten rid of their two greatest obstacles to free expression: a single-party system and a multi-national state that protected the interests of certain political elites rather than the nations that comprised it. In the now obsolete regime, which had been very interested in film (particularly as a means of ideological propaganda), this had meant unfinished projects, police confiscation of recorded material, the bunkering of films, bans on work, and fear of censorship. But then commenced a period which was one of the most difficult stretches for documentary filmmakers since the beginnings of organized cinematography in Croatia, yet documentarians fought for and won their piece of the pie and public acknowledgment. Instead of providing generous room for freedom and exploration, the early 1990s brought with them wartime aggression, and, instead of freedom of speech, there were new kinds of limitations and (self) censorship. At a moment when they should have been opening their eyes wide and pricking up their ears, the senses of the documentarians were deafened by Greater Serbian guns and nationalist rhetoric. Meanwhile the Croatian politics of the period, dominated by the presidential will of former Yugoslav general Franjo Tuđman, swiftly devised ways to further clip the wings of filmmakers: throughout the mid-1990s and up to the new millennium and the change of government, documentary film was given no state funding, although everyone knew full well that even with the new market-driven system, in this devastated and impoverished transitional country of four and a half million inhabitants, the film industry would not survive without state support. The true advent of a *new* day was therefore put off by nearly a decade. Until documentary production was brought back under the umbrella of government funding during the mandate of Minister of Culture Antun Vujić (2000-2003), those who were the most persistent and the most loyal to documentary film did their best to sustain at least some continuity of production and bring credibility back to this first and foundational film genre which even the most rigid dictatorships never give up on — precisely because images speak louder than words.

In other words, despite it all, documentary filmmakers went on filming, in anticipation of the day when they would be able to show how engaging reality can be, as demonstrated by the film *New, New Time* (*Novo, novo vrijeme*). It predated the Croatian importation of Michael Moore's full-length documentary provocations aimed at the American establishment. This full-length film, made by Rajko Grlić and Igor Mirković in 2001, was one of the first documentaries subsidized in part by the post-Tuđman government,[1] and one of the first documentaries in Croatian history which the people of Croatia paid to see at the ever-declining number of non-commercial movie theaters. At the same time this is a film which pioneered a move across mental "barbed wire" and went behind the scenes of the hitherto untouchable topic of high politics in order to expose the dynamics of the multi-party "marketplace" on the eve of and during the first presidential election after Tuđman's death. At a moment when filmgoers were steering away from domestic movies, and the critics were not fond of them either, the reactions to the stripping bare of politicians using the up-close observation method (measurable in box office sales of about 27,000 tickets, fabulous for a film of this genre)[2] were unexpectedly encouraging. After that move (which was not merely nominal and symbolic!) there were similar strides into a *new* time, and in Croatian documentary filmmaking many things would never be the same.

At the start of the millennium, both cultural policy and filmgoers began to recognize the importance and potential of the documentary, and this mood spurred production. Government funding (channeled today through the Croatian Audiovisual Centre [Hrvatski audiovizualni centar]),[3] as well as funding from certain local (municipal) administrations, took a firmer hold in the years leading up to 2010, and this contributed to the emergence of producers who make documentaries either regularly or intermittently. Today there are some thirty of them. This is identical in number to the current record number of projects receiving government funding in a single year, though only in 2008, which was at least three times the size of the average annual quota in the 1980s and many times

---

1] The commissioner for documentary film within the Ministry of Culture, who proposed subsidizing the film was Vinko Brešan.
2] See: Ivo Škrabalo, *Hrvatska filmska povijest ukratko, 1896-2006* (*A History of Croatian Film in Brief — 1896-2006*), Zagreb: V.B.Z., Croatian Film Association, 2008: 226.
3] The Croatian Audiovisual Centre (HAVC) is a "public institution established by the Government of the Republic of Croatia pursuant to the Law on Audiovisual Activities (NN 67/07) for systematic promotion of audiovisual creative work in the Republic of Croatia. The center prepares and runs the National Program for Promotion of Audio-visual Creative Work, spurring the management, organization and funding of preparation, development, production, distribution and presenting Croatian, European, and World audiovisual works. The Centre secures funds for its work and the implementation of the National Program from the state budget and from a part of the total annual gross income realized through audiovisual activity: Croatian Radio Television, national-level television broadcasters, regional-level television broadcasters, operators of the cable distribution network, operators in mobile and non-mobile telecommunication networks, providers of Internet access services, and the persons who publicly show audiovisual works."

larger than that in the 1990s. When one adds to the number of subsidized projects the television, non-professional, student, and *non-budget* documentaries the total annual output may reach as many as a hundred short and full-length titles,[4] and today these can be distributed through a number of different channels. Aside from state television and the growing number of local, national, or international festivals with competition or special documentary programs (Split, Motovun, Zagreb Film Festival, Human Rights Film Festival, Bjelovar's Docuart, Liburnia Film Festival, and others), the growing and increasingly popular ZagrebDox with a regional and international selection, the surviving non-commercial movie theaters are showing a rising interest in non-fictional film, including the first Zagreb movie theater specialized in documentaries, Doku-Kino Croatia. Because of all of this, the documentary "base" is stronger than it ever has been in the history of Croatian cinema. Documentarians have recently been participating in international co-productions and pitching sessions, insuring a growing visibility for films on the world festival scene. In the regional context they are now prominently recognized, on the world scene they are increasingly recognizable, although they have still not reached the ratings of the 1960s, 1970s, and even 1980s, when Croatian documentaries, in tandem with or alternating with the Zagreb School of Animated Film, regularly won prizes at the Oberhausen festival, still an important venue where even now Croatian titles enter competitions though with greater difficulty. Currently Croatian documentaries enjoy more success at the influential Netherlands IDFA. Over the last ten years through the Jan Vrijman Fund this Amsterdam mega-festival of documentary film has financially supported, and then screened, eleven films which were either produced or co-produced by Croatian companies such as Factum, Croatian Film Association [Hrvatski filmski savez], Nukleus, Milva Film & Video, and others. In this regard Croatia has far outstripped the other members of the former Yugoslav federation.

Television Time and War Themes

From the perspective of the years leading up to 2010, when the severe economic downturn cast a shadow over the film industry with predictable consequences for domestic production, the dividing line between the "new" (Tuđman) and the "new, new" (post-Tuđman) era is not so clearly defined that it could be encapsulated in a single film. *New, New Time* and other similar production-intensive forays into the political and day-to-day commonplace are more likely to be a consequence or continuation of processes and phenomena that were visible or nascent during the 1990s in documentary film, experienced at that time as dissonant tones in an otherwise constrained and controlled mainstream.

Croatian Radio Television largely set the standards in terms of main-

---

4] This information is based on a list of all documentary films submitted to the Days of Croatian Film festival for 2010, while the number of titles subsidized by HAVC in the previous production year was four times less.

stream production, aesthetics, and world view in the first years of sociopolitical and cinematographic transition. At that time state television was the only producer of documentaries with stability in terms of funding and infrastructure, but it was also a controversial shaper of public opinion, particularly during the years of open hostilities by the Yugoslav People's Army and Serbian paramilitary units in Croatia and Bosnia and Herzegovina (1991-1995). Until the mid-1990s those who had survived the demise of the socialist system were intermittently present on the documentary film scene. Among these were Jadran Film (which had invested a part of its capacities in documentary film from funds created by state investment after World War II), Zagreb Film (the famous Studio for Animated Film. In parallel to animated film they also cultivated educational and creative documentaries), Filmoteka 16 and smaller regional production houses. The war also kept on their toes the amateurs who were gathered around the surviving film clubs and the Croatian Film Association, and spurred the involvement of independent authors and new, specialized producers in documenting the destruction wrought by the war and the human suffering from Osijek to Dubrovnik (Art film, Studio ZNG, and others).

But professional cinematographic production began to feel the impact of the demise of public funding in the second half of the decade, in which politically influential director Antun Vrdoljak[5] — author of the most expensive and controversial documentary project in the history of Croatian cinematography, a television series, both documentary and acted, on Josip Broz Tito (*Tito*, 2010) — played a decisive role. After successfully purging the "politically incorrect" staff and subject matter from Croatian Radio Television programs during the first (wartime) half of the 1990s, as commissioner for film within the Ministry of Culture in the second (postwar) half of the decade Vrdoljak eliminated the institution of competitions for and subsidy of documentary filmmaking, retaining only discretionary right as commissioner to support something now and then with government funding. Hence the ball was in the court of "filtered" state television, whose documentary program, closely affiliated with the information services, was in the service of government policies throughout this period, with the goal of a homogenization of the public around national history and culture, military objectives and strategies, the displaced persons crisis, and, more broadly, the suffering of the civilian population. Aside from its role as an articulation of information policy, Croatian Radio Television documentary production was most closed toward "unverified," independent, out-of-house professionals. At the same time, most television authors, particularly the occasional documentarians recruited from among journalists, gave in far too readily to the pressures of propaganda rhetoric and the conventions of what is known as the *sandwich* structure (a series of statements — then illustrations — then statements, etc.), which were used to fill the closely watched programming minutes. Ethically and aesthetically articulate documentarians were exceptions to the rule, often shunt-

---

5] In the 1990s Vrdoljak was, among other things, the foremost film director of Croatian Radio Television, a representative to the Croatian Parliament, and vice-president of the Republic of Croatia.

Petar Krelja: *On a Sidetrack* (*Na sporednom kolosijeku*), 1992
Suzana's Smile (*Suzanin osmijeh*), 1994

ed off to some of the second-tier educational, scientific, or cultural programs. But nevertheless, fortunately, there were a number of them, and thanks to this fact we can speak today of a sizeable corpus of early war documentary.

Petar Krelja's presence as an author was more than visible in this period. His filmography numbers more than two hundred titles today, among other things because even after 1990 he continued to work a great deal for Croatian Radio Television and (affiliated) independent (co)producers (Zagreb film, Filmoteka 16). Cultivating the high humanist and creative standards set by his socially engaged films from the late 1960s and in the 1970s, Krelja dedicated himself to the fates of victims behind the combat lines (*On a Sidetrack / Na sporednom kolosijeku*; *Zoran Šipoš and His Jasna / Zoran Šipoš i njegova Jasna*, 1992; *Corn Road / Kukuruzni put*; *Suzana's Smile / Suzanin osmijeh*; *The Third Christmas / Treći Božić*, 1994, and others), and repeatedly to artists and ordinary people with creative hobbies. With an average of three documentaries per year, he was perceived during the first five years of Croatia's independence as almost the only active professional from the "old guard," although there were other documentarians who occasionally came out with films (such as Berislav Benažić, Zvonimir Berković, Eduard Galić, Branko Lentić, Miroslav Mikuljan, Edi Mudronja, Zlatko Sudović, Vladimir Tadej, Šime Šimatović, Bogdan Žižić, and others). The focus of most of the more experienced documentary filmmakers in the new circumstances skirted the actual events or entirely sidestepped them, pursuing a series of harmless or socially tried-and-true themes and more conventional approaches, most often making documentary portraits of artists or cultural-historical inventories with what were known as *kultur* films, a genre that was frequently used before the 1990s as well. Be-cause of the circumstances at hand (the humanitarian crisis, political control of the electronic media, the authoritarian government) it was difficult to expect that authors would sharpen their critical spears and tangle with those aspects of reality subsumed in the wartime events. These began surfacing in the late 1990s: the unsanctioned murders of civilians of Serbian nationality, the involvement of Croatia in the war in neighboring Bosnia and Herzegovina, war profiteering, criminal privatization of what had been publicly owned, the birth of the "nouveau riche," the presence of the mafia and criminal activity in general. This earlier period was a time when a single, collective, i.e. national, identity, was privileged. Consequently, these types of problems as well as those concerning threats to human rights and individual identities, traumatized as people were by the recent events and totalitarian environment, could hardly break through onto the documentary film agenda. In documentary film as in everyday life, truth and the person/individual meant far less than political interests and the nation, in whose name through the ether flew words that had no place in a democratic, tolerant society. Hence Krelja's "wartime" opus, zeroing in on the fates and emotions of individuals — who, after all, represented the most threatened crosssection of the population — shone as an exception, giving wartime documentary film a measure of universal humanity.

On the margins of production at the same time a (counter) revolution of a new, depoliticized and ironic post-modern generation was smoldering. The revolution was primarily aesthetic in nature. A breath of fresh air had blown in at the start of the 1990s from the Zagreb Academy of Dramatic Art, whose student production, thanks to the newly founded national review/festival Days of Croatian Film had reached a broader audience by the second year of the war. A generation came onto the scene from whom, as formulated by young director Lukas Nola, "... the war had been stolen";[6] but it became clear that they had a more sober and engaged attitude about the war and reality than did television journalists and the on-duty watch dogs. The new relationship implied avoiding the pathetic rhetoric of victimhood, homeland homilies and spoken commentaries which had been the recognizable features of television production, sometimes taken to the limits of tastelessness.

Of the young Academy students who were prevented from going to the front with film crews and equipment, the first to shine was Ivan Salaj. After his macabre observations on the proximity of life and death (the hospital obstetrics ward on the second floor and the hospital morgue in the basement) in his student film *Second Floor, Basement* (*Drugi kat, podrum*, 1991), Salaj attracted attention in *Hotel Sunja* (1992) with *vérité* confessions by defenders in the field, recorded during breaks between war operations. Jelena Rajković of the same generation defied television conventions with a distanced and stylized note on the inoperative presence of highly organized *blue helmets* (UN units) in chaotic Croatia during the Homeland War (*Blue Helmet*, 1992/1993). Rajković (1969-1997), who died far too young, went on to grapple with the surfacing of PTSD among war veterans, first in a fictional treatment (*Wish You Could Hear / Noć za slušanje*, 1995), and then in the reconstruction documentary *Radio Krapina* (*Krapina, poslijepodne*, 1997), addressing an event that is anticipated in her senior film project. Some recent Academy graduates contributed to the documentary inventory of events happening behind the front lines, such as Neven Hitrec in *Hall* (*Dvorana*, 1993) who observed with tact and compassion the lives of patients displaced from an institution for the mentally handicapped and accommodated in a gymnastics hall, or Goran Dukić in *Special Guests* (*Po-*

6] This formulation is in part a commentary on the fact that Drama Academy students were not allowed to go off to the front with equipment to document the war.

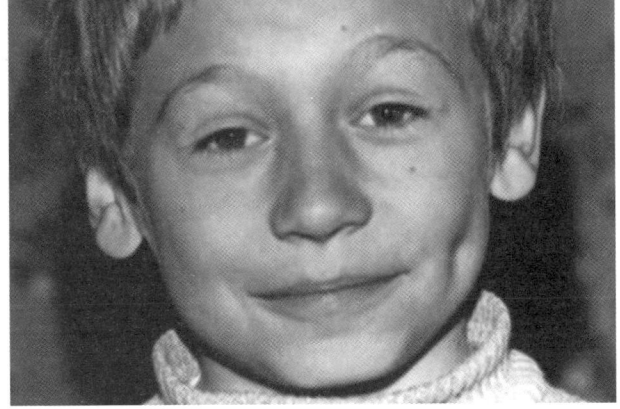

Ivan Faktor: *Das Lied Ist Aus*, 2002
Biljana Čakić-Veselič: *The Boy Who Rushed* (*Dečko kojem se žurilo*), 2001

sebni gosti, 1992), with a similar approach to refugees from war-devastated rural areas placed in an orderly Adriatic hotel.

Out of a need to promote the "truth about the war" by documenting destruction or honoring victims, among whom were a large number of cameramen who were killed on the job, emerged a series of hybrid-genre documents/films and poeticized reporting war vignettes (such as *Mozart 1991* by Krasimir Gančev, 1992). The war provided a wealth of documentary themes even for the first years of the new millennium, when war-related material, and particularly psychological and spiritual consequences, could be observed from a distance. Associated with lived experience, this necessary distance in time brought with it a series of emotionally mature, formally inventive and cognitively powerful films using very varied styles, such as the confessional *The Boy Who Rushed* (*Dečko kojem se žurilo*, 2001) by Biljana Čakić-Veselič — on a search of many years for a brother who had disappeared; *Das Lied Ist Aus* by Ivan Faktor (2002) — a noir essay on the absurdities of war in the border town of Osijek, its sound track taken from *M* by Fritz Lang, or *Bad Blue Boys* (*Panj pun olova*, 2007) by Branko Schmidt — disturbing observations on the infatuation of veterans with weapons even after the war is over.

The Distance Generation

With the new generation whom the current events mentally damaged and physically undid, there is a general sense of a need for distance and a move away from normative representation, not only of the war, but also of other less extreme manifestations of the new reality. State television, as the only producer and screener of documentaries during most of the 1990s, was prepared to tolerate this only in part, while more agile independent producers able or willing to support this need for distance were nowhere to be found until the later years of the war decade. Hence the young authors were left to try to air their conceptualization of the creative documentary on targeted, educational, cultural, and other programs of state television. Only a few in the wartime and early postwar years broke through to the documentary program of Croatian Radio Television and succeeded in preserving creative autonomy while working with it.

Goran Dević: *Imported Crows* (*Uvozne vrane*), 2004
Happy Country (*Sretna zemlja*), 2009

Vinko Brešan, for instance, one of the most successful Croatian directors today, did not address the war until 1996 when his debut feature *How the War Started on My Island* (*Kako je počeo rat na mom otoku*) came out, but with the socially sensitive *Lunch Together* (*Zajednički ručak*, 1993) he covered a sample of the retired population which, at the time he was documenting meals for the poor at a Zagreb soup kitchen (and later), was one of the greatest examples of collateral damage of the transition brought on by the war and the changes in the economy. Afterwards, in the style of his later bitter-sweet features, he played with the "victims" of the endless Croatian judicial waiting room in the television piece *The Corridor* (*Hodnik*, 1994). Just as with his feature films, in *The Corridor* Brešan allowed humor, performance and playfulness to mingle with real situations and people, while steering clear of politics and politicization, an approach that was welcomed as something new. Moreover, it could be said that by making this poetic choice he oriented a significant portion of the subsequent television and independent documentary production toward irony, the grotesque, playfulness in performance and fabulation. These traits help one recognize a directorial signature and the directors of the younger and middle generation, who seek the bizarre in people, nature, and/or society, whether working on television or as independents: Branko Ištvančić (*The Cormorant Scarecrow / Plašitelji kormorana*, 1998), Tomislav Mršić (*Rio Bravo / Machinist / Rio Bravar*, 2002), Hrvoje Hribar (*There Once Was / Bil jedon*, 2002), Ljiljana Šišmanović (*The Last Bay of the Pannonian Sea / Posljednji zaljev Panonskoga mora*, 2003), Dražen Žarković (*Office Window / Šalter*, 2000; *From Dawn till Dusk / Od jutra do mraka*, 2005), the former trio Matanić-Rukavina-Tomić (*Bag; Good Luck / Sretno*, 1999) and Goran Dević (*Imported Crows / Uvozne vrane*, 2004; *Happy Country / Sretna zemlja*, 2009).

At the time when Croatian Radio Television began to relax its nation-building autism, Brešan would be followed in his march on the propaganda machine of state broadcasting by his colleagues of the same generation "assigned" to various television programs, given the chance to make relatively "painless" and harmless but creatively worked documentaries from the top list of the 1990s. Among them were a carefully structured and stylistically refined ethnographic essay on lace-making by Vlatka Vorkapić called *Lace-Making Designs* (*Pogačica, ročelica, mendulica*, 1997) and *Grandpa, Batek, Granny* (*Dedek, batek, bakica*, 1998), filmed for the television department of folk music and folk customs; a poetic-anthropological observation of life on Mount Velebit in *Mirila* by Zadar video artist Vlado Zrnić (1997), or the ethnographic films of Branko Ištvančić, a productive and traditionally themed filmmaker, particularly *The Cormorant Scarecrow*, a humorous depiction of people of an unusual "occupation" — shooing birds away from the Pannonian fish-breeding farms. Jelena Rajković used the training ground of television for practice, making a costumed documentary and acted construct *The Zagorje Region, Castles* (*Zagorje, dvorci*, 1997) and a subversive reconstruction (*Radio Krapina*). However, the Academy was not the only place to launch future documentarians. For instance, Damir Čučić, who worked on film editing for state television, made a debut threesome of socially engaged films which takes as its theme depression and hopelessness among workers who have lost their jobs in *Četvrta smjena* (*The Fourth Shift*) or among the people of Split, the Croatian "case city," in *Sea over Split* (*More nad Splitom*, 1999). That same year he articulated a remarkably tactful and sensitive approach to the existential tragedy of a Vukovar veteran, who, after nearly his whole family is killed, finds the strength for a new beginning as a displaced person, to which he testifies in the independently produced *Creatures in the Pictures* (*Bića sa slika*), one of the best Croatian documentaries of the 1990s.

While advanced students and graduates of the Drama Academy fought for their first professional projects under the existing conditions, the beginnings of a "new" documentary were continuing to germinate among the new generations of students. Students were allowed to work with increasing ease, innovation, in different styles. They even (ab)used the production impoverishment and freedom creatively, showing that a documentarian needn't necessarily be "objective" and serious, that seriousness and playfulness can go hand-in-hand, that "fiction" is sometimes missing from "faction," and that the "truth-based" approach to reality does not exclude a subjective position or personal "style." Although the social and cinematographic environment were hardly encouraging, Drama Academy students and their mentors were the ones who, in fact, created the new mood that began to be felt just at the time when the greatest restrictions were being imposed on the documentary mainstream, as early as 1996.

Those years, for instance, two student films were made which appear on critics' lists in the survey *Croatian Cinema Chronicle* (*Hrvatski filmski ljetopis*, 2003) of the best documentaries following Croatian independence. The first is *Mother's Name: Orange* (*Ime majke: Naranča*, 1995) by Jasna Zastavniković, an example of a fake documentary or "mockumentary," a genre which in Croatian documentary film, as focused as it had been on "serious" or (socially) tried-and-true themes, had not until then asserted its civil rights. The second one, *The Sky below Osijek* (*Nebo ispod Osijeka*, 1995) by Zvonimir Jurić, offers a subjective and pessimistic view of the postwar city of Osijek from the perspective of members of the disillusioned younger generation. Both films question the previously ruling dogma of "objectivity" of documentary representation, and mark the very beginning of a new wave of thematically and stylistically divergent documentary work. The somewhat later omnibus *Metropolis* (*Metropola*, 1997) by student trio D. Matanić, T. Rukavina, S. Tomić could be understood as a sort of documentary manifesto of the new generation that was looking at the postwar reality of the Croatian metropolis and its demi-monde without flinching or prettifying. Similarly, *Duel* (*Dvoboj*, 1998) by Zrinka Katarina Matijević, done in the direct film style, could be viewed as a manifestation of documentary skill in almost banal everyday situations (a verbal duel between a mother and her little son over a meal), a film style which, like the minimalist form in general, had completely disappeared from professional production, owing to the expansion of television minutage. The Grand Prix at Days of Croatian Film for *Duel* in 1999 was yet another confirmation of the uninventiveness of the professional documentary, which lost in competition with this film, and which until the late 1990s was still fending off challenges from the politically and spritually entangled postwar reality, and from aesthetic and world-view provocations of the "young filmmakers," even when they were not reaching for dangerous themes.

Political and Personal: Factum and the Facts

Nenad Puhovski had returned to the scene at this point and, as founder, director, and producer of the Factum documentary film project, set out to provoke discourse on the painful points and taboo themes of post-socialist Croatia. He came out of the documentary workshop at the Imaginary Academy (Imaginarna akademija) in Grožnjan, begun in 1995 with support from the Soros Open Society Institute. Factum appeared in 1997, at a moment when inaccessible and powerful Croatian Radio Television and the Academy of Dramatic Art, accessible but with modest production capabilities, were almost the only producers of documentary film in Croatia. At that point the only other relatively active independent producer was Gral Film (from 1993), making an average of one film a year in discontinuous production, broaching many sensitive topics (the exhumation of war victims, the de-mining of mined areas, the life of displaced persons, the life of refugees, and so forth), but Gral Film's filmography is largely tied to the name of author and producer Tomislav Žaja, noted for his authored films, who frequently worked for state television as well. Puhovski decided to attract as large a number of authors as possible for production, so after his "inaugural" film *Graham & I, a True Story* (*Graham i ja*, 1998) which he directed himself, he provided opportunities for proven students (Podgorelec, Korovljev, Budisavljević, Jurić, Matijević-Veličan, Mirošničenko, Matanić, Rukavina, Tomić and others) and went on apprenticing promising documentarists to production into the years of the last decade (Danko Volarić, Goran Dević, Nikola Strašek, Igor Bezinović, and others).

Graham & I, self-reflexive, self-aware and radically subjective in its treatment of a politically motivated incident (the self-immolation of Graham Bamford of Britain in front of the British Parliament as a protest against the policies of the western powers toward the war in Bosnia and Herzegovina), caused controversial reactions, and suggested which direction Factum's production would take. Its focus on the political, socio-critical, activist (in a humanistic sense), and creative (authorial) documentary assumed possible initial "misunderstandings" in the reception of Factum films. There were quite a few of them, because this is a production which opened new chapters in the Croatian documentary and, more broadly, in the perception of reality. Croatia was portrayed for the first time as a conflictual and fragmentary place composed of different social groups, entities and identities, and not as a monolithic, orderly community, while Factum, with its average annual output of five films, has imposed itself as a factory of various authorial approaches.

The first essential chapter of Factum's documentary production are films that are politically explicit in a way in which they had not been before that, nor could they have been, with the exception of films of overt ideological or nationalist propaganda. Factum dedicated itself to themes that had been swept under the rug by the majority of filmgoers, official policy, and even filmmakers, although international organizations such as Helsinki Watch had been addressing them. These were largely films on human rights issues, or, more explicitly, on the unsanctioned crimes that the Croatian side had perpetrated against Serbian civilians during and at the end of the Homeland War. Puhovski addresses them himself in *Pavilion 22* (*Paviljon 22*, 2002) and *Lora: Testimonies* (*Lora: svjedočanstva*, 2004), Božidar Knežević does so in *Operation Storm* (*Oluja nad Krajinom*, 2001), as does Goran Dević somewhat later in the Sisak doc-noir *I Have Nothing Nice to Say to You* (*Nemam ti šta reć' lijepo*, 2006). Political motivation or provocation is present in Factum's early project *BBB* (1998) by Saša Podgorelac, a documentary about Dinamo soccer-club fans, whose subversive behavior in the 1990s was a litmus test for the mood of the public toward the authoritarian policies of President Tuđman. Less "noisy" but also politically motivated was *A Life in Fresh Air* (*Život na svježem zraku*, 2001) by Danko Volarić, a view of life and preparations for local elections in an ethnically mixed Croatian village after what was known as the "reintegration" of the occupied zones. Playful *Pescenopolis* (*Peščenopolis*, 2003) by Zrinka Matijević-Veličan can be seen as a carnevalization of Croatian democracy through "dramatization" of relations among residents of an outsider city-state and its ridiculous "chief," situated in Peščenica, a Zagreb neighborhood. In Factum's political "program," there was space for both "old" and "new time." "Then" and "now" were appealingly bridged by the three-part croquis, *Drinking Water and Freedom III* (*Pitka voda i sloboda III*, 1999), by Rajko Grlić — on the fate of a city fountain and plaque after the government which had placed them there changed, filmed at three different times over a span of 27 years, and by *Poetry and the Revolution* (*Poezija i revolucija*), Branko Ivanda (1971/2000), incorporating "liberated" material on the 1971 student strike which had been kept under lock and key for almost thirty years.

A second essential orientation of the new production house was an offshoot or continuation of the existing tradition of socially engaged film: testimonies about handicapped people, people on the margins and outsiders, the bizarre aspects of life and social abberations of all profiles in

Zrinka Matijević-Veličan: *Pescenopolis* (*Peščenopolis*), 2003
Zvonimir Jurić: *Jurić: Fortress* (*Jurić: Tvrđa*), 2000

engaged and/or stylistically self-conscious documentaries. This series was begun by young authors and includes: a) short films in observational mode such as those by Zrinka Matijević-Veličan (*Of Cows and People / O kravama i ljudima*, 2000), Andrej Korovljev (*Una Storia Polesana*, 1999; *The Years of Rust / Godine hrđe*, 2000), Silvio Mirošničenko (*Dreams from the Railway Station / Snovi na peronu djetinjstva*, 2001); b) playful, humoristic and stylistically coy films such as those by the trio Matanić-Rukavina-Tomić (*Bag and Good Luck!*, 1999); c) films in an interactive-confessional register by Aldo Tardozzi (*Think Pink / Terra Roza*, 1999), Igor Mirković (*Orbanici Unplugged*, 1999) and Dana Budisavljević (*Straight A's! / Sve pet!*, 2004).

The third model inaugurated by Factum's production and perhaps the one most significant for new Croatian documentary filmmaking is in the use of the subjective discourse of the documentary as self-portrait or autobiography, the sort of thing that only amateurs, avant-gardists and video artists had tried their hand at earlier, hence this model was on the margins of industry. The "center" generally preferred hiding behind "neutral" impersonal speech, or speech in the name of an imaginary "we" which was believed to guarantee "truth" and "objectivity." The heretofore invisible or implied subjective "filter" of reality in the documentary suddenly became visible, and instead of presenting the predominant collective identity it pushed to the surface disparate, fragmentary, changeable, and insecure (post-modern) identities. In that sense *Graham & I* acted as a release mechanism for the trend of documentary self-inscription into history, memory, confession, personal jottings, self-examination, and seeking. One of the first to succeed at this form was Zvonimir Jurić, rounding out a three-part urban anti-symphony of his native city, started with the student piece *The Sky below Osijek* (1995), and continuing with the self-aware, metamedia-programmed films *Jurić: Fortress / Jurić: Tvrđa*, (2000), and *Blacks Have Endured* (*Crnci su izdržali, a ja?*, 2001). Biljana Čakić-Veselič sparked a collective catharsis with her documentary search for her brother who had gone missing in the war in *The Boy Who Rushed* (2001), at a time when there were still searches underway for Croatian defenders who had disappeared. In the process she earned for herself the flattering title of "Croatian Antigone." Filmmaker Silvestar Kolbas then strode boldly into the realm of women's experience, filming a journal of the artificial insemination and pregnancy of his wife and co-screenplay writer Nataša Kraljević (*All*

Ante Babaja: *Good Morning* (*Dobro jutro*), 2007
Tomislav Gotovac: *Dead Man Walking*, 2002

About Eve / Sve o Evi, 2003), while dramaturge Lana Šarić felt the need to reconstruct a traumatic battle with serious illness in *Category: Optimist* (*Klasa optimist*, 2010). This trend itself a reflection of similar worldwide tendencies in literature, the visual arts and film, was launched by Factum using genuine individual stories and preeminent directorial methods. The self-documentary suddenly became remarkably interesting for other producers, while authors from the alternative margin and particularly women authors continued to cultivate the subjective discourse they had inherited from the avant-garde. The list of filmmakers and audiovisual arts who support the "first person singular" is growing longer. Ivan Faktor (*Željko Jerman — My Month / Željko Jerman — moj mjesec*, 2005), Tanja Golić (*Wait, Wait... / Čekajte, čekajte*, 2005), Tomislav Gotovac (*Dead Man Walking*, 2002; *Cesar Franck — Wolf Vostell*, 2005), Ana Hušman (*House / Kuća*, 2003), Kristina Leko (*IDon'tRememberHisName*, 2001), Tanja Miličić (*Patchwork*, 2003), Igor Mirković (*Happy Child / Sretno dijete*, 2003), Renata Poljak (*Great Expectations / Velika očekivanja*, 2005), Ljiljana Šišmanović (*Half Sister / Polusestra*, 2006), Ksenija Turčić (*Residency*, 2002), Robert Zuber (*An Accidental Son / Slučajni sin*, 2008) and others. At a point when the trend had already taken off, the filmmakers were joined, camera in hand, by Ante Babaja, a long since "retired" eighty-year-old veteran of modernist film, with *Good Morning* (*Dobro jutro*, 2007) his testamentary self-portrait from an old-peoples' home, with which he sums up and rounds out his opus. As the aesthetic pinnacle of the subjective and intimate documentary, Babaja's film provided a synthesis bridging the most potent stylistic periods of the "old," meditative-essayist (modernist) and "new" meta-medial (postmodern) documentary filmmaking.

Confessional Documentarism as Activism

From the signatures of self-documentarians one can also see a relatively symmetrical presence of men and women filmmakers, to which the gender structure of short-film authors in general is gradually catching up. Moreover, having begun their advance on cinematography in the 1990s, women documentarians (as well as other women filmmakers) have been many times more provocative, inventive, and open over the last twenty years than in the period prior to it, and at the Days of Croatian Film festival they have taken several Grand Prix and other awards (Jelena Rajković, Zrinka Matijević-Veličan, Biljana Čakić-Veselič; Vlatka Vorkapić, Ljiljana Šišmanović, Dana Budisavljević, Ivona Juka, Tanja Golić, Irena Škorić, and others). The growing cinematic presence of women's and personal voices with "political" reverberations is comparable to the phenomenon of feminist, peace, gay and other forms of activism through civil society associations, which are all the more numerous and evident at the advent of the new millennium. In tandem with their appearance on the public scene, awareness is growing of Croatian society as disorderly and intolerant, a society which is not in a geographic or historical vacuum, but is, instead, part of an imperfect regional and transitional context.

By coming forward with debate and activism, Factum has, doubtless, spurred other filmmakers, particularly those of the younger generation, to gather around similar projects, and even state television can no longer behave autistically when faced with the social facts. The Factum example was followed after 2001 by Fade-In (first an association, and then, in 2008, a company), defined as a "platform for young people interested in socially engaged and artistic video." Human rights, equality, youth culture, ecology and the individual are the thematic priorities for the new independent house whose authors/producers Nebojša Slijepčević and Hrvoje Mabić have begun the *Direct* (*Direkt*) documentary series along with their educational and experimental films. The series of mosaic shows is conceptualized as representing various samples of the younger population, "marked" by a certain "problem" or problemmatic choice, such as minority (ethnic, national, etc.) identity, alternative sexual orientation, life in a dysfunctional family or with no parents, dependence on harmful substances or behaviors, an unusual life style and world view, and others. The realities captured by a dozen men and women authors in about a hundred episodes of *Direct* filmed with a dynamic camera, using a combination of interview and observational methods, touch on all the essential problems of Croatian society, particularly daily life in the city. The series was also shown by Croatian television in the late evening time slot. Dana Budisavljević initiated a similar project called *Changing the World* (*Mijenjam svijet*, 2007-2011) as producer and author at Hulahop, an additional place for young directors to gain experience (Saša Ban, Jurić, Matijević-Veličan, Zastavniković and others), expanding the space on television for (activist) confession.

Unlike traditional "talking heads" who testify to or speak of themselves in drab television documentaries, the "independent" confessional subjects of the new Croatian documentary do this with more immediacy, in their own environment, movement or action, and the films are made all the more interesting by the authentic and eccentric life experience they convey, almost always paradigmatic of an outsider. Such films can be found in the notable recent production lines of almost all the key producers of documentary films, which would include the Academy of Dramatic Art with films *World Heritage Site* (*Spomenik nulte kategorije*) by Zvonimir Rumboldt, 1999; *Wolf* (*Vuk*) by Nikola Ivanda, 2000; *I'll Kill You* (*Ubil bum te*) by Nikola Strašek, 2007, and *Above Average* (*Natprosječan*) by Igor

Bezinović, 2008, Factum productions with films such as *Three* (*Tri*) by Goran Dević, 2008 and *Together* (*Zajedno*) by Nenad Puhovski, 2009, as well as Maxim Film with *The Last Genuine Petrović* (*Posljednji autohtoni Petrović*) by Damir Terešak, 2006 and *The Sign on Kain* (*Znak na Kajinu*, 2009) by Ljiljana Šišmanović and Tihana Kopsa, and 4 Film, with *Facing the Day* (*Što sa sobom preko dana*, 2006) by Ivona Juka, the Croatian Film Association with *My Neighbor Tanja* (*Moja susjeda Tanja*, 2006) by Petar Krelja, and the documentary program of Croatian Radio Television with *Anxiety* (*Tjeskoba*) by Damir Čučić, 2010. All these documentaries share a common feature of giving the right to a public voice, emotion, and a personal truth to people on the margins of society, outside the law, losers, rejects, those who have been written off. Speaking of themselves the subjects speak of the society in which they live. The immediate methods of *cinema vérité* and interview used with provocative subjects have become a dominant and powerful modus for contemporary Croatian documentary, just as, in the best years of "Yugoslav" documentary filmmaking in the 1960s and 1970s, the preeminent method was direct (observational) film.

Shifting the Borders: Between Para-Dox and Mega-Dox

Documentary essays and poetic-experimental-documentary hybrids date from roughly those years, 1960s and 1970s, with followers among the avant-garde and modernistically oriented authors ranging from Babaja, Tadić and Galić to Martinac, Gotovac, Mikuljan and Zafranović. In the new constellation of subsidized cinematography in the first years of the new millennium the possibility arose for perpetuating this tradition under professional conditions. The authors who first seized the opportunity were from the alternative and video-art enclave, which went into action with the first air raid sirens in the early 1990s, reacting with video-recordings to the aggressive hostilities launched against Croatia. As the war operations subsided and new producers surfaced (The Croatian Film Association, Milva Film & Video, Pangolin, and others) they began to integrate into the professional mainstream. Vlado Zrnić was dedicated at the time to visually poeticized meditations on the rudiments of (rural) life (*Mirila*, 1997, and the feature *Day under the Sun / Dan pod suncem*, 2000), Zdravko Mustać chose observational documentaries without narrative interventions or commentaries (*Ludar*, 1999; *Purgatory / Purgatorij*, 2005), as did Damir Čučić, when he was "taking a break" from state television (*The Forgotten / Zaboravljeni*, 2001; *La Strada*, 2004; *City Killer*, 2007) and Boris Poljak (*The Split Watercolor / Splitski akvarel*, 2009), and both Poljak and Čučić were interested in experimental visually stylized observation and a poetic-experimental structuring of documentary material. Tomislav Gotovac bridged alternative (multimedia) and documentary praxis in a series of self-portrait films (*Labor Day / Praznik rada*, 2001; *Cesar Franck — Wolf Vostell*, 2005 and the found-footage self-portrait *Dead Man Walking*, 2002), as did Ivan Faktor, Željko Kipke and Nicole Hewitt (*In Time*, 2008), and women filmmakers with a feminist bent or self-reflexivity who document (their own

Igor Mirković: *Happy Child* (*Sretno dijete*), 2003

or someone else's) female experience such as Breda Beban and Rada Šešić working abroad, Renata Poljak, Krstina Leko, Ana Hušman, Vlasta Žanić, Martina Globočnik, Jelena Bračun, Ksenija Turčić and others. What the Amsterdam IDFA has termed the "paradocumentary," a mixed-genre of experiment, document, fiction and/or animation, is one of the most vital documentary genres in Croatian cinematography, to which otherwise conventional authors sometimes flee, as do others outside the "alternative" circle. The paradocumentary genre has never relied on a large budget, it has lived outside the sway of ideological influence and control, and today it is supported by the joint efforts of art, media and film circles.

Along with student production, alternative production can be credited with keeping alive the short form, which was threatened first by the documentary being dropped from the preview cinema repertoire in the 1970s, and then by imposition of the strict 30-, 50- and 70-minute television time slots. But with the return of the documentary to movie theaters, where it used to be shown as an opener for feature films, it can now enjoy a much broader reception, with a large and perhaps even entertaining subject, and in full-length (or even longer) format. It is no surprise, therefore, that there are a growing number of full-length titles by Croatian documentarians following the world production trend. Documentaries are now longer than they used to be in the late 1990s. *New, New Time* was followed by a second box-office hit, *Happy Child* (2003) by Igor Mirković, a nostalgic evocation of the late 1970s and early 1980s on the Croatian music and media scene, as well as the "rockumentaries" *When Miki Says He's Scared* (*Kad Miki kaže da se boji*, 2005) by Ines Pletikos and *The Rhythm of the Rock Tribe* (*Ritam rock plemena*) by Bernardin Modrić, 2005, the farcical *Pescenopolis* by Zrinka Matijević-Veličan and *Radio 101 Independence Day* (*Dan nezavisnosti radija 101*) by Vinko Brešan, 2007. Aside from being sometimes involved with escapism and tabloidization of the public realm, full-length documentaries have also been used for dramatization of serious themes and hermetic approaches in films such as Babaja's *Good Morning*, Kolbas's *All about Eve*, Zrnić's *Day under the Sun*, and *Return of a Dead Man* / *Povratak mrtvog čovjeka* by Petar Orešković and others. Faced with the lack of a screenplay development fund and the paucity of interest on the part of Croatian Radio Television for co-production with independent producers they often reached for help in broadcast minutage within or

Atans Georgiev: *Cash and Marry* (*Plati i ženi*), 2008

outside the region, but the cross-border traffic went in many directions. Factum's *New, New Time*, *Day under the Sun*, and *Together* were funded by western sources (such as the Jan Vrijman Fund) as was *Return of a Dead Man* by Petar Orešković (2006) produced by Nukleus, a young production house which would expand the documentary horizon in the territory of the former Yugoslavia with its co-production efforts, and would take part with minority involvement in projects indirectly touching on the Croatian situation but led by authors from neighboring countries. An example is the film *Cash and Marry* (*Plati i ženi*, 2008), by Macedonian director Atans Georgiev, a humorous dramatization of the attempts of several young men from the Balkans to secure legal residency in Austria for a friend through marriage. Now, when Marina Andree Škop's co-produced *Sevdah* is reverberating across the Croatian documentary screen (2009), and the gaze of Croatian producers is being drawn "far, far away," to the Serbian *Village without Women* (*Selo bez žena*) by Srđan Šarenac, 2009, perhaps such films should be understood as the prototype of a new documentary for a "new, new time." After some twenty years of seeking, a search still underway for an identity or identities in the wasteland of imperfect societies, an awakening from passivity, and a spread of documentary boundaries, our gaze today turns to the space beyond the borders, that very space of which politics and state cinematography wished to be rid some twenty years ago. In any case, documentary and "historical reality" are finding themselves faced with new challenges.

Translated by Ellen Elias Bursać

Croatian Animation, Then and Now: Creating Sparks or Just a Little Bit of Smoke?
by Sanja Bahun

In one of their collective statements, the members of the Zagreb School of Animation Borivoj Dovniković, Ante Zaninović, Zlatko Grgić, Vladimir Jutriša, Aleksandar Marks, Dušan Vukotić and Nedeljko Dragić defined animated film as a protest against rigidity. Animation breathes life into a drawing, they argued, and thus there is a particular continuity between what we call life and the making of animated films:

"Life is warmth. Warmth is movement. Movement is life. Animation can be lukewarm or boiling. Cold animation isn't animation; it is like a stillborn child. To make animated cartoons means to rub tree trunks against each other until there is a spark perhaps or just a little bit of smoke. Take a kilogram of ideas (if possible not too confused), fifty kilograms of talent, and a few thousands of drawings. Stir it well and then with a bit of luck you won't get the right answer to your question." (quoted in Petzke 1996: 53)

For the Zagreb School of Animation, one of the arguably most significant phenomena in both Croatian and Yugoslav cinematography, to animate never meant to imitate reality, but rather to give it a design, or, better still, an "interpretation" (Vukotić 1978: 15). This vigorous challenge to the simplistic perception of the relationship between art and reality (including historical reality) is a particularly adequate overture to the present article for a number of reasons. First, to assess Croatian animation, in terms of either historical or contemporary practice, would be inconceivable without serious reflection on the production of the Zagreb School (so termed by the French critic Georges Sadoul) and the subsequent filmmakers' negotiation of this legacy. The symbolic capital and energy generated by the Zagreb School provided not only a creative impetus, but also the infrastructural developments enabling the growth and international recognition of Croatian animation: the founding and activity of the Zagreb Film production studio, the establishment of the Zagreb World Festival of Animated Film — Animafest (the second oldest festival of animated film in Europe), and the introduction of animation in the national curriculum in higher education. Most importantly, perhaps, to understand the particular artistic and ideological context of the practices within which Croatian animation has developed and is developing, one needs to address precisely the issue that vitally informed the production of the Zagreb School: that of the essential yet volatile relationship between reality and an interpretation thereof. In what follows I shall therefore first survey the history of Croatian animation, with a detailed excurse into the years 1958-1980, the so-called "Golden Age" of the Zagreb School of Animation, then probe the artistic, commercial, and political vicissitudes of the relative interregnum in the late 1980s and during the 1990s, and finally examine the paths open to the old and new animators active in Croatia today.

Scholars tend to trace Croatian animation (then, Yugoslav animation) to the period between the two world wars and the activities of a series of immigrants: the cartoonist Sergej Tagatz, a Pole who emigrated from the Soviet Union to Yugoslavia in 1922, and his collaboration with Aleksandar Gerasimov, another emigré from the USSR, on a series of educational silhouette-animated films for the School of National Health, and the Jewish-Croatian-German brothers Zvonko, Ivo and Vlado Mondschein, who ran a successful film commercial production company called Maar Ton. Properly speaking, however, Croatian animation was "born" in the late 1940s with two rather different authors: Bogoslav Petanjek, an apprentice in Quirino Cristiani's animation studio in Buenos Aires, who returned to Yugoslavia to a career in the production of educational films for Jadran Film (and, in addition to them, a successful gag film called *Blackman Miško* [*Crnac Miško*, 1949]), and Fadil Hadžić, the editor of the satirical magazine *Kerempuh*, who had no previous animation experience but had a work force of enthusiastic cartoonists and caricaturists employed at the magazine. In the wake of Yugoslav split with the Soviet Union, Hadžić and his crew decided to make an animated anti-Soviet satire. The result was The *Great Rally* (*Veliki miting*, 1950, dir. Hadžić, anim. Walter and Norbert Neugebauer), a 20-minute long film that scored well with both the political committees and the cinema audience. Its success allowed Hadžić to found a film production company dedicated exclusively to animated film, Duga Film, and assemble around himself the most distinguished animators of the day: Walter Neugebauer and the authors whose names will soon become synonymous with Yugoslav animation — Dovniković, Jutriša, Marks, Vukotić, and others. In the five years of its existence Duga Film produced a number of short films, notable of which are Neugebauer's take on the Disney short, entitled *A Cheerful Event* (*Veseli doživljaj*, 1951), and Vukotić's first probing of the stylized, "limited" animation, titled *How Kićo Was Born* (*Kako se rodio Kićo*, 1951).

After the dismantling of Duga Film, the center of animation activities transferred to the newly formed Zagreb Film (est. 1953). It is there that the Zagreb School of Animation came into being, against the backdrop of a developing film industry that focused its creative efforts on the realistic-sentimentalist representation of the Second World War and the resistance struggle. The Zagreb School offered new thematics — modern, everyday, universal — and a new type of expression, a stylized, minimalistic, crossover between art and cinema (Prouse 1959: 136). The "Golden Age" of this school (1957-1980) spanned three waves, each characterized by the artistic dominance of a different group of authors-animators: Dušan Vukotić, Vlado Kristl, Nikola Kostelac, Vatroslav Mimica (the first wave, app. 1957-1962); Zlatko Bourek, Borivoj Dovniković, Nedeljko Dragić, Zlatko Grgić, Aleksandar Marks and Vladimir Jutriša, and Pavao Štalter (the second wave, app.

 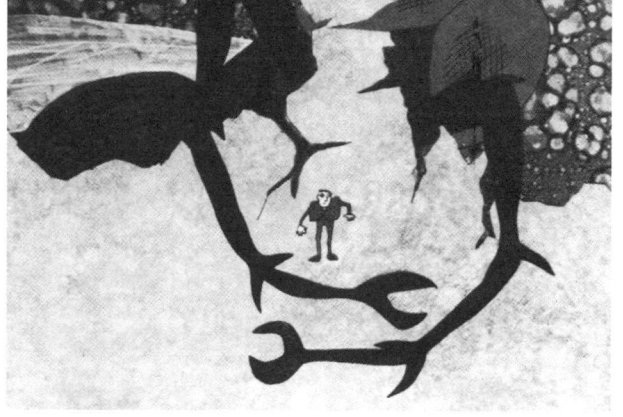

Aleksandar Marks, Vladimir Jutriša: *The Fly* (*Muha*), 1966

1965-1969); and Nedeljko Dragić (again), Zdenko Gašparović, and, towards the end of this period, Joško Marušić (the third wave, 1972-1980; see the interview with Joško Marušić on page 129). During these years the Zagreb animators garnered an unprecedented amount of national and international attention, and its authors won awards at all major animation and film festivals — from Annecy to Teheran — including the 1961 Academy Award for the Best Animated Short Film, the second ever given to a film created outside the US and the first given to a film produced by a non-US film company (for Vukotić's *Ersatz*), as well as two further nominations for the same award (Dragić's *Tup-Tup*, 1972, and Zlatko Grgić and Bob Godfrey's *Dream Doll*, 1979). By the end of 1970s the New York Museum of Modern Arts had already organized two retrospectives of the Zagreb School (1968; 1978).

To call the Zagreb group a "school" means to employ a misnomer, though. The "School" had no overarching spokesperson or "house style": while they were all committed to "cel animation," the Zagreb authors deployed a surprising variety of styles — from the Paul Klee-inspired shapes and palette of Vukotić's *Ersatz* to the reduced stick drawings of Dragić's *Tup-Tup* — and from the graphic austerity of Jutriša and Marks's *The Fly* (*Muha*, 1966) to the almost impenetrable abstraction of Gašparović's *Satiemania* (1978). Yet insofar as being a "school" presupposes collaboration, sharing of a more or less unified worldview, and generation of particular narrative models and aesthetic choices, the Zagreb group could indeed be called a school. The Zagreb authors worked as a shapeshifting team, where the director of one film was often the screenwriter, or the main animator, or the editor, for another. The Zagreb school scripts of the 1950s and 1960s are dominantly based on visual gags, with an anecdotal focus on the "small man" defying (but most often succumbing to) an alienating "big world" (Munitić 1975: 3). Vukotić's famed *Ersatz* is a case in point. Here, a semi-abstract humanoid figure, caught in consumerist fantasies and all-too-human desires, creates and destroys his little world (a "perfect holiday") in a series of visual gags — until he, too, incidentally steps on a nail and deflates.

The "warm" small man vs. the "cold" big world gag-template soon became recognized as the thematic trademark of the School, one that Midhad Ajanović correctly identifies with the ideology of the "third way," or the non-aligned cultural-political reality, of Yugoslavia (2004, pp. 95-6). The narratives of the Zagreb School involve a tone of satire but the latter rarely concerns the immediate political reality of the 1950s-1970s (unlike, for instance, Czechoslovakian animated films of the same period). Rather, the Zagreb animators of the 1950s and 1960s targeted global problems — the two contrasted worlds intent on annihilating each other, the issues of colonialism, racism, dignity-challenging poverty — in short, the problems against which the "small man," or a "small," non-aligned nation, can struggle by highlighting their absurdity. Due to the changes in the global political landscape and structure of experience in the 1970s, the "small person" narrative gave ground to a loosely testimonial narrative structure, where the subject's interior landscape interacts with the objective world in a string of visually or auditorily commanding phantasmagorias (Dragić's *Diary* [*Dnevnik*, 1974] and Gašparović's *Satiemania*). Finally, the horror-based, or anxiety-inducing, narratives took hold in the work of the School in the late 1970s and the early 1980s, and are identifiable in the masterpieces of the uncanny such as Marks and Jutriša's *The Fly* and Marušić's *Fisheye* (*Riblje oko*, 1980).

But these disparate script-models can be hardly said to constitute a "school" of narration. The most important common denominator to the various artistic practices of the Zagreb School, however, was an intention to probe the limits of animation art by challenging the naturalistic representation. Committed to two-dimensional drawing-based animation (animation not involving tri-dimensional objects such as puppets or clay, or the effort to achieve tri-dimensional effects through computer manipulation), the Zagreb School was specifically engaged in the technical and stylistic practice of so-called "limited animation." In full animation, every drawing in a production is used only once, and quick editing assures the constant movement and metamorphosis of shapes (the ideal of such animation is the creation of 24 different images for each second of the 24 frames-per-second running time of a motion picture film). Limited animation is more economical: it cycles or re-uses the same drawings, thereby reducing the number of drawings needed to tell the story, and its appropriation as an artistic strategy is oftentimes caused by some material necessity like a scarcity of drawing foil (Furniss 2007: 134). The movement necessary for the unfolding of the story is oftentimes generated by the camera: limited animation tends to involve long takes and extensive camera movements (panning, zooming in and out), or even, with particular effects, long static frames (see, for an excellent example, *The Fly*). As a consequence, limited animation abrogates the medium's aspirations to verisimilitude: it "limits," or reduces, the details of representation in a fashion reminiscent of abstract art. Insofar as the Zagreb animators' decision to use limited animation was premised upon the belief that the paucity of material resources creates the preconditions for innovation, and the conviction that art should interpret, rather than mimetically represent, reality, the Zagreb School could be best contextualized in relation to a signature cinematic movement the rise of which coincided closely with that of the Zagreb School of Animation — the French *Nouvelle Vague*.

Dušan Vukotić: *Ersatz* (*Surogat*), 1961
Vladimir Kristl: *Don Quixote* (*Don Kihot*), 1961

Drawing specific parallels between the Zagreb School and the French New Wave aesthetics would be well beyond the scope of the present article, but it merits a note that the Zagreb animators used limited animation in comparably creative ways, exploiting the specific potentials of animation to be unconstrained by physical laws (Vukotić 1978: 15) and to incorporate and re-semanticize other art forms such as painting and music. The most notable of their innovative strategies was the examination of the fluid boundaries between the foreground and the background and the consequential emancipation of the "white space." In Dovniković's *Curiosity* (*Znatiželja*, 1967) the white background actively interacts with the foreground where we observe a constrainedly sketched bench, a sleepy "small man," and a bag. As objects and people emerge from various angles of this whiteness (a ship with passengers, a fire brigade, a military unit), all intent on seeing what is "hidden" in the bag, the foreground and the background become indistinguishable; and they project forward beyond the screen boundary, since viewers, too, are swept by a desire to see what is in the small man's bag. Wittily exploiting what Christian Mc-Crea has called "the dimensional excess of animated bodies" (9), the Zagreb School animators also let their humans and other objects expand, shrink, transmogrify, merge with and emerge from this white background, as a result of their desires (*Ersatz*) and constellation in a multi-media aesthetic world (*Satiemania*). Such representation can pose a profound challenge to the figurative nature of film art.

The abstract painter and filmmaker Vladimir Kristl had the ambition to create an animated film that would be structured not by the demands of cause and effect, or any requirements of visual probability, but by its own artistic rhythm. The result was *Don Quixote* (*Don Kihot*, 1961), a film that could be interpreted variably as an ode to the non-figurative "essence" of the world and as a visualization of its own music score — a practice subsequent Croatian animators were keen on advancing. To make an entirely abstract film such as *Don Quixote*, however, means to produce an extreme of what Umberto Eco called "the open work of art" (*opera aperta*) and to unlock the cinematic text to the viewer's free associations, personal and political. Writing in 1967, Ralph Stephenson, for instance, had no doubts that the proliferation of "dots, shapes, creatures, trailers, wheels [...] forward lines [...] and projectiles" in Kristl's film signaled "radars, can-

Zlatko Grgić: *Professor Balthazar*, 1967-1978
Zdenko Gašparović: *Satiemania*, 1978

nons, tanks, aircraft, patrols, and armies [...] a vision of chaos, at the same time eccentric and terrifying" (Stephenson, quoted in Ajanović 2004: 88).

In fact, limited animation commonly relies on the music score and rhythmic patterning to generate meaningful connections between the frames. The Zagreb School animators were consistent in their avoidance of dialogue, or even voice-over, but they intensely used the music score as an actively operative interlocutor and creator of meanings. In films such as Vukotić's *Ersatz* the score, strongly based on leitmotif-development and/or featuring refrains, provides a controlled chronotope for the anti-hero's activities. Music is also used diegetically to bridge the storyline and the form, as in Zlatko Grgić and Pavao Štalter's *The Fifth One* (*Peti*, 1964), a short that follows the ordeals of an endearingly persistent musician to become the fifth member of a quartet. At its most innovative, the Zagreb School would radically exploit the property of music for both expansive meaning-giving and fundamental shape-shifting. The case in point is Gašparović's fantasy *Satiemania*, where the animated world — scenes of a woman getting bored, of bars, butchers, steaks, shopping malls, steaks, ships in the rain, of Grand Canyon and Montparnasse — is continuously reshaped through Eric Satie's music. It is probably for the reasons of this interpenetration of art forms that Giannalberto Bendazzi praised this highly intertextual and remarkably stylistically diverse film as "the best film ever to come out of the studio on the Sava river" (1994: 338).

While well-supported by government endowments, Zagreb Film was also one of the rare Yugoslav film studios that, from the very start, profiled itself as a commercial institution. In addition to producing short art films aimed at the festival circuit or connoisseurs' enjoyment, Zagreb Film rented out its services and expert author-animators to various companies advertising their products and it achieved particular success with made-for-television series such as Zlatko Grgić's *Professor Balthazar* (57 episodes produced between 1967 and 1978), a children's animated film series that was remarkably popular not only in Yugoslavia, but also in Denmark, Finland, Italy, Iran, the Netherlands, Norway, Sweden.

Despite these commercial injections, however, Zagreb Film became collateral damage of the general economic crisis of the mid-1980s; its funding was cut drastically, and animation activity was reduced and relegated to other Croatian and Yugoslav film production houses. But it may be more accurate to say that the 1980s saw not so much an economy-driven "death" as artistic dissipation of the "Zagreb School." What made the Zagreb group of animators a "school," that is, a shared artistic and ideological premise, diversified into a number of production and distribution practices that could no longer be easily understood within the same cinematic and distributive framework, and no longer spoke to the same audience.

Ajanović has suggested another major reason for Zagreb Film's stagnation: the studio's imperviousness to new techniques in the very period when animation globally underwent one of its silent revolutions (2004, p. 99). From the very beginning, Zagreb Film recruited artists, architects, and newspaper cartoonists for animators and thus based its aesthetic profile on the 2D drawing template. In the 1980s, at a time when international animation was rapidly exploring new techniques — in particular those that engaged the third dimension (stop-motion techniques and computer-based animation) — Zagreb animators showed little interest in any alternative practices. Zagreb Film, however, continued to produce internationally recognized animated films during the 1980s, mainly developing the Zagreb School stylistic and narrative templates I noted above. In *The Skyscraper* (*Neboder*, 1981) Marušić used gag, caricature, and multiplication of focal points to convey a subtly politicized fable on contemporary living. In his coming of age fantasies *Album* (1983) and *Butterflies* (*Leptiri*, 1988) Krešimir Zimonić expanded on the intimistic storyline, dream-sequence structure, and phantasmagoric tenor of Dragić's *Diary* and Gašparović's *Satiemania*. And Milan Trenc's witty and poignant *The Big Time* (*Veliki provod*, 1990) closed the decade with a sudden success at London Film Festival. But the film also announced the beginning of an end — or the beginning of new beginnings: the young animator emigrated to the USA in 1991, like a number of other filmmakers.

It is a matter of historical paradox that the first Yugoslav animated feature film, Milan Blažeković's *The Elm-Chanted Forest* (*Čudesna šuma*, 1986), was released precisely in the 1980s. Produced jointly by Croatia Film and the US-based production company Fantasy Forest, and released in two versions (with the US and Yugoslav audio casts, respectively), the film is based on a children's tale by Sunčana Škrinjarić, relating a painter's visit to an enchanted forest. The film was animated in the Disney-style yet it incorporated certain components of the Zagreb School aesthetics, in tune with Blažeković's earlier film-work like the short *Largo* (co-directed with Branko Ilić, 1970). The latter aspect is mainly visible in the use of relatively shallow space and an easel-like 2D background, a practice which might be alternatively interpreted as purposeful (gesturing the painter's own profession, its tools, and its products) or lacking cinematic ambition. Although *The Elm-Chanted Forest* swiftly became the most commercially successful animated film in former Yugoslavia, the film's simple, underdeveloped storyline and ambivalent animation did not score well at the US box office. The mixture of styles, presumably a consequence of an uncomfortable concoction of artistic and commercial intentions, sent contradictory messages to the international audience, uncertain whether this film aspired to full animation (i.e., competing on the children's animation market with Disney production films) or to limited animation (i.e., affiliating itself with UPA's televised series or the Japanese manga films)? Unsurprisingly, the sequel, *The Magician's Hat* (*Čarobnjakov šešir*, 1989, dir. Milan Blažeković), was released in the original language only. But *The Magician's Hat* was markedly less successful even in the country of its production. The time for magic and appreciation of the plots in which human goodness always prevails seems to have passed in Yugoslavia.

Animation, Paul Wells notes, "has the possibility to tell social 'truths' in a fashion unavailable elsewhere" (1997, p. 43). Thanks to its capacity to equilibrate on the fine line between the realistic and the fantastic, animation challenges the accustomed modes of thought and queries the ideological certainties, suggesting a possible extension of what we perceive as fixed into unpredictable, sometimes ungovernable, realms. In its encounter with socio-political reality animation activates not only the field of the analogically metaphoric (as observable in satire-based animation) but also the semantic scope of surreality, or visual trickery. Therefore the oblique relationship between political reality and animation is most frequently reliant on the genre's inherent surplus of associative power. When, in 1996, Goce Vaskov structured his animated short *Mass in A Minor* (*Misa u A-molu*) around a computer-manipulated, "stained glass" representation of terrestrial and extra-terrestrial landscapes, a simplified background suffused with Christian symbolism, and reiteration of the images of lit matches, or candles, it was difficult to see in the film only a universal parable about the forces of nature. Far more poignantly, the film — which concludes with a shot of Zippo pocket lighters, traditionally used by soldiers — evoked *human* activity, the recent and ongoing wars, the innumerable funerals, and the painfully visible presence of military and paramilitary forces in the region.

By contrast, Blažeković's 1997 feature film for children *Lapitch, The Little Shoemaker* (*Čudnovate zgode šegrta Hlapića*), in production at Croatia Film from 1991 to 1997, strikes one as remarkably dissociated from the immediate historical context of production, even for a children's film. *Lapitch, The Little Shoemaker* follows, now more confidently, the model set by *The Elm-Chanted Forest*: a simple script based on a well-known children's tale (Ivana Brlić-Mažuranić's novel *The Marvelous Adventures of Hlapić the Apprentice*, 1913), a charming set of anthropomorphized animal characters, and a fusion of the traditional Disney-style cel animation of the foreground and limited animation/abstraction of the background. To an audience made up of children who grew up exposed to gory television footage, curfews, and air raid sirens, and adults exhausted by the seemingly perpetual cycles of violence, *Lapitch, The Little Shoemaker* was a welcome escape: it soon became the highest-grossing Croatian animated film ever. The film was seen by at least 355,000 cinema-goers in Croatia, and it spawned a spin-off television series, currently being aired on the UK Tiny Pop television channel; and the dubbed German (1999), French (1999), and US (2000) releases all sold very well globally. The film's humane and uncomplicated script had a certain appeal to international audiences,

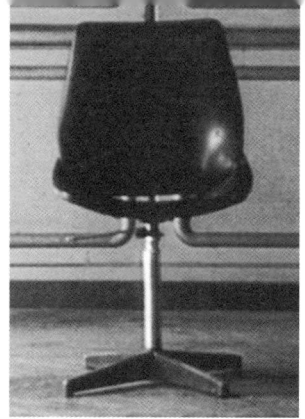

Nicole Hewitt: In/Dividu, 1999

but the marked traditionalism of animation often surprised viewers accustomed to manga, or 3D animation. Taken in tandem, Vaskov's *Mass in A Minor* and Blažeković's *Lapitch, The Little Shoemaker*, provide an evocative picture of the state of Croatian animation, not only in the war-ridden 1990s, but also the early 2000s. Vaskov's short film ushered regional animated art into the world of computer animation, but did so somewhat belatedly and timidly. Blažeković's feature film confirmed that cel, 2D drawing-based animation is the choice style/technique of not only Croatian animators but also their domestic audience. The two films projected the message that the technological aspirations of Croatian animation, as well as the strategies of its production and distribution, are comparatively modest.

A rather different approach to the artistic negotiation of the 1990s was, however, entertained by Nicole Hewitt, a British — and, at times, adopted Croatian — artist and animator. Hewitt's relentless examination of styles and techniques (stop-motion, cut-out animation, drawn animation, object animation, etc.) in her Croatian films such as *Herman's Burden* (*Breme*, 1989), *Notes on Continuity* (*Dnevnik trajanja*, 1991), *Single Viable Fetus* (1995), and *In/Dividu* (1999) exposed Croatian audiences to the potential of abstract animation in confronting political reality through the manipulation of extracts of real life, and posed important questions about identity, temporal change and multiplicity, cultural and media translation, and the role of art in society. While markedly non-commercial, and much indebted to her education in the UK art context, Hewitt's Croatian films nevertheless served as a guide to the forthcoming generation of Croatian animators; her films suggested that it is possible, even beneficial, to produce innovative animation outside big studios and without reliance on state funding.

In their discussion of contemporary Czech animation, Lucie Joschko and Michael Morgan identify a few major factors contributing to the decline of the animated art form in the Czech Republic: the privatization of animation studios, the gradual withdrawal of government funding, and the heightened economic pressure on filmmakers, as well as a change of themes contingent on the transformed political landscape and the fragmentation of domestic audience due to the increased import of international animated films (Joschko and Morgan, 2008, pp. 75-80). With some

 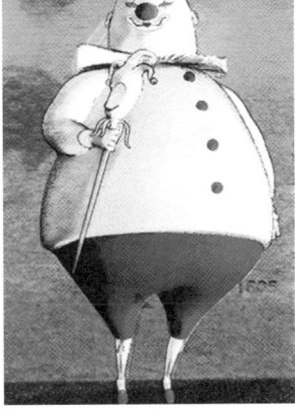

Ana Hušman: *The Market* (*Plac*), 2006
Veljko Popović: *She Who Measures* (*Ona koja mjeri*), 2008

modifications, and taking into account the context of conflict/post-conflict society (as well as a certain cultural lethargy that appears invariably to accompany the prolonged scarcity of resources), the same could be said of Croatian animation. In a 2006 interview young author Ana Hušman rightfully complained about the state of Croatian animation: the paucity of films, restricted scope of topics, limited funding (Hušman, 2006). But it is precisely the mid-2000s that presented us with a veritable turn of events, a turn in which, as we shall see, Hušman herself played an important role. Pragmatically speaking, the most important change that the mid-2000s brought was the reconstellation and consolidation of the financial sector that supports cinematic production, including low-profit genres such as animation. Private production houses, non-governmental organizations, and the Ministry of Culture of the Republic of Croatia, all began showing heightened interest in animation in the early 2000s, both in terms of the preservation of the national animation heritage and the financing of future productions. More significantly, perhaps, these previously irreconcilable financing agents realized that they could work together.

Hušman's animated film *The Market* (*Plac*, 2006) is an exemplary case-study in this respect. The film, which announced a new vibrancy in Croatian animation, was produced by Studio Pangolin (an independent production house she set up with Nicole Hewitt) and was financially supported by the Ministry of Culture. To address both the financial constraints and the fragmentation of audience, the film was published and distributed under the Creative Commons Attribution-ShareAlike 2.5 license and is readily available in good resolution on the Internet. And while *The Market* springs from, and is rooted in, the local context — its framework narrative records a typical day at Dolac, the Zagreb main market place, and the regionally recognizable methods of conserving food at home — the film in fact addresses issues that are universal and exigent: the economic undervalue of local produce, an obsession with cleanliness, xenophobia, and class tensions audible in the documentary, heteroglot voice-over. But the film's key contribution to the reinvigoration of Croatian animation lies in the challenge it poses to our habituation to drawing-based animation. Through its crafty use of stop-motion animation — in the form of "model animation," here, a stilted re-animation of live action footage of the market, combined with pixilation and stop-frame object manipulation (the maneuvering of inanimate objects such as vegetables, kitchen utensils, etc.) — Hušman's film stimulates our visual (and general) appetite. Viewers turn into gluttonous consumers of some haptically accentuated images/objects: carrots, beans, corns. One finds a similar visual language in the author's other stop-motion/live action animated films *Meršpajz* (*Meršpajz*, 2006) and *Lunch* (*Ručak*, 2008) — for food, food preparation, and food intake, and the issues of domesticity and foreignness figure prominently in Hušman's artistic vision.

I am singling out Hušman's animation art because it epitomizes what I believe to be a viable response to the crucial dilemmas of production and distribution sourcing the late 1980s and 1990s decline of Croatian animation. It is fair to emphasize, however, that many other, young and already established, authors have contributed to the rejuvenation of the genre in the 2000s. Nicole Hewitt has continued probing the boundary between the documentary, installation, and animation in a variety of techniques (see, for example, her film *Waltz* [*Valcer*, 2004]), under the auspices of Studio Pangolin. Goce Vaskov made further advances into 3D computer animation, with, in particular, his sardonic computer-assisted clay animation *Bombs* (*Bombe*, 2005). As a vivid evidence of continuity, the Zagreb School émigrés Nedeljko Dragić and Milan Trenc returned to the Croatian animation scene with *Rudi's Lexicon* (*Rudijev leksikon*, 2009; a series of 365 90-second films) and *Loneliness* (*Samoća*, 2010; a short animation), respectively; Borivoj Dovniković and Pavao Štalter teamed to produce the short film *Silence* (*Tišina*, 2009); and Joško Marušić released the feature film *Rainbow*, screened in the official selection of the 2010 Hiroshima International Festival of Animated Films. Judging by the 2009-2010 Croatian Animation catalogue, however, drawing/painting-based animation, either in the form of traditional 2D or computer-assisted 3D films, still dominates the production of animated films in Croatia. This is due both to the heritage of the Zagreb School and to the fact that Croatian animators are still mainly recruited from a cohort of successful illustrators, traditional and computer graphics designers, comic-book writers and painters such as Goran Trbuljak, Simon Bogojević Narath, or, indeed the latter's protégé, young 3D animator Veljko Popović. A compelling postmodern updating of Vukotić's *Ersatz*, Popović's 6-minute long *She Who Measures* (*Ona koja mjeri*, 2008) won the FIPRESCI Award at Annecy 2008, an event that forcefully signaled the return of Croatian animation to the international art animation stage. The film attacks consumerism through a fable about a group of humanoid customers who, armed with "smiley" masks, engage in an eternal shopping spree; they are led by a clownish figure who excretes objects for further consumption. Popović has learnt his Zagreb-School lessons well, so he uses the abstracted background (here, corrugated cardboard, painted and then scratched and 3D manipulated) productively to suggest an infinite wasteland of shopping malls in a dehumanized world. *She Who Measures*, produced by private production house Kenges, is yet another example of a successful diversification of funding: the film was financed by sources that range from private trustees to the Office for Culture of the City of Split, Popović's hometown.

With the belated but convincing rise of computer animation, such mixtures of 2D and 3D (computer-based) techniques have become common in Croatia, but they now also include a self-reflective incorporation of an array of other techniques. The directing-animating pair Davor Međurečan and Marko Meštrović have produced two films that combine 3D, 2D, live action and puppet animation, *In the Gypsy Style* (*Ciganjska*, 2004) and *Silencium* (*Silencium*, 2006); both films are based on, or inspired by, Miroslav Krleža's *The Ballads of Petrica Kerempuh*. In a different fashion, Međurečan and Meštrović (who have in the meantime switched to independent projects) are also good heirs to the Zagreb-School legacy. Subtly political, their films repeatedly return to the issues of personal freedom and the interior and external repression as these get reflected in the life of an ordinary person. They use soundtrack as an agile interlocutor with images, indeed a structuring crux of the film. But the visuality of their films is influenced by an art alien to the traditional Zagreb-School film production (if close to their chosen writer's aesthetic habitat): German expressionism and, in particular, the expressionists' project to exteriorize mental states on screen. All these qualities are easily identifiable in Marko Meštrović's most recent animated short, *No Sleep Won't Kill You* (*Nespavanje ne ubija*, 2010; produced by Kreativni sindikat and Zagreb Film, co-financed by Croatian Audiovisual Centre). *No Sleep Won't Kill You* takes the form of a testimonial narrative: it follows a contemporary insomniac as he explores the features of a recurrent dream by inscribing it on Zagreb public spaces. Yet the dynamic combination of live action and drawing, complex editing, and the experimental jazz music score provided by US artists Jessica Lourie and Abraham Gomez-Delgado defamiliarize this testimony. Described by its meta-cinematic narrator as "arrhythmics with variation," this phantasmagoria transforms the Zagreb city streets into the setting and the material base for animation.

The combination of 2D/3D animation and live action, or animated real-life footage (pixilation), as we find it in Meštrović's film, seems to have gained particular popularity in recent Croatian production. Darko Bakliža's films such as *A Date* (*Spoj*, 2004), *Homo Volans* (2008), and *Format* (2010) compellingly probe the uncanny boundary between the naturalistically plausible and its fantastic, or artistic, extension, through the interface of live and variously animated action. Other techniques start to appear more timidly. Mainly working in Austria, Daniel Šuljić has been experimenting with various alternative techniques such as coffee on glass (*Zlatorog*, 2000; *I Can Imagine It Very Well*, 2003) or oil on glass (*The Cake*, 1997; *A Film with a Girl*, 2000) for more than a decade. More recently, Michaele Müller, a Swiss native studying and working in Zagreb, used painting on glass and enhanced sound design in her graduation piece *Miramare* (2009) to associatively recount the complexities of life on the Croatian Mediterranean shore. The artistic boldness paid off: the film was selected in the category of graduation films for both the 2010 Cannes Film Festival and 2010 Annecy Animated Film Festival and it won the Spirit Award for Animation at the 2010 Brooklyn Film Festival. The cases of both Šuljić and Müller — as well as that of Dragić, Trenc, and Hewitt — also highlight the need to conceive of contemporary Croatian animation as not only, or not even primarily, a national cinema practice, but as a product of international transits, exchanges, and culturally diverse routes of social and artistic identification.

Such a proliferation of new animation art has not passed unnoticed. In 2009 the London International Animation Film Festival featured both a Zagreb Film tribute and a panorama of new Croatian animation. In 2010 a comparable program was mounted at Fantoche, the International Animated Film Festival in Baden, Switzerland. As I write this text, encouraging news is coming in. Popović's *My Way* (*Moj put*, 2010; based on a novel by Svjetlan Junaković) and Meštrović's *No Sleep Won't Kill You* were featured in the highly selective competition programs of the 2010 Annecy festival; and the latter won the 2010 EUNIC Award for the Best Experimental Film at the I've Seen Films Festival in Milan. Bakliža's *Format* won the 2010 Best Experimental Film at the Golden Boli Festival in Adana.

I started this article with a quotation from a Zagreb-School manifesto. In the words of Zagreb-School authors, animation should be warm — which means creating sparks, or, simply, a bit of smoke. What these lines call for is not so much an inflammation as a subtle working with everyday social and political reality, so that the coldness of the world — our petrification in certain modes of behavior or certain structures of feeling — can be challenged anew. Does contemporary Croatian animation live up to this project or even subscribe to the same view of film art? While it would still be difficult to offer a definite answer to this question, the recent evidence of increasing experimentation with animation styles and multiple-audience messages, as well as the new inventiveness in the production-distribution strategies, confirm, convincingly, that Croatian animation is alive and ambitious. It does not purport to offer a unified worldview and it values and gradates its own artistic practices differently. In all its forms, however, it appears committed to an engagement with the external world: to be "warm;" to create, at least, a little bit of smoke.

Works Cited

- Ajanović, M. 2004. *Animation and Realism*. Zagreb: Hrvatski filmski savez.
- Bendazzi, G., 1994. *Cartoons — One Hundred Years of Cinema Animation*. Eastleigh: John Libbey & Company Limited.
- Furniss, M. 2007. *Art in Motion: Animation Aesthetics*. Revised edition. Eastleigh: John Libbey & Company Limited.
- Interview with Ana Hušman, 2006. Kuhinja (TV programme). Pro.ba.
- Munitić, R. 1975. "Krotitelji divljih crteža." (Tamers of Wild Drawings). *Filmska kultura* (100): 3.
- Petzke, I. 1996. "Četrdeset godina studija crtanog filma Zagreb filma." (40 Years of Zagreb Film Animation Studio). *Hrvatski filmski ljetopis* (7): 53-57.
- Prouse, D. 1959. "Yugoslav Cartoons (In the Picture)." *Sight and Sound* 28 (3/4): 136.
- Vukotić, D. 1978. "Scenarij crtanog filma." (The Screenplay of Animated Film). In Z. Sudović, ed. *Zagrebački krug crtanog filma, tom 2: Odabrani scenariji i knjige snimanja filmova zagrebačke škole*. (*The Zagreb School of Animated Film, Vol. 2: Selected Screenplays and Shooting Scripts*). Zagreb: Grafički zavod Hrvatske.
- Wells, P. 1997. "The Beautiful Village and the True Village: A Consideration of Animation and the Documentary Aesthetic." *Art and Design* 12 (53): 40-45.

Gender in Contemporary Croatian Film
by Mima Simić

Although films have been made in the territory of Croatia for nearly a century now (the first Croatian feature film, *Brcko in Zagreb*, dates back to 1917), the period since 1991 frames an independent national film industry that, despite its cultural roots still protruding from the fragmented Yugoslav soil, can nevertheless be analyzed as an organism, or rather (to stick to the metaphor) — an artistic and ideological celluloid body. As all bodies, it had to go through various stages of development to reach "voting age," when it can finally be held fully responsible for all the political decisions it does — or, indeed, does not — make today.

In my analysis of contemporary Croatian film and its treatment/reflection of what is popularly known as "gender issues," I focus mostly on mainstream feature films, in particular those that had unusually high budgets, attracted large (inter)national audiences, won awards at film festivals and/or have been distributed worldwide with government endorsement. My selection is informed not only by lack of space, but also by the fact that these films, in light of their production, distribution, and government support (being sponsored by the Croatian Ministry of Culture and its institutions, Croatian National Television and/or international production companies), are representative of Croatian official politics, that is, the dominant ideology regarding the question of gender; i.e. gender roles and identities.

The (Re)Birth of a National Cinema

Observing the process of the Croatian film industry's metaphorical coming of age, we should (despite the embarrassment it may cause) stop to consider the "birth pains" of new Croatian film during the War of Independence (1991-1995), with emphasis on the celluloid construction of gender in this ideologically charged period. Indeed, in order to express and underscore its autonomy and independence from Yugoslavia the new Croatian state needed to formulate the image of the new Croat man and the new Croat woman — the specific Croatian masculinity and femininity — which can be read in the films produced during the war and immediately following it.

In *Women Nation State* (1989) Nira Yuval Davis and Floya Anthias analyze the relation of the nation state to the woman, the function of the woman within the nation state, and the "ways in which women have tended to participate in ethnic and national processes and in relation to state practices" (1989: 7). The woman produces members of the ethnic community and is the central figure of the ideological reproduction of the community. In perpetuating its culture she is the marker of ethnic and national differences, and a symbol in the ideological discourse used in the construction, reproduction, and transformation of ethno-national categories (8-10). Cynthia Enloe, too, highlights how "[w]omen are relegated to minor, often symbolic roles in nationalist movements and conflicts [...] as icons of nationhood, to be elevated and defended." The woman's body as "a booty or spoils of war, to be denigrated and disgraced" becomes "the *sign* through which men communicate with each other" (Das 1995: 212). Furthermore, Robert M. Hayden observes that women's bodies exposed to violence are "constructed [...] as ethnic territories themselves" where rape marks, defiles, and excludes the female body from the geographical territory (2000: 32). All these theoretical findings clearly show the "sexual division of labor" in warfare, where the woman is typically a symbol, a sign and a means for the transfer of power, rather than a powerful and active subject. As if based on these ethnographic studies the two most expensive cultural products of the Croatian war era, Oja Kodar's *A Time For...* (*Vrijeme za...*, 1993) and Jakov Sedlar's *Our Lady* (*Gospa*, 1994), reflected this gender division and dynamic to the minutest detail.

Although of questionable artistic value (as is any pamphlet or propaganda), Kodar's and Sedlar's films were estimated to be of the greatest symbolic importance at the time, due to their ideological function, judging by the exceptionally high budgets they managed to raise in a period of serious political and financial crisis. These films, as I will show in more detail, are textbook examples of the gender-prescriptive, restrictive, and regulatory function culture plays in a time of war, being, like war, a continuation of (here: patriarchal/nationalist) politics by other means. And as nationalism and religion were the foundation stones of the new nation state, their common denominator, patriarchy, needed to be (re)affirmed through clearly delineated gender boundaries/roles, best exemplified through crude (gender, ethnic, religious) stereotypes. And naturally, as One is defined in relation to an/the Other, this relation with the (then) ultimate Other (Serb/Yugoslav) needed to be depicted in a strongly monochromatic and simplistic manner.

A Time For... Our Lady

Interestingly enough, Oja Kodar's *A Time For...* was one of the few "new" Croatian films both written and directed by a woman and the first film about the Croatian War of Independence. This, unfortunately, made no ethical or aesthetic difference in the execution of the project. Evoking the Bible in the very title, the film denotes the Croatian bond to Christianity (i.e. Roman Catholicism), placing the Croatian nation both in the realm of the spiritual and the anti-communist. All the Serbs (including their religious leaders) are depicted in the worst possible light, physically and ethically alike. Croats, on the other hand, are noble, good-looking, pious, brave, and self-sacrificing. This symbolic representation of the characters in the film signifies not only what the Other is like, but what the One, i.e. "ideal" Croatian (male and female) citizens, (ought to) look/be like. As women function as "boundary markers" between different national, ethnic, and religious groups (Kandiyoti 1991) in times of ethnic conflict they can be expected to play a significant (yet, as "markers," necessarily passive) role. The Croat woman (a hardworking, self-sacrificing, and virginal mother, who is also a nurse) will be granted a moment of action, incredible and insane courage, only through motherhood. Moreover, the power of her symbolic representation lies exactly in her passivity; in order for the climax of the film to work effectively, she needs to be exposed to the ultimate act of (ethnic) violence, rape. Here she stands not only for all Croatian women but even more so for the Croatian land itself, stripped and ravished by the enemy.

The other key female character is the Son's girlfriend, poetically nicknamed Cinderella, blonde and beautiful, unspoiled and pure. She and the Son lose their virginity to each other and, having served this designated purpose, she remains out-framed for the rest of the film, waiting for him to return. Drawing on the fairy-tale tradition, which reflects the patriarchal symbolic frame, Kodar neatly fits this younger female character within it as a structural (generational) predecessor to the Mother figure. In contrast to these two epitomes of Croatian womanhood, the Serb nurse-spy is represented as uncomfortably fleshy, vulgar, and promiscuous. To demonize a woman efficiently is thus to portray her as (over)sexualized, and overtly physical. Interestingly enough, both Serb (ugly and evil) and Croat (beautiful and virtuous) women will be granted the same scope of action, limited to either their sexual or asexual (motherly) practices. In this world females are politically insignificant and are recruited in their most traditional roles. It is men who carry the weapons, make the decisions and, if necessary, take lives.

In 1994 Tuđman's favorite director, Jakov Sedlar, made *Our Lady*, a film blessed with a high-budget and an incredible cast. Apart from Martin Sheen, *Our Lady* hosted Michael York, Morgan Fairchild and Paul Guilfoyle. This was a cast that the domestic film industry could not have imagined since the 1970s and Tito's reign. Despite its title, which suggests contemplation on the question of faith, the film is actually an anti-communist manifesto, and a propaganda tool for upholding Tuđman's political and territorial interests in Bosnia and Herzegovina. This, to be sure, was no place for women. The one female character of any significance is subservient nun Fabijana Zovko (Morgan Fairchild), who is given a handful of lines and a few more suffering, dramatic looks. All the agents are men, occupying all sorts of powerful positions, whether in Church, government, the army, the secret police, the law and similar. The hypertrophied nationalist imperialist patriarchy that this film stands for in the end, much like *A Time for*, could perhaps be redeemed only if it were to be read as camp. However, for the elementary school pupils (eight graders) for whom it was compulsory viewing at theatres this kind of a reading was most certainly unavailable and the political climate of the time did not allow for much distance from the "patriotic" and "pious" topic of this film.

A Happier Childhood

With the economic recovery following the war, and the emergence of a new generation of filmmakers (known as the Young or New Croatian film), things slowly started looking up for the Croatian film industry. As the previous, war years had (understandably?) determined the subjects, the genre, and the shape of gender roles in the handful of films made in this era, the beginning of a happier childhood for the new Croatian film was marked by another film dealing with the war, but in a much lighter mode and genre. Vinko Brešan's prewar comedy of character and customs *How the War Started on My Island* (*Kako je počeo rat na mom otoku*, 1996) was (and remains to this day) the biggest grossing Croatian film. At the time of its making it was also a social signal that the child was finally allowed to go out and play.

However, the postwar world that this celluloid child encountered was perhaps different in genre, but not much different in gender ideology. The benevolent community of a Croatian fictional island that Brešan's film depicts (much like the one in a later Croatian cinematic hit, *What is a Man Without a Moustache* by Hrvoje Hribar which I analyze in more detail in another article in this book) is but a gentler (comic) version of the same patriarchal society with the adherent ideology of the previous era; yet, as the genre demands, less crude and seasoned with a lot of charm, and seductive in its quaint ways. The island community is a palette of picturesque character types, yet what binds this bunch of bizarre individuals is a common ideology. Indeed, much like in the celluloid "tragedies" (in every sense) analyzed earlier, this comedy leaves all the military/political business to men, whereas women perform the familiar kind of auxiliary function. The only two female characters in this ensemble piece are the wife and the mistress of the Yugoslav Army major Aleksa who is about to start the war on the island (and Croatia as symbolized by it). Probably the most quoted line from any contemporary Croatian film, "Aleksa, come home, I've made *pasta sciutta*!" is exclaimed by the wife; her cooking skills, symbolically, being her most potent weapon. When the wife fails to get the major to come home, the major's mistress attempts to do so, with the same result. There is an implication that the major will not leave the post and keeps threatening to blow up the island because he is afraid of his wife's rage at his having a mistress. This, however, seems more of a mark of the Serb commander's lunacy and idiocy than the actual power of the wife/woman. The comic co-existence of the wife and the mistress on the same stage, in the same symbolic plane, and with the same (lack of) political relevance/influence implies that the women's position in the power structure had not changed with the genre. And the celluloid child that is Croatian film has not learned much about the complexities of gender in the process.

Regarding this dual subject (of gender and genre) it is extremely interesting to observe an example of probably the only "chick flick" among contemporary Croatian films (its predecessor can be found in Rajko Grlić's 1984 hit *In the Jaws of Life* based on Dubravka Ugrešić's postmodernist bestseller), made by the only female director who makes feature films

Rajko Grlić: *In the Jaws of Life* (*U raljama života*), 1984

on a relatively regular basis (meaning three feature films in six years, 1996-2002, not counting her TV films). The woman in question is Snježana Tribuson and the film is *The Three Men of Melita Žganjer* (*Tri muškarca Melite Žganjer*, 1998). This Croatian anticipation of *Bridget Jones's Diary* came as a celluloid refreshment and drew comparatively large audiences. The film tells the story of an overweight thirty-something woman, desperately unhappy for the lack of a man in her life, obsessed with a Spanish TV soap and in love with a character from it. Melita is thus both a stereotypical fan of trivial literature and the protagonist of these types of texts. In this way the narrative relies on (gender) stereotypes twice as much, but this indeed is the point of the game, the game being postmodernism. Unlike most of the Croatian film production of the time, operating within the traditional frames of the genre and generally lack self-reflexivity or self-irony, Tribuson plays freely with and ironizes the ("women's") genre within which she works: the inserted Spanish TV soap here is an excellent lighthearted narrative maneuver rarely seen in the more "serious" and generally mimetically obsessed Croatian film production of the time. There are indeed many layers to the film's narrative, this complexity being further proliferated and emphasized by the film's form. All of this considered, one will wonder if the ideological effect of such a story is not to maintain the existing social relations and (patriarchal) system, as would be suggested by all the stereotypes it plays/builds the narrative on. Yet, the many disruptive elements in the film (at both the diegetic and the structural levels) can in fact be said to be preventing the viewer from escaping into the text as easily as they would into a less self-reflexive work; being constantly made aware of the constructed nature of both film and its "filling," genre and gender. *Three Men of Melita Žganjer* proves that form indeed can make all the difference in meaning, and if served with a ton of pink icing on top, stereotypes necessarily become indigestible.

Of The Birds and the Lez-Bees

Within two months of Tuđman's death in 1999 the political life of Croatia changed dramatically. This turn in political outlook had many benefits for filmmakers, one of them being the implementation of a non-governmental board to oversee subsidies, film archives, education, film publishing, and international sales, as opposed to the infamous Minister-dependent film committee of the Tuđman regime. With the fall of the Croatian Democratic Union (the HDZ) the whole system of subtle prohibition began to dissolve. The authors from this era proceeded to break free from the chains of self-censorship and started producing films more complex in form as well as in their political outlook. With Tuđman on his death bed Vinko Brešan's *Marshal Tito's Spirit* came out, another successful, mildly provocative, populist political comedy dealing with the Croatian past and the present, again located on an island among colorful natives, former partisans, and a young policeman investigating an alleged appearance of Tito's ghost, i.e. the ghost of the Croatian past. It followed the successful formula of the previous hit and relied on lively characters (with mostly male agents) and the spirit of the community — and although its satirical blade turned against politics past and present, the politics of patriarchy was left unscathed.

This was also a period when Croatian movie-going audiences could see two quite interesting, apparently critical studies of Croatian society by Dalibor Matanić, the director who is probably the only one who regularly (and bravely!) places women in the focus of his film narratives. His films *The Cashier Wants to Go to the Seaside* (*Blagajnica hoće ići na more*, 2000) and *Fine Dead Girls* (*Fine mrtve djevojke*, 2002) brought a fresher approach to "women's questions." The latter was the first (and so far the only) film in Croatian mainstream cinema to take up the subject of lesbianism, placing a homosexual couple at the center of the narration. According to the director, it took six years and a change of government for this film to be made — it was too shocking for both National Television and the HDZ Ministry of Culture to fund it. In the sensitive, constitutive postwar period, when heterosexuality is not only an ethical (in the context of the religious "revival" which accompanied the establishment of the new state), but also a demographic imperative, and the Woman the symbolic and literal mother of the nation, lesbianism embodies the ultimate threat to the re/construction of a land devastated/liberated by war. This can explain the unwillingness of the (right-wing) government to subsidize a cultural project that "promotes" homosexuality by depicting lesbians in a favorable light. Considering the obstacles this film had to overcome (it was finally made with the help of an independent producer), as well as its theme which suggests the possibility of a different structuring of gender roles and relations, a closer reading is due, in order to ascertain how subversive this film actually is.

The *Fine Dead Girls* are Iva and Marija, a lesbian couple moving into a sublet apartment in a crumbling Zagreb building, which is a grotesque mirror image of postwar Croatian society inhabited by bizarre characters — a violent nationalist, a crazy old woman, a prostitute, a rapist, a doctor performing illegal abortions, a mentally retarded young man — in this context the lesbians are in fact depicted as the most "normal" of them all. In such a clearly oppressive environment, when their lesbianism is discovered Iva is raped and Marija dies at the hands of tenants who push her down the stairs. Iva returns to her former boyfriend and has a child by him, but as the film title indicates, in the end she, too, is symbolically dead after choosing a false existence.

Despite the fact that it does not judge lesbianism and avoids the well-known and well-worn perspective of pathologizing it, the film associates it with experiences of trauma so intense that it becomes, in fact, an impossibility. As previously suggested, the symbolic meaning and literal function of the (postwar) woman as the (re)producer of the nation and ethnicity cannot be endangered — in the moment of crisis lesbianism becomes something a woman must reject in order to survive; she herself as well as the nation whose procreation her body guarantees. Women's ultimate emancipation from patriarchy (symbolized by lesbianism) must be put "on hold," or entirely rejected for the greater goal — the reproduction of the nation/state. This result may be depicted as tragic for individual women, but their sacrifice seems necessary and unavoidable.

Fine Dead Girls proved to be a film that in fact had a little to do with homosexuality and could hardly be said to have challenged any stereotypes. Moreover, by introducing helpless lesbian victimized heroines to Croatian celluloid, it managed to affirm a few more. As a vehicle for critique of the new militaristic, traditionalist, patriarchal, and nationalist discourses and practices, it symbolically sacrificed the woman/lesbian (and paradoxically) served to perpetuate the *identical* ideology and discourses it aimed to critique, ultimately preventing the establishment of the woman/lesbian *subject*. In the end, the film did not deal with lesbianism in any way more complex than do mainstream media — using the controversial subject to attract audiences, only to avoid it in the body of the text, transforming it into a metaphor or a means for meditating on, but also (despite his best intentions) of mediating and affirming, a familiar (postwar) ethos.

In 2003, as Croatian cinema was about to hit puberty, the "reformed" and EU-oriented HDZ was again back in power. Fresh, politically and culturally relevant themes were introduced in film — such as dealing with Croatian war crimes (Brešan's *Witnesses / Svjedoci*, 2003), and multiculturalism with its endless challenges (of a darkly comic nature in Ognjen Sviličić's *Sorry For Kung Fu / Oprosti za kung fu*, 2004 and traumatic and tragic in *The Melon Route / Put lubenica*, 2006, by Branko Schmidt). Yet, how fresh or novel was the approach of these filmmakers to gender roles and relations? Let us briefly discuss each of the lauded and awarded examples.

Brešan's *Witnesses* was the first Croatian mainstream feature film that dared raise the controversial issue of Croatian war crimes against Serbian civilians during the Homeland War, a subject long disregarded and/or suppressed by politicians, the media, and the people of Croatia. Its symbolic relevance was acknowledged at the 2004 Berlinale where it received a special Jury's Peace Prize, and it is still one of the most successful Croatian contemporary films in the international arena.

The (modernist, *Rashomon*-like structured) narrative depicts the murder of a Serbian civilian by a group of Croatian soldiers, the only witness being his little daughter whose life is now also in danger because of what she has seen. The ultimate evil of the film, however, is not the killers/executors (they are soldiers who got a little too used to war), but the one of the killers'

Ognjen Sviličić: *Sorry For Kung Fu* (*Oprosti za kung fu*), 2004
Vinko Brešan: *Witnesses* (*Svjedoci*), 2003

mothers who cold-bloodedly agrees that the Serb child should be liquidated. As she has already lost her husband to the Serbs and her two sons are all she has and lives for, to save her own child she will willingly sacrifice another's. This can, of course, be interpreted as a critique of patriarchy that makes monsters out of women when their social role is reduced to motherhood/wifehood, yet very few viewers will arrive at this reading, as the Mother character is already too complex to deal with at the very first (extra-filmic) level, being played by Serbian film superstar Mirjana Karanović.

The other important female character and a rare female protagonist in Croatian cinema who is finally granted some traditionally "masculine" agency, i.e. agency beyond the scope of her sexuality/motherhood, is the character of the journalist who stubbornly investigates the case of the murder of the Serb, even though she is constantly met with censorship and the hostility of her professional and private surroundings. One should be grateful for an emancipated female character propelling the narrative with her inquiry, forcing the male protagonist (a Croatian soldier, brother of one of the murderers and war invalid himself) to search his own conscience and act to save the little girl (thus indicting/sacrificing his own brother). Of course, the female journalist character is not the one who in the end will/can save the little girl; the actual saving is done by the man, a decision-making and active agent of patriarchy; which he remains even when he is actually half a man, symbolically castrated in the war (he loses a leg). The emotionally and visually overdone epilogue of the tragedy is a symbolic restoration of a (now mixed!) Croatian family, as the Croatian man, Croatian woman and Serbian child are riding into an orange sunrise.

The clash of cultures, ideologies and ethnicities was handled somewhat differently by Ognjen Sviličić in his *Sorry for Kung Fu*, a black comedy set in rural, i.e. hyperpatriarchal, Croatia, where a girl/woman returns from the west (Germany) to her parents' village, only to be met with an avalanche of accusations for being pregnant yet husbandless. As her parents try to find her a husband and the many men line up one after the other trying to woo her, she more or less silently puts up with this abuse (for the benefit of the film's comic potential, presumably) but the real shock to the community comes when she gives birth to a child — and a Chinese one at that (hence the title). At last realizing she cannot bring her child up in these surroundings, she returns to Germany. The reunion takes place a few years later on her father's deathbed, where he ostensibly accepts the child. This film, much like Schmidt's *Melon Route*, brings in the Other (in both cases it is Chinese as the ultimate object of Orientalization) to reflect the xenophobia correctly located in the patriarchy of Croatian insular society. In *Kung Fu* the woman is the mother of the Other; and the One who accepted and embraced (in more ways than one) the Other (in Germany, where both, in fact, were Other — implying that the only way to learn to accept another is to be in their shoes). The woman is thus the agent of the reconciliation, the softer side of society through which multiculturalism (in Croatia it is symbolized by the EU) will be accepted, whereas at least one generation of men will have to pass away before this idea is integrated in the society. In the *Melon Route*, however, a Chinese woman is saved by a war veteran haunted by PTSD, first from the water, later from criminals he kills in a bloody showdown. His love for an Other here is, however, hopeless. His mission for them to escape to Germany (as their relationship is impossible in Croatia) fails and she leaves on her own. Both the comedy and the tragedy treat the subject of multiculturalism as something that is on the border of Croatia (as Croatia is now on the border of the EU) but is not as yet its "proper" integrated reality.

Bringing these novel, socially and politically relevant topics into Croatian film definitely diversified its thematic landscape, yet the symbolic and auxiliary function of the Woman continued to haunt Croatian mainstream cinema throughout the stages of its development. Furthermore, the string of films that were made in the following (i.e. past) few years, in the period from Croatian cinema's late puberty to its adolescence, proved to be (as is any young man of that age, and the Croatian film industry most definitely, and proudly, proved to be of male gender) brimming with testosterone. So much so that the most popular, most successful, and outstanding films of this period had barely any female characters in them — and more than one had *none*.

Rajko Grlić's *The Border Post* (*Karaula*, 2006), Kristijan Milić's *The Living and the Dead* (*Živi i mrtvi*, 2007), Sviličić's *Armin* (2007), Dalibor Matanić's *Kino Lika* (2008), Goran Rušinović's *Buick Riviera* (2009), Zvonimir Jurić & Goran Dević's *The Blacks* (*Crnci*, 2009) and Branko Schmidt's *Metastases* (*Metastaze*, 2009), all these films in their own right proved that Croatian cinema has indeed finally matured. Directors collaborated with eminent novelists (Grlić worked with Ante Tomić, Kristijan Milić with Josip Mlakić, Dalibor Matanić with Damir Karakaš, Rušinović with Miljenko Jergović etc.) creating celluloid texts of an undeniably better quality, finally building a body of national cinema worthy of note (if only, as yet, on Croatian territory). However, almost all of these films are so male-centered that one can rightfully wonder if Croatian film will soon start reproducing though cell division.

Grlić's film takes place (as the title suggests) in a prewar Yugoslav army barracks — it's a co-production financially backed by almost all former Yugoslav republics (this is a practice many directors nowadays recognize as a potent strategy for winning back some of the cultural and financial territory lost in the war); where the only female character is an officer's wife who serves as a (erotic) tool for the protagonist's sexual coming of age. She also pays a hefty price for her love and sexual misconduct since she is tragically killed in the rampant shooting that concludes the film. At the narrative level this expulsion of the central female character precludes any possibility of a genuine choice for her lover, a handsome medical doctor, and ensures that the military experience remain a truly male undertaking. On the other hand, her lover, manages to leave the army unhurt (at least physically) and return to his native Dalmatia. The earlier part of the plot comically deals with men's life in the army and, of course, with politics (another male territory).

Milić's *The Living and the Dead* as well as Zvonimir Jurić & Goran Dević's *The Blacks* are remarkable examples of war films that go beyond the stereotypes (of genre and ideology), and that have finally brought a complex (formally, structurally, thematically) perspective on the war to domestic film production. (Un)surprisingly, there are no female characters in either of the films. For better or worse, the men are the doers, agents, and whatever their agency, they are always in the shot. Sviličić's *Armin* and Rušinović's *Buick Riviera* are both films about a male-male relationship the development of which drives the plot. The former is a story about a father and son (and the media industry in the postwar zone), the latter is about a chance meeting of a Serb war criminal and a Bosniak refugee on the US territory, bringing back into play the dynamics and complexities of the past war. Schmidt's *Metastases* is another surprisingly well-written, well-directed and acted film about urban (moral) decline, told through four stories of four young Zagreb males in their everyday lives of drinking, betting, soccer-watching and wife-beating. The men that inhabit this world may be the victims of an ethically deteriorating society, but women are the ones who take the worst beatings. And accept them as something natural.

The sad paradox, we could say, of the recent years of Croatian cinematic production is that the better the films are getting, the less space for women there seems to be in them — in front of and behind the camera alike. Whereas in its beginnings it was both the ideology and the form that we could hold against Croatian film, today we are tempted to dismiss the question of (gender) ideology more easily, blinded by the light at the end of the tunnel. But perhaps it is time we face the truth. It's a train, baby. And it has gender written all over it.

Works Cited

- Das, Veena. 1995. "National Honor and Practical Kinship: Unwanted Women and Children." In *Conceiving the New World Order*. Ed. Faye Ginsburg and Rayna Rapp. Berkley: University of California Press, 212-233.
- Enloe, Cynthia. 1990. *Bananas, Beaches, and Bases: Making Feminist Sense of International Politics*. Berkley: University of California Press.
- Freeland, Cynthia. 1996. "Feminist Frameworks for Horror Films." In *Post-Theory. Reconstructing Film Studies*. Eds. David Bordwell and Noell Carroll. Madison: University of Minnesota Press, 195-218.
- Kandiyoti, Deniz, ed. 1991. *Women, Islam, and the State*. London: Macmillan.
- Interview with Matanić. 2003. *Kinoeye*, Vol. 3, No. 6, May 26.
- Interview with Jurica Pavičić. 2000. *Central Europe Review*, Vol. 2, No. 19, May 15.
- *Hrvatski filmski ljetopis*. 1995. Vol. 1/2 (1).

Conversations

A Conversation with Rajko Grlić:
Films Are Stories About People, Not About Ideas
by Aida Vidan and Gordana P. Crnković

Rajko Grlić (b. 1947) made his first amateur film at the age of fourteen, his first professional acted film at eighteen, and his first award-winning film, *If It Kills Me*, at twenty-seven. Since then his accomplishments have spanned several continents, and included a number of highly acclaimed movies, multiple festival awards, recognition in the area of education, and the founding of the Motovun Film Festival. Born in Zagreb, Croatia, where he spent his youth, he went on to study at the renowned *Academy of Performing Arts* in Prague (FAMU) along with several other important South Slavic film directors, such as Goran Paskaljević, Srđan Karanović, Lordan Zafranović, and Emir Kusturica. His experiences at FAMU left an indelible imprint on his directorial style and made him recognizable for his remarkable sense of humor, meta-narrative commentaries, and an interest in the fates of ordinary people who come to stand out under the burden of social and historical circumstances.

Rajko Grlić's sensibility for political issues doesn't manifest itself in open proclamations. Rather, he tends to focus on simple individuals and their foibles, on characters who exist within a well-rounded social and political environment. As they cannot escape the intricacies of their own temperaments and habits, much in the same way they are entrapped, sometimes even without knowing it, in the circumstances dictated by a specific historical and political moment. His films point to the obvious, the absurd, the ridiculous in our lives — to which we have become oblivious. He has a keen eye for everyday passions, but in front of his camera our little, carefully constructed universes crumble, typically in a rowdy manner, only to reveal undercurrents, traits, and thoughts which, turn out to be not so funny. It is this precarious balance that gives Grlić's films their particular flavor.

Titles such as *Bravo Maestro* (1978), *The Melody Haunts My Reverie* (*Samo jednom se ljubi*, 1981), *In the Jaws of Life* (*U raljama života*, 1984), *Three for Happiness* (*Za sreću je potrebno troje*, 1985), *Charuga* (1991), *Border Post* (*Karaula*, 2006) and most recently *Just Between Us* (*Neka ostane među nama*, 2010) — to mention just the most important — have entertained, provoked, and amused his large domestic and international audience and made them reflect at the same time. He has also directed many documentaries which have resonated profoundly both on the film and political scenes such as, for example, his series *Drinking Water and Freedom* (*Pitka voda i sloboda*, 1974, 1986, 1999), while one of them (co-directed with Igor Mirković) entitled *New, New Time* (*Novo, novo vrijeme*, 2001) literally defined a new era in development of artistic and political democracy in Croatia.

Despite some common stylistic and cinematographic denominators, Grlić's opus is too diverse and complex to summarize in a few lines of introduction. It must be noted, however, that already one of his earliest films, *The Melody Haunts My Reverie*, was recognized in the category Un Certain Regard at the Cannes Film Festival for its "original and different" vision. This feature about a young Partisan hero rising quickly in the post-WWII socialist hierarchy of Yugoslavia only to be brought down by apparatchiks envious of his love for a woman from the wrong social class is a provocative and passionate commentary on socialist practices and ideological blindness. That it roused political ire is not surprising. More importantly, it has also been pronounced by many critics and audiences to be the best Yugoslav film of all time.

His *Charuga* was made at a time when Croatia was in the process of seceding from Yugoslavia and when its political scene was undergoing tumultuous change. The film focuses on a legendary rebel-outcast figure from the northern part of the country and it examines another turbulent period, that of the 1920s, which was similarly unstable in terms of regional political orientation. Through playful probing of the notion of political leadership and the need for local populations to have a fatherly "hero-figure" who will dominate the political scene regardless of background, Grlić's film in many ways pre-figures and comments on the events that were to unfold in the 1990s.

In the Jaws of Life is a film with a number of meta-levels which in a mockingly reflective manner does not leave any Yugoslav stereotype unturned. Based on Dubravka Ugrešić's novel *Steffi Cvek in the Jaws of Life* (*Štefica Cvek u raljama života*, 1981), itself a parody of romance novels, Grlić gives us an East European *Bridget Jones' Diary* long before Hollywood did. And being East European and non-commercial, it is profoundly richer and more reflective: it has a pronounced political dimension which does not shy away from exposing the typical profiles of a conformist, anarchist, activist, etc., poking at gender issues, playing with local ethno-types, introducing a folk dimension to clashes between urban and rural mentalities, examining characters against their fictional and meta-fictional Doppelgänger, and parodying both literary and filmic procedures.

There is also a political dimension to his *Border Post* (analyzed in detail elsewhere in this volume), a film which bursts with comedic energy at the beginning only to implode in a vortex of tragic events that sweep away both individuals and the country. In addition to the many other fine attributes *Border Post* deserves, the degree to which its humor hinges on a complex political backdrop is interesting to observe. This humor reveals incongruities, injustices, biases, indoctrinations, and calculated schemes which devour those who do not know how to play the system. The fact that Grlić's most recent film, *Just Between Us!*, is apolitical is a decision which is perhaps a commentary in itself, for in the author's own words: "there are no politics any more, it is all about money" (see below). In it he returns to the tradition of the family comedy that brings him close once again to the Czech tradition, but which is nonetheless marked with riskier and more provocative, sometimes even astringent, South Slavic humor.

Particularly admirable about Rajko Grlić's career is his devotion and commitment to teaching. He is currently Eminent Scholar in Film at Ohio University, Athens, USA, and has previously held positions at Zagreb Academy of Dramatic Art, and New York University. His teaching engagements also include Art School in Amsterdam, the Central European University in Budapest, Centro Cinematografico Central in Mexico, UCLA, and Harvard University in the U.S., among others. The importance he ascribes to film education is evident not only in the fact that he brings students along to his sets and includes them in the process of making his films, but also in the interactive CD-ROM set he designed — a virtual classroom for anyone interested in film — "How to Make Your Movie: An Interactive Film School". One of his favorites, this project was named the best multi-media project in the U.S. at the New York Festival in 1998 and has won many other forms of recognition. While it never claims to replace practical experience, this amusing primer with over two thousand instructional graphics and a hundred QuickTime clips provides solid beginner-level training for aspiring film students and cinephiles.

Last but not least, Rajko Grlić is co-founder and artistic director of the Motovun Film Festival which, in 1999, breathed new spirit into Croatian film at a moment when, owing to political circumstances, it was on its deathbed. Gaining over the years in popularity and reputation, Motovun has re-introduced polyphony to what had been the increasingly monophonic film life of the region and has transformed it into an alternative scene that brings local filmmakers together and opens a window to the treasure trove of non-commercial world film. The festival is more than a film event; it is a series of cultural happenings that take place every July in a bucolic medieval town in the heart of Istria.

Rajko Grlić is loved by his audiences, closely monitored for his innovative approach and provocative topics by his critics, and followed (even literally) in his footsteps by his devoted students, all of which we saw with our own eyes during our stay at the Motovun Film Festival in July 2010 when this interview took place.

—— *You are known to have made your first film very early, at the age of fourteen. Could you tell us about how your interest for film developed and what drew you to film?*
—— Well, I had an uncle — in all good stories there is a good uncle — I had an uncle who worked for the UN in the pharmaceutical industry in Switzerland. With a Japanese colleague he developed a system which is still used today by Interpol for tracking drug routes by chemical analysis. In their free time, however, they started making amateur films. He was so drawn to it that he gave me a Bell & Howell camera as a Christmas present when I was fourteen. That camera more or less defined my life. Around then I joined Cinematheque (Kino-club) Zagreb. The cinema clubs at the time were places where various intellectuals, painters, doctors, architects made strange little films. There was the official grand-scale state film industry, while at the other end of the spectrum there was the intellectual underground. From this underground later sprang the GEFF (Genre Film Festival) and the other festivals attended by various people like Mekas and others who came to Zagreb. I was very impressed by all of this, finished some coursework and started making my first little films. This is the period starting with 1964 and on.

I was in my sophomore year of high school when, along with several friends, I made my first film entitled *The Brick* (*Cigla*). In Zagreb at the time street urchins liked to ambush couples. They would attempt to sell the guy a brick, which often, out of fear, he would consent to buy and pay for. I made a few small films like this, went to some festivals and received a number of awards. This would have been 1965 or 1966. I was given the award for the best Croatian amateur film. If I passed the entrance exam in Prague at FAMU — the Film and TV School of the Academy of Performing Arts — the award would include the possibility of a scholarship. In this context I also met Lordan Zafranović with whom I shared the award. One cannot enter the FAMU straight away, but must wait for a year after finishing high school, which is quite clever. Then there was an endless entrance exam which was likely the most difficult exam I have ever taken. In the course of several months culminating in the final exam which lasted for two-three weeks they whittled it down the list of thousand applicants to ten people. There was a clear rule that only five would make it to their second year, while the other five would not be able to continue. This was a very harsh game, but I passed with enough points to be accepted directly into the second year. So for the first year I had only to make films and could go on.

—— *In addition to your uncle, what other influences did you have in your formative phase?*

—— It was only when I came to the Academia that I started falling deeply in love with the works of different directors. The Prague Academy had a great custom of showing new films all day every Friday, while during the week the *Kinoteka* (Cinematheque) was active and they had and probably still have one of the finest film archives. They would show retrospectives for a week of, for instance, Buñuel. They would screen some thirty films, you'd spend the week watching these films all day and after that week you were absolutely convinced that this was the only way to make a film, that there was no other poetics that could be relevant. A few weeks later you'd watch Bresson and you were persuaded that this was the only way to go. At such an age one goes through many loves not unlike falling in love with different girls. One of my big loves — and not only mine — was Godard and the French New Wave along with the Italians from Antonioni to Fellini, who somehow had a spirit that resonated with this part of the world. Parallel to this, we were studying in Prague during the flourishing of the Czech wave. My professor Elmar Klos received an Oscar for his *The Shop on Main Street* (*Obchod na korze*, 1965) the year I became his student. Czech cinema was experiencing major growth at that time and we were being groomed to stay a part of it, which would have been likely had it not been for 1968.

—— *You have received many awards from your earliest years and up to the most recent ones in both Pula and Karlovy Vary (2010). Is there an award you would like to single out, an award which has had special meaning for you or perhaps brought you a special type of recognition?*

—— There are a few rules of thumb: one is "Never believe positive criticism." And then: "Receive an award, but promptly forget about it." These rules set us on the right track. Awards are endlessly cherished, they are a wonderful thing, the ego is stroked, but awards in the film industry are measured by how much they make it possible for a given film to "enter" the world. Personally, there are many awards I value, but if I had to single out one, it would be the award I received for my educational CD-ROM — *How to Make Your Movie: An Interactive Film School* — because it took me to another world, another medium. When I was given the award for the best multimedia project in the world, that meant I had managed to master yet another medium. I was convinced during that period that I was never going to shoot films again, and for that reason, too, the award had special meaning.

—— *We have touched on your contribution in the area of film education, but of course, this is only a part of the picture since you are also a professor at Ohio University.*

You are known to take your students to the sets of your own films and you generally hold the educative aspect at the center of your activities.
—— The first time I entered the educative role was after I returned from Prague. Professor Belan, who was teaching at the Zagreb Academy had some health issues, and asked me to take over his class — I was twenty four or five and the cleaning ladies would often try to kick me out after hours as they thought I was a student. I taught for two years and was just beginning to make my first film. Professor Babaja warned me that I would have to choose whether I want to be an educator or a filmmaker and I thought it was a strange division. I, of course, chose to make my first film. This is how my first love affair with the Zagreb Academy ended. In 1989 Krešo Golik retired and insisted that I inherit his last generation of students. I was back at the Academy for two years, went off on a Fulbright and came back in 1991 only to be informed that my position no longer existed. After that I received an invitation from NYU after I showed *Charuga* (*Čaruga*). I was there, talked for several hours with students, and was offered the position. I came back, realized that I could not do anything in Zagreb anymore because I was on all kinds of lists, black, white, pink... so I went to NYU and was asked to teach the first-year directing class. I had a fantastic group of students! NYU asked me to stay and soon afterwards I started getting various offers — I was completely unaware that America had a market for professors! In the end I received the offer from Ohio University which was entirely different because they were willing to support any project I wanted to work on. Also I could combine teaching and my own work, which the position of eminent scholar allows. That's what eventually brought me to Ohio University and there I worked on the CD-ROM for five years. They invested a large amount of money in it and luckily they got it back.

This is roughly my academic geography, but it has always seemed to me that it is incredibly stimulating to have some kids around with whom one exchanges and sharpens one's ideas. I always insist that they work only on their own films. I have avoided showing and explaining my own films and that is, I believe, the only serious way to teach film. They work on their own film, and I put them to the test and through this common process certain things are learned. In Zagreb and New York and Ohio I have had a few fantastic students who have received awards all over the world for their school films and I have truly enjoyed this aspect. I have the privilege of choosing my students and I must say, it is, as a rule, a very pleasant partnership. When I do work on my own projects, I try to include them because this is typically their first contact with the real film world: when they are on the set with a hundred and twenty people, when they see the camera work — these are experiences which stay with them.

It was out of this same way of teaching that I developed my CD-ROM. When I was at NYU, a publisher contacted me. I must say, I enjoyed the process of teaching and that was the first time that I really developed a set of notes and tried to rationalize what the person does automatically. It is indeed a strange turning point when one has to distance oneself from the things one simply does and has to explain them as a part of a rational system. So a publisher contacted me and asked whether I would put together a book based on my lectures. For days I was roaming around bookstores and saw that there was an astonishing number of manuals telling you how to make a film for two cents, how to make a film in three days, etc. And I thought: why do another one? But then I got a computer that had a CD drive and I got a instructional book on film which was unbelievably boring and I also purchased some sort of computer game and just from looking at these two things I came to the conclusion that if I wanted to do anything, I would likely to try to combine these two things. I had no idea when I started the project in which direction to go and it took me year and a half just to write the script. It was about 1200 pages long. My office at Ohio University was huge and I was putting all sorts of post-its everywhere to organize my ideas since this was the first time I had to jump from a linear narrative into a non-linear one. We received the funding, found the right people, and worked on the project for four and a half years. It was a huge amount of work! When I embarked on the project I thought it was going to take some six months, but the project really resonated and it was pronounced the American film product of the year. It was shown in many places, from Cannes on, at numerous festivals. This work also gave me some lightness of living in the sense that I found a new toy during a time when I was not making films.

— *You mentioned earlier the political context of your career which forced you to relocate to America and prompted you indirectly to exploring the new media. It would be interesting to discuss this aspect of your work. In your films* The Melody Haunts My Reverie *(Samo jednom se ljubi),* Charuga, Border Post *(Karaula) there is a political element, while in your latest film* Just Between Us *(Neka ostane među nama) this element is not there.*

— I think there are no politics any more, it is all about money. Politics have been reduced to money. The element of utopia has disappeared as well as the element of the social category in politics. Politics represents the process of arriving at a position of power that can be calculated through money. In particular, in transitional countries which have a portion of the new capital that was generated by crime, politics has become an empty category. Whoever is closer to the money takes it. For many, politics is the simplest way of getting money. It can all be reduced to these clear-cut parameters.

— *Did you ever feel anxiety, especially in the 1980s, for the consequences you might suffer as a result of your films? This, of course, particularly concerns* The Melody Haunts My Reverie?

— No. When one is working on a film, and many would agree with this, the censorship is within us. We either liberate ourselves or not. I do not believe in external

Rajko Grlić: *The Melody Haunts My Reverie* (*Samo jednom se ljubi*), 1981

censorship. I don't believe that someone can press you to that degree that they cripple your convictions. If you want to say what you believe in, you will find a way of saying it. Thus while making the film I was never thinking about its consequences. I tell stories and it seems to me that each of them has its own context. Just as this last one, *Just Between Us*, exists in a political vacuum, the previous ones were immersed in the political context of their time. Only when things related to the film (as with *The Melody Haunts My Reverie*) started happening, did I understand that these are things that hurt more than I could have suspected. When the film was banned, when the police locked up the negative, when I was told not to travel anywhere, when it all acquired much more drama than I had anticipated, of course, I did realize that we have something that is "the merchandise." We had to put up a long fight, and it if hadn't been for Cannes, that film would not have become available for years.

— *A few years earlier some other filmmakers from Yugoslavia had had major difficulties, Stojanović was imprisoned, Makavejev, with whom you have a long-term friendship, experienced major difficulties and eventually had to leave. How would you comment on what came after this first wave of trouble?*

— There were problems, but they were different. The government initially committed what is likely one of the biggest crimes against film in this region. They attacked the "black wave" movement bringing about as a result the "pink wave," which revolved around turbo-folk and colorful joy that had as its main task muddying up the waters. We came somewhat later and it seems to me that in the meantime they had learned not to attack frontally. They attacked, but they did not have the same power. Their power was evaporating and so was the fear. In the eighties the situation was slipping out of their grasp and they had more important things to worry about. They left film alone for a while and fell in love with TV since they realized that this was a powerful medium which could be used and later was used on as the basic vehicle for [the 1990s] war. The politicians thus turned their attention to another toy.

— *If we look at the years of the eighties and your two films,* The Melody Haunts My Reverie *and* In the Jaws of Life, *although these two films are stylistically different they both foreshadow a major crisis. It seems that it was quite clear to you back then from which corner and how the crisis was going to hit us. In addition to the political context, especially your film* The Melody Haunts My Reverie *could be interpreted as a story of a "loss of innocence," of maturing and understanding what the world is about.*

—— Yes, that is a story about utopia tripping over reality.

—— *Do you think that once people lose their idealism (whatever their ideals may be) this is what happens — a loss of politics, a loss of social values. Can society be shaken up again through certain types of stories, in particular through film?*

—— This is indeed the main reason for making films. My goal is to shake you, or make you laugh, or make you think so you feel that you want to go on living. I made *The Melody Haunts My Reverie* at a moment when I felt I was standing before a wall in a system of non-functional values. I asked myself: what is the source of all of this. I simply wanted to see how it all went wrong, where this utopia, once it touched ground, took a wrong turn and how it ended up in a swamp instead of a river. My parents were leftists and dreamed of living in a just society and ended up in gulags. I had a need to see how this illusion fell apart and that's how *The Melody Haunts My Reverie* came about. My next film, *In the Jaws of Life* (*U raljama života*), was made in one of the most depressing moments, 1984-85, when we had major shortages, were driving our cars on alternating days, etc. Deep desperation took root. I had a gut feeling that many good communists were going to become good nationalists since this is the shortest path from power to power. So I started playing with this idea and that's why in the film I have a brave Serb, a cerebral Croat, a punctual Slovene — these are the clichés with which we were playing at the very moment when it was clear that the country was stumbling. However, *Charuga* was actually the film I made with the feeling — whether rational or subconscious — that things in the country were going down the drain. *Charuga* was my political statement because it was about a leader. It was also about us and the fact that we need this "Daddy-leader" who is also a little bit of a criminal, but nonetheless he is ours. By coincidence, the signature of the real historical Charuga was found on the first document that mentions socialist Yugoslavia. His is a story about the end of a utopia and when it entered movie theaters, although it's a feature, its effect was documentary — there was not much difference between this character and the characters who in the 1990s piled logs up near the [Croatian city] of Knin. The images on TV and the images in my film strangely overlapped. The protagonists looked alike and said the same things. It was sobering to start making a film using historical elements and turning them into fiction only to hit upon reality. *Charuga* was my statement about the end of illusion and for this reason it is very dear to me. Also, it seems to have resonated well with younger generations since every time I visit regional drama academies, the kids are familiar with this film in details.

— *When we talk about your film* Border Post, *there is a political message in the film, but there is also a statement in the way the film was produced. It was the first co-production in the region which included all six former republics. Similarly, the Motovun Film Festival which you conceived and brought to life, is also a political statement.*

— Well, when I left here in 1991 to teach at NYU, I left with a clearly stated message of why I was leaving, as did many others who left at that moment. It seemed to me that nationalism served as a cover-story for theft. I am a person who in 1968 lived through the process of disillusionment during the Prague Spring and I had a difficult time getting excited about any type of political concept, especially a nationalist one. I thought it was a dark period and the strong nationalist vein that reigned during this time was something completely foreign to me. So I left convinced that I was never again going to be making movies. I did not even try because I had been telling stories for twenty years and they were seen by so many — those films were really watched! We had millions of viewers and successfully beat American films at the box offices. We had an illusion that we were telling something to someone and that these films, although not really changing anything in people's lives were still advancing awareness perhaps by a millimeter with regards to what was going on. But nothing had really changed. The war was organized and executed with the help of TV in no time. I was truly convinced that I would never make another movie and then started feeling the hunger when I was back in Croatia during the time when Tuđman was hospitalized. Igor Mirković and I placed a camera in front of the hospital and then added another nine cameras and for three months followed the fall of an empire. The playfulness of the camera got me back into the game and I started making films again.

When I started making *Border Post*, I thought that if I ever had my own stance towards the war it did not make any sense to be making a typical war film which would end with "our guys are the good ones, and those on the other side are vicious." It seemed to me that it would be much more interesting to see where and why the whole thing happened, how the people were prepped through the process of socialism for the war, how simple it was with the aid of a small TV set to pour hatred into people, and how the same TV set turned people into victims, blood-spillers, murderers. *Border Post* is about 1987, a moment which, it seems to me, was the turning point in what ensued. I wanted to tell a story about it and after that decided not to deal with history again since I have dealt with all the points that have interested me in the region where I spent a good part of my life — from 1918 in *Charuga* to 1987 and Milošević. After that I had the enormous pleasure of making this last film where I focus on five people and their love problems.

— *Documentary is an important part of your opus. Your* New, New Time (Novo, novo vrijeme) *had one of the largest audiences in the post-war 1990s in Croatia. Could you comment on the role of documentary*

Rajko Grlić, Igor Mirković: *New, New Time* (*Novo, novo vrijeme*), in 2001

films which have acquired, in the last fifteen years, a very important and powerful role in Croatian cinema?

—— I started my career with the documentary. When I returned from Prague, I first made a series of films for Angel Miladinov which were banned, then I did a full-length documentary *All Men Are Good Men in Bad Society* (*Svaki čovjek, dobar čovjek*) which was also banned. I have tried to make documentaries in between each feature film. In a similar way in which a musician tries to get just the right quality of sound, a filmmaker through documentaries sets out to find the sound of reality what will resonate in his feature film. I have always thought that this is an indispensable part of filmmaking. The documentary camera in a sense probes reality and after this process it is much easier for me to make my fiction films. This allows me to be aware of the scent of reality. The same thing actually happened with this particular documentary, *New, New Time*, which was essential for me in order to make *Border Post* later on. After all I had not made a film in this region for a full ten years and I needed to feel the reality. At the same time I needed to capture a moment when the type of reality which forced me to leave was still there in some form, regardless of how much varnish was laid over it. People were telling me: "No way, this is not going to work. Who in the world would go to the movies to see the same faces they watch every day on their TVs?!? Why would I pay for a ticket to see that?" But still, movie theaters were packed because we managed to show those same faces from a different perspective. We stepped out of the sterility of TV, out of wearing politically correct suits, and it seems that this documentary helped set the stage.

The stage is, however, inconceivable without the name of Nenad Puhovski. On one of these Istrian hills, not far from Motovun, we ran a school together called the Imaginary Academy (*Imaginarna Akademija*) which lasted for seven years. I received $15,000 from Ohio to go to Prague and hold a workshop. I managed to persuade them to bring the funding here. The Soros foundation matched it, and for seven years continued to match everything I was able to raise. Nenad Puhovski, Vjeran Zuppa and I organized a school which generated Motovun

[Film Festival], ZagrebDox, Factum. This school also propelled Matanić, Jasmila Žbanić, and many others. It was a very healthy small summer school and at times also included fifteen days in Ohio. The young people who attended the school were terribly burdened with the experience of war and burdened with the images through which they lived. We started making films, initially documentaries because they are the least expensive in terms of production. Nenad [Puhovski] gave a documentary workshop, which later grew into Factum, which later grew into ZagrebDox, possibly one of the most interesting festivals in the region. World film industry is getting to be sharply divided into $100 million and over projects and $1 million and under. The space in which I have spent my life, the zone of independent film (which is between these two categories), is slowly disappearing. Through the web, YouTube and numerous other IT forums the documentary camera will be the food of the future. Whether this will also generate fiction film, I do not know, but if I were a producer, I would try to persuade young filmmakers who dream of feature projects to first make ten documentaries.

—— *Since we are discussing reality and ways of probing it, perhaps we could turn our attention for a moment to your features. In many of them you have an overlapping of multiple narrative levels: a meta-narrative level, the level of "true reality," the ironic level. It appears that in many of your features you probe reality from different angles and with different instruments.*

—— I am a child of central Europe by origin and by my background, I spent my formative years in Prague, one of the most wonderful and most cynical of cities — thus it is not surprising that my *Weltanschauung* has irony, playfulness, and the need to tell the most serious stories with some distance, laughter, and ambiguity. I do not believe in one-dimensional stories, but rather I think that stories ought to have several layers and that film is precisely a tool that plays with this multiplicity of levels. The viewer essentially chooses how many and which layers he wants to pursue. Films should not force people into this or that, rather they should be interesting and one should be able to follow them even at a superficial level. However, if one wants to use a shovel and dig for more layers, that, too, should be possible. Film should not be didactic or contain political propaganda because films are stories about people, not ideas. Of course, people live in certain contexts, in certain circumstances, in a political reality or a political bubble, so all these elements are contained in various layers.

—— *Many critics recognize in your films a strong tradition of Czech family film that often addresses the fates of common people. These are unassuming but complex everyday stories and this trait is visible in your last film,* Just Between Us. *However, after the film was released, you were also accused of pornography.*

—— Let me give you another example of my earlier film *The Melody Haunts My Reverie* with which I had enormous problems. If we had cut out all the parts that the police wanted us to cut out, there would have been perhaps five minutes left of the entire film. But we survived. I arrived in America and had the premiere of the film at Carnegie Hall, which included a discussion with the audience after the screening. Ninety nine percent of the questions concerned the sexually explicit scenes in the film. I thought this was incredible since back home, in Yugoslavia, nobody mentioned a word about the erotic scenes and they wanted to decapitate me for the politics. In America, it was the other way around. But you see how the world has changed. Now here [in Croatia] nobody is interested in politics but they have become obsessed with bare bottoms. Croatia is divided these days in terms of its morality. At the state level it is shaped by the Church and, on the other hand, the media live primarily from their scandal sheets. The two (the Church and the media) try to patch it up from time to time. It is a strange situation. In the end, all the fuss ended up being good advertising for us.

—— *We are sitting in the extraordinary town of Motovun which, over the years, has become one of the most vibrant international movie scenes. Yet, its beginning was not easy and the nearby national Pula festival initially created many obstacles for you. How did you manage to get this far?*

—— As I mentioned earlier, it all started with the Imaginary Academy which included students from some thirty countries. We had professors, filmmakers, students and people who were bringing different films along. Eventually we ran out of space to show these films and started looking for a more suitable location. We (Imaginary Academy's student Boris Matić with whom I started the Festival and I) found it on the next hill, in Motovun, which, having being a town of wealthy families, has wide squares and spaces which could be used for screenings. We started with one movie theater there, Bauer, and that's how it got off the ground. But there is a pre-history since even before the Motovun Film Festival was conceived, I used to come here with friends and other filmmakers for two months over the summer and I can't tell you how many scripts were cooked up in this very room. So, naturally, Motovun was our logical choice and when we proposed our idea to Motovun's mayor he was taken aback because the town was completely bankrupt at that time. It had one grocery story that worked for two hours twice a week. It was neglected and sad. I thought if we managed to pack one outdoor movie theater, this would more than suffice. After six years of the Imaginary Academy, the Ministry [of Culture] still did not want to know about us and we lived off of foreign funding. But at that point we managed to involve the local officials and things got going.

That's the factography. However, one should know that at the time Croatia was a claustrophobically closed country from which young people were massively emigrating because they were not in touch with the outside world. We wanted to have a locale where we had the right to our own form of happiness. Motovun was not envisioned as just another film festival, it was imagined as an event. All these years I structured it in such a way that the films are, naturally, at its core, but also I wanted to have ten recognized writers, painters, musicians. I wanted to have a space in which visitors feel good and can choose with what, in addition to great food and wine, they wish to nourish themselves.

—— *You have mentioned that several younger Croatian directors became involved with the Academy and later on with the Festival. Would you comment on the new generation of Croatian filmmakers who are being more and more recognized for their work and some of whom took their first steps here? Related to this, how would you assess the status of Croatian film abroad? Does it have any characteristics that set it apart? We talked earlier about the Czech wave, these days a Romanian wave is going strong. What about Croatian film and film in the Balkan region in general?*

—— In order for a film industry to have a profile, you have to start with the area of production. That has not happened here. Croatian film industry simply took over the structures that existed during socialism. As a result it is organized as it was in Yugoslavia, when, after all, each republic had its own cinematic structures. So nothing changed. Yugoslavia ran its film-financing program modeled on Russia's. These are models that have roots in the 1930s and are based on the strong control of the state over funding and associations of the so-called "film workers." Croatia continued to rely on this system which, for the first ten years or so was in the hands of [Antun] Vrdoljak. This arrangement produced strictly controlled films which chased audiences out of the movie theaters. Croatia committed a huge crime against its own film because it lost its audience. Film-goers still go to movie theaters in fear that they may have to face political propaganda of this or that sort. Croatian film thus went through a very unfortunate phase which is still in the foundations of the so-called new film industry. Since then not much has happened at the organizational level. We have HAVC [the Croatian Audio-Visual Center — *Hrvatski audio-vizuelni centar*] because one of the conditions for entering the EU is having centers such as this. However, the division was done mechanically. In other states it is such centers that have absolute control over their funding, here everything is funneled through the Ministry [of Culture]. Here the Minister handpicks the Center's employees, provides the funding, etc. Accordingly, HAVC is just another branch of the Ministry of Culture and structurally we don't really see any changes.

In order for a film industry to gain its identity, it has to have room to build its profile starting with ideas, scripts, stories. It has to have people who know this type of craft and can participate in the process. Film is an inherent creative process and if the state is the only producer and does not care about the process but only who gets the money and who doesn't, this situation definitively does not help its film industry.

In the last ten years there have been several extremely interesting films and outstanding young directors in Croatia. But these are the exceptions. These people did what they did despite the system, on their own, through their own persistence, strength, determination. I had the same objection during the period of Yugoslavia when we had republic industries which weren't very functional. We can talk about individual opuses such as Žika Pavlović's, Dušan Makavejev's, Boštjan Hladnik's, but we did not have a cinema which had its own identity. We can contrast this, for instance, with Danish cinema. They have a structured system which allowed their film to become the second export industry of this fairly small country. Our changes are not fundamental but superficial changes when it comes to production. For Croatia, Pula is an interesting venue so the state can assert that six new Croatian films were shot — nothing else. There is no purpose and organic system, film is in the domain of politics and until it starts living in its own domain, Croatian film will find it difficult to acquire an identity. However, this is not to say that we will not have talented authors who will be and are recognized in their own right. We already have names such as Jurić and Dević who made his extraordinary film *The Blacks* (*Crnci*), Rušinović with *Buick Riviera*, Milić with *The Living and the Dead* (*Živi i mrtvi*), etc. etc. There are local directors who are making surprisingly good films considering the film environment in which they are growing.

— *Distribution plays a huge role and, as you mentioned earlier, it is very difficult for those who fall in the category of projects around $1 million. How closely related is the question of distribution and winning at the big vs. small festivals for small film industries?*

— My generation had the opportunity of seeing how Polish, Czech and Hungarian film industries dealt with this issue. First, in the world of film criticism there is a hunger to "discover" someone new every three or four years. For instance the Romanians now, the Austrians, etc. As a generation we had the luck to have had our turn at one moment. One needs to go to fifty small festivals, bring awards home and then slowly one gets to Cannes and such. There is a logical pyramid of growth behind all that. Back then films could win all this with their quality — or at least so I believed. Film is nowadays, just like politics, solely and exclusively tied to money. Nobody without a large distribution is going to enter Cannes these days. A little film simply cannot stray there on its own. My last two films were in the orbit of the so called "A" festivals because we had a serious sales agent. But I have to repeat again, the festival serves its function inasmuch as it gets the film to the movie theaters. Cinemas have disappeared and we have multiplexes and one hundred American films which hold on tight to 95% of the world screens. There is only 5% of the cinematic space in the world for you to enter with a non-studio film. There are about 2000 films competing for 5% of the space. Our win in Karlovy Vary this year meant five different distribution contracts and invitations to perhaps twenty festivals which all happened in a matter of hours. Festivals are big markets, nothing else.

— *You mention students both here in Croatia and in the U.S.*

several times in the course of the conver-sation. You are one of the very few directors with such rich teaching and filmmaking experience. Could you comment on your students on both continents and similarly on American and European or East European audiences?

—— I think that students everywhere in the world are the same especially since the media have forced them to read the same books, listen to the same music, watch the same YouTube clips. They grow up watching the same material and no more is there the difference that there was in my generation. We leaned towards European films, while students in America were more exposed to American films, etc. Simply put, the world has erased these borders and students share the same curiosity. There is, however, a substantial difference: an American student who has patience, desire, persistence, stubbornness and a bit of talent can come to a point where he can realize his projects. Here, in Croatia that is much harder. Students here become disillusioned much earlier because they see that their options are to go to TV to work on soap operas, or wait for ten years to get small change from the Ministry. When such an amount of negativity and cynicism enters a young person so early it can turn into a type of poison which can be destructive for hope and determination and hope and determination are the positive substances from which films are made. Small environments are in general prone to backstabbing, everyone knows everyone. Small environments have the curse that they are small, while the big ones have the advantage of multiple options. So my students here and there, in Croatia and in the U.S., are in two different systems. Here, in Croatia, considering the small numbers, there is a remarkably large number of excellent young directors. In the U.S. there are some ten thousand students studying film and media while here we have five-six students per year. If in Croatia we have a promising director every two or three years, that is fantastic success.

To answer the second part of your question regarding audiences, I would say that people everywhere watch films in the same way. If the film is sufficiently rooted in the reality of one milieu, it will be understandable to everyone. Since I have the good fortune of living in the U.S., I have "test-screenings" of my films there and I can observe the degree of understandability. I believe that any film should have a level of comprehension that can be appreciated in South Korea and in Ohio, but I do not buy into Hollywood's principle where the film is set apart from reality in order to force everyone to perceive it the same way. As a result Hollywood films exist in a fictive, post-production universe. Small films can survive only if they anchor themselves deeply in reality and say: ok, I am sitting here eating truffles and home-made pasta in front of a stone house, and that's it — from this anchorpoint the story can flow on.

Introduction and translation
by Aida Vidan

A Conversation with Vinko Brešan:
No Aesthetics without Ethics
by Aida Vidan and Gordana P. Crnković

The cinema of Croatian director Vinko Brešan (b. 1964) has the unique ability to garner large domestic audiences on one hand while experimenting with and exploring the formal potentials of the medium on the other. Aesthetically consummate and ethically pertinent, his dynamic films have communicated well internationally and have won prestigious awards (e.g., at the Berlin Film Festival) as well. Son of prominent Croatian playwright Ivo Brešan, Vinko Brešan comes from the city of Šibenik on the Adriatic Coast. He studied comparative literature and philosophy at the University of Zagreb's School of Humanities and Social Sciences (*Filozofski fakultet*), and earned a degree in film and TV directing at the University of Zagreb's Academy of Dramatic Art. Brešan started his film career by making documentary films, some of which received the Oktavijan award, the highest Croatian award for documentaries (*Lunch Together* [*Zajednički ručak*] and *The Corridor* [*Hodnik*] in the mid-1990s, for more on them see Diana Nenadić's chapter article in this volume). He also worked on documentaries later on in his career, most notably in directing the influential 154 minute-long documentary *Radio 101 Independence Day* (*Dan nezavisnosti radija 101*, 2007).

It is Brešan's first feature film, however, that made him a household name and placed him firmly in the group of the most prominent and interesting film directors of new Croatian cinema. The Mediterranean setting, color, and temper, familiar to Brešan from his home locale, find their parodied rendering in his 1996 comedy, *How the War Started on My Island* (*Kako je počeo rat na mom otoku*), which revisits the beginning of the Homeland War in a way that had until then seemed impossible, or was even deemed, officially or not, politically suspect — that is, with humor and laughter. This comedy proved to be an enormous success with domestic audiences, and is still the top-watched domestic film in Croatia since independence. His second feature, *Marshal Tito's Spirit* (*Maršal*, 1999), was, like his first, based on a screenplay written by the director in collaboration with his father, Ivo Brešan. The film is built on a fantastic premise of the appearance of the ghost of long-time president of Yugoslavia, Josip Broz Tito, on one of the Croatian islands. A pleasure to watch, this lively and intelligent comedy combines a fast-paced suspenseful story, marked by a hilarious grotesque twist, with amusing but cutting political and social commentary. *Marshal Tito's Spirit* was also a hit with domestic audiences, becoming the third most-watched domestic film in the country since its independence. Brešan's third feature, *Witnesses* (*Svjedoci*, 2003), is a drama revolving around difficult ethical choices put before the people of Croatia during the Homeland War. The film is characterized by both its involvement with an issue crucial for the Croatian community, and by its elaborate non-linear directing and editing. Sandra Botica Brešan, Vinko Brešan's wife, who edited this masterfully as she did Brešan's other films and has herself won the highest Croatian award for editing (the Golden Arena for editing at Pula Film Festival in 2008), is to be credited for much of this and Brešan's other achievements in film. *Witnesses* won a score of international awards, and is one of the most aesthetically and ethically successful films made in Croatia in the contemporary period. Brešan's most recent feature to date, *Will Not End Here* (*Nije kraj*, 2008), again challenged some firmly entrenched taboos of new Croatian society, revolving around an unlikely love story between a Croatian Serb woman and a Croat man who are both — in their different but existentially related ways — involved in and permanently affected by the recent war in Croatia.[1]

The following interview was conducted in June 2010 at the Zagreb-Film building, where Mr. Brešan proved a lively, engaging, and generous interlocutor.

---

[1] A review of Brešan's war trilogy is included in this book on page 196; for a more extensive earlier discussion of his cinema see Gordana P. Crnković's "The Battle for Croatia: Three Films by Vinko Brešan," in *Democratic Transition in Croatia: Value Transformation, Education & Media*, eds. Sabrina P. Ramet and Davorka Matić (Texas A & M University Press: College Station, 2007).

—— How did you become attracted to directing?
—— My father is dramatist and screenwriter Ivo Brešan. The first script he wrote was an adaptation of his own drama *Acting Hamlet in the Village of Mrduša Donja* (*Predstava Hamleta u selu Mrduša Donja*). This film was on the official program of the Berlin Film Festival at some point in the 1970s and generally won all kinds of awards. It was directed by Krsto Papić. I was eleven at the time of the shooting and my father invited me to come to the set one day. This was probably the most boring day in my entire life! The only person who has fun at a shooting is the director, I thought. So I was not at all impressed.

Later on, however, a series of Papić's documentaries was shown on TV and I was a bit older by then, perhaps thirteen or fourteen. Since I knew the director, I wanted to see the films and I really enjoyed them. So I decided I would like to make documentaries. That was my primary motivation when I entered the Academy of Dramatic Art (University of Zagreb). I made quite a few documentaries, some of which had a significant success. One of my student films, *Our Stock Market* (*Naša burza*), was even entered in a professional competition of short film at Oberhausen which was the most important festival for this genre at the time. In 1994 and 1995 I received the highest recognition in Croatia, the Oktavijan award, for documentaries *Lunch Together* (*Zajednički ručak*) and *The Corridor* (*Hodnik*).

I started working on a feature, in fact, because of the impossibility of solving certain problems in the documentary. There was a war in Croatia, as you know, from 1990 to 1995, and there were many protests in front of military barracks. I was in Šibenik at the time and witnessed many bizarre situations. You could really see how humor was clashing with tragedy — these were fantastic scenes! Unfortunately, I had no camera to record any of it. In 1995, when I got my chance to shoot, there were no protests. Reconstructing all of it through someone's narrative simply did not have the same energy. So I decided to make a feature and spoke with my father, Ivo Brešan, who is a seasoned screenwriter, and together with him I wrote *How the War Started on My Island* — and that's how I entered feature film.

—— Do most of your films start with an idea and then you approach someone to write the script, or do *you rework an existing novel as in the case of your last film* Will Not End Here (Nije Kraj, *2008) based on a play by Mate Matišić?*

—— One reads literary things, of course, but I generally have a need to tell a particular type of a story first, and then I immerse myself in literature, seeking the right kind of material. Literature helps me tell the story in the best possible way. For instance, this was the case with *How the War Started on My Island* and *Marshal Tito's Spirit* [Maršal, 1999]. The latter got going from a joke. A friend of mine came and said, "You know, two fishermen in Novi say they have seen the ghost of Josip Broz Tito." We were sitting in a bar and it just occurred to me that this was a great premise for a film. So, little by little, we built a comedy around this joke.

The same goes for *Witnesses* (Svjedoci, 2003) — I really felt the need to make a film that speaks about a different aspect of the war. Mind you, this was in 2002, when the topic of war crimes by Croatian soldiers could not be read about in the newspapers. The situation is now different. But, back then, there was a change on the political scene in Croatia, Tuđman had died recently and the Social Democrats came to power, only to be disappointing in a way. The new government simply did not address the burning issues in society and I felt the need to say something about this. My wife spoke of the novel by Jurica Pavičić, *Alabaster Sheep* (Ovce od gipsa), and I recognized in it what I wanted to focus on in the film. Now, Pavičić's novel is broader in scope and I tried to refract the story through a family drama so that it has a firmer structure. The emotions are also more dense given that this is simply the nature of film. The same thing happened with *Will Not End Here*. When I initially spoke with Mate Matišić, I told him that first and foremost I wanted to make a love story based on his play *Woman without a Body* [Žena bez tijela]. But this play is not a melodrama, it is not dealing with love at all. The author established a relation between a young man and a prostitute whom the man wants to help, but there is no love story. So the playwright and I started reading the play in a different way because I really wanted to have a narrative in which the solution for the hatred between two nations would precisely lie in love.

—— *Were you surprised by the tremendous success of your first feature,* How the War Started on My Island? *Also, do the critics and the filmgoers agree in evaluation of your films or are there discrepancies?*

—— I would lie if I said I was completely taken aback. The final number did surprise me, but throughout the whole process of making this film I said that I had an enormous need to establish communication with the audiences. Let's face it: film is an art in which the audience is a part of its definition. The audience was of utmost importance to me at that particular moment. The final number was about 350,000 people, which is 8% of Croatia's population! Imagine if an American film were seen by 8% of that country's population! I know, it's a different frame of reference, but again, the only film that did better at the box office in Croatia over the last twelve years was *Titanic*. In terms of reviews, well, each review, good or bad, is the opinion of one person. I have seen one Hollywood critic say for one of my films that it is "a masterpiece of narration." Of course, I was happy as a kid when I read that, but ultimately this is the view of one individual and nothing more. Someone else will say for the same film that it's totally chaotic and incomprehensible — that too is the view of one person. There is always some sort of balance with my films, and at the end of the day I am happy overall with their reception.

In terms of the audience, as I said, communication with them was essential, especially regarding *How the War Started on My Island* and *Marshal*. The question of genre is relevant here as well, because these two films are comedies and as such are more appealing to audiences. On account of the political situation, however, things stopped being funny for me personally. During the time of Franjo Tuđman, who was a very serious person and nearly impossible to get a laugh out of, things were funny. He perceived culture as a mortally serious business so I took pleasure in being a court jester, in carnevalizing life under such circumstances. But later on, things changed. It is only now, while working on my current script, that I am turning again to the genre of comedy. In my first two films it was the audience who mattered, in my next film, *Witnesses*, strong emotion was what I was going after. I also started exploring a particular form and this specific form is quite unusual for Balkan film in general and is not frequent in world film either. The film is an hour and a half long and every half hour it starts anew. The perspective shifts just a little bit each time and this was very demanding. But I had a need for this kind of exploration.

—— *We have already touched on our next question which is about humor in Croatian film.* How the War Started on My Island *is already perceived as a hallmark film not only in terms of its popularity but also for its humor. How do you see Croatian comedies in relation to this genre in the region? For instance, Serbian cinema is known for its "black wave" and darkly colored humor, while Croatian cinema is celebrated more for its cerebral achievements. Where do you see your work in this dichotomy?*

—— I am Mediterranean, from the city of Šibenik. This is a place where humor is simply a part of life. A person with no sense of humor will not feel comfortable in Šibenik, and may even suffer there. People there love humor, even if it's sometimes harsh, so this is somehow a part of my *Weltanschauung*, of my perception of life, it's a part of me. I lived there as a young man and this perspective cannot simply disappear. Frankly, it's harder for me to work on a serious scene such as, say, in *Witnesses*, knowing that I have no right to joke around. The theme does not allow me to have an ironic relation to reality. For such a theme I have to strip myself naked, in a sense, and stay naked with the rest of the [characters] in the problem that is being dealt with. In humor, you have distance, you have removed yourself a bit, and you look at the world from an ironic angle — sometimes with love, sometimes without it, but that is yet another question. When it comes to humor, it's all in the timing. It takes a cool hand to hit on the right timing and make things funny.

I often see how certain things could be rendered both seriously and comically but I have other reasons that direct me in my choices. Why do I say this? Because humor is a part of me and I have a need for the jester, the comic dialogue, that is the way I actually think. When both *Marshal* and *Will Not End Here*, which also has comical parts, were shown in Karlovy Vary, it was interesting for me to make a comparison with Czech humor. The Czech audience recognized the humor in my films, and Slavic humor at that, but also identified it as different from their own because it's harsher.

—— *To continue in the same direction — you have mentioned carnevalization. Some of the critics even mention your films as structurally related to commedia dell' arte. We even have our local prototypes of comical characters coming all the way back from the Croatian Renaissance, which also stems from the Dalmatian, Mediterranean milieu. Do you relate to this background at all?*

—— I don't dare make such comparisons! In terms of my generation, we somehow grew up on a Monty-Python diet of humor, which is the absurdist type of comedy. In film I don't really go in that direction, their form was entirely different, but I am related to it. I do seek absurdist situations and then, of course, I have to bring the viewer through the narrative to recognize the situation as absurd, but the absurdity is there. So my characters may be related to Croatian Renaissance prototypes at the level of narrative or *fabula*, but the humor itself is of different nature.

—— *How is it to keep the business within the family, so to say? You have had your father, Ivo Brešan, as a principal collaborator on some of your scripts, and your wife, Sandra Botica Brešan, as editor, but these family relations also seem to, in a way, extend to the entire team which remains more or less consistent from one film to the other. This is interesting because it creates an opus that has not only a recognizable directorial imprint, but also a tangible style coming from the other artists who participate in the project.*

—— This does not happen automatically or by chance. As a film director you always want to make the best film in the world. If that is not your starting point, you're a fool. This is a kind of business in which it's not wise to make compromises. I've had the luck to have a father who is an established dramatist, but I would wish to work with him even if he weren't my father; I have the luck to have a wife who is an outstanding editor, but I would continue working with her even if we were to separate in our private life. Furthermore, Mate Matišić, a good friend of mine, has also worked as a scriptwriter with me, including the latest project to be called *The Priest's Children* (*Svećenikova djeca*), a comedy dealing with the [Catholic] church's stance towards sexuality. I have surrounded myself with people of talent and that is not by chance. I really do think that my wife is about ninety percent of my talent — no irony here. My father is eight percent,

Vinko Brešan: *How the War Started on My Island* (*Kako je počeo rat na mom otoku*), 1997

Mate [Matišić] another few percent, and so forth. Mine is one tiny bit. This is nothing strange: I bring my life into my films, I work with individuals whose talents I appreciate in general. They share with me certain views, so it is indeed not surprising that I want to work with them on a continuous basis. On the other hand, we do not have identical tastes. The tastes of my father are not identical to mine. The same goes for my wife, who actually does not like comedies at all! And it is good that it is so, we need differences as well.

—— *As you are aware, the topic of war has been preoccupying many Croatian directors in recent years, to the degree that we can speak of generational differences in the perception of the war, especially when it comes to the so called Young Croatian Film. You have also contributed to the pool of war films yourself, with your war trilogy that exploits different genres.*

—— You have now said something that is making me pause for a second: you've mentioned a war trilogy. I guess you have in mind *How the War Started on My Island*, *Witnesses*, and *Will Not End Here*. I have actually never thought of these films as a trilogy, but now that you mention it, it is indeed intriguing that one film is a comedy, one is a drama/thriller, and the last one a romantic comedy with elements of tragedy. It's a vast jump in terms of the genre and I made this jump completely unintentionally. I really had no grand plan, it just happened that way. My next film takes place again on an island, so, perhaps, there will be an island trilogy as well!

With regard to the war, the fact that I examine the last war through three different genres says that within myself I have different perspectives on the war. The war started when I was twenty-seven and lasted for four years. These are mature years when you can think about a problem in depth, but you are still young enough to have a defense mechanism that shields you against the evils that surround you. Maybe one day I will tackle war topics again, but I am pretty sure that for a while I would like to explore other things.

—— *In some of your films there are layers that can be directly associated with older Yugoslav — and also Serbian — authors such as Aleksandar Petrović and Slobodan Šijan, especially the function of Roma characters in their films. Even in your last film you use a Roma character in a comic manner, and he*

actually carries and organizes the narrative both as a character and a voice over.
—— Of course, Saša [Aleksandar] Petrović and his film *It Rains in My Village* (*Biće skoro propast sveta*, 1968) begins with three Romas singing the following lines: "The end of the world is coming, let it come, there's nothing to lose" [*Biće skoro propast sveta, nek' propadne nije šteta*]. I can't think of a better opening for a film than these lines — in the first twenty seconds you learn everything about the director's world view, it's ingenious. So, of course, nothing is by chance. I like Petrović. And Šijan. For instance, in *Marshal*, one of the characters is called Miško and when he can no longer run, someone else tells him "Drive on, Miško" ["Vozi Miško"]. Šijan is definitively a part of the humor of the absurd, the surrealist type of humor which was a part of my growing up as well. He himself is under the influence of Monty Python, etc., etc. We grew, so to say, out of the same overcoat. I've never been shy in recognizing Šijan's influence; on the contrary. His films make me feel good.
—— *In conjunction with* Marshal: *it's a great film for watching but it also gives much substance for thinking, in particular regarding its historical aspect. You have a specific relation to history — in a very accessible, comical, but at the same time clever way you tell your viewers that our history is like the museum shown in your film, in which all the pictures are crooked or turned upside down, everything is chaotic and we haven't really figured out how to organize this or what has been happening. This is particularly palpable when you show Tito's figure. You use archival shots, speeches...*
—— *Marshal* is a film which looks at our current attitude toward historical figures. I joked around and showed the development of communism retroactively — I started with the period of transition and went backwards to the socialist revolution. This dramaturgical playfulness was very entertaining for me. I like history, at one point I even wanted to study it [at the University], so I feel a connection to historical themes. Now, the film was made in 1999. Our vision of history in that moment was like the ultimate circus and that was incredibly funny. So I tried to convey on film my perception of the way we relate to history and turn it into a comedy of the absurd.
—— *What were some of the formal challenges you faced or created for yourself in your films? For instance, the narrative structure of* Witnesses *is quite complex and it is not presented in the same way in Jurica Pavičić's novel* [Alabaster Sheep / Ovce od gipsa] *on which the film is based. The novel is linear and chronological, so what was the reason for the departure? We have of course seen this type of approach, although rarely, in some other foreign films, but there it does not often have the ethical dimension it has in your film.*
—— The motivation was indeed very simple: it was the question of truth and what the truth is. In the three stories that make up the film, I give pieces of the truth. It is possible to grasp the truth only at the end when all the puzzle pieces fall into place. This is my general stance towards the problem — it's necessary to perceive the whole

truth, the guilt, the relations — in order to dissect our emotional response to it. This kind of thinking guided me in choosing that particular form. I wanted the viewer to develop his emotions and to have to flip them over and over again from one story to the next. In the first story, to remind you, I give indications that there was a witness to a war crime and that the witness was killed. In the second story I give indications that the witness is a girl and that she was killed. In the third story we learn that the relations between people are far more complex than one would think and that a brother may pull a gun on a brother. Thus I spin the viewer's emotions, trying to pull him into the story precisely through this type of structure. I wouldn't have been able to convey all of this through a different form. I was aware that if I told the story in a linear way, I would not succeed in triggering the catharsis in the viewer nor would I have been able to flip his emotions so suddenly and cause surprise.

—— *After the screening of this film, it is not unusual to have five minutes of silence before any reactions. The audiences, including student viewers, seem to pause upon watching it and ask "What just happened here?" And then there is a realization that, when we need to explain why events took the course they did, it comes down to an individual and his conscience and actions. We are constantly told that an event happens because some other event triggers it, because of these or those circumstances that justify certain actions. This film puts forth the question of individual responsibility. What is your take on this reading of the film?*

—— There is no aesthetics without ethics. I have never seen a piece of art which is strong aesthetically without containing an ethical component. Ethics is a constituent part of art and if it is not a part of artistic striving, then the piece is definitively not going to become art.

—— *To come back again to your war trilogy, it appears that you force the viewer to examine him/herself. You toss him from one corner to another, be it comically, or through a thriller-like uncertainty, or through the emotional charge of a romantic narrative, making him constantly question his views and check the other side of the coin.*

—— In my films I always pose questions that I ask of myself. I make the viewer examine his position inasmuch as I ask myself to do the same. This is the only path that can lead us to answers or potential answers. Of course, here we come back again to the ethical component. For me it is essential, but at the same time I don't set out to make a film by thinking how to convey this or that ethical dimension. I've never worked that way. The script either contains this dimension or it doesn't, there's no help there. If you as a spectator recognize it in my film, this will make me enormously happy.

—— *In some systems or situations, as we know, too much re-examining is not a desirable quality. This was the case with some of your films, and they ended up caught in the arena of political discourse.*

—— Yes — and let them be a part of political discourse! I am from Croatia, which is a part of the Balkans. The key question in this part of the world is the question of

Vinko Brešan: *Witnesses* (*Svjedoci*), 2003

individual freedom. Regardless of what your profession is. Every time I am about to make a film, I have to ask myself: how free am I going to be? Will I be free within the already established frameworks or will I try to push the line of freedom by some ten centimeters? Or maybe a meter, or two? But I tend to think, let's push it at least for a bit. Whoever works in film and has managed to push the line of freedom, be it political, artistic, or some other type of freedom, does good things. I always have the need to push this line, although, of course, I can't tell how much I have really succeeded. Now, whoever has this kind of need has to accept the fact that pushing the limits creates resistance on the other side. This is natural. I no longer get upset about this. Perhaps when I was younger, I would have gotten worked up, but now I am aware of these social moments. This is, after all, my decision. The point is that you push the limits, then there is a fuss over it, but it has happened and there is no going back. That is a good thing all around.

— *Since you are involved with some of the important film institutions in Croatia, we would like to touch on the technical question of distribution. Is there any hope that it may become easier to obtain Croatian titles, especially abroad, although even at home it is tricky if not impossible to get hold of some of the older films?*

— A Portuguese poet once said that his native Portuguese language is a tomb for thoughts given that, in his view, nobody really cares to hear what is said in his language. And we are talking about Portuguese which is used by 230 million people! What should I say, I who speak Croatian! The problem here is that we make films in Croatian and, if it does not happen that a film makes it into important festivals such as Berlin where my film *Witnesses* was on the official program — and is, as a result, available abroad — that film will not have a place for itself on the international scene. Simply put, an enormous quantity of films is made every year and the decision of what to buy and show is a delicate one for distributors. They, of course, do the simplest and easiest thing: they go to Cannes, to Berlin, to Venice, and that's more or less that. This is not a problem unique to Croatia, but is true of world film in general. Of course, there are smaller film industries that we hear about, but it's not an easy game and they need extraordinary films with generally recognizable human issues to make it.

— *Has an idea of making a film in English ever intrigued you?*

— I have had some interesting exchanges in the US. The idea was to have a remake of *Witnesses* done, but it would have been a story about the American-Iraqi war. In terms of the narrative, it's plausible: two soldiers come back from the war for a friend's funeral, they kill an American of Arabic background, etc. etc. so it's doable. The problem was that in that moment the Americans could not see their soldiers as bad guys. This could still be seen from the situation with the relatively recent releases: *The Hurt Locker* [by Kathryn Bigelow] and Brian De Palma's *Redacted*. De Palma's film has disappeared, while Bigelow's has all the Academy awards of the universe. De Palma asks some very serious and interesting questions and at the emotional level it is similar to *Witnesses*.

— *Our next question concerns the attitude that the domestic audience has towards domestic films, which is not always positive or full of interest. With your* How the War Started on My Island, *you turned that attitude on its head, at least for a while.*

— Well, film is primarily entertainment. You pay your ticket and you don't want someone to beat your kidneys with an iron stick. People for the most part do not yearn for this kind of experience. Comedy is different and you have a different chance there. The three most watched domestic films of all times in Croatia are comedies [*How the War Started on My Island*, *What Is a Man Without a Moustache*, and *Marshal*]. Of course, you cannot build a serious film industry only on comedy; you need other topics, you need playing with the form, and so on. What Croatian cinema really needs is to have a domestic hit every two years which the general audience will recognize as its own, and that is not happening.

— *But on the other hand, the last twenty years in Croatian film have brought about a big change at the aesthetic level, and the domestic film industry is beginning to show characteristics that set it apart.*

— I would agree and I personally like what I see in domestic film more and more. There are interesting authors and interesting films. It's just that we need to do more to both bring the domestic viewer to the movie theaters and to make it to the important festivals. There are political factors as well, this region is becoming less interesting politically and filmmakers here have to start exploring new topics.

— *Production questions loom large over the Croatian film industry. How do you address this problem? How do you produce your films?*

— Well, let's take a specific example, my last film *Will Not End Here*. The funding came from the film fund of the Republic of Croatia, the city of Zagreb, Croatian Radio-television, the Ministry of Culture of the Republic of Serbia (it was a Croatian-Serbian co-production), the city of Belgrade, Eurimages, and several sponsors who all contributed fairly modest amounts. The film ended up costing 1.5 million Euros, which is a typical budget for the region, while in other, western parts of Europe budgets tend to go to 7-9 million Euros because the costs are greater. If making a film here costs 1.4 million Euros, in Holland, for instance, it would cost 7 million Euros. So we do as best as we can.

— *How much influence does a European producer have on the actual film?*

— That really depends on the producer. But, in general, in Europe the producer does not have the final cut. That is likely the biggest difference between how American and European movies are made. In Europe the final cut is the director's. It is the director who raises funds based on his name, on the script, and on the concept of the entire project. So it is logical that final decisions tend to be in the hands of the director. Now, of course, there are diverse producers and some exert a greater, some a lesser influence. I did my last three films, and probably will do the current one, with Interfilm and producer Ivan Maloča. He is a person who likes film very much and, consequently, his production remarks are often also relevant in terms of dramaturgy.

— *The question of your favorite directors is inevitable. Who do you look up to?*

— In Croatia definitively Krsto Papić. In the region, as I mentioned earlier, Saša Petrović, Slobodan Šijan, Žika Pavlović, and then even more broadly, Fellini as a Mediterranean kindred spirit. Definitively Coppola and his *Godfather*. This is just to scratch the surface, it'd be hard to mention all the favorites here.

— *Could you describe your method of work, literally, the "hands-on process?" For instance, we know that Polanski is obsessive in terms of managing details. At the other end of the spectrum we have Mike Leigh who gives his actors a character and simply tells them to live with the character for a while and figure it out. What is your style? How do you come up with the openings such as in* Witnesses *where the first shot lasts for a full six minutes?*

— Well, I am not a great supporter of exhibitionism which is in the nature of long shots such as the one you mention from *Witnesses*. I prefer when the director is a bit more hidden. But we had a different problem in that particular film. It takes place mostly in dark interiors, through close-ups, and closed situations. I had to somehow open up the film so that the viewer feels a certain amount of energy — and a long shot like that does bring exactly that — the camera goes from the square through a window inside a house, pans over the dead body, goes out through the other window, you have an atmosphere of wind, empty streets, three conspicuous characters, and so on, and you know immediately [as a viewer] that there will be some hustle there. On the other hand, I needed that shot for the formal reasons as well, so that I could point that this was going to be a story that will follow different people through whom we would get a complex structure. Such types of shots are prohibitively expensive in the production sense and demanding of the crew, but we really needed it here. I was aware that I had to open the film with a tense scene which would continue growing in order for the viewer to be able to sustain all the anxiety, silences, and questions that ensue. So this opening shot is the initial push to the viewer, so to say, something that draws him deeply into the story. But this is an exception; generally I tend to remain more hidden as a director.

To answer your question in full, I need to add that I usually have lengthy discussions with my collaborators on the film. We discuss all the details, each shot, lights, sets, and so on, since all needs to be in the function of our ultimate goal. But I am not a person who micromanages, my experience simply tells me that if I have creative people on the set and if I start limiting their creativity with my demands, I will reduce their contribution to the scope of my creativity. As a result, the film will be whatever my creativity has produced and not a sum of the combined creativity of all the people who have worked on the film. This also concerns the actors. Naturally, I choose outstanding artists and then we discuss the character type, the emotions s/he has to generate and in which moment, but I do this for a few days and later on there is generally not much need to intervene. The actor ultimately ends up knowing more about a given character than I do. You essentially set the foundations and watch the whole thing build, hoping that ultimately things will continue standing upright and function. This aspect, for me, is what brings the greatest satisfaction in directing.

Introduction by Gordana P. Crnković;
interview translated by Aida Vidan

A Conversation with Joško Marušić: *Sending Messages to Unknown Friends*
by Sanja Bahun

Long before I discovered Kafka, I had admired Joško Marušić's short animated film *Fisheye* (*Riblje oko*, 1980). Multiple-awarded (Special Jury Award, Ottawa; Grand Prize, Belgrade; Special Award, Rotterdam; International Jury Award, Madrid; First Award in Category, Brussels), the film captures the terrifying prospect of fish taking over a small coastal town — a result of a vaguely intimated disturbance of the natural order of things, or of revenge for fateful neglect, or a previous violation. Clutching my father's hand (he was an admirer of the Zagreb School of Animation), I indulged in Marušić's frightening phantasmagoria. I recognize in retrospect that the horrifying content did not move me as much as the expression — different from anything I had experienced before — an expression that connected the everyday with its (possibly fatal) extension and breathed life into the representation of a species with which we share our habitat. For long time afterwards, I could not eat fish.

Joško Marušić has been actively working in a variety of art media (cartoon, caricature, illustration, literature, film production and television), but his primary interest has always been animation. He has also been an enthusiastic administrator of various regional ventures focused on animation. He was art director of Zagreb Film, the major regional animated film production house, on two occasions, and long-standing art director, and council member of the Zagreb World Festival of Animated Films. He founded the Department of Animated Film in 1999 at the Academy of Fine Arts in Zagreb, Croatia, the first of its kind in the region. His filmography includes the short animated films *Inside and Out* (*Iznutra i izvana*, 1978), *Perpetuo* (1978), *Fisheye*, *Skyscraper* (*Neboder*, 1981), *Over There* (*Tamo*, 1985), *The Face of Fear* (*Lice straha*, 1986), *Home is the Best* (*Kod kuće je najbolje*, 1988), *I love you, too* (1991), *Miss Link* (1999), *In the Vicinity of a City* (*U susjedstvu grada*, 2006) and others. After a remarkable career in short animation, Marušić has recently authored his first animated feature film, *The Rainbow* (*Duga*, 2010), a movie based on two stories by the Croatian turn-of-the-century writer Dinko Šimunović, which he scripted, directed, designed, and produced. Marušić's animated films subtly defamiliarize the world, expose us to both the positive potentials and terrors of a world gone awry, always premised on a deeply humanistic vision. His distinctive animation blends the abstract, the grotesque, and the realistic, and his direction, while always maintaining a basic arc structure, privileges the accumulation of affective content over the laws of probability and verisimilitude. I started by asking him why he chose animation as his mode of expression in the first place.

—— *Why have you chosen animation? What is it in the nature of animation that attracts you to this mode of cinematic expression?*

—— When my interest in animation was first stirred, the charisma of the Zagreb School of Animation was so strong that it was impossible for any Croatian artist to ignore it. I was finishing my BA studies in architecture at the time, and my work in comics and caricature was already professional and published widely enough to secure a more-than-stable living for myself. An intrinsic connection between animation and caricature was an important aspect of the Zagreb-School tradition of animated film (in terms of graphic art, the Zagreb-School aesthetic was based on drawing). During the year of mandatory military service that followed my graduation, I had some time to "reflect." It is in this period that I decided to make what might have been a passing love affair into a lifelong profession.

In contrast to the job prospects in architecture, working in animation offered the possibility of swift career progress (to the ambitious young man that I was at the time, this promise was not negligible). More importantly, perhaps, animation appeared to me to be a perfect medium for the kind of messages I was intent on conveying. It is interesting, I reflect now, that my early fascination with animation did not stem from an interest in either drawing or animating but from a belief in the potential of this medium to "relay" my messages to unknown friends throughout the world. Although, over the course of the years, I have developed a distinctive style of graphic drawing and animating, animated film is still primarily the "message in the bottle" for me.

—— *You are also a well-recognized cartoonist and caricaturist, with multiple awards to your credit. How do these forms, cartoon, caricature and animation, relate in your work? Do they inform each other, and, if so, how?*

—— Whatever media I am working in — comics, caricature, or animated film — I relay the same kind of messages. These are messages of encouragement aimed at the fearful and the intimidated. Through my art I tell those afraid of grand manipulations (political, economic, emotional…) that they should not be scared, that they should live their own life, that the world is where they themselves are and not contained in utopias and mystifications.

Animated film is an expensive endeavour and the production takes a long time, so the medium of caricature allows me to send these messages on an everyday basis; I publish about 500 caricatures a year, and produce an animated film every four-five years. But I do not analyze my artistic style any more. It's like handwriting. I sit and work. Every day. People say I sometimes send messages that will reach no one, or that the addressees may reject them, for various reasons. But I know many of them will be greeted with a smile by that distant, unknown friend, and this promise keeps me going.

—— *As a visual-art form, animation extends reality, commenting on it or offering alternatives, social, politi-cal, or, simply, universally human. Eastern European animation tends to position itself as an active agent in a political semio-sphere, and animation in the countries of the former Yugoslavia is no exception. What are your thoughts on the poli-tical role and operation of Croatian animation in its various stages, and your own animation practice?*

—— As you probably know (you have seen it in a film at least!), prisons tend to have — in addition to cells — a space where prisoners meet their relatives and friends. Those prisoners who behave well are even allowed to use a room where they can have intimate intercourse with their partner who lives outside, free. This prison story is, of course, symbolic. Many years after the fall of the Berlin Wall I realized that Yugoslavia had operated as one such "room" for intimate encounters. We were a space of osmosis where the East and West met. At the time I myself was not aware how much this factor was part of my genome, but today I understand that political ideas dominate everything I have ever done. My first animation (I call it a "student work"), a two-minute film called *Inside and Out* (1978), recounts the story of a man who spends his life creating wings and one day succeeds in getting off the ground. The numerous inquisitives assembled around him do not follow his example but build a gigantic cage where they confine both him and themselves; but the cage is so huge that he continues to fly in it...

I have sought and held out this space of freedom in every [socio-political] context. But I am really not a revolutionary; nor have I ever been one. Revolution is like war, a tragic fact, and when the smoke has cleared, when the dead have been buried and the tears have dried, we realize that the actual advancement is minute.

—— *Your work spans decades of the development of animation, and culture in general, in the region. You belonged to the younger cohort of the famed Zagreb School of Animation (roughly 1970-1990), a group of auteurs of otherwise divergent styles assembled around postulates such as rejection of rigid mimetic forms, the enthronement of creativity and authorial autonomy, but also an intrinsic and inviolable relation between animation and human life. Could you comment on this legacy and its role in your own work?*

—— The Zagreb School of Animation had its specific technological and "worldview" coordinates. The technological characteristic of the School was the so-called "limited animation," which, in digest, means

Joško Marušić: *Fisheye* (*Riblje oko*), 1980
The Rainbow (*Duga*), 2010

a complete commitment to stylization. It is customarily contrasted with the Disney-style "full animation", where all characters are animated according to the strictly delineated canons of ("realistic") animation. [*On "limited" and "full" animation, and the Zagreb School's preference for the former, see Bahun's article on page 76.*] In terms of the worldview, the School introduced the genre of animated films for adults, films pregnant with cynicism, auto-irony, and the relativization of divisions between people. [They focused on the fact that], in all great conflicts, our sympathy is with the "small man" who is most frequently subject to manipulation. This "small person" exists in all classes and all societies, and verily constitutes the most numerous sector of society, but remains powerless because he or she is not "networked."

This thematic and technological framework allowed people who previously did not even conceive of working in animation to engage with animated film; but it was a particularly propitious ground for those who believed visual art sophistication was at the heart of their work. Thus, irrespective of the (mis)nomer "school," we can say that Zagreb School animation was created by a rather diverse group of distinct individuals. And this is an important feature, since the School precisely encouraged artists around the globe to use animation to conceptualize their own, rather distinct, messages. My own work in animation is a case in point. Although Nedeljko Dragić had been my "model" at the very beginning, I embarked on my own artistic path rather early. While my films are different in expression (due to my effort to avoid a style which might lead to film industry "confection"), all of them actually tell the same story. The story of one's own life. As I grow old and mature, my films change, too; but the messages remain the same.

—— *You have also been actively involved in the Zagreb World Festival of Animated Films – Animafest Zagreb, one of the most important international animation festivals, as its Art Director of from 1992 to 1998 and the President of the Festival Council from 2000 to 2006. Tell us something about the nature and history of the festival.*

—— The World Festival of Animated Films is an extraordinarily significant institution in the history and development of animation. The first international festival exclusively dedicated to animated films was established in Annecy in 1960, and the Zagreb festival of animated film was the first international festival to follow, twelve years after (founded in 1972). The importance of the Zagreb World Festival of Animated Films lay in the fact that it resolutely drew aside the "iron curtain," opening the door to animators working both in the East and in the West. The strict criteria regularly upheld by the jury of the Zagreb festival promote artistic exploration, and they have therefore also contributed to the most significant development in animation art: artistic animation ceased to be an asylum for lonesome artists and instead started influencing the market and the film industry itself. Thanks to the Zagreb film festival, the mass-market tastes and artistic achievements have become closer than ever before.

To tell you the truth, I had never thought that I myself would be in the position to be the art director of a film festival — and that I would be presiding over it for no less than a decade. I took it on myself as a kind of "war task" in 1992, and, as the festival further developed, this "task" became dear to me. It was also a welcome break in my own career.

—— *What is the situation in Croatian animation now? How much does the new generation live up to this legacy?*

—— I have to admit that a form of crisis in Zagreb-School animation started already in the mid-1980s. There are two reasons for this development. First, the school continued to insist on political messages while global animation shifted focus to graphic experimentation and technological innovation. Second, for ideological reasons, the famed Zagreb Film, devastatingly, did not actually produce anything for the mass market, except the television series *Professor Balthazar*. The crisis deepened during the war. Yet one could say that the foundation of the Department of Animated Film at the Academy of Fine Arts in Zagreb in 1999 positively reinvigorated interest in animation, now also supported by the education system. The results are visible: Croatian animation — and, in particular, student-produced animation — is present again at international festivals. For a more decisive step towards market viability, however, we need a stronger economy in general. Nevertheless, it is fair to say that, as heirs to an important legacy, the young show great interest in media art; and there have always been great talents in this region.

—— *This leads me to my next question. Your most recent film (and your first feature film),* The Rainbow, *pleads for the dialogue between generations, between parents and children. Why is this issue so important for you to make it into the crux of your film?*

—— When I decided to dedicate three precious years of my life to a single project, I asked myself: what is a message worthy of that commitment? And my response to myself was as follows. Of all the problems our world faces every day there is one we speak about least, and it is precisely that one that will cost us much. The problem concerns a complete discrepancy of opinion between different generations when it comes to the conceptualization of the future of our world. This problem stems from a lack of dialogue. The contemporary world has been constructed by the hedonistic and conformist measures of an old generation. The old are ashamed to admit this fact to their own children, and so they have created a whole set of mechanisms whereby children will be led to seek the causes of their frustration somewhere else. Here, that is the actual theme of *The Rainbow*, however much the film may be based on an archaic legend and rooted in a specific historical context.

—— *The Rainbow is also a film that argues for a dialogue at the level of form. Its dialogic structure becomes visible as an exchange between 2D and 3D animation, and pastel on paper. In effect, the film becomes a polyphonic structure, a loving historical compendium of animation styles, modes, and technical possibilities. How did you make a choice for such a structure? More important still: how do you see your own position as a teacher and a practitioner today in the context of the interplay between heritage and new possibilities, technological and creative?*

—— I have to admit something: the great challenge I posed to myself was to make a "commercial film." Yet, even though *The Rainbow* is the first Croatian film that was on a regular Cineplex repertoire, I have not really achieved this goal. I was restless and had to give in to my exploratory instincts. The film ended up having too many "risky features" at all levels (narrative, design, and animation) for the taste of a conservative mass market. Thus happened what I hadn't actually wished for (because I am also the producer of this film): *The Rainbow* became primarily — and exceedingly — interesting to the juries of international film festivals. It is now a film that everyone would like to see but no one wants to buy!

But I am satisfied. At this moment, to produce, uncompromisingly, a high-budget animated art film is an epoch-making statement, a move whose positive effects will only be assessed in the future.

—— *The Rainbow, like all your other films, distinguishes itself by its emphasis on a humanistic message. You recently became involved in the international Human Rights Animation project. Could you comment on this component of your work?*

—— Indeed I am a philanthrope; I help wherever I can. There were times when I would have gone "to the end of the world" if only there were people who would be interested in my encouragement to the young to break the cycle of prejudices. Now, as a middle-aged gentleman who has his own hedonistic and conformist pleasures, I allot the same importance to my career as to, say, having a portion of nicely grilled sea bream; and, beyond good animation, I do love soccer. I would like to demystify my profession. I've had the luck to work in a field where my talent could flourish, and thus to reach the hearts and minds of many. But the same could be done in other ways, and every person has the ability to do it. Truly everyone.

Translated by Sanja Bahun

A Conversation with Nenad Puhovski: *Documentarism as a Personal and Social Mission*
by Diana Nenadić

An amateur film enthusiast in the 1960s, a student of theater and movie direction and a young author in the early 1970s, a teacher at the Academy of Dramatic Art in the late 1970s, a theater and television director and award-winning documentary filmmaker during the 1980s, since the mid-1990s a producer of his own Factum documentary film project, and, in the new millennium, founder of the ZagrebDox international documentary film festival and a course of graduate study in documentary filmmaking. There will be more to add because Nenad Puhovski, the filmmaker who has dominated Croatian documentary film production for the last fifteen years, has not yet accomplished everything he set out to do over the many decades he has spent focused on popularizing documentary film in a country of 4.5 million relatively poor people, who until recently preferred to close their eyes both to reality and to creatively shaped documentaries. For now what remains is an unresolved battle with Croatian Television, because state television has been ignoring independent production both in terms of funding and broadcasting, and the founding of an institute for documentaries. Even without this, Puhovski is one of the rare Croatian filmmakers, perhaps the only one, to commit himself to documentary film, although in his earlier days he did have an inclination for what we call fiction.

—— Even as an amateur I started off with documentary film. I made my first film when I was fifteen and a student at the Fifth Gymnasium where we started a film club with the help of the Film Clubs' Association [Kino Savez] and its head, Kruno Heidler. I remember going to see Comrade Tito as a representative of the amateur filmmakers, an event that was recorded on several rolls of 8 mm film. So there has always been interest in documentary film. As a student at the Academy in 1972 I made a film called *Činča*, the title being the protagonist's nickname. My film had much in common, both in structure and its use of the *vérité* method, with Tomislav Radić's full-length film *Living Truth* (*Živa istina*) which he made that same year. They each even have a nearly identical scene: in Radić's movie Vjeran Zuppa, managing director of the &TD Theater, explains to actress Boždarka Frajt why she cannot join the repertory ensemble of the theater, while, in mine, Činča asks Professor Joško Juvančić to explain why she failed the entrance exam for the degree program in acting. Yet Radić had never heard of me nor had I heard of him. We were simply doing the same thing at the same time. He categorized his film as a feature, I called mine a documentary. Radić's was screened that summer at the Pula festival of feature films, while mine was screened at the Belgrade festival of documentary and short films, from where I get a call from a dear professor of mine, himself a prominent filmmaker, and he tells me that if I allow him to move *Činča* into the "feature" category I will get the "gold medal." I answered, "Professor, with all due respect, this is a documentary." "Oh, I know, but they all think this is the current craze, everyone in Zagreb is doing it. Hey, say the film is a feature and you get the gold!" "No," I said, "I won't." And so it was that *Činča* remained a documentary, and I "only" got honorable mention.

Now, cut to the future! Several years later, the Academy posted a job announcement for two teaching assistants, one to teach television, the other for acting. As I had already worked a lot in drama, I submitted my application for the drama teaching job as I had been assisting in the drama department as an "external." Žiro Radić, on the other hand, applied for the television job. The Dean of the Academy called us in for a conversation with an unusual offer: Radić had done more work in drama, while I had worked more with television, so he proposed we switch our applications. And so it was that Radić ended up teaching drama, and I ended up teaching in the television and later the film department. Life does make the weirdest films!

—— *How much were you helped by the fact that you started teaching at the Academy at a young age and managed to make a living. Did that allow you to go for film, documentary film no less? It is widely known that the documentary is only a stepping stone here to mainstream production of full-length feature films.*

—— It is true that my job at the Drama Academy gave me a certain degree of financial security, particularly in the 1990s when I was briefly completely cut off from the possibility of directing anywhere. So setting up Factum was supposed to allow people who had found themselves in a similar situation to be able to work and do so without the kind of compromises that would be necessary if they were working somewhere else. When I started off with my own production in Factum, I swore that I would not work only on my own films, that I would be primarily a producer, opening for others space for their work, and that only every tenth film would be under my direction. And there you go, there are currently about sixty movies in Factum production. I have directed four, and am currently working on the fifth. Beyond that, I deliberately focused on production but also making my own films about things that no one else wanted to "touch" before that, most of all films about war, war crimes, and similar themes. It was clear to me that, with the other risks that were quite quickly proving to be realistic, I had shot myself, as the Americans say, in the foot.

First of all, I antagonized a whole series of people, from those who were sincerely opposed to my positions on ideological grounds to those who saw with the films I was doing at the time that it was possible to do something that was needed and important and for which they did not have the courage. On the other hand, perhaps more pertinent to this conversation, I knew I was significantly limiting my maneuverability as an author. I had agreed to do something that was so thematically challenging that no one would think of analyzing whether it was good or bad, whether it was done one way or another, what sort of structure it had, and so forth. And besides, when someone you are interviewing wets himself while he is speaking of how he was tortured, aesthetics become secondary. So the decision to handicap myself was deliberate. It is only with my most recent film, *Together* (*Zajedno*), that I have come back to what I really find interesting, and, if I may say, gratifying. And so it is that the last twenty years of my work as an author have, in large part, been devoured by locusts. But, I am fine with that. I created Factum, gave my colleagues, especially younger people, a chance to work, broached some themes at a time when no one else in the entire region dared to, started ZagrebDox, raised a generation of young documentarians… It has been worth it.

—— *That authors have stages in their work is something completely normal, something that makes the early films different from later ones. In your case, the 1990s seem to be a time for a turn toward politically engaged and provocative films, in which you took a firm stand on the new social situation in post-communism and the wartime and post-war conditions in the new state. How do you define and compare the "before" and "after," in both the thematic and formal sense?*

—— Before the 1990s I worked on two kinds of documentaries: films about art and films about social problems. Regarding the first group, it is important to say that I tried doing them differently than others do. At that point people were mostly making films on art history, looking at art from a historical perspective, a touch professorial, heavy on the narration and so forth; Radovan Ivančević was fantastic at that. Since I am not an art historian, and such films didn't move me much, I decided that instead of making films "about" art, I would make films "from within" art, from my own feeling of the art. For example, in my film about Šutej (*U potrazi za Šutejem / In Search for Šutej*), which was showered with awards, I used *stop-frame* technique in animation of his mobiles, inspired by the story "Pale sam na svijetu" (*Pale Alone in the World*), about how these mobiles had a life of their own that was parallel to the life of people, and which we cannot see simply because of the different dimensions in which people live in relation to mobiles. In a film about Bućan (*Bućan triptih / The Bućan Triptych*), inspired by a phase when his posters had human faces, I had the posters speak. A film about painter Nives K. K. was in fact a collage of five different films and in the last one we animated drawings of a hand which Nives often drew on the margins of larger sketches. We did all that, my team, cameraman Enes Midžić, editor Maja Rodica, composer Igor Savin and I, using ordinary, classic film techniques, without the technological wonders that exist today. That was an intriguing film game that satisfied and pleased me at the level of pure film aesthetic.

But as I was always socially sensitive, I also made films about social issues, with varied success. For instance a film I am very fond of, *Dead Harbour* (*Mrtva luka*), sat on a shelf at Zagreb Television for fifteen years because it was about a shelter near Zagreb, and the editor, in a classic case of switching the messenger and the message, accused me of what I was using the film to expose — the inhumane conditions under which the "wards" of this institution were kept. Then *The Borderlines of Hunger* (*Rubne slike gladi*), a film dealing with the problem of hunger in Croatia during the 1980s, a time of economic chaos when people's salaries were quoted in the millions. But when the war broke out, I felt I no longer had a choice. Films about art would have to wait. And they are still waiting... After 2005 and in the context of social themes, I came back in a way to what I really liked doing — a combination of the social and the intimate. My most recent film, *Together*, is about people who are on the margins in a variety of ways, even handicapped, but want to

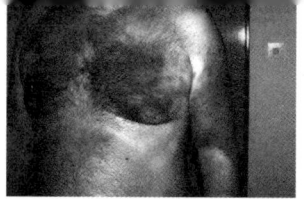

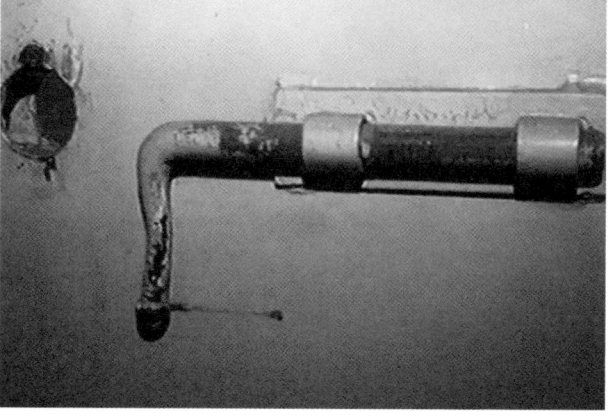

Nenad Puhovski: *Lora: Testimonies* (*Lora: svjedočanstva*), 2004

live in partnerships with others. I have worked on it for four years and it has taken me back in a sense to the time and method of *Činča*... It seems to me, when I look at this from the outside, that the *vérité* style is what suits me. I hadn't thought about it as a style, because it is normal for me to talk with a person in front of a camera about things, we converse, communicate, and I try to get something from them that this person might not say in another situation. I made use of this in the movies I made during the war as well, for example in *Lora*, talking with people who were tortured. I was fascinated by the possibility of conversation with people in front of a camera, when you see in their eyes that they want to say something, to communicate, to forget the camera...

— *The past is often idealized, especially at difficult moments, and we think that things used to be better, and then the current situation changes and again we think maybe it wasn't so good back then because there wasn't the freedom. On the other hand, it looks as if cinematography functioned better back in the day, perhaps by inertia, but it functioned. How do you relate to the period before 1990?*

— First, I was never a member of any one group. As far as I'm concerned, as far as short and documentary films are concerned, there were only two places to go in Croatia, maybe three. One was Kinoklub Zagreb, a very strong center for alternative film, but simply too aesthetically radical for me. I did not believe in "anti-film," which was very strong at the time. I was a member of the club, took courses, went to the club, hung out with the people, but that kind of experimental film which went *ad absurdum* in terms of karyokinesis, burning film, was not something that drew me.

The second circle, which evolved in a sense from the first and was much more interesting for me, was the Film Authors' Studio (Filmski autorski studio) or FAS, also started by the Film Association and it worked to establish a different modality of production which would give younger authors a chance to venture into more professional terrain. However FAS collapsed when it tried to produce a film about the 1971 student strike at Zagreb University during the time known as the Croatian Spring. The fate of that film was simply the last nail in the FAS coffin, because it had already become clear that there was no support for such an independent production system. I always say that Factum tried to be the spiritual offspring of FAS, a place for people with different ideas to gather, although FAS had also been involved in quite a few feature films as well. I repaid my debt to FAS and the people who made the film about 1971 in a sense when I produced the documentary *Poetry and Revolution* (*Poezija i revolucija*) which was made from material that was filmed then and shelved for years.

The third place, very interesting at that time, was Zagreb Film. Kruno Quien, who, if you ask me, is one of the key figures though often forgotten, had a personality trait that I was particularly fond of. He liked to talk about film and do something that is called *brainstorming* today. I "stole" that, too, when I created Factum. So there were three sub-systems which I knew and respected. But personally I was always outside of them.

—— *But there is a fourth, Croatian Television, Zagreb Television.*

—— Croatian Television was making better documentaries back then than they make now. Not because there was more freedom, but because authors were valued in a different way. And because they worked in a very simple, actually very socialist way and that was, if you'll pardon my language, work until you screw up! So until you make a cardinal error you can do more or less whatever you want. In that sense things were easier. I made *Dead Harbour* on television, a documentary which I agreed on with Angelo Miladinov, known as a very open-minded man and someone who promoted young authors. When I received an honorarium that was 50% higher than what we had agreed, I worried that something bad would happen to the film. And, indeed, it ended up on the shelf, only to be "released" in 1991, which turned out to be appealing as an anecdote because it was "liberated" by Obrad Kosovac, a man whom many had experienced as a major censor. To cut the story short, I would say this: before 1990 the system functioned quite simply. There was a certain degree of freedom, but self-censorship was such that people knew full well what could not be done. From that time we have terrific socially engaged documentaries, but they were socially critical only up to a point, to the limit of what was allowed, and that was something that was built into socialism, something that one "drank in with one's mother's milk." It was something known. Well, now, there are people who claim that limits are a healthy thing. I disagree. That is a story for little children. It seems to me that something else matters, which is that we still have taboo topics today.

—— *The story about Factum and your production undertaking begins in the second half of the 1990s, just as your film* Graham & I (Graham i ja) *was coming out. From the early 1990s until then you were completely invisible. Why?*

—— Up to 1990 I was working a lot in theater, on television and in film, all sorts of things. It was in the theater that I did the most subversive work, Orwell's *1984* or Stoppard's *Travesties*, for which there were quite a few problems and political reactions. And they were really brilliant performances! But in 1990 there was a split into those who were politically correct and those who were not, which was not, in my opinion, necessary. It was a fabrication. It was created, unfortunately, at least as far as culture was concerned, by the "creeps on our side," culture people, and a few of my colleagues from the Academy. This was a time when it was key to prove one's true faith, devotion to the idea of the Croatian state, regardless of the fact that at times this meant stomping on someone else's work. For instance, in the fall of 1991 I made four films about the Homeland War: on wartime Dubrovnik, war reporters, wartime medicine in cooperation with the Ministry of Health, etc. I did what was the most normal thing in the world to do at that moment. I promoted the truth about what was happening in Croatia. Among these there was also a film about Vukovar which I made for the Vukovar Club, using amateur material which they got for me, while Pavao Pavličić wrote the text that went with it. And in the end, when Vukovar fell, I made a closing sequence to "Pie Jesu" from Lloyd Webber's *Requiem*, and the premiere was only a few days later at the Zagreb Culture and Information Center. The film was then appropriated by the Ministry of Information and distributed in hundreds of copies all over the world. It was the first film about the war in Croatia which was screened at the Alpe-Adria festival in Trieste, and later at the World Congress of the United Nations on Human Rights in Vienna, etc. But within the country this film did not exist. I was under pressure at the time not only because I was given "friendly advice" to leave the country, but because my family was openly threatened. I had to leave the country for two years. And so... these films of mine were not screened at the Days of Croatian Film festival, they aren't in a single survey of the films from the period, they aren't at the Kinoteka [Croatian Film Archive]... that part of my biography simply does not exist. People in the field clearly knew of them, but as if it didn't agree with them that I was the one who made them... When I came back, I started from zero, or rather at less than zero, soon I was proclaimed to be an opponent of the Croatian state who had never done anything for Croatia, among other things because these films simply did not exist. It did not occur to me, of course, to pound my chest and shout.

—— *Maybe you could have continued doing films about artists, as some other documentary filmmakers did during the nineties?*

—— Sure, but that isn't what I wanted to do. I felt these weren't times for that. During the 1990s I was supposed to decide what to do in a situation when the only work that could be done was what I didn't want to do. You know, there hasn't been a generation for a very long time in this part of the world that has been able to live out life without going through a war. I thought and think that I owe my children and grandchildren a chance at that. And work was needed. I did what I know — movies. The only source of funding which imposed no conditions was the Soros Open Society Institute. Factum (first as a part of the Center for Dramatic Art) was started in parallel to the Grožnjan summer school, some of the films

Nenad Puhovski: *Pavillion 22* (*Paviljon 22*), 2002

were begun there, some in Zagreb and from then until now some sixty films have come out of it which have been signed by authors of all the generations, from Čejen Černić, who worked with us when she was only eighteen, to Branko Ivanda who finished the 1971 film on the Croatian Spring at Factum.

— *Your return as an author to the documentary filmmaking scene in 1998 with the film* Graham & I, *also Factum's first production, was quite tempestuous. The film was not included in the Days of Croatian Film competition, you protested vociferously, and the commentaries were controversial. You speak in the first person singular in the film, which was unusual here. Was that perhaps one of the taboos you mentioned and the reason why the film was not understood?*

— The movie is about Graham Bamford, an Englishman who took his life on the lawn in front of the British Parliament in protest over the war in Bosnia, particularly the Ahmići massacre. Since Graham and I belonged in a sense to the same generation, and I didn't want to make a journalistic, factographic film but wanted to bring the story closer to the region for which he killed himself, I decided to tell parallel stories about him and myself, feeling that this could give the film a new quality. I was careful to keep my story smaller, more modest, etc. All the materials from my story were visually reduced, "framed" within the shot, while those from the story about Graham were presented in full format. The critic at the newspaper *Slobodna Dalmacija* wrote that my insertion of myself alongside Graham was, in fact, war profiteering. It seems to me that this reaction shows they didn't get the movie, what it says and the way it says it. I don't think this is a brilliant film, but I do think it is good and raises questions to which, just then, we did not have ready answers.

There is something else at work which is par for the course here and which I have often experienced. When they want to get to you politically, then they say you are a bad, untalented director. This shuts you up, of course, because they put you *a priori* on the defensive. That is what happened when a preeminent intellectual, someone with a liberal orientation, was on a Croatian TV talk show and the conversation turned to a later film of mine, *Lora*, which takes as its theme the fact that there was a camp during the war in the city of Split where prisoners of war were tortured. At one point he said, "We won't talk about this, the film is bad." This is typifies the discourse, a way of talking about certain things. On the one hand the members of the association of defenders were publicly calling for me to be kicked out of the country and demonstrated in front of the television building because of the showing of the film, while on the other hand there are people from whom you'd expect an argumented position who simply fall back on: it's a bad film. All this is happening in an environment in which intellectuals, and particularly my colleagues, generally keep their mouths shut. I would say that this silence is a constant in the environment in which I work. Whenever there has been trouble about movies on which I worked, none of my colleagues, intellectuals, film critics, theorists or authors, with the possible exception of two or three, ever once said: "Hey people, let's discuss this!"

This was the most drastic in the case of the movie *Operation Storm* (*Oluja nad Krajinom*), directed for Factum by the late Božo Knežević. At one moment the film was even lambasted in the Croatian parliament. All of them spit on us, both those in positions and those in the opposition. Not only did not a single filmmaker step forward in our defense, at least in defense of the right for such a film to exist, but something happened which was far worse: Božo Knežević died in the way he died, in a car accident, a truck ran into his car. After that a film was made which was actually an open pamphlet against Knežević with the premise that since he wasn't a Croat he had no right to make a movie about the Krajina. What happened next was interesting — the Council for the Days of Croatian Film, the central national festival of short and medium-length films, decided that (among other things) they would open the festival with this film. I wrote an email to a colleague, today a respected middle-generation director, and asked him that they not do this, because the man against whom the filmed pamphlet had been made was dead. I was for screening it, but not for opening the festival with it. I get the answer: Colleague, you are wrong, all films and all terms are the same to us. So the national festival opened with this film. I am not saying all this for my own sake, but because the situation in our film industry would be entirely different if filmmakers, other artists, and intellectuals would take a principled position and if they would have the courage to speak up, rise, stand for something. Do you remember what happened in the Netherlands when filmmaker Theo Van Gogh was killed? I have no need to be a revolutionary, I didn't want to then, nor do I want to now. But I simply was brought to having to fight my own battles. And I fought them the best way I knew: in the name of something I believed in, a person must speak the truth. Unfortunately, until a few years ago I was absolutely the only one — not only in Croatia — in the entire region, who was doing that. In documentary film, of course.

—— *You drew a large number of your students into Factum production, a generation which was perhaps not as engaged in a political sense, but was defiant in terms of both the production of the time and their social surroundings. In that generation we mark the first successful attempts at making fake documentaries, of broaching the subjective perspective, for instance in the work of Zvonimir Jurić, and women directors, a playful, provocative approach to themes found with authors such as Matanić and Mirković, Korovljev, and others. Interesting that a year after your* Graham, *there were similar issues with Jurić's* Fortress (Tvrđa) *which was not included in the Days of Croatian Film competition. This would seem to be due to a lack of willingness among filmgoers to embrace the new model of the documentary which resists the dogma of the "observational" documentary, which is seen as being more truthful because of its alleged impartial observational position.*

—— For a long time here — I have to say until Factum appeared — the existing dogma was that the documentary is something happening to someone else, it tells an objective story. This is, of course, nonsense. But that so-called objectivity is partially — let's be honest again — the heritage of a more or less rigid social system such as socialism. We all hid behind objectivity then, behind a reality, which, in the end, became dogma. Of course this reality was very often counterfeit, especially in the early phases of socialism, with cheery workers and grinning miners. What is called *observational documentary, fly on the wall, direct cinema* or whatever you like, is something which came in very handy, both in an aesthetic and a political sense, for authors, we ourselves, to hide behind. So now, once you have been hiding for a long time, as any psychologist will tell you, you begin to believe that this is reality, and when you have to say "I," you run up against a problem. There are many Croatian documentarians who have never tried to say "I" in a film of theirs.

Of course this has swung, in some instances, to the opposite extreme today, and anyone who has a home video shot ten years ago thinks he or she is an author and that something ought to be done with it. It is a fact that today the documentary is something which is in the first person, something very intimate, personal and which speaks of personal engagement. So Factum made three series of films. The first are films on social themes which no one else wanted to touch, mostly war crimes and similar topics. The second are autobiographical films which are made systematically, so that at this moment we have as many as four new autobiographical documentaries in production. The third is something which was always typical of Croatian cinematography until the 1990s, and those are films about people on the margins, outsiders. But after 1990, especially in the Tuđman era, there was a new push for uniformity — we are all Croats, we are all Catholics and all of us are Dinamo fans.[1] And if someone isn't, whose fault is that?! And it was at this moment that we started a series of films about small people on the margins

---

1] Dinamo is a popular Croatian soccer team, which was controlled by Franjo Tuđman in the 1990s. Tuđman's attempt to change the name of the team caused a major revolt among its fans.

with filmmakers such as Budisavljević, Matijević, Mirošničenko, Strašek, Tardozzi, and others and so we brought the focus back to something that Croatian documentary film has always favored.

— *It seems as if in recent Croatian documentary film and at Factum there are many more women authors and directors than there are in domestic feature film. Why is this?*

— One of the essential tenets of Factum's philosophy is that we give voice to those who are a minority in society — whether in numbers, or influence. Therefore, as far as we are concerned, it would be completely normal for us to encourage women filmmakers to make documentaries and until now some fifteen of them have been working at Factum. As far as the others are concerned — I don't know, but I believe we are getting back to the old theme of the documentary as less important so let the "kids and the ladies" have their fun! Factum's *The Boy Who Rushed* (*Dečko kojem se žurilo*) by Biljana Čakić Veselič, *Straight A's!* (*Sve 5!*) by Dana Budisavljević or *Category: Optimist* (*Klasa optimist*) by Lana Šarić, are definitely some of the most interesting Croatian documentaries.

— *Factum was the first to produce feature-length documentaries even before Michael Moore's films were shown in Croatian movie theaters, which is also important, and is something completely new here. It started with* Poetry and Revolution*...*

— It started even earlier, with a film about the Bad Blue Boys, which was shown at the former Kinoteka in 1998. While it was on, the crush of filmgoers almost smashed glass on Kordunska St. That was the first time someone had faced off with Tuđman using a theme such as fans. The fans were constantly clashing with the authorities and they were the first to dare to voice their discontent with official politics. We made a simple but strong film and showed it for five days to a packed Kinoteka. We headed in that direction quite early, proceeded with *New, New Time* [by Rajko Grlić and Igor Mirković], my movie *Together*, we are working on Bezinović's *Blockade* (*Blokada*) about events at the University, and we have just started work on the film *Danke Deutschland* by Miroslav Sikavica. This film takes a look at wartime music — from the song *Danke Deutschland* and all the way to all the *band-aid* bands, and all the naiveté and iconography produced between 1990 and 1995, on what happened later to the people who sang the songs, and so forth. The film speaks of those years from an entirely different, mildly ironic and mildly nostalgic, perspective.

— *You said something already about how the first Factum films were budgeted. We know that before 2000 the documentary was not part of the system of financing of public funds. How did you manage to cobble together a budget for those first films?*

— My wife began working in the education section of the Soros Institute when we came back from England in 1994. I spent time over there, I talked with people, got involved in the work of the Culture Committee, so I got to know Diane Weyermann who is working today for Participant Media, an exceptionally important American production house which connects the commercial documentary and social activism in a very interesting way. At the time she was in charge of the fine arts at Soros. In conversation with her I mentioned that something ought to be done about documentaries, and she answered that Soros was not interested in film because he felt film was commercial and shouldn't be supported. I said that I agreed, but not when documentaries were in question. Out of this conversation, though not, of course out of this conversation alone, we got to the fact that: first, Soros began gradually to fund documentaries, and second and more important, the Soros Documentary Fund was created with time which became one of the most important documentary funds for socially engaged film. So a possibility was created to begin using some sort of minimal funds for documentaries and I tapped into that. I should say that the sums were very small, but also — contrary to what my colleagues often say — no one ever asked for anything in return. It is important to say something else here: I have not produced a single film to this day which has had a budget over 50,000 Euros. Not a one! So we are truly working with *low* and *non-budget*. At the moment, for instance, we are making three films with no budget, no money.

—— *How frustrating is that?*

—— There is a real danger here. The way we have learned to work is: you pick up a camera and go shoot. This kind of production within the system of European co-productions, pitching, seeking international funds and co-productions, is becoming a dinosaur, something that is dying out. I am sorry to see it go. Of course I am well aware that we will have to enter the system and adapt to it. But, on the other hand, I think one should leave open the possibility that some kids be handed 5000 kunas ($ 1000), a camera, and montage to make a film and see what they make of it. In co-production with Restart we are currently working on a full-length documentary on the student blockade. They covered the costs of filming, we provide post-production support. We didn't get a kuna from anyone, not from the city or the Croatian Audiovisual Centre and this is a full-length documentary, which would cost 500,000 Euros or more anywhere in Europe. But the crux of the whole story is something different. Here we come to my favorite subject, Croatian Television. What there should be within the whole system is *support*, partnership, with Croatian Television. Film funds or institutes do not necessarily need to be partners for documentary film, but public television must be that partner. What is fantastic is the fact that not a single one of the sixty films we have made was done in cooperation with Croatian Radio Television.

—— *How many of them have been shown by Croatian Television?*

—— About fifteen, perhaps as many as twenty, have been broadcast on television, but television did not come forward with money for any of the sixty films. It would be logical that in this situation I would go to Croatian TV and say: listen, people, you have no way of following this subject for two years, give us a little money and we'll do it, and together we'll make something. No! No way! If there is something frustrating, then it is the fact that the institution whose job it is, among other things, to support independent production, is not doing so in the case of documentary production. And they are spending five times as much as everyone else combined on documentary film in Croatia, with results at zero or near that.

— *This is not only frustrating for Factum, but for all the other independent producers, and there are a number of them. You have mentioned several: Restart, Nukleus, the Croatian Film Association, etc. How do you explain this blossoming of the independent scene? And how much of a role in all of this outside of film industry have civil society associations played which are louder and more active than ever?*

— At one moment we were essentially the only one, and then with time, as the situation relaxed and as we tore down some of the taboos, a generation appeared that was not impressed by the past, and then the ranks of independent producers swelled. I will say something which no one likes to hear: per capita there are too many producers in Croatia. Just look at the last page of the catalogue for Days of Croatian Film — dozens and dozens of them! I am of the opinion that a producer needs more than just a bank account, a producer is something much, much more important, and that is what I have always tried to be: the person who develops projects, talks, helps, jumps in, who has the essential technical wherewithal to get something going even with no funding. I think that everything is far too particularized. There are too many little producers who make one film a year or maybe two in three years. Our average is four to five films a year, we've been doing that for fifteen years now, and right now we have a dozen projects at various phases of production. But this is a moment, essentially a healthy situation, which will, I believe, lead with time to some sort of consolidation, a merging of the smaller producers.

— *You launched graduate study in documentary film direction at the Academy of Dramatic Art. Do you think this will more firmly bond certain directors to documentary film, since here it has mostly been nothing but a transition or stepping stone to feature production?*

— An article appeared over the last few days [July 2010] in all the Croatian newspapers about the catastrophe of Croatian film, because not a single (feature) movie was included in the selection of the Sarajevo Festival. It is a fact that four documentary and three short feature films were included in the festival selection, but these were ignored in all the fuss. Unfortunately this manifests an obsession with feature film, which can be laid at the feet of film critics, as if that were the only genre of film worth its salt. This is insulting to all those people who have chosen documentary film as their calling. Small environments, poor environments, they always take a position like that. On the Zagreb streets you will see a far larger percentage of BMWs than in Frankfurt. It is typical for the small and poor that they want to parade how rich they are. So we think documentary film is not good enough to show the wealth of our talent and our intelligence, and feature film is what we need, it has to cost 10 million somethings, etc. I disagree,

I have never thought that way and I have been battling for a very long time for acknowledgment of the legitimacy and equality of documentary film. Graduate study on documentary film is also a facet of this battle, as is ZagrebDox, which, if I might paraphrase, is an expression of Factum by other means. Interestingly no one who has taken the entrance examination for the masters' in documentary filmmaking so far studied film direction for their undergraduate degree; these are people from other circles: producers, amateurs, cameramen, journalists...

—— *Perhaps this is good and healthy for the documentary...*

—— I am pleased about it, but still it shows that people who come to study direction at the Academy come only for feature film and dream of becoming "rich and famous"... What I find interesting is that in the history of the Drama Academy, from my *Činča* and on, more documentary films have been given awards at festivals than feature films have. However the pressure of the Academy, the pressure of the world in which we live, the pressure of colleagues, is such that only feature film is worth working on. Everything else is a stepping stone to it. As if someone were to tell Satie that everything he composed for the piano was really just a stepping stone to the symphony he never wrote!

—— *Unlike the traditional media, such as the dying breed of newspapers, the Internet is becoming a new form of communication with great possibilities, such as the possibility of more intimate conversations, where people who have something to say open up to a broad audience, but through a conversation with one person, or they parody social situations as Michael Moore did. This is terribly important and has a powerful influence on the whole social and artistic situation. For this inside situation, which is obviously moving with a completely new and great energy, do you see something similar going on in Croatia as well? Do you see a place where it would be possible, outside of festivals, to support and sustain contact with the public?*

—— In Croatia there is a widely held belief that we have too many festivals. There are more than 40 in this country of 4.5 million inhabitants. However the fact is that festivals here are a form of alternative distribution. They have the role that art-house cinemas should be playing. People don't feel like going out just to go to the movies. They can watch a movie at home. They go on family outings which include movies, shopping, dinner, and so forth, or as a festive event when they see a lot of films and run into interesting people. At ZagrebDox, which exclusively screens documentaries, we had an audience of 25,000 people this year, a respectable number indeed in a city the size of Zagreb. People come to see films, and very important for us is the fact that people of all ages come — young, middle-aged and old, grandmothers and grandfathers, and not just students who are a specific sort of audience. People have had it with false Hollywood reality, they are interested in what is really going on. A movie theater dedicated to documentary film, Doku-kino, is now up and running in Zagreb, and at movie theaters such as Tuškanac and Europa they are showing more and more documentary films, simply because they have all realized that this matters. These last few days I have had three or four offers for Internet distribution and cable television. I am having serious discussions about this because documentaries can be watched on the Internet as well. That works well as a medium for documentary film, because a large screen, Dolby Surround, etc. are not *conditio sine qua non* as they are for many acted films. I am a member of the European Film Academy and this year we will view online a third of the films we are voting on. This is something unstoppable. Whether I like it or not is another question. At this moment in Croatia we have no portal which would only be for documentaries, but that will come with time. It is a necessity. I think that we are quite close in these matters to what is going on in the world though, of course, with much less money, but there is a real interest. I repeat that 25,000 attended ZagrebDox, and we are a festival without a big party. I am very optimistic as to audience reception, their hunger for quality documentaries, their interest. I think that this is very, very OK.

Translated by Ellen Elias Bursać

Reviews

Dalibor Matanić: *Fine Dead Girls* (*Fine mrtve djevojke*, 2002)
reviewed by Marko Dumančić

Since his debut feature *The Cashier Wants to Go to the Seaside* (*Blagajnica hoće ići na more*) in 2000, Dalibor Matanić has become one of the most talked-about Croatian filmmakers. Domestic critics not only praise his films but also point to him as the type of bold and innovative artist that could raise the industry's reputation abroad and revive the interest of local audiences in national cinematography — no small feat, to be sure.

Indeed, one cannot but marvel at the moviemaker's productivity and duly deserved critical acclaim; in a decade he has produced six feature-length films[1] and a couple of award-winning shorts. Although all of Matanić's films have created a buzz and several stirred heated controversy at home, this review focuses on his 2002 feature *Fine Dead Girls* (*Fine mrtve djevojke*). This motion picture is significant not only because it reflects his artistic philosophy but also because it provides critical insight into the representation of queerness in Croatian and Balkan cinema since 1989. *Fine Dead Girls* cemented the director's reputation at home and in Europe as a filmmaker who challenges injustices, conservatism, complacency, and uniformity of modern societies. Despite the fact that various commentators regularly treat Matanić's films as a reaction to the monotonous propaganda pieces that dominated Croatia's silver screen under the censorship-happy regime of Franjo Tuđman, *Fine Dead Girls* in particular and Matanić's opus in general offer more than a straightforward condemnation of ubiquitous parochialism and intolerance in Croatia. Rather, this young director wrestles with more demanding questions about everyday evils, social isolation, and the possibility for redemption.

Matanić's oeuvre has dealt with what he terms "invisible" people and spaces (whether interior or geographic) which the general population overlooks or dismisses as irrelevant. Asked about how he feels about being called "the protector of those who are different" (*"zaštitnik onih koji su drukčiji"*), Matanić somberly responded that he generally likes to depict people who live on the margins because in today's world all reasonable individuals — not only targeted minorities — are marginalized and tossed to the side (Simić, T. 2008). On another occasion Matanić more pointedly

---

1] These include, in descending order: *Mother of Asphalt* (*Majka asfalta*) in 2010, *Cinema "Lika"* (*Kino Lika*) in 2008, *I Love You* (*Volim te*) in 2006, *100 Minutes of Glory* (*Sto minuta slave*) in 2005, *Fine Dead Girls* (*Fine mrtve djevojke*) in 2002 and *The Cashier Wants to Go to the Seaside* (*Blagajnica hoće ići na more*) in 2000.

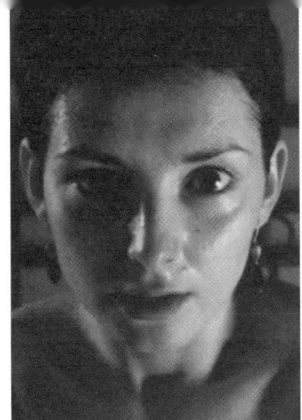

Dalibor Matanić: *Fine Dead Girls* (*Fine mrtve djevojke*), 2002

declared that he is "a man who shocks" (*"Ja sam čovjek koji šokira"*). The tremors this director unleashes with his motion pictures, however, stay clear of cheap sensationalism and are instead aimed at stirring the listless public life in Croatia from its indulgent and costly moral hibernation. Matanić declares that life in Croatia is a bit stale: because everything moves at a snail's pace, audiences need a thunderous wake-up call to become aware of contemporary problems (Prica, 2008). In 2003 this young Croatian director outlined a cautious "activist" agenda: "I would like to help the whole of society if I could, but I don't know how powerful art is to help at present since it is so marginalized. How is it possible to cleanse people, to galvanize them into action?" (Trajkov, 2003). Six years and three feature films later, Matanić expressed the same level of dismay at the reactionary impulses of Croatian society while exhibiting the equal level of determination to fight them with his films. He observed: "Instead of some sort of evolution, some sort of progress... our civil society is gradually disintegrating. But one thing is for certain: each of my subsequent films will continue to dissect this society ever more forcefully."[2]

True to his word, each of Matanić's films has tackled a topic either neglected or purposefully ignored in the public discourse. In 2000, his quirky *The Cashier Wants to Go to the Seaside* looks at how long a modest, kindly cashier suffers injustice from people less noble than she when her only desire is to take her daughter for much-needed medical seaside convalescence. Becoming one of the most watched films of the year,[3] *The Cashier* secured Matanić the caché with which to advance his point of view even more vigorously in his next production. In 2002, *Fine Dead Girls* became the first postwar Croatian film to deal explicitly with the issue of same-sex love and homophobia. In this macabre film noir, the moral depravity consuming Croatia's "upstanding citizenry" costs a lesbian couple their lives. The 2006 *I Love You* — another first in Croatian cinematography — deals head-on with the issues of HIV transmission and society's intolerance of the HIV-infected population. As with other of Matanić's

---

2] Luketić, Željko. Interview broadcast as part of Radio 101's show "Cultural Interview" on 30 October 2008.
3] The film sold approximately fifty thousand tickets in Croatia and had astronomical ratings when televised, earning it the title of the most watched film of the year. See the director's website (www.dalibormatanic.com) for further information.

films, *I Love You* addresses larger social ills; in the director's own words: "I wanted to deal not only with AIDS... but also consider... a society in transition in which everyone wants to make up for the years of want under communism by voraciously consuming everything they can swallow... which inevitably leads to emotional and spiritual breakdown..." (Simić, T. 2008). His latest feature, *Mother of Asphalt* (*Majka asfalta*) takes a long, hard look at the bedrock of Croatia's Catholic society: heterosexual marriage. Matanić deftly juxtaposes the traditional/institutional views of heterosexual marriage with a humanist/personalized perspective to flip conventional wisdom about this "institution" on its head.

Of all his films to date, *Fine Dead Girls* arguably left the deepest mark on Croatian society and the cultural scene. First featured at Croatia's main film festival in Pula, the movie achieved an impressive feat by winning the Grand Golden Arena for best film, the Golden Gate of Pula Audience Award, and the Critic's Choice Award. The film not only signaled the coming of a cinematic master but also announced the arrival of a bold new perspective in Croatian cinema. Representing an unapologetic "dressing down" of Croatian society, *Fine Dead Girls* features two lesbian lovers as protagonists in this fast-paced *noir* thriller.

The narrative begins ominously with a knock at the door. The dweller of the musty, stifling apartment in a derelict building opens the door to find a detective and two police officers accompanied by a short-haired and strikingly beautiful Iva. The policeman coolly asks the inconspicuous middle-aged tenants — Olga and Blaž — whether they have kidnapped Iva's son. Having found no trace of Iva's child in the building, the detective later encourages Iva to reveal why she has accused a seemingly harmless, ordinary couple of such a heinous crime. In a series of flashbacks, Iva reveals how she and her girlfriend, Marija (Mare), moved into one of the apartments Olga was renting. Although it seems at first that the pair has found a perfect love nest, it soon becomes obvious that they are surrounded by a gallery of unsavory characters. The ghoulish cast of neighbors signifies the ills besetting contemporary Croatian society: a xenophobic veteran suffering from PTSD who physically abuses his wife for not bearing him sons; the "gynecologist" Perić who performs illegal abortions in a primitive, unhygienic attic; a pensioner who hides the rotting corpse of his wife in the apartment (à la *Psycho*) in order to continue receiving her retirement checks; and a young, petty, self-satisfied prostitute. The individual misdeeds these characters commit are compounded by their collective guilt as they turn a blind eye to each others' misconduct. The ringleader of this ninth circle of hell in the outskirts of Zagreb is the sadistic Olga, who keeps everyone under her thumb and worships only her son Daniel, who is a coarse skinhead. After Iva rejects Daniel's insistent advances and Olga discovers that her two new tenants are lesbian, the stage is set for disaster. Goaded by his mother, Daniel rapes Iva while Marija is away. Once aware of the crime, Marija confronts the rapist and in the course of their struggle Daniel meets his end under the wheels of a train. A witness to her son's death, Olga immediately rouses the tenants who, in a fit of mob psychosis, push Marija down the stairs (and to her death) as she tries to escape them. Iva survives the episode but, as the plural in the title suggests, dies a different kind of death: she marries Dalibor, the man she dated before meeting Marija.

Although several aesthetic and narrative aspects of this motion picture call out for analysis, the treatment of lesbian characters and their relationship jumps out as the film's most unique aspect in the context of postwar Croatian cinematography. As one of a handful of Balkan films that places same-sex lovers center-stage, *Fine Dead Girls* continues to evoke lively and constructive critical and scholarly discussion in regard to its treatment of lesbianism. Like many other domestic film critics, the inimitable Nenad Polimac positively evaluates Matanić's attempts to deal with the dynamics of a lesbian relationship. He argues that: "Although *Fine Dead Girls* is not a typical gay film that auto-reflexively concerns itself with the hidden nuances of homosexual relations... the film succeeds precisely because of the realistic portrayal of the heroines' personal relationship" (Polimac, 2002). Film scholar Mima Simić, however, unearths a more sinister side to Matanić's "queer movie." Through an incisive feminist and queer reading, she convincingly demonstrates that showing same-sex desire as natural does not automatically qualify *Fine Dead Girls* as a "lesbian film." In fact, Simić contends that Matanić produced a "sexist and patriarchal product that operates within the same repressive film tradition which represents lesbian (and female) characters as victims and establishes lesbian relationships as an impossibility.[4] (Simić, 2006) Building on the works of K. Moss and D. Iordanova, she observes that much like the Yugo-era films that featured the Roma population — which were made neither *by* nor *for* the Roma — "queer films" serve as a metaphor for the patriarchal and sexist processes that are transpiring in the Balkans. As Kevin Moss also notes in his work: "In Central and Eastern Europe and the Balkans... gay and lesbian characters are used as a metaphor for nationality." (Moss 2008: 136)

Faced with the postwar demographic crisis and an EU enlargement that threatens the purity of the nation, the lesbian celluloid heroine is forced to uphold the nation's demographic, ethnic, and nationalistic agenda by denying herself the same-sex contact she craves. Thus, Simić's analysis demonstrates that Iva's and Marija's death is not a cautionary tale about what happens when a society tolerates/condones patriarchal and sexist attitudes; instead, *Fine Dead Girls* becomes another cultural product promoting female heterosexuality as the only acceptable mode of behavior for women in a country obsessed with a declining birthrate and the inviolability of its national identity as it fears being swallowed whole through EU enlargement. Even though Simić acknowledges that heterosexuality is presented as the grotesque opposite of the innocent

---

4] In another equally stimulating essay "Čuvarica granice" (also referenced here), Simić broadens her argument to include two other "lesbian films": the Slovenian *The Guardian of the Border* (*Varuh meje*) by Maja Weiss and Dragan Marinković's *Take a Deep Breath* (*Diši duboko*). Simić argues persuasively that these works criticize the patriarchal and nationalistic discourse/practice while simultaneously upholding the very same traditional ideology. By disabling the establishment of the female/lesbian subject, films that seemingly undermine the racist and sexist discourse ironically enable it in different ways.

Sapphic love between Iva and Marija, she maintains that *Fine Dead Girls* nonetheless represents lesbianism as something to be rejected in order for the nation to secure its existence. What is more, Simić asserts that Matanić presents lesbianism as *a choice* and a condition that can and must be overcome (Simić, 2010: 213).

However compelling Simić's arguments are (and they are indeed persuasive), this reviewer could not but notice that for a movie aimed at promoting traditional female roles (as a way to symbolically ensure the [procreative] health of the nation), *Fine Dead Girls* takes great pains to portray male heterosexual characters as chronically incapable of assuming patriarchal roles. Throughout the narrative the progeny's behavior and women's (procreative) choices are effectively out of men's hands; they are symbolically impotent to perform basic patriarchal duties. Daniel's rape of Iva (his attempt to impregnate her and "teach her to love cock") ends in his death; the "gynecologist" Perić not only performs abortions (thus depriving the Nation of offspring) but also fathers a mentally handicapped son; the veteran with PTSD drives his wife to terminate pregnancies that will not yield male offspring; Blaž is ashamed of his son throughout the movie but cannot help him because he turns a blind eye to Olga's every crime; and even Iva's husband Dalibor — the only untainted male in the narrative — has no idea that his picture-perfect marriage is a sham. In fact, one of the last exchanges in the movie suggests that all married men know precious little about their spouses. When asked whether Dalibor knows about her lesbian relationship, Iva shoots back a question of her own to the detective: "Do you think you know everything about *your* wife? You know other people better than your own family." In short, Matanić produces masculinities that are damaged beyond repair; the gendered system he presents is so thoroughly dislodged from its heterosexist axis that the impossibility of homosexual unions would hardly be sufficient to compensate for the masculine lack. If indeed Matanić introduces a lesbian couple only to have them sacrifice their same-sex love on the altar of the Homeland, it is necessary to note that he also makes men incapable of receiving/making use of such a sacrificial offering.

Although *Fine Dead Girls* is not a "lesbian film" since it casts Marija and Iva as metaphors for larger socio-political processes rather than flesh-and-blood characters, it seems to this reviewer that (based on Matanić's oeuvre and his artistic philosophy) this film should not be judged (exclusively) from a "queer perspective." Rather than being evaluated on the merits of motion pictures made by and for queers, it might be worthwhile to weigh it against the standards of its own category; i.e. to motion pictures such as Jen Nemec's *A Report on the Party and the Guests* (*O slavnosti a hostech*) or Andrzej Wajda's *Sewer* (*Kanał*). By conveying a sense of a fragmented and angst-ridden collective consciousness, these cinematic parables certainly neglect to offer individual psychologies of particular characters, but nonetheless perform an indispensable task of transforming the silver screen into a mirror and forcing audiences to confront their era's moral crises.

Works Cited

- Anon. 2008. "Nova hrvatska generacija: Moćni prije četrdesete." *Nacional*, December 29. <http://www.nacional.hr/clanak/50856/mocni-prije-cetrdesete> Accessed on January 28, 2012.
- Lamble David. 2007. "Global Lens Festival Highlights." *Bay Area Reporter*, November 1. <http://www.ebar.com/arts/art_article.php?sec=film&article=415> Accessed on January 28, 2012.
- Moss, K. 2008. "Three Gay Films from Former Yugoslavia." In: David M. Bethea, ed. *American Contributions to the 14th International Congress of Slavists, Ohrid, September 2008. Vol 2: Literature*. Bloomington: Slavica, pp. 125-38.
- Polimac, N. 2002. "Fine mrtve djevojke — najbolji hrvatski film od Maršala." *Nacional*, July 30. <http://www.nacional.hr/clanak/13172/fine-mrtve-djevojke-najbolji-hrvatski-film-od-marsala> Accessed on January 28, 2012.
- Prica, B. 2008. "Dalibor Matanić: Od tate sam naslijedio preciznost a od mame smisao za loš humor." *Nacional*, September 24. <http://www.nacional.hr/clanak/48764/dalibor-matanic-od-tate-sam-naslijedio-preciznost-a-od-mame-smisao-za-los-humor> Accessed on January 28, 2012.
- Simić, M. 2006. "Fine mrtve djevojke: Zašto su prve hrvatske celuloidne lezbijke morale umrijeti?" *Cunterview: Women Art Media Space*, November 2. <http://www.cunterview.net/index.php/Filmska.net/ Fine-mrtve-djevojke-Zasto-su-prve-hrvatske-celuloidne-lezbijke-morale-umrijeti.html> Accessed on January 28, 2012.
- Simić, M. 2010. "Čuvarica granice: Celuloidna lezbijka kao dvostruka metafora u re/konstrukciji postjugoslavenskih nacionalnih identiteta." In: Edin Hodžić and Tarik Jusić, eds. *Na marginama: Manjine i mediji u jugoistočnoj Evropi*. Sarajevo: Mediacenter, 205-24.
- Simić, T. 2008. "Filmska provokacija buntovnika s kamerom: Kako shvatiti ličke redikule." *Nacional*, June 30. <http://www.nacional.hr/clanak/46924/kako-shvatiti-licke-redikule> Accessed on January 28, 2012.
- Trajkov, Igor Pop. 2003. "I Love Actors: Dalibor Matanić Interviewed." *Kinoeye*, May 26. <http://www.kinoeye.org/03/06/trajkov06.php> Accessed on January 28, 2012.

Fine Dead Girls (*Fine mrtve djevojke*), Croatia, 2002. Color, 77 min.
Director: Dalibor Matanić
Script: Mate Matišić, Dalibor Matanić
Director of photography: Branko Linta
Art director: Željka Burić
Music: Jura Ferina and Pavle Miholjević
Editing: Tomislav Pavlić
Cast: Olga Pakalović, Nina Violić,
Inge Appelt, Krešimir Mikić, Ivica Vidović, Jadranka Đokić, Milan Štrljić, Zdenko Sertić Krieger, Marina Kostelac, Boris Miholjević, Mirko Boman, Janko Rakoš, Ilija Zovko
Producer: Jozo Patljak
Production: Alka Film

Kristijan Milić: *The Living and the Dead* (*Živi i mrtvi*, 2007)
reviewed by Nikica Gilić

During the 1990s, Croatian-Bosnian soldier Tomo with his group tries to reach his comrades and approaches a location called Graveyard Field (Grobno polje), unaware of a similar destiny shared by his grandfather Martin in the 1940s. The film concentrates on the two groups of soldiers fighting in wars at different points in history (with different enemies and even against one another), only to face the same tragic consequences at the end. In both wars, the military units lose more and more troops to the enemy, until, in the end, everybody meets at Graveyard Field, where dying Tomo (the last of his group) is surrounded by the ghosts of all the warriors who were killed.

This Croatian-Bosnian co-production uses the two most recent wars in Bosnia and Herzegovina as its centerpiece, focusing mostly on the role and destiny of the Croats indigent to that country (the screenplay was written by an ethnic Croat from Bosnia and Herzegovina), but also taking into consideration the complex political and ethnic relations in the entire region. It is important to note that in the story from the last war of the 1990s, the featured Croats are fighting against Bosniaks, more or less following ethnic lines of division, while in the story from the earlier war (World War II), to make things more complex, Croats and Bosniaks mix in a Croat-led army, fighting the Partisans (the anti-fascist resistance army that was itself ethnically "mixed," that is, composed of Croats, Bosniaks, Serbs, Jews, and so on), who appear in this film though they are not developed as a theme or defined as a political or social force. This, of course, may be contrary to the expectations of local viewers and possibly even more so of viewers from abroad whose notion of war films about the former Yugoslavia and its region was formed by the popular Partisan genre and directors such as Veljko Bulajić (Orson Welles and Yul Brynner, among others, starred in *The Battle of the Neretva*), Hajrudin Krvavac, Žika Mitrović, Stipe Delić, Fadil Hadžić and many others. The war films from the socialist era were generally ethically clear-cut, with good guys and bad guys as easily recognizable as in a western; some of these films (particularly those made by Žika Mitrović) were even openly compared to American westerns (for more on this genre see the article by Ivo Škrabalo on page 21).

The Living and the Dead crafts a more complex picture through a particular distribution of narrative threads. To make things more easily comprehensible to viewers, this action-packed and often violent war film

Kristijan Milić: *The Living and the Dead* (*Živi i mrtvi*), 2007

chooses a strategy that is not frequently used in recent films dealing with these topics. *The Living and the Dead* takes the tradition of genre cinema (mostly American war films, action films, and thrillers), mixes it with the tradition of the fantastic, and, in addition, uses a modernist mixing of temporal planes thus artfully interweaving segments of recent and less recent history. This storyline strategy works well concurrently, and the viewer of *The Living and the Dead* not only easily understands the reasons for a direct juxtaposition of the two wars, but is also forced to generate an ethical perspective that questions the purpose of warfare in general. For instance, the first jump from 1993 to the past is motivated by a discussion of a cigar-case with a picture on it of Travnik (Travnik is a Bosnian town associated in the 1990s with Muslim-Bosnian community and identity). The cigar-case was given to the 1990s character by his grandfather, who in turn had received it during the tumultuous events of 1943 (the same actor plays both characters).

In this film where all sides lose, there is no real hero, rather the narrative relies on a conglomeration of characters all of whom play important roles. The viewer can nonetheless easily recognize the typical profiles of the genre — a seasoned war hero, a confused novice who might endanger himself and others, a wise older commander, etc. On the other hand, the cinematography (often strikingly beautiful despite the limited production budget) will remind viewers of Walter Hill's, John Carpenter's, and John McTiernan's best cinematic achievements, particularly those taking place in the forests (*Southern Comfort* or *Predator*, for instance). The Yugoslav, Croatian, and Bosnian traditions of war films dealing with World War II in a modernist or otherwise unconventional way (some of the films by Antun Vrdoljak, Vatroslav Mimica, Bata Čengić, or Puriša Đorđević), interestingly enough, seem to be far less consequential for Kristijan Milić's film.

In addition to showcasing all the political intricacies of the story (difficult, perhaps, to grasp for those viewers unfamiliar with the complex history of the region, but whose viewing pleasure will be unaffected), *The Living and the Dead* clearly reveals personal and family histories often hiding behind political turmoil, thus allowing the central problem of the characters to become the central problem for the viewers as well, regardless of their cultural background. There are at least two main techniques facilitating this narrative — but also political — strategy. First, as mentioned above, World War II in Bosnia and the Bosnian war of the 1990s are constantly intertwined in the storytelling, with events from the two periods reflecting, explaining, and mirroring each other, and with the ghosts of victims of both wars uniting in the narrative finale. Also, the very title of the film itself suggests some sort of leveling among the characters.

The second technique that makes the characters' fates more immediately relevant for the viewer lies in the astute decision to cast the same actors for roles in both historical periods. They are sometimes explicitly playing the members of the same family, sometimes they just appear in the chaos as a familiar face and voice. For instance, the supporting walk-on character of a Bosnian soldier in the 1990s war gets killed by a Croatian soldier, who himself is the grandson of the man who was, at least apparently, in the same unit with the Bosnian soldier's grandfather, Ferid, during World War II. The two different generations of Bosnian Croats are played by Filip Šovagović (in the roles of Tomo and Martin) while Enes Vejzović plays the two Bosnian Muslims ("Bošnjaci") — Ferid and his unnamed grandson. Some of the casting choices further frustrate the horizon of expectation for a viewer who wants to see a clear-cut ethnic division. For instance, despite his Muslim name and ethnic heritage, Enes Vejzović, who plays Ferid, is one of the better known younger Croatian actors, a fact that may easily escape an international viewer but is immediately apparent to local filmgoers.

Taking these directorial choices into consideration, one can underscore with a certainty that the entire structure of Kristijan Milić's film supports its essential anti-war orientation. Not only that the theme of mindless killings in wars in general is laid bare and criticized on moral grounds in this film, but also the very fabric of its narration and characterization skillfully carries the heavy burden of explaining the particularities of the recent wars in Bosnia and Herzegovina, rendering history as a series of cyclical tragedies. War in this artistic vision is not, in my opinion, linked exclusively to the region depicted in *The Living and the Dead*; Milić's film reveals war as a universal human occurrence — with equal horrendous consequences no matter when and where it takes place.

As the film reaches its logical end, probably at least partly hinted at by the genre aspects of the story, the fact that a character belongs to a specific army (the Home Guard, Croatian Defense Council, BH Army, etc.), or even his ethnicity, becomes increasingly more irrelevant for the viewer, because it is conveyed as less and less significant for the remaining characters. Their only aim becomes to survive, rather than to achieve anything significant or prove something to "the other side," whatever the side may be. This change of focus is also a very effective narrative strategy for achieving an emotional connection between the viewer and the character regardless of the character's ideology or other characteristics. In addition, the different visual styling of the past (sepia) and the present (more-or less "realistic" color) helps not only to differentiate events and eras, but also to suggest to the viewer that, although so similar, these events are still not easily understood or reducible to simple explanations. For instance, although the commanding officer of the Ustashi (a World

War II fascist force), played by Robert Roklicer, is extremely unlikeable, to say the least, and unpleasant, even this group is shown as lacking homogeneity and several other individuals among the Ustashi project quite a convincingly human motivation.

The general fatalism and pessimism of Milić's film is particularly evident in the dwindling number of surviving characters (a tradition that includes McTiernan's *Predator*, but goes back at least to John Ford's *The Lost Patrol*). As the characters die, the visuals get darker and the camera slowly closes in on the remaining figures, conveying the claustrophobic sentiments they are feeling until everything is leveled by death, the only thing everyone has in common regardless of religion, ethnicity, or ideology.

The Living and the Dead (*Živi i mrtvi*), Croatia, Bosnia and Herzegovina, 2007. Color, 87 min.
Director: Kristijan Milić
Script: Josip Mlakić (based on his own novel)
Director of Photography: Dragan Marković, Mirko Pivčević
Music: Andrija Milić
Editing: Goran Guberović
Set Designer: Kemal Hrustanović
Cast: Filip Šovagović, Velibor Topić, Enes Vejzović, Borko Perić, Slaven Knezović, Marinko Prga, Miro Barnjak, Robert Roklicer, Božidar Orešković, Izudin Bajrović, Ljubomir Jurković, Nermin Omić.
Production: Mainframe, Olimp produkcija, Uma, Porta, Croatian Radiotelevision, Bosnia and Herzegovina Radiotelevision

---

Rajko Grlić: *Border Post* (*Karaula*, 2006)
reviewed by Vida Johnson

Border Post (*Karaula*) is the tenth feature film by Rajko Grlić, one of the best Yugoslav/Croatian directors, who belongs to the well-known Prague School of filmmakers. When asked in an interview (see page 100) about this film's "multiple narrative levels: a metanarrative level, the level of true reality, and an ironic level," Grlić answered that he is a child of Central Europe, that he spent his formative years in Prague, and developed his world view which has "irony, playfulness, and the need to tell the most serious stories with some distance, laughter, and ambiguity. I do not believe in one-dimensional stories, but rather I think that stories ought to have several layers and that film is precisely a tool that plays with this multiplicity of levels. The viewer essentially chooses how many and which layers he wants to pursue."

In a close textual and visual analysis of the film, I will attempt to demonstrate how an ostensibly comic story, full of realistic details of life in a military outpost in the far reaches of Yugoslavia several years after Tito's death, becomes a metaphor for Yugoslavia's demise. Aware of the many war films about Yugoslavia's disintegration in the 1990s, Grlić did not want to make a typical war film with good and bad guys, but chose 1987, one of the last years before the war, as "the turning point in what ensued. [...] It seemed to me that it would be much more interesting to see where and why the whole thing happened, how the people were prepped through the process of socialism for the war, how simple it was with the aid of a small TV set to pour hatred into people, and how the same TV set turned people into victims, blood-spillers, murderers." But in this film, Grlić does much more than explore the causes of Yugoslavia's break-up. In the opinion of this reviewer, he takes a nostalgic trip down the memory lane of Yugoslav cinema itself — the multi-national Yugoslav film industry that produced world-renowned black comedies, tragic-comedies, farces full of social and political critique, as well as sex, and rich, juicy language. For native speakers, this film is a reminder that no language has such creative swearing as the mother tongue — Bosnian/Croatian/Serbian as it is now called! (Viewers who must rely on subtitles, unfortunately miss much of this linguistic richness). In this sense, the film is also about the language(s) and the dialects that both united and separated the various nationalities of Yugoslavia.

Many reviews have noted that this is the first post-Yugoslav "Yugoslav" film, in whose production almost all parts of the former Yugoslavia

Rajko Grlić: *Border Post* (*Karaula*), 2006

participated. Private companies and ministries of culture in Croatia, Serbia, Slovenia, Bosnia and Herzegovina, Macedonia, and Kosovo (Montenegro is absent) provided funding and support, along with, Hungary, Austria, and England. The long list of production credits that opens the film attests to the multi-national nature of small-budget filmmaking in Europe, but is also a statement on the part of the director that cooperation among the former Yugoslav republics, the new countries in the Balkans, is possible. Moreover, the well-known and new names among the actors span the former Yugoslavia, and at the film's end, the full credits of the production teams reveal, if one studies the names, representatives of all the former republics. Thus the theme of "Yugoslavism" is introduced in the credits on a black background even before a single frame of the film's action is screened, and it is repeated again in the film's concluding credits. This theme is openly re-stated in the introductory note that follows the credits, still on a black background (in my translation): "The Yugoslav People's Army was founded during World War II by communist leader Josip Broz Tito, and for the following 50 years it was a symbol of the unity of multi-national Yugoslavia. All men between 18 and 27 had to spend at least 12 months in one of the units which numbered representatives of all the Yugoslav nationalities." An abbreviated translation of the latter part of this statement (seen on the screen) that the men had to serve "in one of its multi-ethnic units" loses the director's emphasis on "all" — that the army was a true unifier of Yugoslavia.

Only after the titles and this statement does the film actually open with a long tracking shot over water, culminating in an enigmatic and symbolic explosion in the water, which is never explained in the film's realistic narrative plane, but which clearly has metaphoric meaning and presages the explosion of Yugoslavia to come. The film is shot in widescreen, foregrounding in the repeated tracking shots of the lake and the surrounding countryside the pristine beauty of the landscape that was once Yugoslavia. The explosion is reflected in an eye, shot in close-up with a cut to the actors' credits, and a tilt shot up to the sky. This sequence is repeated at the very end of the film, thus creating a circular metaphoric and stylistic connection.

After a fade to black, there is a repeated cut in close-up to the eye of a soldier, lying in a boat as he watches another soldier having sex with a woman. Sex, it seems, is all that is on the minds of these young soldiers, and as they joke around about women, the film's "stud," soon to be identified as the Serb Ljuba Paunović, speaks, in the official socialist clichés that will mark the ironic linguistic level in the film. Berating his friend for seemingly not taking the opportunity to have sex with a local girl, he tells the young "doctor," in a double entendre, that the soldier's primary task is: "the sweet dreams of the population." As the naked men run and dive into the water, the final critical piece of information that places the film in its historical place and moment is written across the screen: "Lake Ohrid, 1987, Yugoslav-Albanian border." Could this heedless jump into the depth of the water by these bare-bottomed innocents, serve as a metaphor for what, perhaps, awaits them in the future?

As the more experienced man continues to joke about the other soldier's innocence, the younger man produces a pair of woman's panties with teddie bears on them, with the afterthought, that "gentlemen don't tell…". It is precisely this seemingly innocent, handsome, and beguiling young man, the "doctor," who will bed the wife of the commander of the outpost, and set in motion events that will lead to tragedy. As the men race to get back to their outpost, to arrive before their lieutenant, Safet Pašić does (his name suggesting he is a Bosnian Muslim), the more-experienced man continues his well-practiced official jargon, now describing the men's race as an Olympic event, and identifying himself as the Serb Paunović and his buddy, the "doc," as Siniša Siriščević from Split. So a Serb and Croat could still be bosom buddies in this prewar Yugoslavia. What unites them is not only their age, but clearly their middle-class upbringing, their education, and their light-hearted, and ironic attitude towards their military service and, by extension, the country that required it of them.

The men arrive in time to line up, but without a lost boot that Paunović lies to the commander he has had to clean. As Paunović clearly pokes fun, the commander asks: "Are you screwing with me?" (Or literally: "Are you fucking me?"), and then answers his own question with a yes. (He employs the most frequently used verb not only in the film, but in army jargon, and the broader society at large). It is here that the struggle begins between the smart-ass soldier and the frustrated, clearly outwitted commander, a struggle that will take a tragic turn at the film's denouement.

The everyday details of the soldiers' daily lives in this god-forsaken border post — what they eat, how they exercise, but mostly how they relax and horse around listening to contemporary music — are given in an almost documentary fashion, with an energetic moving camera following their activities in mid-shot and close-up. The real-life nature of this place and time is underscored by repeated TV reports which document the larger social and political events that reach even this distant corner of Yugoslavia. Barely heard, as the men go about their business, is an announcement that there is to be a scholarly conference titled: "After Tito: Tito," and that workers have visited the birthplace of this "greatest son of the nations and the nationalities" and that a Slobodan Milošević was to visit Kosovo… This seems to have absolutely no effect on the men, and is part of that official jargon that, on the one hand, still retreads the

Titoist past, and on the other, presages the major events to come, of which the men, and, the population at large, are blissfully ignorant.

Once the director has invited the viewer to relive the last days of innocence, or at least, ignorance, in a Yugoslavia that is still clinging to its socialist past, the plot, as the saying goes, thickens. In a comic scene, the commander Pašić, orders Siniša, the "doc" (who has graduated from medical school but never practiced), into his office to show him (and us!), in close-up, the sore on his penis. Syphilis, says the doc. A telling conversation takes place as Pašić asks for the doc's "communist word of honor," to keep things quiet, only to find out that the doc is not a party-member, and moreover, isn't sure he can give his word, because he "doesn't want to die." Pašić, for all his flaws, belongs to the older communist generation, while the baby-faced doctor is part of the cynical generation which seems to believe in nothing. When the commander discovers that it will take three weeks of shots to cure his syphilis, he orders a lock-down and full combat preparedness at the outpost, cancelling all passes (including his own) because "Albanians are lining up on our border," and "the enemy never sleeps." When the soldiers ask how long this will last, his answer is, at least three weeks. It is not farfetched at this point to identify the commander's made-up Albanian threat (so he can hide his syphilis) with the imaginative and deadly warmongering of higher-ups that lead to Yugoslavia's disintegration.

In order to be cured and to fool his wife, Pašić sends Siniša, the young doc, to town to get the necessary medical supplies, and to tell his lonely and suspicious wife that he, as commander on duty, cannot visit her. Back at the border post some soldiers fall for this ruse, training for a fight with Albanians, while Paunović (Ljuba), who continues to horse around, points out that none of them has ever seen an Albanian. Siniša's trip to town (shot on location in Macedonia) yields an image of useless, frenetic military activity, and a Serb colonel, nick-named Rade the Orchid (the director's ironic nod to a well-known war criminal of the 1990s from the region), who worries about his flowers, which "produce oxygen without which we cannot breathe." In the outpost, suspicions about the non-existent Albanians and Pašić's motivations for the lock-down are merged with continuing TV news that on "the 42rd anniversary of the victory over fascism and the 7th anniversary of Tito's death" a Yugoslav youth relay was to be run from Kosovo all the way to Belgrade to "demonstrate that we are still following in Tito's path." Much of the film's black humor is found not only in the situational comedy ("until we heal his prick, we are at war with Albania" says the town doctor), but in the various linguistic puns, the raw, juicy, swear-laden language of the recruits, and the stultifying and soporific official government jargon, delivered on television, and repeated with wonderful irony by the doctor's buddy, Ljuba Paunović. The ever-present mother-swears, addressed by everyone to everyone, may be funny, but they also point to the deeply patriarchal machismo culture, not only of the military, but of the whole Balkan society. Everyone gets either literally or metaphorically "screwed" in this film.

As the men believe and don't believe the story of the Albanians, some practice their drills and others, primarily Siniša and Ljuba, horse around, and smoke hash, deciding, however, not to give it to the guard dog, because "someone has to protect Yugoslavia." When Paunović decides to rearrange the words of an official slogan on a building about protecting "brotherhood and unity," into "electrical orgasm," (the title of a musical band in Belgrade, he tells the commander), he sets in motion the conflict with authority that will end in tragedy. After Pašić slaps him for the offense, Paunović slowly seeks revenge by insisting, in his best socialist lingo, that he must go on foot to Tito's grave in Belgrade to pay respects "for everything that he (Tito) has done for the brotherhood and unity of our peoples and our socialist collective." The gullible Pašić wavers between belief and disbelief, but must, in the end, send Paunović to the colonel (Rade the Orchid) in town, to carry out his homage to Tito.

As Pašić continues to send the doctor on errands to town and to his wife, the physical attraction between the young doctor and the lonely, abandoned wife takes on a life of its own. Official public life and private fates intersect as the siren marking the anniversary of Tito's passing is heard in the town marketplace over a private, sexually charged conversation between Siniša and Mirjana, who finally learn each other's names, well on their way to their inevitable affair.

During his repeated meetings with his commander to give him shots in the behind (with some comic physical elements), the doc, Siniša becomes the lieutenant's confidante, learning of Pašić's own story, a typical biography of socialist progress from a poor peasant shepherd to a university-educated officer. Of course, in Pašić's drunken retelling, he ran away from the sheep and the Bosnian mountains only to find himself in this mountainous, sheep-infested god-forsaken hole elsewhere in Yugoslavia, from which he is so desperately trying to escape. To keep the men at combat readiness, Pašić destroys the radios the men use to listen to pop music (but which also keep broadcasting Tito announcements), and seemingly believing in his own propaganda about the Albanians, works himself and some of the men into a paranoid frenzy, with night maneuvers in camouflage gear.

In the meantime, during their third meeting, as Siniša delivers Pašić's salary to his wife, the two lovers finally consummate the visual and verbal affair they have been having since the moment they met. Their passionate coupling seems to be a momentary escape from this stultifying, provincial hell-hole, with Mirjana's self-aware commentary on how "stupid it is to be a woman" (with your dowry, sheets, and towels stowed away even before you can walk). When Siniša tries to calm her, saying "everything will be fine," she responds with "nothing will be fine," a comment that foreshadows not only the fate of their relationship, but of the whole country as well.

Back at the border post, Paunović continues his campaign to go to Belgrade to pay homage to Tito, clearly playing Pašić for a fool. As he and Pašić get drunk together, they rope in the sober doctor to drive them to the local *kafana* to celebrate their last night before Ljuba is to report to Rade the Orchid for his trip. While Pašić still cannot decide whether Paunović is kidding about walking to Tito's grave and is going to "screw him over" with this stunt, the two men, in a drunken stupor, make up, despite the fact that, when asked, the doc says that Ljuba will in fact screw the lieutenant. It is no surprise, then, that when told by the colonel that a TV crew is all ready to accompany this pilgrimage to Tito's grave, Paunović disavows the trip, saying he doesn't want to go and with copious tears tells the colonel Rade the Orchid that Pašić made him do it. While the doc and Mirjana, in bed, discuss the possibility of telling Pašić about their affair (he might kill you, she says), the colonel is apologizing to the journalists for this fiasco, telling his assistant to "give them flowers and drinks" and then, back in his office, proceeds to beat Paunović as he continues to cry.

The physical and verbal comedy in the "homage to Tito" narrative line is interspersed with the increasingly serious repercussions of the affair between the doc and the commander's wife. Moreover, the farcical tone of the film (carried out beautifully in the outstanding, over-the top acting of Sergej Trifunović as Ljuba Paunović), takes on a sinister note with a cut to the now dark lake accompanied by ominous whooshing sounds, and, in close-up, the dripping water from a leaky roof back at the border post.

The rest of the film takes place in darkness and in the rain, as Pašić, berated by the colonel for supposedly making Paunović go on the pilgrimage to Tito's grave, finally breaks down: seeing his career in ruins, with no hope of ever getting a transfer out of this hell-hole, he swears back at his superior. Now the raw swearwords and the ethnic slurs, which were funny throughout most of the film (as when the Macedonian Mirjana pokes fun at her Croatian lover from Dalmatia), acquire a life-ending fatality which is soon fulfilled. The sad Bosnian music that accompanies this scene announces an imminent tragedy. After saying to his underling, "bring me that circumcised idiot on a chain like a dog," the Serb colonel smiles knowingly as he hears Milošević speak on the radio in Kosovo that "it was never in the nature of the Serbian and Montenegrin people to retreat when faced with obstacles, to demobilize when it is time to fight…" Once again individual personal conflicts foreshadow and parallel the larger conflict yet to come.

As everything begins to fall apart and take on a tragic tone, the lovers also feel the end is near: Siniša, looking at Mirjana's half-packed suitcase, ponders his commitment to her, and in vain tries to console her, telling her to wait until this is over, when "normal life" will come. She responds with a knowing finality that "there is no normal life," that "everyone talks of normal life, but something more important always comes up." As he makes love to her for what we know to be one final time, it becomes clear that even that life-affirming passion can no longer provide escape from the literally dark reality that surrounds them.

When Siniša leaves, a desperate, half-dressed Mirjana, fearing that her husband will kill her lover, races off into the night after him, hitching a ride to the border post on the army vehicle sent to fetch Pašić to the colonel.

A series of rapid events and misunderstandings, all played out in the dark, all but abandon the comedy in this tragic-comedy, or perhaps render the comedy, in the Yugoslav tradition, truly black. The rain-soaked meeting between Pašić and Paunović ("I was only joking," the soldier tells his commander) takes a deadly turn when Pašić savagely beats Paunović after hearing from him that his wife is "fucking" another man. Paunović responds in kind, beating Pašić to death with a heavy stick. As the doc sees Pašić die, he nods to Paunović who is hiding in the bushes, and who presumably runs away, as we never see him again or find out if there were repercussions for his, now, deadly prank and fight. Is it coincidental, we might ask, that it is the Bosnian who dies, the Serb who kills and the Croat, perhaps somewhat wiser, is relatively unscathed at the film's end? This seems too simplistic an explanation for the overall tragedy played out in the film's final scenes.

As some soldiers come running to see the fight, others yell "Albanians," mistaking the army vehicle sent by the colonel for the enemy. (The intermittent, poorly working car lights are seen as enemy signals). In the rapid firing that ensues, accompanied by bravado shouts of pride in Yugoslavia, one lone officer who escapes the army vehicle single-handedly gets the border post to surrender — a no longer funny commentary on the preparedness and commitment of military and its future in the coming war. The soldiers seem not to notice that this supposed Albanian enemy is swearing at them in their mother tongue. Unfortunately, other soldiers in the vehicle and Mirjana herself fall victim to the shooting. As the doc leans over Mirjana's dead body, looking up at him with innocent, open eyes (the first of many innocent victims of the war to come), the film's main narrative ends with a close-up of her eye and then a moving train reflected in it.

This reflection serves as a transition in time and space, and from darkness to light, in the film's epilogue. In overhead, panoramic tracking shots, the rushing train, with the Yugoslav red star prominently displayed on the locomotive and carrying the demobilized doctor (we ask where?), cuts through the bright, magnificent landscape, ending over the now blue water as credits roll. Presumably the doctor is headed back home to Dalmatia and the beautiful Adriatic Sea which he had promised to show Mirjana. Coming from land-bound Macedonia, she had never seen the sea and was fated never to see it, just as her now dead husband was fated never to escape the mountains. The last sequence of the film shows that rushing train of socialist progress taking the beautiful country into an uncertain future. The accompanying haunting music, heard intermittently in the film, of Bosnian sevdalinke, sad love songs, does not bode well for that future.

The Border Post (*Karaula*), Serbia, Croatia, Slovenia, Macedonia, Bosnia and Herzegovina, Hungary, Austria, UK, 2006. Color, 94 min.
Director: Rajko Grlić
Script: Rajko Grlić and Ante Tomić (based upon the novel *Nothing Can Suprise Us* by A. Tomić)
Director of Photography: Slobodan Trninić
Music: Sanja Ilić (composer), Suzana Perić (editing)
Editing: Andrija Zafranović
Cast: Toni Gojanović, Sergej Trifunović, Emir Hadžihafizbegović, Verica Nedeska, Bogdan Diklić
Producer: Ademir Kenović
Production: Refresh production, Sarajevo; Vertigo / Emotionfilm, Ljubljana; Sektor film, Skopje; Propeler film, Zagreb i NP7, Zagreb; Croatian Radiotelevision, Zagreb; Yodi movie craftsman, Beograd; Film & music entertainment, London

Ognjen Sviličić: *Sorry for Kung Fu* (*Oprosti za kung fu*, 2004); *Armin* (2007)
reviewed by Hana Jušić

In the late 1990s Croatian cinematography slowly started emerging from the now already proverbial "dark ages" with the appearance of films that sought to distance themselves from the sway of dark topics, clichéd portrayal of the war, and naïve propaganda about the post-war era. These new films attempted to re-build credibility that had been lost with the domestic audience. A part of this wave was *Wish I Were a Shark* (1999), a debut comedy by Ognjen Sviličić (born 1971), which drew filmgoers back to the movie theaters at a time when most of them were rather unenthusiastic about domestic production

One of the biggest objections to the Croatian film of the nineties was rigid acting and imposition of a form of the standard language which did not reflect reality. Sviličić's film, by contrast, was announced as sparkling with the southern mischief of the Split region and featuring colorful personages and tricksters. It was also spiced up with an ironic perspective on the rural penetrating the urban milieu. The film, however, did not quite live up to expectations. Its mosaic composition (used as well by Gonzáles Iñárritu) was handled in a somewhat unsophisticated manner and the directorial choices are often unpolished and unelaborated. Regrettably this is not done for the purpose of stylization, which would later become one of Sviličić's strengths as a director. The biggest problem are the characters who are reduced to clichés of a particular mindset. An almost notorious example are two characters from the hills (*Vlaji* as they are known in the local jargon) who have come down to the coastal urban area of Split in search of fun. Ridiculing precisely such individuals fit well with the widespread wave of intolerance in the 1990s towards the local "hillbillies" and Herzegovinians who had moved into the urban areas, some of them making profits in shady dealings, and locals felt they brought with them an unwelcome cultural influence. This made them an easy target for derision, and Sviličić too shows them as one-dimensional characters trapped at the level of caricatures or *stand-up* imitators without providing any critical distance despite his amicable jabs.

When Sviličić made his next feature, *Sorry for Kung Fu*, in 2004, the idea of it being situated in the Dalmatian highlands (*Zagora*), among those same "hillbillies" was somewhat worrisome as was the fact that the film was announced as yet another comedy, this time with a dark slant. However, it was precisely this film that came to be praised by the critics as an exceptionally subtle work with a finely calibrated directorial touch that introduced new ideas to Croatian cinematography. On the surface of things the film depicts a specific mentality and its system of beliefs and values — which made Sviličić vulnerable to stereotyping and generalizations. Nonetheless he succeeds in creating exceptionally refined and nuanced characters, while the directorial coarseness from the earlier film is employed here as a part of overall stylization which stands in a dialogic relation to the subject of film.

The plot follows Mira (Daria Lorenci) who comes back to her village in the Dalmatian hinterland from a lengthy stay in Germany. Her recently renovated parental home is situated in a rugged and barren area surrounded by mountains and this landscape (just as in Papić's *Handcuffs*) appears to be one of the principal protagonists. The father is a typical product of the environment — strict, patriarchal, verbally parsimonious, protective of his value system — while his wife accommodates to his every whim but also holds the upper hand. Mira is in the final stage of pregnancy and does not feel inclined to discuss the baby's father. Her traditional parents make an attempt at accepting this, but at the same time they seek the services of a spirited matchmaker. Bizarre suitors keep showing up at Mira's doorstep, but she turns every single one down, protesting her parents' efforts and sinking ever more into desperation as she no longer belongs to this mindset. She ends up giving birth to a baby with Chinese features which causes a full-blown scandal in the small provincial hospital. The father is shocked and hurt and Mira has to leave along with her new-born. When she comes back after a few years with the little boy, her father is on his deathbed with lung cancer and the two finally bond and make their peace.

The narrative line of this film is entirely stripped down and minimalistic: we follow Mira from her arrival to her departure in a series of scenes that function almost as tableaux. Sviličić is a great storyteller and in a chain of linear scenes that provide the basic set-up he builds an organic narrative whole that draws the spectator in despite a certain amount of restraint and distance. It may be relevant to mention that this film preceded the so-called stream of *slow cinema* which is currently rather visible at the festivals and in independent films in general. In Europe, for instance, the leader in this category is Romanian film, and this same tendency can also be observed now in Croatian cinematography, in particular with younger directors and in debut short films by the students graduating from the Zagreb Academy of Dramatic Art.

The basic feature of this orientation is minimal use of stylistic devices, a prevalence of lengthy medium shots without camera movement, with an imperfect perspective on the subject or scene. The focus of the dramaturgy is on everyday and accidental situations, and dialogues are measured and not subordinated to the spectator's understanding of the story. In Sviličić's films we see an inclination towards the same stylistic choices and narrative approaches. From the very beginning he plays with the bleakness and ruggedness of the landscape which is often shown in long shots with characters who appear small and lost in the harsh and barren terrain.

Ognjen Sviličić: *Sorry for Kung Fu* (*Oprosti za kung fu*), 2004

In addition, Sviličić tends to depart from a customary organization of dialogic scenes in which he does not show close-ups of the characters, but prefers a broader perspective. There are instances when the central character has his back turned towards the camera or the vision of the scene is not ideal. Similarly, the editing cuts are deliberately rougher. It is unfortunate that Sviličić is not consistent when it comes to his directorial decisions and after deliberate minimalism in some segments of the film there follow scenes with an almost sit-com perspective such as unmotivated camera drives, close-ups when a character makes a humorous remark, a spot-like shot of the matchmaker's expensive car, etc. A similar mixed approach is visible sometimes in the dialogues and characterization. Dialogues are elliptical on occasion and cut short just as the shots are, but sometimes they reveal the type of humor we saw in his *Wish I Were a Shark* where the primitivism and customs of the region are foregrounded. This at times makes the supporting characters into one-dimensional caricatures, and dialogues resonate with replicas from a TV series. Luckily there are not many such moments in the film and for the most part they surface in scenes with Mira's suitors of whom one is childishly silly, another a covert Muslim (nearly forced by Mira's father to take his pants down), and yet another, mildly retarded.

These infrequent forays into uni-dimensionality are saved by the actors whose performances are subtle, and this especially goes for Lorenci about whose character we actually don't know much and who keeps silent most of the time. This, however, does not prevent the spectator from empathizing with her. We could say the same for Filip Radoš, an actor who became known for his comical interpretations of people with a traditional worldview. He manages to subdue his character adequately, creating a touching portrait in this film of a man who is slowly losing his race with time and has to watch his system of values disappear before his very eyes.

The plot of the film revolves around what is essentially a socio-ethnological problem: how an "undeveloped" environment lives up to challenges that fly in the face of its entrenched values. Sviličić does not fall victim to setting forth any theory. At all levels this remains a story about individuals with a narrative line that is simple, stripped-down, and devoid of the author's commentary or any type of ancillary connotations. The plot is essentially tailored to the contours of the characters and in a sense fol-

Ognjen Sviličić: *Armin*, 2007

lows their own simplicity. Precisely because of this quality it might be fruitful to apply the literary category of *free indirect speech* to this film. Although in the third person singular and seemingly neutral, the narration is marked with the character's cognitive processes, his/her beliefs and even speech habits. In the case of Sviličić's film the camera shows the action in an ostensibly unbiased manner, however directorial choices such as broad unempathetic angles, absence of camera movement, abrupt editing, barren landscape and an ugly gray set of interiors correspond to the characters' perceptions and the general mindset of the region. One has a sense therefore that the very texture of the film was filtered through the minds of the highlanders. Sviličić speaks of them by coloring his stylistic choices with their vision of the world.

Three years after his *Sorry for Kung Fu* Croatian filmgoers eagerly expected Sviličić's film *Armin* (2007) which, in terms of the author's *Weltanschauung*, is rather similar to its predecessor, although its realization differs substantially. *Armin* was quite successful in movie theaters and at various film festivals, and perhaps the only criticism one could voice from a dramaturgical point of view is that it would have been better off as a mid-length feature.

Armin could be compared to the films of Mike Leigh more readily than to those of *slow cinema*. In this film, just as in Mike Leigh's, we cannot speak of a marked directorial stylization. The shots are simplistic, one might even say they underscore the aesthetics of the ugly, while the visual style is unmarked with stress on the mise-en-scène. Compositionally, the perspective is subordinated to the action. The dramaturgy is linear just as it is in *Sorry for Kung Fu* and it unfolds around a trip to Zagreb undertaken by a father and a son. The opening of the story picks them up and the end drops them off at exactly the same location. The plot centers on their relationship, their failure to communicate, as well as the father's inadaptability to the big city. They set off from a small Bosnian town for Zagreb so that the son, Armin, can audition at a hotel for a west European film crew which is preparing a film on the Bosnian war. Sviličić reaches again here for a mindset as the framework for the film (instead of Leigh's English working class these are Bosnians lost in Zagreb).

The irony is twofold: wealthy and alienated westerners shoot a film on the war in Bosnia, while the audition takes place in Zagreb which, with its cold and modern contours, appears to two Bosnians to be an extension of Western Europe. The father-son pair feels out of place although the film-in-film is supposed to be about people exactly like them. In the end, the principal role is given not to an authentic actor, but to a boy whose father is depicted as a typical snobbish dweller of Zagreb. Despite the rejection, Armin's father insists that the film crew at least give Armin a chance and hear him play his accordion. Reluctantly, they agree, but during the performance Armin has an epileptic seizure. Perplexed by this unexpected situation, the western director offers to make a documentary about the young man's illness which was worsened by the war, but Armin and his father firmly turn this offer down.

For the sake of metatextual interpretation, we should mention an external detail: Sviličić spotted Armin Omerović (the young actor playing the part of Armin in the film) at an audition for Branko Schmidt's film *The Melon Route* when he came from Bosnia with his father. This real-life event was used by Sviličić as the core for the project. For a moment we may be tempted to think that Sviličić condescends towards his character just as does the director in the movie who wishes to make a film about Armin. On second thought, however, we see that the real director ironizes his position through self-reflection in the character of the foreign director eager to make a film about "a sorry human fate" (similarly, just as the putative film, *Armin* is a Croatian-Bosnian-German coproduction).

Mike Leigh's films are recalled not only in connection to the style, but also because of the problems between father and son, who are emotionally deprived and fail to establish a valid relationship up to the point when they are both rejected and thus forced into an emotional catharsis. Sviličić employs a typical Leigh-style relationship between parent and child in which the former is touchingly lost while the latter has an almost animal-like aggression and lack of articulation owing to his own helplessness and failure to assimilate. One need only recall relationships between fathers and sons in Leigh's titles such as *Meantime*, *All or Nothing*, or relationships between mothers and daughters such as in his films *Life Is Sweet* and *Secrets and Lies*. The incompatibility of the characters is doubly underscored in Sviličić's film because of their otherness (Bosnians in Zagreb). The undercurrent that juxtaposes the two different milieus and perceptions of the world, provincial and westernized-urban, is thus present also in this film and becomes more palpable in the scenes of the father and the son in the cold hotel environment, the father admiring McDonalds, or buying a drink for complete strangers who mock him, or lighting up a cigarette at breakfast in an expensive non-smoking establishment. Luckily Sviličić escapes creating stereotypes. For instance, Emir Hadžihafizbegović, the actor who plays the role of Armin's father, has been perceived in contemporary Croatian popular culture as the embodiment of a typical Bosnian (from various sitcoms to commercials), but in this film he depicts clashes of mentalities with great emotional subtlety.

In this contemplation of Zagreb as an alienated westernized metropolis one could perhaps object to the occasional long shot of the urban skyline or exteriors of the sterile-looking hotel which serve as superfluous directorial comments and slow down the action unnecessarily. Another objection, as pointed out earlier, is the length of the film which contributes to dramaturgical imbalance. Considering that the film relies on classical structure rather than a more meditative *slow cinema* narration, one can pinpoint segments that could have been imbedded more firmly in the plot. For instance, the first part of the film leads to the moment of audition and generates a certain amount of tension. After Armin does not come anywhere near to being considered for the role, the viewer begins to expect a conclusion, but the film is, in fact, just half-way through. Armin's playing of the accordion along with the epileptic seizure come as an unexpected peak. Following this, the German director in the putative film suggests making a documentary about Armin, which produces another peak-reversal-humiliation sequence just before the end.

But these minor objections aside, Sviličić appears to be a stylistically and dramaturgically thoughtful director who has introduced to Croatian film emotional subtlety particularly visible in virtuosic elliptical dialogues and stripped-down narrative structures, and who has proven to have just the right touch when it comes to a minimalistic use of stylistic devices.

Translated by Aida Vidan

Wish I Were a Shark (*Da mi je biti morski pas*), Croatia, 1999. Color, 75 min.
Director: Ognjen Sviličić
Script: Ognjen Sviličić
Director of Photography: Vedran Šamanović
Music: Ognjen Sviličić
Editing: Staša Čelan
Set Designer: Goran Stepan
Costumes: Ruta Knežević
Cast: Josip Zovko (Mate), Vedran Mlikota (Kristijan), Elvis Bošnjak (Ive Dumanić), Bruna Bebić-Tudor (Dode Dumanić), Edita Majić (eccentric painter), Siniša Ružić, Mate Ćurić, Ecija Ojdanić, Jasna Jukić, Vanča Kljaković, Saulle Ashimova, Ichiro Takana, Snježana Sinovčić
Production: Croatian Radiotelevision

Sorry for Kung Fu (*Oprosti za kung fu*), Croatia, 2004. Color, 70 min.
Director: Ognjen Sviličić
Script: Ognjen Sviličić
Director of Photography: Vedran Šamanović
Music: Maro Merket, Ognjen Sviličić
Editing: Vjeran Pavlinić
Set Designer: Mladen Ožbolt
Costumes: Ruta Knežević
Cast: Daria Lorenci (Mira), Filip Radoš (Jozo), Vera Zima (Kate), Vedran Mlikota (Veliki), Luka Petrušić (Marko), Ivica Bašić (Mate), Yong Long Dai (boy), Josip Zovko (Ćaćo), Davor Svedružić (Begić), Zoran Ćubrilo (doctor), Jadranka Đokić (Zorica), Barbara Vicković (nurse), Mate Ćurić (Krule), Milivoj Gaće (Jović), Branimir Rakić (Tadija), Ivan Brkić (Ljubo), Jolanda Tudor (Mare), Trpimir Jukić (boy), Boženko Dedić (waiter), Marija Škaričić (woman having a baby 1), Ecija Ojdanić (woman having a baby 2), Emil Glad (patient), Jadranka Matković (Jehovah's Witness)
Production: Croatian Radiotelevision

Armin, Croatia, Bosnia and Herzegovina, Germany, 2007. Color, 82 min.
Director: Ognjen Sviličić
Script: Ognjen Sviličić
Director of Photography: Stanko Herceg
Music: Michael Bauer, Georg Karger, Peter Holzapfel, Zoran Kesić
Editing: Vjeran Pavlinić
Set Design: Mladen Ožbolt
Costumes: Blanka Budak
Cast: Emir Hadžihafizbegović (father), Armin Omerović (Armin), Marie Baumer, Barbara Prpić, Jens Munchow, Daria Lorenci, Enis Bešlagić, Ranko Zidarić
Producer: Damir Terešak, Markus Halberschmidt, Mirko Galić
Co-producers: Ademir Kenović, Marcelo Busse
Production: Maxima film, Croatian Radiotelevision

Antonio Nuić: *Sex, Drink and Bloodshed* (*Seks, piće i krvoprolić*e, 2004); *All for Free* (*Sve džaba*, 2006); *Donkey* (*Kenjac*, 2009)
reviewed by Mario Kozina

Antonio Nuić's entrance into Croatian cinema was greeted with general approval. As a student of the Academy of Dramatic Art in Zagreb he made two short films, *On Site* (*Na mjestu događaja*, 1998) and a TV drama *Give Them Back Their Dinamo* (*Vratite im Dinamo*) in 1999 for which he was conferred an award at the Academy of Dramatic Art Students' Festival (FRKA). His debut on the big screen was as a director of one of the three soccer-related stories from the omnibus *Sex, Drink and Bloodshed* (*Seks, piće i krvoprolić*e, 2004).[1] Although the quality of the omnibus was uneven, critics praised its move away from (post)war themes and its focus on contemporary, urban subject matter. Many critics praised Antonio Nuić's story as the most successful of the three, and luckily,[2] his good fortune continued in his feature works: *All for Free* (*Sve džaba*, 2006) and *Donkey* (*Kenjac*, 2009).[3]

The appeal of these films stems in part from the way Nuić depicts the everyday life of his characters. Croatian cinema of the nineties was heavily infused with contemporary politics. The films were burdened with (post)war themes and their authors often used them as an ideological vehicle to *spread the truth* about everything that happened during and after the war. In Nuić's films the war is a part of their diegetic universe, but in terms of the plot and ideological stance, it is relegated to the background. For example, one of the most surprising elements of his story in *Sex, Drink and Bloodshed* is the lack of an explicit link between the characters and the postwar period, especially when compared with other works of popular culture situated in the same milieu of the Dinamo [Za-

---

1] The omnibus was a debut for two more people who placed contemporary Croatian cinema in their debt. Zvonimir Jurić is currently one of the most promising Croatian film directors, and Boris T. Matić helped to develop the domestic festival scene. He also produced this one, as well as two of Nuić's feature films.

2] For example: On the cover of the DVD there is a quote of Dragan Jurak's, film critic for the political weekly *Feral Tribune*, who said: "Antonio Nuić is definitely a promising boy. A savior. Croatian film hasn't seen a feature-film debut as good as this one not only since [Dalibor] Matanić's, or since [Vinko] Brešan's, but since Zoran Tadić's *Rhythm of the Crime* in 1981."

3] *All for Free* was awarded four Golden Arenas at the national festival of feature film in Pula (for best film, director, screenplay and the supporting actress, Nataša Janjić), while *Donkey* won three awards at the same festival. Nuić won The Golden Arena for best screenplay, Mirko Pivčević was given an award for his brilliant cinematography, while Srđan Gulić was awarded for his touching score. *Donkey* also won an Oktavijan, the diploma awarded by the Croatian Society of Film Critics.

Antonio Nuić: *All for Free* (*Sve džaba*), 2006

greb] soccer club fans — the Bad Blue Boys.[4] These characters were often depicted as a group of individuals who hadn't found their way during the period of economic transition, who drown their frustration in alcohol, drugs, violence, and crime, and who transfer ethnic tensions from the battlefield to the soccer field. Nuić kept only their aggression and addiction to alcohol, and these function as a buffer that keeps them from confronting their personal problems. Similarly, *All for Free* shows a country ruined by bad postwar politics, although the unfortunate socio-political climate isn't as important as the consequences of the destructive patriarchal mentality that shapes the lives of the characters. The plot of *Donkey* takes place in the summer of 1995, the summer of the Storm military operation that marked the end of the war in Croatia.[5] The echoes of the war can be seen and heard on news broadcasts on the radio and TV-screens, while the distant gunfire in the dark increases the feeling of emotional anxiety which dominates the plot. Also, the characters of disabled people are important to mention because they reflect the detachment of Nuić's poetic from the cinema of the previous decade. Miro (Bojan Navojec) from *All for Free* and Boro's brother Pero (Emir Hadžihafizbegović) in *Donkey* lost their limbs during the war, but they are not presented as pathetic reminders of enemy aggression. Their physical disability is analogous to the emotional disability of the main characters. The drama of both films comes from the protagonists' subconscious need to confront the reasons that brought them to the state of emotional impairment. Nuić articulates their efforts through plot construction, mise-en-scène, and visual solutions, and the roots of his thematic and formal preoccupations can be traced back to the omnibus *Sex, Drink and Bloodshed*.

Choosing to place the plot of his first big-screen film in urban Zagreb may seem atypical for the rest of Nuić's work which takes place in the provincial parts of Bosnia and Herzegovina; however, here he introduces key motifs he will continue to develop in his later films. In the opening shots

---

[4] For example: Borivoj Radaković's play *Welcome to Blue Hell* (*Dobrodošli u plavi pakao*, 1994), (the soundtrack for its theater adaptation, as well as for the omnibus, was developed by *Pips, Chips & Videoclips*, a band that holds an important place in soccer pop-culture), and Alen Bović's novel *Metastaze* (*Metastases*, 2006) and its film adaptation of the same name (2009) directed by Branko Schmidt.

[5] One can even draw a parallel between the end of the war in a broader historical sense and the tensions that have been relieved between the characters.

we see a group of soccer fans beat up a man.[6] Through the fast exchange of medium shots of the four people involved, filmed with a hand-held camera, Nuić creates a strong sense of a closed male group grounded on exclusion whose members are united by their aggression. We don't see the person they are hitting, nor do we see the setting where the action takes place. The impression is heightened when the plot moves from unidentified urban exteriors to the more intimate space of one of the character's living room. The choice of space can be understood literally (motivated realistically by the plot), but Nuić uses the mise-en-scène to heighten its metaphorical dimension.

The characters talk about Njonjo's marriage and his relationship with his wife Martina (Leona Paraminski). Her presence is mostly felt off-screen. She very rarely enters the circle where the guys talk, smoke and drink, never crossing the living room threshold. In fact, she gives the impression of being an angry harridan, always yelling and cursing, who haunts the apartment and the men's conversation. The guys in the living room discuss the fact that the day Martina supposedly got pregnant with Njonjo she had also slept with both Mario (Bojan Navojec) and Goc (Rakan Rushaidat), which makes them potential fathers of the baby. This knowledge could have led to a confrontation among them, maybe even to the disruption in their friendship, but it does not. With the help of alcohol, cigarettes and soccer chants, the subversive potential of the information is toned down through friendly teasing, which reaffirms the mechanisms of patriarchal mentality that led to Njonjo's discomfort. This also explains why he married Martina. It was to prove his maturity and sense of responsibility, although he lacks both. Martina's presence reminds Njonjo of his own weaknesses, which is why she becomes an object of loathing. The anxiety that lurks beneath Njonjo and Martina's relationship is emphasized by the ambiguous ending: Njonjo leaves the circle of his friends to look through the window, and then the film cuts to the bedroom where his wife and child are trying to sleep. Seeing these two shots together brings back the metaphorical dimension of the living-room drama, while the ominous final fade-out once more destabilizes the false reconciliation among the friends.

The emotional interplay between a man, his family or friends, the mentality of the society he grew up in, and a woman will be the dominant motif of the rest of Nuić's works, although he plays his cards differently each time. His next film *All for Free*, set in central Bosnia, begins with a story about four deadbeat friends stationed in the town of Vareš, who, much like the soccer fans from the previous film, find themselves in a situation where the paternity of one of them is brought into question. Josip (Franjo Dijak) has slept with Marko's (Enis Bešlagić) wife and she is pregnant. While in the previous films friendly teasing releases the tension of the situation, here one of Josip's comments results in Marko killing Jo-

---

6] The first part of the film is concentrated on the Bad Blue Boys who get beaten up by Torcida, fans from their rival club, Hajduk, from Split. They blame Njonjo's wife Martina for the beating, because she called him on his cell phone while they were in hiding, exposing them to the angry Torcida.

sip and Miro, and he himself ends up in jail. Only one of them, Goran (Rakan Rushaidat) survives the bloodshed. He decides to sell his house and leave his hometown to travel the unknown.

The part of the film before the credits has several analogies with Nuić's previous film. The plot deals with the problem of friends and paternity, and the characters are played by the same actors.[7] However, the revelation of infidelity, partly because it happens after the wedding, has different consequences here than it did before. It destroys their friendly/familial community.[8] The locus of the revelation is once more at the table where friends/brothers gather to drink together, while the presence of a woman again haunts the conversation. Unlike in the earlier film, in *All for Free* the anxiety that smolders underneath the friendship is brought to its logical end, literally destroying their lives. Goran's voyage can therefore be understood as a search for a new family. Having sold everything he owns, he travels from town to town with a luncheon van offering drinks for free in exchange for his collocutors' life stories. Thereby he reconstructs the situation where men gather to drink, smoke, and sing together as a way of forgetting their problems and channeling their suppressed discontent. It is no wonder that during his travels he witnesses different faces of the same oppressive mentality which led to his unhappiness in the first place, and from which he tried to escape.

However, Goran's voyage stops when he meets Maja (Nataša Janjić), a woman imprisoned in the same situation. After her fiancé is killed she lives emotionally and financially dependent on his brother. Like Martina from Nuić's previous film and Marko's wife from the beginning of this one, Maja is perceived not as an individual, but as a material possession that can be transferred from brother to brother. However, Goran sees her as a person, and the sparks of his romantic interest change something in her own understanding of herself. Contrary to the audience's expectations Goran and Maja do not end up together, but Maja, as suggested by the last shot, manages to leave the oppressive situation in which she has been living. However, her future remains precarious. As suggested by Goran's unsuccessful travels around the country (and by the title itself),[9] one can only wonder if it is possible to break free from the chains of patriarchal mentality.

To answer this question Nuić again "rotates" some of his cast in his next film. In *Donkey* Nataša Janjić plays the lead female character. This time she is Jasna, a woman from Zagreb who hasn't finished her studies because she marries an emotionally distant man. We meet her on a trip to Drinovci, a village in the ethnically Croatian part of south Herzegovina (in Bosnia and Herzegovina) where her husband Boro was born and to which they travel with their son Luka (Roko Roglić). Although the casting of Nataša Janjić in some ways represents a link between Nuić's first and second feature, the dramatic tension of *Donkey* is again related to his male

---

7] The only exception is casting of Enis Bešlagić who replaced Hrvoje Kečkeš.
8] In one part of the film Goran states that his friends were the only family he had.
9] The meaning of the title in Croatian can also be understood as an irony, because it can also mean *all in vain*.

Antonio Nuić: *Donkey (Kenjac)*, 2009

protagonist. Furthermore, because of the way the cinematic techniques are used to present its plot and character(s), *Donkey* is Nuić's first film that could be completely understood as the inner drama of its main male protagonist. The plot builds upon the archetypal conflict between father and son. Boro's father Paško (Tonko Lonza) has never loved him, nor has he loved Boro's mother. As a matter of fact, Paško had behaved so viciously toward her that she committed suicide by drowning herself in a local lake. Boro repeats his father's mistakes, although he is not aware of his own behavior.

Similarly to Goran's voyage in *All for Free*, the story of Boro's return to his native village has a strong psychoanalytical subtext that is now enriched with the smart use of cinematic techniques. The opening, which is filmed in black and white, suggests that the story takes place in another space and time that do not have to be understood in a literal, historical sense. This kind of opening could also suggest that the viewer is entering the subjective space of one of the characters. It is not by chance that once the color appears the image is dominated by a washed-out yellow, completely devoid of green, which suggests summer heat but also Boro's suppressed emotions. The color is further connected to the limestone that dominates the landscape and that too has a symbolic meaning. In fact, if we accept the visuals as an exteriorization of Boro's inner world, then the complete architecture of the space, and even some of the characters and motives, have symbolic meaning. Limestone area rocks become the male element standing for the stubbornness and emotional remoteness of Boro and his father, while the lake becomes the female element, connected to Boro's mother.

The subplot that evolves around the discovery of a drowned boy's dead body announces the emergence of long-suppressed material from Boro's subconsciousness. The catalysts of these events become Boro's brother Pero and his wife Jasna. Pero is an example of a man who managed to have a normal relationship with his wife and children, despite the tragedy that disabled him. Jasna is even more important, because she takes on the role of his mother. Unlike Boro's mother, Jasna is strong enough to con-front her husband and make him change. The escalation of their conflict takes place in the lake where Boro's mother drowned, and where Boro himself almost drowns. But when Jasna manages to save him, the lake changes its meaning from a symbol of death to a symbol of new life. Boro comes out of the lake as if reborn and ready to confront his father. The confrontation between Boro and Paško reveals the secret behind Paško's emotional unavailability that once again turns out to be the key thematic complex in Nuić's opus. Like Njonjo in *Sex, Drink and Bloodshed*, Paško had to marry a woman he never loved. Her presence reminded him of his own weakness, so he transformed his discontent into a shell of emotional coolness which he used to torment his wife and son.

The communication between Boro and Paško puts a stop to the continuing cycle of emotional torment. The change in their relationship is symbolized by the motif of the animal in the title. In the popular imagination the donkey stands for someone stubborn, but it can also stand for someone who is able to carry a lot on his back. By buying him from a local dealer Paško makes him a pet for Luka, and therefore a token of a new bond between his son and grandson. The donkey, the lake, and limestone, just like Goran's one-day voyages to different parts of Bosnia, symbolize the different faces of a specific mentality that is stubborn, cruel, and unrelenting, but at the same time susceptible to change.

In many ways *Donkey* represents a peak in Nuić's oeuvre. The mise-en-scène, the choice of setting, and the plot structure in his first films showed a tendency to create parts of the film's diegetical universum which functionally complement the main character, but never as successfully as in *Donkey*. The authenticity of locations and the realism in portraying the life, speech, and customs of a small village in southern Herzegovina, thanks to the thoughtful use of cinematography and paced editing, manage to transcend the factographic recording of local exotica and makes this a universal story of the (dis)ability of an individual to confront the restrictive rules of the mentality he comes from. Furthermore, it is important to emphasize that in Nuić's films this individual is always male. This makes his stories "masculine" dramas, although the presence of female characters is of the utmost importance for their emotional development. While his first three films show a gradual improvement in the construction of characters through complex emotional relationships and skillful use of visuals, Nuić's female characters stay somewhat one-dimensional in their passivity of resigned women (Marko's wife, Boro's aunt) or angry furies (Martina, Jasna). However, Maja's getaway at the end of *All for Free* gives us a hint that in one of his next films Nuić's female characters could have a chance to articulate their position through a drama of their own.

Sex, Drink and Bloodshed (*Seks, piće i krvoprolice*), Croatia, 2004. Color, 76 min.
Director: Boris T. Matić, Zvonimir Jurić, Antonio Nuić
Script: Boris T. Matić, Zvonimir Jurić, Antonio Nuić
Director of Photography: Vjeran Hrpka, Thomas Krstulović
Music: Saša Lošić
Production Designer: Nedjeljko Mikac
Editing: Marin Juranić, Veljko Šegarić
Cast: Admir Glamočak, Matko Fabeković, Bogdan Diklić (first story), Leon Lučev, Krešimir Mikić, Daria Lorenzi (second story), Franjo Dijak, Leona Paraminski, Rakan Rushaidat, Hrvoje Kečkeš, Bojan Navojec (third story)
Producer: Boris T. Matić
Executive Producer: Hrvoje Osvadić
Production: Propeler film

All for Free (*Sve džaba*), Croatia, Bosnia and Herzegovina, Serbia, 2006. Color, 95 min.
Director: Antonio Nuić
Script: Antonio Nuić
Director of Photography: Mirsad Herović
Music: Siniša Krneta, Hrvoje Štefotić
Production Designer: Nedjeljko Mikac
Editing: Marin Juranić
Cast: Rakan Rushaidat, Nataša Janjić, Emir Hadžihafisbegović, Bojan Navojec, Franjo Dijak, Enis Bešlagić, Sergej Trifunović, Vanja Drach, Pero Kvrgić, Daria Lorenzi
Producer: Boris T. Matić
Co-producers: Miro Barnjak, Miroslav Stanić, Zijad Mehić
Production: Propeler Film, Magic Box Multimedia, Porta produkcija, Television of Bosnia and Herzegovina

Donkey (*Kenjac*), Croatia, Bosnia and Herzegovina, UK, Serbia, 2009. B&W, Color, 88 min.
Director: Antonio Nuić
Script: Antonio Nuić
Director of Photography: Mirko Pivčević
Music: Srđan Gulić Gul
Production Designer: Nedjeljko Mikac
Editing: Marin Juranić
Cast: Nebojša Glogovac, Nataša Janjić, Tonko Lonza, Emir Hadžihafisbegović, Momo Kiki Kapor, Asja Jovanović, Roko Roglić
Producer: Boris T. Matić
Co-producers: Mike Downey, Srđan Golubović, Jelena Mitrović, Antonio Nuić, Vanja Sutlić, Sam Taylor
Production: Propeler Film, MaNuFaktura, Croatian Radiotelevision, Film and Music Entertainment, Film House Baš Čelik, Zagreb Film Festival

Lukas Nola: *Celestial Body* (*Nebo, sateliti*, 2000); *Alone* (*Sami*, 2001)
reviewed by Bruno Kragić

From a ten-year vantage point, the historical relevance of Lukas Nola's film *Celestial Body* is exceptional. Having in mind titles such as Vinko Brešan's *Witnesses* (Svjedoci), and especially Kristijan Milić's *The Living and the Dead* (*Živi i mrtvi*), and Goran Dević and Zvonimir Jurić's *The Blacks* (*Crnci*), Nola's film could and should be considered the originator of the postwar-themed films in Croatia and Bosnia and Herzegovina. The qualification "postwar" has broader connotations here, reflecting a non-monolithic depiction of the war, an aesthetic departure from linear narrative in favor of the associative narration more commonly found in art-films, and the dominance of ambiance over plot.

In this respect, Nola's film is not only a hallmark of the revitalization of Croatian war film (and feature film in general), but it also draws on a tradition which, at the time of its creation, had been almost completely abandoned. It reaffirms the poetics of one of the pinnacles of modernism in Croatian film, Vatroslav Mimica's *Kaya* (*Kaja, ubit ću te*) from 1967 which also focused on the theme of war. While Mimica's film was a part of a Croatian and Yugoslav modernist orientation, and at that, one of its most radical examples in terms of form, Nola's film stood out as an exception at the time of its creation.

From the very beginning, through the monochromatic blue-hued long shots of the river and its surroundings, Nola demonstrates that his principal goal is depiction of ambiance. And indeed, the story about the wartime wanderings of his reticent protagonist, Jakov (Jacob) Ribar, is quite a direct allusion to the Bible. Following the itinerant movements of his central character who runs into lonely soldiers, brave women, and crazed enemy commanding officers, Nola entirely discards causal narrative organization and realistic dramaturgy. As a "travel film" *Celestial Body* is characterized by a mosaic-type dramaturgy, fragmentary narration, and a specific circular structure. The end of the film takes us back to its beginning and the principal female character, director of a home for orphans and the infirm, who was rescued by the protagonist immediately before (and in keeping with the Biblical allusions and anti-realist dimension of the film, literally brought to life by him) and is now observing a disturbance associated with an exchange of war-prisoners. The conclusion repeats the opening but with the difference that the spectator could not be aware of all the ramifications of the scene at the beginning of the film. The dis-

Lukas Nola: *Celestial Body* (*Nebo, sateliti*), 2000

turbance erupts because one of the prisoners, Jakov, leaves the group and starts walking through a mine field. The scenes of crowd from the beginning are replicated to be followed by ones in which Jakov advances through the field and then through water. These mid shots and long shots, however, leave the impression that Jakov is walking not *through* the water but *on* the water, which can be experienced and interpreted as yet another direct parallel with Christ. In charge of supernatural powers which he uses for the good, the protagonist of this film is, as we see, both unusual and passive, which fits him into the category of "weak" characters in Croatian feature film. He alters his surroundings more by chance than by force of will. Apart from the two situations when he is shown as a healing figure (when he appeases a sick man who is in shock and when he revives a murdered woman), his only specific active deed is at the beginning — i.e. end — of the film when he abandons the group. The separation, however, unmistakably positions him as the protagonist since it initiates the action which consists of episodes, fragments, and narrative moments originating in the protagonist's wanderings. These segments are tied together by the main character, the space (a swampy, valley-like area in proximity of the sea), and wartime. In addition to having specific allusions to the delta of the Neretva river by the Croatian-Bosnian/Herzegovinian border, the space through which the protagonist roams is shown with stylized faded photography and is used as a universal symbol of the general atmosphere captured in the film.

War is clearly portrayed in Nola's film as a world of chaos, shock, and terror, a demonic vision which is further underscored by images of a sanatorium, and especially, towards the end of the film, by images of a prisoner camp, scenes with soldier-occupiers presented as a drunk mob, and formally with darker shades of photography, and sharp cuts. The circular structure implies the permanence of this state and also allows the film to be discussed as an example of a Fryeian mythos of irony since the prevailing feeling is an absence of any heroism and effective action (also their diffusion and predetermination for defeat), as well as a general sense that the world is ruled by chaos and anarchy. In this vein and considering the focus on the general theme of wandering, the film appears as an *ironic* variant of a romance with Jakov Ribar as a chance protagonist who embarks on a journey that, rather than ending, starts anew. This is emphasized by the omnipresence of water (in various forms: lake, water in a tub or barrel, rain, the sea), an element which traditionally belongs to the realm of the afterlife and the state of chaos or dissolution accompanying death (this is further underscored by images of dead or killed fish which repeat and vary in several scenes). Still, the film escapes such unambiguous classification. The fact is that life is not enslavement with no way out, the demonic epiphany can be overcome, and this hope — as weak as it may be — still exists as shown through the scenes of Jakov's miracles and the symbolic shots of doves which traditionally stand for harmony, love and hope and which gather around the protagonist or land on him, such as in the last scenes of reviving.

Owing to its strong symbolic dimension, *Celestial Body* is a film which can be elegantly interpreted with archetypal, structuralist or psychoanalytic approaches, but at the same time a piece which functions paradigmatically as an art film because a classical plot is being suppressed in favor of ambiance. This is also a film in which atmosphere is conveyed in an extremely suggestive manner, not only at the level of stylized photography, but also in terms of the mise-en-scène, music (always present in the background), editing (where an important role is also given to the short shots which have an associative and aesthetic function), as well as the acting (extroverted episodes which are on the edge of a stylized grotesque complement the minimalism and subdued appearance of Filip Nola as Jakov). These are all the reasons why this particular film has been recognized as a novelty in newer Croatian cinematography at the very end of the twentieth century and one could assert that Nola's aspiration to portray the war in archetypal and universal terms was indeed best realized through his choice of art-film.

Having proven to be a master at direction, Nola radicalized this kind of approach in his next project, *Alone* (*Sami*), made only a year later. In this film directorial intentions are even more resolute and secure, but at the same time abstraction is far more pronounced, on account of which (unlike with his praised previous film) Croatian film critics mostly reacted with confusion. Reviews ranged from accusations of the extreme eccentric approach (at least in terms of Croatian cinematography) which was impossible to evaluate in relation to anything else, to objections to the hermetic style loaded with difficult-to-understand symbolism reflecting Nola's proclivity for poster-like and literal symbols, to descriptions of the film as a work of high aesthetic tonality with the purpose of parading semantically exhausted signs, and finally to reviews which perceived the film as a strained pose dwelling in the death of visual beauty.

Although the critics univocally praised the visual aspect of the film, this recognition was accompanied by objections to the lack of social context in the plot and the unclear spatial-temporal situation of the story. One could argue in general terms against this kind of negativity by pointing out that Nola's earlier film provides some kind of context in a sense, but one could protest more specifically against such a perception of *Alone* on the grounds that it disregards what is essential in the film itself: what one sees on the screen. This is precisely the aspect that is emphasized in *Alone*, especially since the verbal dimension is almost absent (there are only about twenty brief exchanges). If we glance again in the direction of archetypal interpretation, *Alone*, like its predecessor, could be discussed as an example of the ironic mode: the film is dominated by anxiety and an almost funebrial atmosphere, which is further weighed down by photography dominated by a dark color scheme. Furthermore, the setting is a forest and a series of dilapidated underground spaces (a subterranean apartment), it takes place at some unspecified time in the future after an ecological catastrophe, and finally, its main theme is the impossibility of escaping traumatic experience.

The protagonist, who is tormented by the fact that his negligence at the wheel caused the death of a boy, ends up with his throat slit, entirely in keeping with the spirit of the image of human life as slavery with no way out, while the characters' unsuccessful pursuit of emotional contact and communication appears from this perspective as an ironic mirror-image of the romance. Furthermore, if one considers this line of interpretation, symbols once again acquire dramaturgical functionality and become charged with a deeper meaning. One could even say that they establish a context in relation to Nola's earlier film: here too dominate symbols possessing strong links with Christian iconography and iconology (such as images of fish, water, crucifix, but also milk as a general theme of redemption and spiritual healing).

Ending the film without the possibility of redemption, at least not for the protagonist, and giving only to some characters the chance of finding peace through revenge, Nola seems to have reached the utmost limits of such archetypal preoccupations just as he exhausts an exploration of what were for him inspirational art-film poetics, most notably those of Andrej Tarkovskij and David Lynch. In his subsequent feature, *True Miracle* (*Pravo čudo*), he decided to return in a less hermetic and far more populist way to the postmodernist eclecticism he employed in his first feature, *Russian Meat* (*Rusko meso*). The eclecticism in the later film, however, manifested itself in the direction of a love-erotic grotesque, or a type of artistic populism in the spirit of Lordan Zafranović. For this reason, I would prefer to leave *True Miracle* outside the scope of the present essay and to establish that it was precisely *Celestial Body* and *Alone* that, in addition to their poetic and aesthetic kinship, remain the most elaborate and refined examples of different stylistic choices in Croatian feature film since independence.

Translated by Aida Vidan

Celestial Body (*Nebo, sateliti*), Croatia, 2000. Color, 85 min.
Director: Lukas Nola
Script: Lukas Nola
Director of Photography: Darko Šuvak
Music: Legen
Editing: Slaven Zečević
Set Designer: Velimir Domitrović
Costumes: Ksenija Jeričević
Cast: Filip Nola (Jakov Ribar), Barbara Nola (Lucija), Filip Šovagović (Uzelac), Rene Bitorajac (zapovjednik), Ivo Gregurević (Škaričić), Lucija Šerbedžija (Iva), Leon Lučev (Johnny), Goran Grgić (Senna), Predrag Vušović (Hans), Leona Paraminski (Jelena)
Production: Interfilm, Ban film, Croatian Radiotelevision

Alone (*Sami*), Croatia, 2001. Color, 81 min.
Director: Lukas Nola
Script: Lukas Nola
Director of Photography: Mirko Pivčević
Music: Svadbas
Editing: Slaven Zečević
Set Designer: Velimir Domitrović
Costumes: Ana Savić Gecan
Cast: Nina Violić, Jakov Nola, Leon Lučev, Nerma Kreso, Inge Appelt, Ksenija Ugrina, Bojan Navojec
Production: Alka film

Snježana Tribuson: *The Three Men of Melita Žganjer* (*Tri muškarca Melite Žganjer*, 1998)
reviewed by Karla Lončar

All her life Melita wants to take the cake. Especially when it comes to finding a perfect mate. Shy, passive, with low self-esteem, but fanciful and hungry for love, she is a fictional character we often meet on the screen of movie theatres, especially romance movies or romantic comedies. Snježana Tribuson's film *The Three Men of Melita Žganjer* (*Tri muškarca Melite Žganjer*, 1998), praised among Croatian critics and very well received by domestic filmgoers, surely belongs to the latter genre. A multiple national prize-winner in several categories, this well-directed and written film represents a stylistically impressive and humorous portrait of a wallflower in a search for the object of her desire.

At a time when most of the Croatian films were occupied with recent wartime or postwar struggles, Snježana Tribuson, an acclaimed director and screenwriter, offered a considerable detachment from the harsh socio-political reality, and brought about an intimate and escapist celluloid fantasy, which got through to tens of thousands of people in Croatia and beyond. Although preoccupied with a plot which could best be described as a modern fairy tale, Tribuson spiced up the narrative with ironic comments on the delicate line between fiction and reality and parodied many aspects of Croatian culture.

And the main protagonist, played by Mirjana Rogina, indeed does not quite understand which verbal or non-verbal messages belong to a true, or real, lovers' discourse and which ones are just fake or belong purely to fiction. She fantasizes about having a passionate relationship with a sweet-talking macho man like Juan (Filip Šovagović), the star of a Latin soap opera, at the time a very popular TV genre in Croatia, called *Slave to Love* and savior of a beautiful diva-like victim, played by the late Ena Begović (also a star in the extra-diegetic world), with whom Melita would gladly switch places. Apart from daydreaming, Melita, a chubby confectioner from Zagreb, socializes with her two roommates with whom she shares an old Upper-Town flat. By representing the antique interiors of Zagreb's middle class and the romantic exteriors of the old Upper Town, as well as the contents of Melita's flights of fancy focused on the wishful world of bonne-etiquette, the film is remarkably reminiscent of Krešo Golik's *One Song a Day Takes Mischief Away* (*Tko pjeva zlo ne misli*, 1970).[1] Much

---

[1] According to a number of polls among various film critics, one of the best Croatian films of all times.

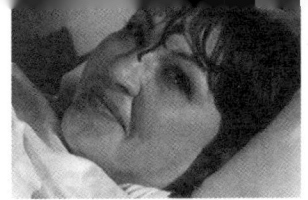

Snježana Tribuson: *The Three Men of Melita Žganjer* (*Tri muškarca Melite Žganjer*), 1998

like the slowly dilapidating Zagreb Upper Town and socially deteriorating middle class, Melita is also somewhat outdated in her expectations of love. Mentally she lives in a world similar to Golik's fictional 1935 Zagreb, where relations between men and women are traditional, women submissive (just as she is), men expected to be bold and courteous like Juan, and where love is expressed in a rather deprecating manner.

However, *The Three Men of Melita Žganjer* also resembles another great Croatian film. Namely, the character of Melita seems very similar to Štefica Cvek, fictional TV series character and a counterpart of sorts of filmmaker Dunja, from Rajko Grlić's film *In the Jaws of Life* (*U raljama života*, 1984), an adaptation of Dubravka Ugrešić's novel *Štefica Cvek u raljama života*. All these female characters experience trouble finding a compatible partner, regardless of their different wants, needs, social or "fictional" status. Calibrated with a witty postmodern ironization of typical women' genres and gender stereotypes, Grlić and Ugrešić, as co-screen-writer, inspired generations of women to question their feminine roles under the conditions of the constant social commands to have a skinny figure and a gorgeous prince in shining armor by their side. In addition, Tribuson was clearly also inspired by Grlić's and Ugrešić's humorous representation of Dunja and Štefica and their adventures with different men in a topsy-turvy collision of fiction and reality, and decided to make her own artwork by loosely following a similar formula.

As the title of Tribuson's film suggests, Melita had a few interesting situations with men as well. Structurally divided into three parts, due to the three objects of Melita's romantic interest, the film introduces the principal man of her life, Janko (Goran Navojec), a confectioner like Melita, as seemingly the opposite of the man of her dreams. He stutters and is therefore reluctant to speak with women, especially Melita, with whom he is in love. He falls for her because, among other things, she is not aggressive, which is a personality trait he dislikes and fears. Melita likes him too, but is pretty unaware of his feelings. So she tries to find another, more masculine man with the help of her two friends and roommates: co-worker and outgoing coquette Višnja (Suzana Nikolić) and cold, strict policewoman Eva (Sanja Vejnović).

After Eva brings Melita to a police party at a restaurant, Melita meets the second object of her desire — Jura (Ivo Gregurević), a pettifogging

Don Juan, or even a Mr. Fulir from Golik's film mentioned above, who uses his verbal skills to get to sleep at Melita's place because his wife has thrown him out. Fortunately or unfortunately, he does not have sex with Melita, who, ultimately, finds out he was also involved with Eva in the past. However, after learning that the actor who plays Juan, Antonio Mullero, the third man in the story, is about to act in a film shot in Zagreb, surprisingly self-assured and primly dressed Melita rushes onto the set, where she gets to act a wounded and unconscious woman in a hospital scene with Antonio. What is more, she even gets a chance to speak with the actor, utterly mesmerized by everything he says. That is, until he accuses her of stealing his sunglasses. Disappointed by the unfortunate revelation of his true character, she rushes into the arms of Janko, who is accidentally catering on the set. And, from then on, they live happily ever after, in their own perfectly frosted world.

The sweetness of the sentimental entanglements between characters corresponds with Tribuson's depiction of bold colors, especially shades of pink, and an iconography that reminds us of the aesthetics of women's magazines, cookbooks, and old-fashioned interior decoration. A combination of these elements inevitably evokes glimpses of nostalgia for a past time when the roles of women (and men) were strictly determined. In several instances Tribuson goes over the top and approaches the aesthetics of camp. Hence, her character representation aims to be exaggerated, which serves her humorous and ironic detachment from stereotypes well. Even if you feel sympathy for Melita and the man of her dreams and fall under the spell of the feel-good conventions of romantic comedy, the director makes you consciously or subconsciously revise your learned expectations of the peculiar film genre by putting the same musical performance of Davor Radolfi from the impressively reconstructed telenovela *Slave to Love* to the credits of the film. In this way, film's fictional elements are exposed once more, for the sake of the viewers' sense of humor and, for some, for the sake of their critical minds.

The most illuminating scene, regarding the dismantlement of the illusory aspects of the fiction, takes place at the film's metafilmic sequence — when Melita accepts the role of an extra on the film set. The scene shows Antonio lecturing Melita on the proper words and modes of acting, in order to see to it that she look more "genuine" for the love scene. Although she hears him, she doesn't quite understand what he is saying. Just as if she had a real wound on her head (but not in her heart), made for the purpose of filming a scene of a film inside the film, she listens to Antonio and hears only what she wants to hear: his declarations of love which, up to that point, were always directed at a lovely looking co-star of his, not her. Eventually, she wakes up from her somnolence, but not as a result of realizing she is succumbing to the alluring nature of fiction, but rather as a consequence of Antonio's harsh accusations flung at her. Revolted by the brutality of her idol, she escapes into the safety of Janko's embrace, who reacts in a rather instinctive and emotional manner, relieved that he doesn't have to put any mental effort into informing Melita of his intentions.

In this way, their relationship becomes a union between two people who wish to escape unpleasant and aggressive reality, and who remain unaware of the conditions that are making reality so complex and, at times, unbearable. Just as in Philippe Barry's definition of love: "Love is two minds without a single thought," Melita and Janko, too, are mindlessly bound together in a free-flowing wellspring of emotions. Their communication is only seemingly contrasted to the one from the telenovela and definitely compatible with their dominantly affectionate personalities, which mirror each other perfectly. Namely, they both represent an ideal by genuinely practicing lovers' discourse at its best; they are primarily emotional, sincerely devoted to each other. More so, traditionally viewed, they are quite feminine in their expressions, passive, and in search of a soul mate with whom they could live in a protected world. That is, in a world relatively free of alienating social pressures, but sometimes made a bit difficult because of pranks and teasing by Melita's benevolent friends.

Of course, almost everyone fantasizes about this kind of romantic relationship, only by readjusting one's gender role in it, according to one's inclinations. And it is definitely easy to feel good about the happy ending. Tribuson also seems aware of the escapist quality which she proposes in her dream factory. To please the part of the audience who seeks more than light amusement, however, she has an ace up her sleeve. And that would be the previously mentioned irony, through comments which imply that it is ok to want to live a life that looks like a hybrid of a telenovela and a fairy tale, where everything ends in a joyful and pleasant way, where people survive a plane crash as do Maria and Juan, or perhaps, miraculously walk after spending years being disabled, find their siblings in an unexpected way and/or become intensely joined to the ideal partner. But, with the sounds of Davor Radolfi's voice, the director wants us to step back and realize that this is all just a fantasy, including the characters with whom we eagerly want to identify with, which does not need to, or even have to, be implied in the real world.

So, by combining these two aspects — conventional romance and irony, Snježana Tribuson's function is somewhat of a confectioner, too. She made a visually lovely cake, which the audience could have and eat it, too, but, like the non-substantiality of the characters, the wonderfully crafted cake, lacking in just a little bit more critical substance, has not resulted in a distinctively tasty mash which will be remembered long after the film is consummated.

The Three Men of Melita Žganjer (*Tri muškarca Melite Žganjer*), Croatia, 1998. Color, 97 min.
Director: Snježana Tribuson
Script: Snježana Tribuson
Director of Photography: Goran Mećava
Music: Darko Rundek
Editing: Marina Barac
Costumes: Vesna Pleše
Cast: Mirjana Rogina (Melita), Goran Navojec (Janko), Sanja Vejnović (Eva), Filip Šovagović (Juan), Suzana Nikolić (Višnja), Ivo Gregurević (Jura), Ljubomir Kerekeš (Žac), Ena Begović (Maria)
Producers: Josip Barlović, Vesna Mort; Executive producers: Irina Damić, Sanja Vejnović
Production: Kvadar, Croatian Radiotelevision

Arsen Anton Ostojić:
A Wonderful Night in Split
(*Ta divna splitska noć*, 2004)
reviewed by Inna Mattei

A Wonderful Night in Split (*Ta divna splitska noć*, 2004) consists of three interconnected stories unfolding simultaneously in the center of the ancient Croatian city of Split on New Year's Eve. These stories are linked through characters and the mesmerizing pathways of coincidence that characterize the film. The sense of order stems from the compact, triptych structure of the narrative, from the aesthetic continuity of the black-and-white palate, and from the repetition of motifs — staircases, alleys, rooms, birds — and other visual and narrative devices. Temporal and visual interlinking creates a sense of cohesion that brings the stories together. Yet, it is not order but transgression that is the driving force behind the stories and their protagonists. And, as we shall see, this transgression is encircled by Chaos, the opposite of order, or "Cosmos", as conceptualized by Greek mythology. My analysis does not aim to imply that the film falls neatly into a given mythological framework; such frameworks are in themselves synthetic. Rather I use the themes from classical mythology as clues for interpreting the structure of the film to yield more insights into the director's vision, highlighting the richness of interpretations that can be found there.

Transgressive behavior is possible only in opposition to order, since it entails challenging a set of norms. Consequently, the interplay between order/Cosmos and transgression, represents, in my view, the central tension of the film. Visually, as well as cognitively, this tension can be linked to background-foreground pictures, such as those of M.C. Escher. Yet, this film is not merely an elegant maze, or a puzzle with a key. A maze is a kind of mini Cosmos. *A Wonderful Night in Split*, as we shall see, is a maze floating in the sea of Chaos.

The first story includes several transgressions. First is the implicit transgression of war, which took the life of little Duje's father. Second is the transgressive relationship between Marija and Nike (Duje's Mom and her lover), as seen through the eyes of the boy, who erroneously thinks that he can control the status quo. Thirdly, Nike's transgressive drug smuggling leads him back into the city to kill Blacky the drug dealer and eventually return to Marija's apartment, where he finds his death.[1]

1] Here it's worth noting that Ostojić came back to the theme of war in his second film: *No One's Son* (*Ničiji sin*) in 2008. Ostojić's second film is accomplished in terms of characterization and script and overall acting. It is skillfully made, but it is more mainstream visually and takes less creative risks with the narrative.

Arsen Anton Ostojić: *A Wonderful Night in Split* (*Ta divna splitska noć*), 2004

Similarly, the second story consists of a chain of transgressive events focusing on the drug dealer, Blacky, and a young girl named Maja. Suffering from heroin addiction, Maja is ready to do anything to stop her anguish. Without means to pay for the drugs provided by Blacky (whose death an hour later is in the first story), she agrees to be pimped out to a sailor from an American ship. The transgression of the drug user is amplified by the transgression of prostitution and further through Maja's gross indifference to the sailor's suicide. All she could think about is a fix. While the transgressions of the first story include a small group of people, the circle widens in the second story. An old lady provides the room for Frankie, the sailor, and Maja. Three other sailors provide the money to pay the prostitute for their friend. The drug lord/pimp facilitates the transaction. The homeless person tells Maja where to find the drug dealer. "Anyone who needs me knows where to find me," says Blacky, who sees himself as a helper.

The third story is focused on a young couple, Luka and Anđela, intent on finding a place to make love for the first time on New Year's Eve. After a few unsuccessful attempts, they run into Blacky. Luka accepts a key from Blacky to a place which turns out to be a secret junkie hangout on the top floor of a building located in the antique Roman palace that forms the center of the city. This room is not unfamiliar to Luka, since he used to be a junkie and Blacky's client in the past. He is done with drugs now. Ironically, Anđela, who has never tried drugs, convinces Luka to take some acid before their first lovemaking session. Hallucinating, Luka becomes convinced that he can fly. Now he climbs atop of the Roman portico — the very symbol of proportions and order — and gets ready to ascend, when in fact he is falling down. The crowd in the square has gathered there for a rock concert. Chanting in unison the crowd urges the young man toward suicide. As we see, in the third story, the circle of transgression has expanded wider to incorporate the citizens of the town. The transgression of the Chorus is a collective one, just like the collective transgression of war, without which the first story would have not been possible. The locus of the crime shifts from *oikos* (alone) to *polis* — community as a whole.[2]

2] Dylan Sailor, Sarah Culpepper Stroup: *The Translation of Transgression in Aiskhylos' "Agamemnon." Classical Antiquity*, Vol. 18, No. 1 (Apr., 1999), pp. 153-182.

Visually, Ostojić's film is a huge accomplishment attaining textual and visual richness through an aesthetic economy of means. Images like birds, staircases, dark rooms, courtyards, and doorframes gradually mold into recurring motives, and this repetition is productive in terms of creating with repeating elements the atmosphere of the film, as will as a sense of maze or labyrinth. Black-and-white colors do not produce an ironic counter-balance to the black-and-white characterization of the characters; they intensify the moribund nature of the stories. Visually this black-and-white film is more dark than white. But its intense blackness is created, of course, by contrast with light. Thus the narrative tension between order and transgression is mirrored in starkly contrasting visual elements.

While my observations focused on the notions of Cosmos and Chaos, it is possible to build on a Gaia-Eros axis as well as other Greco-Roman motives in the film. For instance, the name of the heroine of the second story, Maja (Maya), means Mother Goddess in Greek. Furthermore, one may even view the film as a medieval tale unfolding in a medieval city (a series of medieval/Renaissance structures were erected within the walls of the Roman palace) populated by allegorical types and pairs: mother and son, the soldier, the sailor, the two lovers, etc. Anđela — the heroine of the second story — is also a name of Greek origin, which means "a messenger of God." But one could add yet another layer of meaning since her name inevitably evokes Catholic/Christian connotations. Dichotomy and ironic reversal of values is lurking here as well since Anđela's behavior is anything but angelic in Ostojić's film. Having tempted Luka to try drugs again thereby causing his death, she is, in fact, a black or fallen angel.

While certainly instructive, these interpretations should not aspire to be definitive or final. *A Wonderful Night in Split* synthesizes narrative, cosmological, and mythological traditions in a unique way. Thus a medieval reading focusing on allegories and angels may overlook the intense physicality of the protagonists connected to death, Eros, and the anguish of drug addiction. Like order and transgression, pain and pleasure are linked to one another and appear to be two sides of the same coin. They are associated with the same source of evil — the drug dealer — who, as the homeless man suggests, "is a legend" in this town. Blacky always seems to have what others want, whether it is money, a key to the room in the palace, women, or drugs. This source of evil is not, however, destructive. On the contrary, Blacky breaks his victims so he can install his own order. Strangely enough, he is himself controlled by the rock singer in the square. If the drug dealer controls a few clients, the rock singer seems to control the drug dealer and the whole town… This brings us to the most enigmatic character in the film. Who is the rock singer in the square?

In real life the rock singer is Dino Dvornik, the rap/pop star from Split, who recently died of a drug overdose himself. Dvornik rose to popularity during the war — a time of chaos. He managed to remain popular after the conflict, thanks to his directness and honesty and unique musical style, which resonated with many of his admirers. Dvornik's music combined a blend of rap, pop, and funk, earning him the title of "King of Funk" and "Funk Daddy."

Two key things happen during the last few minutes of the film. First, the viewer realizes that the point of view of the film was not the point of view of the director/auteur, but the point of view of Luka, jumping off the portico, who becomes omniscient and omnipresent. The crane shots, the soaring perspectives of the narrow well-like courtyards and staircases that are woven throughout as a visual motif become linked to the point of view of the plunging character, who now assumes authority over the point of view of the film-maker.

Secondly, the film concludes with the same song that initially frames the narrative, the gibberish funk-rap of the entertainer/drug-lord portrayed by Dvornik. Thus the final "logos" of the movie is "chaos": The rocker-shaman channels the film out of gibberish, and submerges it into gibberish, because the film's Cosmos is surrounded by primeval Chaos. Therefore the final author is neither the orderly author, nor the transgressive protagonist, but a shaman, who neither creates, nor rebels, but, rather, channels a vision that is beyond his means of control.

Interestingly enough, if not for this framing in gibberish, the interpretations of the film would be completely different. For instance, the focus could shift to questions of poetic justice, probabilities in an improbable world, the role of fate, irony, and even cosmic irony, which entail divine interference. Such interpretations would have been possible, because they would help to explain the cosmos of the stories. But because the cosmos of the stories is surrounded by a sea of gibberish, such interpretations no longer make sense. The linguistic and logical hierarchies are no longer useful given the shaman-rocker framing, since such framing seems to reject the foothold of philosophical *terra firma*. Thus the visuals and language of the first and last few minutes are both chaotic and reduced to a minimum — with maximum impact.

A Wonderful Night in Split (*Ta divna splitska noć*), Croatia, 2004. Black and White, 100 min.
Director: Arsen Anton Ostojić
Art Director: Velimir Domitrović
Script: Arsen Anton Ostojić
Music: Mate Matišić
Director of Photography: Mirko Pivčević
Production Designer: Goran Joksimović
Editing: Dubravko Slunjski
Cast: Dino Dvornik, Marija Škaričić, Nives Ivanković
Marinko Prga, Vicko Bilandžić, Ivana Roščić
Producer: Jozo Patljak
Production: Alka Film and Croatian Radiotelevision

Vinko Brešan: *How the War Started on My Island* (*Kako je počeo rat na mom otoku*, 1996); *Witnesses* (*Svjedoci*, 2003); *Will Not End Here* (*Nije kraj*, 2008)
reviewed by Katarina Mihailović

Vinko Brešan is one of the most important as well as most renowned Croatian filmmakers at home and abroad to have emerged from "young Croatian film," a group of filmmakers within feature and documentary production who began to find articulation in the early 1990s. Along with various other young Croatian directors such as Ivan Salaj, Jelena Ranković, and Lukas Nola, Brešan has dealt with the experiences of the Croatian Homeland War in the 1990s and its aftermath. These filmmakers are united by an eagerness to "rescue Croatian cinema from its pronounced involvement with the narrow propagandist interests of the state," as Pavle Levi explains in his book, *Disintegration in Frames*. In his war trilogy made during and after the war, Brešan experiments with different generic modes of storytelling. *How the War Started on My Island* (*Kako je počeo rat na mom otoku*, 1996) is a dark comedy, *Witnesses* (*Svjedoci*, 2004) is a war drama/thriller, and *Will Not End Here* (*Nije kraj*, 2008) is a postwar drama and romantic tale. With these three films, he rejects the notion that war in the Balkans was inevitable. Moreover, in each of them Brešan audaciously examines the role of Croatian soldiers and ordinary citizens in the bloody wars, an especially difficult task during the Franjo Tuđman rule which ended in 1999.

Brešan co-wrote the script for *How the War Started on My Island*, and for *Marshal Tito's Spirit* (*Maršal*, 1999) with his father, the acclaimed Croatian dramatist and novelist, Ivo Brešan. In *How the War Started*, Brešan comically portrays the outbreak of hostilities between Serbs and Croats in Croatia in 1991. The father of one of the Croatian soldiers, Blaž Gajski (Vlatko Dulić), travels to a small Dalmatian town in order to pull his son out of service in the Yugoslav People's Army and the army's physical space (a barracks), because war between the Yugoslav Army and the Croatian military forces seems imminent. He quickly realizes that his task will be extremely difficult given that the town's inhabitants have surrounded the Yugoslav Army barracks. They are demanding that the Army leave, that the Croatian soldiers be released, and the armaments be surrendered. Similar scenes were happening at army barracks throughout Croatia at that time. Yugoslav Army Major Aleksa Milosavljević (Ljubomir Kerekeš), an ethnic Serb living in the town, passionately defends the barracks, threatening to blow the town to pieces if he is attacked. His rationale, however, seemingly stems from a petty power struggle rather than from any strong political sentiments. When the primary negotiator for the townspeople begs him to surrender the barracks in the name of camaraderie with his fellow citizens, Aleksa replies: "What? Is that why I should surrender to you? So you can be my commander? You a plumber and me a professional?!"

Rather than resorting to violent methods, the townspeople plan to convince Aleksa to release the soldiers by staging a series of comically bad performances meant to tug at his heartstrings. The variety show, which forms the backdrop for the negotiations between Aleksa and the plumber spokesman, along with other hilarities, show Brešan's strength as a comedic filmmaker. Aleksa briefly softens during his wife's sentimental speech about their blissful marriage and wonderful community, until she suddenly remembers his infidelities and begins to curse him. Otherwise, the show consists of kitschy musical numbers, an idiotic skit performed by Aleksa's weight-lifting buddies, and speeches meant to appeal to Croatian nationalist sentiments, a position strangely at odds with Aleksa's mistress' rhetoric of peace and love. With this series of comic events, Brešan pushes the sense of the absurd to its limits.

The stalemate between the two sides is finally resolved towards the end of the film when Gajski, posing as a Serbian Yugoslav Army Colonel, orders Aleksa to release both the soldiers and the explosives. In the last scene, one of the weaker in the film, an enraged, megalomaniacal Aleksa begins shooting at the civilians and Croatian soldiers, accidentally killing the beloved local poet, Dante (Ivica Vidović), who refuses to stop his recitation of the well-known patriotic poem "1909" by the modernist Croatian poet Antun Gustav Matoš as the bullets are flying. The film's last shot shows Dante bleeding to death as he utters the famous last lines of the poem, beginning with "they have hanged my Croatia, like a thief." In an all too sudden switch from the comic to the pathetic mode, the filmmaker reminds his audience of the gravity of the subject matter, but not without succumbing to sentimentality.

The film's success as a satire lies chiefly in the strength and wit of Brešan's caricatures of the small-town *milieu* and the Yugoslav Army mentality. Aleksa typifies the Army buffoon with a blind military loyalty. On the one hand, he seems potentially able to blow up his own wife, his mistress, and his friends out of an exaggerated sense of self-importance. On the other, his *naiveté* is such that he is fooled by Gajski into believing that a Yugoslav Army Colonel would have him release most of his soldiers and all of his explosives in spite of the fact that his barracks are surrounded. The brilliant sequence in which the townspeople give Gajski a tutorial on how to be a convincing Yugoslav Army colonel is a mockery of the Yugoslav military and its mentality. It is very easy, they tell him, as long as he remembers to salute correctly, yell at the infantrymen, and spout official communist slogans, such as "the situation in the country is very complex," or, "the enemy never sleeps." In *How the War Started*, Brešan refuses to show the outbreak of war as inevitable. Instead, war is depicted, in all of its absurdity, as the consequence of a series of banalities, misunderstandings, and wrong turns.

With *Witnesses*, Brešan began to move away from comedy. This drama, co-written with Jurica Pavičić, is loosely based on the journalist's first novel, *Alabaster Sheep* (*Ovce od gipsa*, 1997). The story, set in the northern Croatian city of Karlovac (located in an ethnically mixed region) in 1992, deals with the subject of Croatian war crimes. The film was quite controversial in Croatia, both because of its critical attitude towards some episodes of Croatian involvement in the war and because Brešan hired Mirjana Karanović, a well-known Serbian actress, to play a leading role.

Witnesses opens with a simple long shot depicting a deserted town square at night. A column of army vehicles passes through the square. A roaming camera skims over some windows of a residential building, showing the ordinary activities of the inhabitants, until it stops at an extraordinary scene: a man lying in a coffin in the middle of a living room. Krešo and Joško's father has been killed in the war. All three men were soldiers in the Croatian army. The next scene shows the younger of the two brothers, Joško, killing a local Serbian civilian Jovan Vasić. This is witnessed by the victim's young daughter. Joško and his two friends must now decide whether to kill the little girl, whom they have locked in the garage. Krešo and Joško's mother is adamant that the boys not involve Krešo, who has just retuned home upon recovering from a serious war injury that has left him with only one leg. Meanwhile, a police detective, and Krešo's girlfriend, Lidija, a local journalist, are investigating the murder. They get virtually no help from the local population, and are under political pressure not to proceed since the victim was a highly unpopular Serbian man killed by Croatian soldiers. Eventually, Krešo figures out that his brother is the murderer, and saves the young girl from being killed. In an overly sentimental tone, the last scene shows Lidija, Krešo, and the little girl holding hands as they watch the sunrise.

The film's structure does not conform to a linear narrative logic. Instead, the most important dramatic events are shown multiple times, each time with slight alterations. Moreover, they are focalized through multiple points of view. Because each character has a different perspective on the events, each individual treatment of an important dramatic scene brings new information. In one scene, for example, the mother and Joško see a neighbor talking to a police officer outside their house. Judging by the man's body language, one assumes that the neighbor is incriminating Joško. When the scene is presented from the point of view of the policeman we realize that the neighbor was merely chastising the police for questioning Joško's family on the day of the father's funeral.

The immediate effect of this technique on the audience is a vague sense of fractured storyline. In *Witnesses*, the main dramatic conflict is clearly posited: the murder of the Serbian man is shown at the beginning, and it is also clear that there is a witness. The exposition is fragmented in a way that precludes a full understanding of the background to these events until late into the narrative. The use of this device is, of course, especially well suited to the detective and thriller genres, where the narrative impetus comes from the desire to resolve the mystery. With *Witnesses*, however, Brešan eliminates one of the most important conventions of the genre. In the film, the question that drives the narrative is not who committed the murder. Instead, the central mystery of the film is how a crime

Vinko Brešan: *Will Not End Here* (*Nije kraj*), 2008

like this happens and, as Lidija puts it, "what kind of people do something like this?"

The answer to this question is never really given; instead Brešan develops complex relationships and connections among the townspeople that suggest their multiple levels of complicity. We learn that Joško was always a troublemaker, and that Krešo always helped get him out of trouble; in addition, we learn that Joško's recklessness and carelessness resulted in the accident that cost his brother his leg, and that he, unlike his brother, has had a history of violent behavior since the beginning of the war. Furthermore, it is clear that their mother is prepared to do anything — even orchestrate the murder of the little girl — to save her younger son. The townspeople's callousness and the criminal complicity of the police and politicians paint a dark picture of this *social milieu*, which, as the title suggests, is entirely comprised of witnesses. In this way, Brešan extends the micro-level analysis to the society as a whole.

Brešan's next film, *Will Not End Here*, a tragicomedy, is a love story set in postwar Croatia, in both Zagreb, the Croatian capital, and in the small inland Dalmatian town of Obrovac, which had been largely populated by Serbs before the Croatian offensive known as Operation Storm was launched in August of 1995. A Gypsy porn star named Đuro (Predrag 'Pređo' Vušović) tells the story of Martin (Ivan Herceg), a Croatian war veteran, who fell in love with the Serbian woman, Desa (Nada Šargin). As the narrative unfolds, it becomes clear that Martin was a sniper positioned in Obrovac and stationed for a time across from Desa's house. She was married to a Serbian army leader, whom Martin has to kill. Ruined by the tragedy and forced out of her home, Desa becomes a prostitute in Belgrade. Through Đura, Desa's co-star in a porn film, Martin locates her, and buys her from her pimp for a large sum of money. They return to Zagreb, Martin's home town, where they gradually fall in love. Despite the terrible circumstances that have brought them together, Desa forgives Martin when she realizes that he is her husband's murderer. When she finds out, however, that Martin has hidden a terminal illness from her she leaves him in a rage. In the tradition of the romantic entanglement tale, the conflict is resolved at the end, and the couple comes together once again. Although dark, *Will Not Stop Here* is imbued with a guarded sense of optimism.

Before he begins the story, Đuro declares: "Lucky for me I'm not a Croat or a Serb, but a Roma, a man of the world, since the Croats and the Serbs are too complicated." Đuro's pronouncement is a humorous displacement of the typically held sentiment that the Roma have a tragic fate. Đuro, as an outsider in ex-Yugoslav society, is not embroiled in these regional and ethnic hostilities. Nonetheless, he is drawn into this particular Serbian-Croatian drama.

Brešan paints a dark picture of postwar Croatian and Serbian societies, permeated by crime and war profiteering. Within this sector of society only money has any real value and everyone is selling something: Đuro and Desa sell their bodies, Martin sells personal information (he is a private detective), his aunt sells her kidneys, and former Croatian soldiers sell information about the war. This story about the criminal underworld forms the backdrop to the main plotline. For instance, Martin's friends, his fellow soldiers from the war, sell maps of the graves of Croats who went missing during the war to their families for large sums of money.

If *How the War Started on My Island* is a meditation on the absurdities of war, and *Witnesses* is an examination of the complicity of ordinary people and soldiers in war crimes, then *Will Not End Here* is an unflinching look at the consequences of war on contemporary society. Brešan's films should be seen as social critiques that never shy away from unpleasant discoveries. In *How the War Started* and *Will Not End Here*, which is, in my opinion, the most artistically successful film in the war trilogy, Brešan skillfully blends tragedy and comedy. Although this film is the least polished of the three in terms of visual style, it is by far the most original in its treatment of the subject matter. *Witnesses* and *Will Not Stop Here* are influenced by the narrative modes of Hollywood genres of the romance, the thriller, and the detective story, all of which Brešan adapts to the specificities of the Balkan tragedy. His occasional weakness for a Hollywood-like brand of sentimentality dampens the overall effect of the films but nonetheless, his war trilogy is a heterogeneous body of work that has carried the genre forward. Brešan is clearly a skilled craftsman with a gift for the creation of sophisticated narratives. This, along with his frank and courageous treatment of the realities of war and its effects on a society, make this trilogy an important contribution to Croatian cinema of the war and postwar era.

How the War Started on My Island (*Kako je počeo rat na mom otoku*), Croatia, 1996. Color, 97 min.
Director: Vinko Brešan
Script: Vinko Brešan, Ivo Brešan
Director of Photography: Živko Zalar
Music: Mate Matišić
Editing: Sandra Botica Brešan
Production Designer: Ivica Trpčić
Cast: Vlatko Dulić, Ljubomir Kerekeš, Ivan Brkić, Predrag Vušović, Ivica Vidović
Producers: Ivan Mudrinić
Production: Croatian Radiotelevision

Witnesses (*Svjedoci*), Croatia, 2003. Color, 88 min.
Director: Vinko Brešan
Script: Jurica Pavičić, Vinko Brešan, Živko Zalar
Director of Photography: Živko Zalar
Music: Mate Matišić
Editing: Sandra Botica Brešan
Production Designer: Mario Ivezić
Cast: Mirjana Kranović, Leon Lučev, Krešimir Mikić, Alma Prica, Dražen Kühn, Marinko Prga, and Bojan Navojec
Producers: Ivan Maloča
Production: Interfilm

Will Not End Here (*Nije kraj*), Croatia, Serbia, 2008. Color, 108 min.
Director: Vinko Brešan
Script: Vinko Brešan, Mate Matišić, Franjo Moguš
Director of Photography: Živko Zalar
Music: Mate Matišić
Art Director: Mario Ivezić
Editing: Sandra Botica Brešan
Cast: Ivan Herceg, Nada Šargin, Predrag Vušović, Dražen Kühn, Voja Bajović, Damir Orlić
Producer: Ivan Maloča, Executive Producers: Vesna Mort, Predrag Jakovljević
Production: Interfilm, Croatian Radiotelevision, Vans Films, Eurimages Conseil de l'Europe

Goran Rušinović:
Buick Riviera, 2008
reviewed by Nataša Milas

Goran Rušinović's latest feature, *Buick Riviera*, premiered in the summer of 2008 at the Pula Film Festival where it won the Golden Arena award for Best Screenplay, shared by Goran Rušinović and Miljenko Jergović. Following Pula, *Buick Riviera* appeared at the Sarajevo Film Festival winning two Hearts of Sarajevo, one for Best Feature Film and the other one for Best Actor, shared by Leon Lučev and Slavko Štimac. Since then the film has been making the rounds of the film festivals, including the Seattle Film Festival, Denver Film Festival, Karlovy Vary International Film Festival, where it has been received with great enthusiasm.

Buick Riviera is based on Jergović's nearly eponymous novel, *Buick Rivera* (2002), the first in a trilogy of narratives about people and automobiles, to be followed by *Freelander* (2006) and *Volga, Volga* (2009). Goran Rušinović, a young director from Croatia, who has made films such as *Mondo Bobo*, 1997 and *World Monster*, 2003 decided to follow in Jergović's footsteps when it came to working with the genre of road narratives. After releasing his film *Buick Riviera* in 2008, Rušinović began an adaptation of Jergović's novel *Freelander*.

The film *Buick Riviera* follows the fate of two men, Hasan Hujdur (Slavko Štimac) and Vuko Šalipur (Leon Lučev), two Bosnian expatriates who meet late one night on a desolate road in the middle of America. While Vuko is a man who moves from one situation to another with comparative ease, Hasan is an individual who has trouble overcoming the past and remains "frozen" in time. Both characters let emotions lead the way, and while Vuko expresses his sentiments loud and clear, Hasan internalizes his own, which prevents him from having a healthy existence. This is not a film in which the characters bring out the best in each other. Vuko and Hasan's mutual sabotaging takes the viewers back to the heart of the conflict in Bosnia.

Both the novel and the film treat the relationship between man and his automobile. Jergović comments for the Croatian paper *Nacional*, "for me the automobile is a mixture between a live being, a work of art, a machine, and transmitter of my own psychology."[1] Jergović's sentiment, reflected in his novel, is equally felt in the film. Jergović titles his novel *Buick Rivera*, giving it a common last name, Rivera, an act by which he further per-

---

1] "An Interview. Miljenko Jergović. "Talijanski uspjeh hrvatskog književnika." (The Italian Success of a Croatian Writer) *Nacional*, No. 376. January 29, 2003.

Goran Rušinović: *Buick Riviera*, 2008

sonalizes and personifies the car. The old timer, a 1963 Buick Riviera, is, for Hasan, "his America." It is a place of comfort, something which makes him calm, and collected, better and more patient. While reflecting this in his film Rušinović also accentuates another aspect of this relationship: the car is not a symbol of Hasan's new life, but a refuge from it.

On a more artistic level Buick Riviera works as the vehicle that propels the plot. Due to the Buick's old engine, Hasan is stuck on the road in the middle of the night and that is where he encounters his fellow countryman, the Serb, Vuko Šalipur. Furthermore, the culmination of the movie happens over dinner as the film's only three characters discuss the car, when an almost devil-like deal is made over the Buick Riviera.

The novel begins with a weather report. Jergović is telling us that "spring was coming late in Toledo, Oregon,"[2] which becomes Fargo, North Dakota in the film. There we have, already indicated in the weather, a delay of progress. Even the natural development of climatic conditions has been suspended. Jergović further explains that it is minus 20 degrees Celsius and describes that type of cold. But Jergović lets go of the winter imagery after he has set up the background to the novel. Rušinović, on the other hand, uses the white snow imagery as his main trope, letting it reveal the frozen state of these émigrés, particularly Hasan, whose inability to move on in the new land, his suspended career, his frozen marriage, are all reflected in the images of the winter cold. The audio effects of the harsh winter wind further mimic this dysfunctional reality.

The events in *Buick Riviera* take place, so to say, in "no man's land," which Rušinović represents visually as a desolate white landscape of America. The "no place, no time" is further accentuated by the fact that it is the middle of the night, in the middle of the road, in freezing cold, when the two men meet. What starts as one man helping another in this unfortunate situation (a car broken down) quickly develops into them antagonizing each other. As soon as these two men sit together in the small enclosed space of the car, they bring their past and emotional baggage with them. Vuko, a Serb, who primarily identifies himself with Serbdom and the Orthodox Christian faith, automatically takes Hasan as a Muslim. But Hasan, who considers himself a child of socialism and Yugo-

2] Jergović, Miljenko. *Buick Rivera*. Sarajevo: Šahinpašić, 2009, p. 5.

slavia, tries to deny the labels Vuko provides for him. Everything that happens, that is said in that car, is explained, somewhat fantastically, by the fact that Vuko is a Bosnian Serb and Hasan, a Bosnian Muslim.

The culminating scene in the film occurs over dinner as Hasan, his wife Angela, and Vuko get to know each other better. The Buick, naturally, is central to their dinner conversation. Evoking Bertolt Brecht's poem "Mask of Evil" to help her read Vuko's face, Angela informs us that Vuko is a very relaxed man and such a man cannot be evil, since only grimaces are connected to the notion of evil. There is an overarching sense of evil over the dinner conversation, and the viewers are invited to follow Angela's example and do their own reading of the characters' faces. In the novel, the satanic presence at the table is accentuated through the protagonist's thoughts. Hasan thinks for himself how his meeting with Vuko is no coincidence, "the devil reigns over coincidences," and, as he looks at Vuko at the dinner table, he refers to him in his thoughts as "my devil."[3] This notion is further amplified in both the novel and the film by the deal that happens at the table: the selling of the Buick. If we think of evil's presence in these scenes, we attribute it as viewers to the deal-maker himself, Vuko Šalipur.

Vuko, who has consistently been the movie's main problem-solver — he helps Hasan with his car, gives him a ride, returns his wallet — attempts to resolve yet another of Hasan's issues. Vuko realizes that this car is causing problems in Hasan and Angela's marriage and that the car is a barrier for Hasan between himself and reality. By taking away his Buick (buying the car from Hasan) Vuko is also taking away the only thing that keeps Hasan calm and collected. Vuko bets on the car and wins, and this shift of the car's ownership from Hasan to Vuko marks a major shift in Hasan. Hasan claims throughout the film that he doesn't want to feel hatred, and defends himself by saying that he is not a Muslim when confronted by Vuko. Almost to the end he resists Vuko's offenses but ultimately uses the car for revenge because of everything that has been stowed away in him for the past seventeen years (and has been brought to the surface by Vuko): the war, the death of his family, of his city. Hasan sends Vuko to his death — he cuts the brake line in the car before handing it over to Vuko — thus using his beloved Buick one last time.

As Hasan lies on the floor listening to a recording of his father's voice, his nose bleeds, for the first time directly associating the blood with Hasan. Despite the father's better advice, Hasan acts upon hatred. The music that plays in the background transitions to a scene of Vuko driving the car, thus connecting the relationship between Hasan and the other — Vuko — and his complicity in Vuko's death, or even more significantly, to Vuko himself, equating the two on the scale of (petty) evil. Hasan's face as he lies on the floor assumes a sinister look. Vuko dies and Hasan has blood on his hands. The last image of the film shows blood on the window of the Buick. A window of possibilities, of a new life in America, ends up smeared with blood. Here we are back as viewers in the car as we were

---

3] Jergović, Miljenko. *Buick Rivera*. Sarajevo: Šahinpašić, 2009, p. 159.

at the start of the film. The Buick, therefore, together with us, has witnessed Hasan's transformation and has visually experienced the blood on him. The blood from over there, Bosnia, has finally been transposed here, to America.

One of the more striking features of this film is the emotive use of colors. Rušinović's use of stark white settings has the strongest impact. Extended camera shots often track the movement of a single object, usually the titular car as it passes through a frame suffused by white snow and an equally colorless sky. In fact, the film begins with Rušinović's camera literally incased in the snow-covered car. The viewer discovers the setting only as the windows of the car are cleared of white snow. The whiteness marks the banality and stasis of the main character's life in the mid-western setting. In contrast to this is the color red, which marks the memory trace of blood and violence from the main character's past. Rušinović denotes this landscape of memory with cuts to black and white surrealistic memory sequences. At the film's end, the red and the white finally meet as past violence is transported into the present setting.

Although Rušinović's version of *Buick Riviera* closely follows the plot of the novel — this is a very faithful rendition of Jergović's text — he makes two important changes. Rušinović leaves out the fact that Vuko was a low-level war criminal back home. Even though Hasan and the viewers may allow themselves to assume this fact, Rušinović opts not to point fingers at anyone and instead focuses on transporting the animosity behind the Bosnian conflict to America. Rušinović also provides his viewers with an alternate ending. Instead of having Hasan disappear at the end of the novel and letting Vuko build his new life by inventing Hasan's identity (as a terrorist), Rušinović's ending is more concrete: revenge. Although *Buick Riviera* is most often generically categorized as a road movie, a psychological thriller, or a chamber drama, Goran Rušinović sees the film as a tragedy. As he notes, "the film is a story of two people who cannot have a happy ending."

Buick Riviera, Croatia, Bosnia and Herzegovina, USA, UK, Germany, 2008. Color, 86 min.
Director: Goran Rušinović
Script: Goran Rušinović and Miljenko Jergović
Director of Photography: Igor Martinović
Music: Brane Živković
Editing: Vlado Gojun, Miran Miošić
Production designer: Tommaso Ortino
Cast: Slavko Štimac, Leon Lučev, Aimee Klein
Producer: Kate Bary
Production: Propeler Film in co production with Croatian Radiotelevision, Tradewind Pictures, Referesh Production, FAME

Goran Dević and Zvonimir Jurić: *The Blacks* (*Crnci*, 2009)
reviewed by Lorraine Mortimer

The films' credits scroll on and then — we are in the dark, along with combat men in a vehicle. The driver gets out and breaks a shop window to get what he needs, then gets back in the truck and goes on driving. There are vehicle lights on a dark road, channeling everything into the men's tunnel vision. Once the men are out of the vehicle, the only audible sounds are those of the forest and water. Ivo (Ivo Gregurević), the squad leader, soon identifies an American boot that belonged to one of their men, Alen. The group is then seen on the water, in a canoe, as the sun comes up and the spectator is immersed in the sounds of their paddles, wind in the rushes, bird sounds and crickets at dawn. Light comes down through the trees onto fresh green leaves, black trunks, and sticks on what must be soft, lush earth breaking under the men's feet as they move along. These bucolic images, however, will become the site of the starkly contrasting visual and ethical weight to become apparent in the subsequent shocking sequences.

Goran Dević and Zvonimir Jurić have suggested that Ridley Scott's *Alien* (1979) was an inspiration in their writing of *The Blacks*, with its rising tension, confined spaces, and sudden shift in time — all contributing to a haunting film about tragic realities. Much of *The Blacks* looks and feels like a combat film, combat that is grim, intense, and in the end, hopeless and absurd. But the film's power builds with the unfolding from a flashback of what led up to the fatal mission, and what was going on in the minds and bodies of the combatants, revealed as humans, whose individual fates were not preordained, even if they were likely.

The initial journey that opens the film is punctuated by Ivo crouching to fathom his map, and by a moment in which the new recruit, Vedran (Krešimir Mikić), a "land-miner" who knows nothing about hand weapons, let alone mines (he lied about his skills), has to take a shit.[1] His question about protocol brings some of the first dialogue in this minimalist film, and highlights his nervousness, underlining for the others that it's his first time out. Ivo lays his hand on him, and tells him it's going to be fine. Vedran lies to the seemingly hardiest member of the group, Šaran (Nikša Butijer), when he asks if he has buried the shit. And it becomes increasingly evident that all will not be fine when, after a while, we hear the buz-

---

[1] The land-miner deceived his superiors in order to get out of prison. During the war many petty criminals ended up on the front.

Goran Dević, Zvonimir Jurić: *The Blacks* (*Crnci*), 2009

zing of flies around the excrement, and we see the men anxiously gesture to one another after having realized that they have been going around in circles. An additional signal of a fractured world is conveyed when Ivo stumbles and is irritated as the young men lift him to his feet. His "shut up and walk" becomes his symbolic chant — better to walk in circles, to do anything, than not to act.

The next time we hear flies buzzing will not be for something banal and natural. We are now in flashback mode and the reversed chronology begins to examine the logic and ethics (or lack thereof) that led to the opening scenes we have just seen. Temporally later in the film, but on the day before the mission, Vedran has walked into a space where Franjo (Franjo Dijak) is crouched in the dark, alone by a wall. The newcomer's curiosity is more than sated when Franjo switches on the light, and, to the camera as well, reveals a white room with a large bin and bucket, blood on the floor, on the back of a chair, and across the wall. The camera pans to but doesn't dwell on the bloodied clothing that gives away the crime that took place there. The use of sound, not dialogue, is masterful here too as we hear creaking and buzzing, a light swinging down from the ceiling, and, like one of the perpetrators, Franjo himself, we can't escape into a realm of ideas. Vedran's body will register all this, immediately vomiting up what is not hard for him to imagine, just as he vomits after sighting the dead comrades, who are at last found in the minefield in the woods.

On a second viewing of *The Blacks*, you can more deeply appreciate the economy with which Goran Dević and Zvonimir Jurić crafted this dark gem of a film. Right at the beginning we see more clearly blood-spattered clothing that makes a nest in which a black cat feeds her new kittens, clothing that belongs to people who have been tortured and killed. Like much else in the film, including its title, the garage where these events took place is both a concrete element of a small, claustrophobic world that leads to particular fatalities in this particular story, and a metaphor with historical-political resonance. ("The Blacks" was an actual military unit in the service of the Croatian Nazi-puppet state during World War Two. Croatian Parliament member Branimir Glavaš was convicted of the torture and killing of Serb civilians in the garage of a municipal building in 1992 — in Osijek, the city where Zvonimir Jurić was born.) On a second viewing too, we appreciate so many details of what has led up to the time in the woods which makes up the first third of the film, because we've seen the flashback to twenty-four hours before the mission is undertaken by the men, and know that whatever else it was, it was a journey into self-destruction.

A strong and refreshing aspect of *The Blacks* is that it's rooted in the beauty of nature, but to the opposite ends of those films of the 1990s served up in Western art-houses where a Kusturica-type hystericized viscerality and runaway physicality went along with what has been called "self-Balkanization" or the "Balkanoid" perpetuation of stereotypes. There is no effervescence flowing between the brothers-in-arms here. One of the problems with the stereotype of violence and war being "natural phenomena" in the Balkans, part of a special, mysterious region "trapped in an endless cycle of ethnic conflict and crime,"[2] is a failure to acknowledge that social, like organic, processes are marked by *transformation* as well as reproduction. To refuse to acknowledge this is to perpetuate death by the perpetuation of a myth. *The Blacks*, with that "rough naturalism" Jurica Pavičić describes elsewhere in this book, presents some young men who try to change the fatal course the group is on, who have had enough of killing. They can't shut down reflection about what they have done (the torture and killing of Serb civilians indicated by the bloodied room setting) and what they are now doing, or may do. "Boss, let's talk. What is it we're doing?" Ivo is asked, as they struggle on in the rain and storm, in a nature that is neither malignant nor benign, towards their goal — nominally to get the bodies of their comrades — yet Ivo also wants to blow up a dam though this will be an illegal act since a ceasefire has been called. It is significant that the area into which he can't believe his members went was mined by both Serbs and Croats, as Darko (Rakan Rushaidat) tells him. When the camera tilts to a portion of the sky, releasing us from confusion and claustrophobia, we realize that the birds we see are circling over their comrades' dead bodies.

When Ivo learns that the miner Vedran can't do the job expected of him, he is angry, and it's Franjo, "hopelessly" addicted to drugs, according to Šaran, who makes a choice and aims his rifle at Ivo, who is aiming at Vedran: "No one's going to kill any more." To complete the standoff, Šaran, in turn, lines up "junky motherfucker" Franjo, who still follows through with his stand. Šaran then places the muzzle of his rifle under his chin and kills himself. As Šaran falls to his knees, his head bent over as in prayer, the droning organ used sparingly in the film becomes church- or funeral-like, carrying us across a cut to a corridor of green-tinged light, surrounded by darkness, a cat crossing, halting in doorways, meowing and finally hopping up on Šaran's bed, twenty-four hours before.

In this vastly different setting in a clinical white room, the men are listless and Darko is being told that it's not his fault. We don't know what they mean at this stage, but he is lying on his bed in a fetal position, and we

---

2] The first well-known quotation is from Emir Kusturica, in Dina Iordanova, *Cinema of Flames: Balkan Film Culture and the Media*, London: BFI, 2001. The second is from Zoran Samardžija, "Bal-can-can," *Cineaste* 3: 32, New York, 2007. Both quotations appear in Jurica Pavičić's "Cinema of normalization: changes of stylistic model in post Yugoslav cinema after the 1990s," *Studies in Eastern European Cinema* 1: 1, 2010.

soon learn that he didn't hear a call for help on his comrades' walkie-talkie when they found themselves in a minefield. It's in a supremely cruel way that — like Darko and Ivo after him — we learn of this cry for help and the subsequent carnage. Captured on Serb radio, we hear a supposedly listener-requested replay of a "unit of Croatian fascists who went where they shouldn't go." Alen is desperately calling Darko as his comrades lie dead:

"Do you read me? What am I to do? Call File! Fuck, what did you plot on our map? Call File. Call File, brother."

Once we hear a final explosion, the smooth-voiced female announcer says:

"As for Darko and File, here's a little tune for them." And she plays the song, "It's been a long time waiting for you..."

"Banality of evil" is the phrase that comes to mind, because evil here is not ecstatic and energetic, alcohol-fired violence, but a cold and callous viewing of people as nothing, the part of a perpetuation of hatred over which no person or group in the world has the monopoly.

While the film is bleak, small gestures pass between the men, who aggravate or else look after each other in telling ways. And the cat is in here too, sidling up to Darko, as he sits alone. Ivo threatens Vedran when he kicks the cat, protecting her from random violence that, he warns, must never occur again: and here, with so little dialogue, we learn so much. The first time we see Ivo soften and smile is when he is talking to his son on the phone. But when he speaks to his wife, Silva, afterwards, he gives no hint of that tenderness, his smile evaporating as he accuses: "Why's the kid awake?" Yet we've learned from his conversation with his brother-in-law that Silva will seek a divorce if he keeps taking part in the activity she has heard rumors about. On the phone with her, Ivo swears on his only child that the rumors are not true. We presume it is her he calls shortly after, before going on his mission — telling her it's nothing, just wanting to hear her voice. And he doesn't answer the phone when he is called back, the ring carrying across as Ivo walks through a purple-hued neon doorway and, in a fraction of a second in which we have moved forward in time, as his dead body is being pulled through the grass. The other men's bodies are pulled in the same way, with the dragging and the effort in the breath of the bodies' collectors heard on the soundtrack. Darko is the only one who has survived.

There is something I'd call spiritual about *The Blacks*, though it's a spirituality not necessarily tied to the Catholic or any other church. It's related to the idea of reflection and remorse, and of sinning no more. When Franjo goes missing from the bunker-like headquarters, he walks down the aisle of a church to its altar. Instead of white walls and neon, all is quiet, warm, and ordered. Peace can descend. When he meets his old drug dealer there is the small friendly gesture when Franjo taps the taxi roof as the car leaves, and when the dealer backs up, Franjo gladly gives him the Blacks' emblem from his uniform that the man's son has requested. When he starts to prepare the drugs, however, he no longer has the stomach for them. A nice detail is that he can't take part in a last, unholy communion when Ivo offers each of the men a swig from a bottle before they go on their suicide mission. When Franjo says that he cannot go on killing, Ivo replies: "You think it's easy for me?" And he's right, of course, given that, as military experts tell us, parts of us have to be broken down and conquered for us to lose our "normal" inhibitions about taking other people's lives.

I was surprised to hear that this film had an "all-star ensemble cast." We're not getting enough films from Croatia and other Yugoslav successor states to know these actors, which is a great pity; and it also means we could be learning much more than we are. But the acting in *The Blacks* is so understated, so perfectly natural, that we can believe in these characters completely. They are just one of the great strengths of this small, unpretentious film that is a significant triumph in itself.

Works Cited

- Pavičić, Jurica. 2011. "From a Cinema of Hatred to a Cinema of Consciousness: Croatian Film After Yugoslavia." See page 49.
- Pavičić, Jurica. 2010. "'Cinema of normalization': changes of stylistic model in post Yugoslav cinema after the 1990's." *Studies in Eastern European Cinema* 1: 1.

The Blacks (*Crnci*), Croatia, 2009. 78 minutes, color.
Directors: Goran Dević and Zvonimir Jurić
Script: Goran Dević and Zvonimir Jurić
Director of Photography: Branko Linta
Music: Jura Ferina and Pavle Miholjević
Editing: Vanja Siruček
Art Director: Mladen Ožbolt
Costumes: Ivana Zozoli
Cast: Ivo Gregurević, Krešimir Mikić, Franjo Dijak, Rakan Rushaidat, Nikša Butijer, Stjepan Pete, Emir Hadžihafizbegović, Saša Anočić
Producer: Ankica Jurić-Tilić
Production: A Continental Film release of a Kinorama presentation in co-production with Croatian Radiotelevision

Krsto Papić: *When the Dead Start Singing* (*Kad mrtvi zapjevaju*, 1998)
reviewed by Boško Picula

At the small apartment of two Croatian guest workers in Berlin, one of them watches in amazement as his friend steps out of a coffin, and asks him: "What do you need a coffin for when you're alive?" His roommate answers handily: "But I am not alive any more. I died this morning at eight o'clock..." These are the opening lines in the film that marked the year of 1998 in the eyes of critics and filmgoers alike. The film's author is Krsto Papić, one of the most significant Croatian film directors, whose contribution to the seventh art in Croatia is mirrored in feature films and documentaries of equal importance. Furthermore Papić chalked up a series of international successes: participation in the Berlin festival, nomination for the Golden Globe, an award at the Montreal festival.

Born in 1933 in Vucidol, Montenegro, Papić earned his university degree at the School of Humanities and Social Sciences, University of Zagreb, and began to work in film in the mid-1950s as an assistant to directors such as Fedor Hanžeković and Veljko Bulajić. Ever since he made his debut in 1965 as director of the segment *Waiting* (*Čekati*) in the New Wave omnibus *The Key* (*Ključ*) (the other two segments directed by Vanča Kljaković and Antun Vrdoljak), his films are regularly considered to be creations manifesting a unique opus despite the variety of film types, genres and themes he takes on. This variety within his recognizability as an author has remained a constant of Papić's creative work until the present as he is preparing a new film project. Established as a Croatian cineaste in the years and decades in which Croatia was a federal unit within the former Yugoslavia, Krsto Papić shot his first feature film in independent Croatia in 1998. This was the tragicomedy *When the Dead Start Singing* which in many respects draws on, interprets, and unites his thematic, generic, and ethnographic preoccupations from his most famous and familiar earlier films, be it feature or documentary. It is therefore hardly surprising that *When the Dead Start Singing* was greeted at its premiere as the great return of a great director.

Having declared that he likes mixing the tragic and the comic in his films, Krsto Papić chose the the play *Cinco and Marinko* (*Cinco i Marinko*) by prominent Croatian playwright and musician Mate Matišić for his return to film after a seven-year absence dating from the movie *Story from Croatia* (*Priča iz Hrvatske*, 1991). He had already worked with Matišić as screenplay writer on *Story from Croatia*, and this cooperation logically extended to the next film. As soon as Papić saw the play performed, he decided to adapt it as a film. Ever since his first movie, Papić had himself written or co-written all his screenplays, which made him, among other things, one of the leading representatives of what is known as authorial cinema. Thus as co-screenplay writer he can be credited with the adaptation of Matišić's original play which was given new sub-plots and screenplay solutions. The film *When the Dead Start Singing* is a true tragicomedy, and it is a tragicomedy of confusion in which the comic is first in the lead, and the tragic comes at the end of the story. But independent of the prevailing intonation, the film does not pull back for a single frame from the synergy of the humorous and the sad. Regardless of which part of the story he tells, or which character he works with, the director, also co-writer, firmly remains in the position of creating an atmosphere of the interwoven nature of human comedy and tragedy. Even in the funniest situations, one tastes bitterness somewhere. *Shakespearean*, one might say: in a manner adapted to this part of Europe.

The central protagonists of the film are two Croatian emigrants in Germany who have been sharing an apartment for a year. They are Cinco, who went to Germany for economic reasons, and Marinko, whose main reason was political, fleeing the Yugoslav communist regime as a Croatian nationalist. 1991 was the year when the Yugoslav federation reached its turning point after the democratic changes in which several of the republics, including Croatia, opted for independence, while a part of the Serbian minority in Croatia opted for armed rebellion. This is what was happening at the moment when Cinco and Marinko set out from Berlin for their homeland, though they were making the trip for prosaic reasons. Cinco has falsified his death so that he might enjoy a German pension at home upon his return, while Marinko happens to help in getting the coffin over the international borders. What looked at first like a perfect plan soon comes upon a series of obstacles: Cinco's physician who signs the fake death certificate is actually involved in the sale of human organs; Marinko is attacked by a Yugoslav secret agent who ultimately kills him, while Cinco in his coffin ends up in a vehicle headed for Turkey instead of traveling in a hearse to Croatia. And finally, the destination of the two friends is becoming a war zone in which the Yugoslav army and Serbian rebels are attacking the Croatian village…

The play from which the movie was filmed premiered in 1992 at the Zagreb Kerempuh Satirical Theater, and was honored as the best dramatic text at the Days of Satire. Krsto Papić had already been successful at filming theatrical work in the past. One of his best films, *Acting Hamlet in the Village of Mrduša Donja* (*Predstava Hamleta u selu Mrduša Donja*), with which he participated in the official program at the Berlin film festival in 1973, is an adaptation of a play by noted Croatian writer Ivo Brešan, also with a tragicomic approach. Papić definitely plumbed the experience of working on that film, drawing from the original the most cinematic aspects, building them into a new cinematic form of expression applicable to the whole. The movie *When the Dead Start Singing* unfolds at a lively pace in which various plot settings easily follow one after the other, and their

Krsto Papić: *Acting Hamlet in the Village of Mrduša Donja* (*Predstava Hamleta u selu Mrduša Donja*), 1973

interchange — from the peaceful and prosperous German capital city to a little town in Dalmatian Zagora facing wanton wartime destruction — signal the shifts in coordinates of the tragicomedy. As the saying goes, the further south you go the sadder things become, but with no loss of wit. And furthermore, when he was a young director in the late 1960s and early 1970s, Krsto Papić stepped forward as the strongest film interpreter of the rugged Dalmatian landscape and the people who live there. His film *Handcuffs* (*Lisice*) of 1969 is on all the lists of the best Croatian feature films of all time. This is a case of a unique melding of a modernist approach, a documentary-like atmosphere, and ethnographic authenticity which uses the example of the regime settling accounts with a dissident to enunciate a concrete setting and concrete politics. Intimate and contextual at the same time.

There is a similar connection as well in *When the Dead Start Singing*, but more as a dedication to Papić's entire opus than as a determining factor of the story. In this sense the film is the breeziest piece in his career, whose feature films, with the exception of this one and, in large part, *Acting Hamlet in the Village of Mrduša Donja*, grapple with serious themes and discourses, and portray society in dark tones. From *Handcuffs* which speaks critically about the nature of Yugoslav totalitarianism clashing with Soviet totalitarianism after World War II, through *The Rat Savior / La Nuit de la Métamorphose* (*Izbavitelj*, 1976) as a metaphor for the birth of fascism in inter-war Central Europe, to *My Uncle's Legacy* (*Život sa stricem*, 1988) which, again, from the perspective of an individual speaks on the nature of the Yugoslav variant of communism and anti-individualism (nominated for a Golden Globe). Always informed by the reactions of viewers as the key arbiters, Papić has attempted to create as fluid a communication as possible with filmgoers in his *When the Dead Start Singing* by grounding the film in the comic plot.

This is what sets this movie apart from the rest of Papić's feature films. What makes it typical of Papić is the uninterrupted interfusion of human destiny and social context. There is hardly a film in which Krsto Papić hasn't used the characteristics of the environment and period in which the story unfolds to determine the fate of his characters. Setting his story in 1991 at the onset of the Croatian war for independence from Yugoslavia, whose federal institutions had been taken over by the regime of Ser-

Krsto Papić: *When the Dead Start Singing* (*Kad mrtvi zapjevaju*), 1998

bian president Slobodan Milošević, later indicted for war crimes, Papić gives us a unique moment in Croatian history with a keen and acerbic take. His personifications are the main characters of the movie: economic emigrant Cinco who risks his life and liberty to enjoy life with his family after years of privation while he lived and worked abroad, and political émigré Marinko who, despite the democratic changes in the country, harbors no illusions that anything will change in terms of the social status of people like himself. Their journey home is the journey of two of life's losers or, as it was later often called, losers in the democratic transition, of which there were millions in Central, Eastern and Southeastern Europe after the fall of the Berlin wall. The specifics of losers in the democratic transition in Croatia is that their position was made all the more difficult by the war, the outbreak of which is re-interpreted, also tragicomically, in the movie's finale. In doing so Papić supplements the genre of tragicomedy with wartime action drama, taking care not to lose for a moment his critical tone and ironic overtone. Although it is very clear who started the war, not all defenders are innocent. This complexity makes the film all the more relevant and profound although some of the critics faulted the film for its sudden and unnecessary transition to a war-related theme.

Yet another important link between *When the Dead Start Singing* and the rest of Krsto Papić's creative opus is the theme of Croatian guest workers in Germany. Papić dedicated some of his finest documentaries, for instance, to this topic, such as *Hello, Munich* (*Halo, München*, 1968) and *Special Trains* (*Specijalni vlakovi*, 1972). Regardless of whether they are documentaries or features, the Croatian economic emigrants in Papić's films are almost fatalistically pre-determined for a bitter fate, in which they do not experience satisfaction in the place they have moved to, nor in the place they left behind. This is why the choice of preeminent Croatian actors with whom the director has worked before — Ivo Gregurević (*Story from Croatia*) and Ivica Vidović (*The Rat Savior*), playing the roles of Cinco and Marinko — is key to the final impact of the film. The characters of energetic swindler and melancholic stoic are given optimal interpretations, just as the macabre use of deceased singers from Sinj *rera* ensembles in the background of the story (hence the movie's title), resembling a Greek chorus, effectively rounds out the depiction of the destiny of people from that time and place. And finally, the poster designed by Boris Ljubičić, himself from this region, was successful in promoting the movie.

The movie *When the Dead Start Singing* brought its director the Golden Arena for Best Director at the 45th film festival in Pula, 1998, at which composer Zrinko Tutić was also honored with an award, while the film itself was given the Golden Arena, an audience award conferred at the Pula arena, one of the largest open-air movie theaters in the world. Triumphing at the national festival in 1998, Krsto Papić confirmed that after Croatia's independence the continuity of his creative works meant that he remains one of the leading names in the domestic film industry.

Translated by Ellen Elias Bursać

When the Dead Start Singing (*Kad mrtvi zapjevaju*), Croatia, 1998. Color, 102 min.
Director: Krsto Papić
Script: Mate Matišić (based on his play *Cinco i Marinko*), Krsto Papić
Director of Photography: Vjekoslav Vrdoljak
Music:Zrinko Tutić
Editing: Robert Lisjak
Set Designer: Mario Ivezić
Costumes: Ruta Knežević
Cast: Ivo Gregurević (Cinco), Ivica Vidović (Marinko), Mirjana Majurec (Maca), Ksenija Pajić (Stana), Boris Miholjević (Dr. Lučić), Matija Prskalo (Ana), Žarko Savić (Vlajko), Dražen Kühn (Ante), Đuro Utješanović (agent), Ivica Zadro (driver), Ljubo Kapor (Petar), Peter Carsten (Kurt Müller)
Producer: Ljubo Šikić
Production: Jadran Film, Croatian Radiotelevision

Goran Dukić: *Wristcutters: A Love Story*, 2006
reviewed by Maxim Pozdorovkin

Goran Dukić's *Wristcutters: A Love Story* begins with the suicide of lovelorn Zia (Patrick Fugit) and the revelation that those who commit suicide end up in an afterworld that is just like the world they were escaping but a little worse. In this desaturated land, nobody smiles, the appliances are finicky, and people make small talk about how they "offed themselves." It goes without saying that this is a fantastic premise.[1] Absurdist potential aside, the dramatic possibilities are endless. "Who could think of a better punishment, really?" Zia wonders soon after ending up there. Dukić has Fugit pause for a moment before giving us the real kicker, "I've thought about suicide again, but I haven't tried it. I didn't want to end up in a bigger shithole than this one." The union of Fugit's slacker nonchalance and the existential weight of the situation are a match made in heaven.

Much like Harold Ramis' *Groundhog Day* (1993), *Wristcutters* begins as a satire about the eternal return and ends up as a romantic comedy. Twenty minutes into the film, as feelings of existential dread start to overwhelm Zia (i.e. dive bars begin to seem like a drag), he discovers that his ex, Desiree (Leslie Bibb), had also "offed" herself, thus becoming — at least ontologically — available. Zia sets off on a road trip to find her.

Desiree — attractive in a shampoo-commercial sort of way — is a glaring mismatch for the pale and disheveled Zia. The possibility of their ever being a couple seems remote, the likelihood of one party being driven to suicide — minuscule. In his quest to find Desiree and restore what was so clearly not meant to be, Zia is joined by Eugene (Shea Whigham), a Russian-American rocker, who plays the assertive yet clueless best friend. Soon after setting out in their junker, they pick up sexy and mischievous hitchhiker Mikal (Shannyn Sossamon). At this point the film goes into cruise control. Amorous indecision replaces philosophical anxiety and it is only a matter of an hour or so before Zia realizes that it is Mikal, and not Desiree, he wants.

Wristcutters, which premiered at Sundance and had a successful festival run, is a familiar romantic comedy/buddy road-trip hybrid. More interestingly, it is also a premise film, an extended *what-if* proposition, a forking-path reality that resembles our world in all but a few crucial ways.

1] The film's screenplay is an adaptation of Etgar Keret's story "Kneller's Happy Campers," which Keret himself adapted into graphic-novel form as "Pizzeria Kamikaze."

Goran Dukić: *Wristcutters: A Love Story*, 2006

Unlike elaborate science-fiction fantasies that delight in the spectacle of unfamiliar worlds, *what-if* films are only slightly fantastic, limiting themselves to a single aberration and its spatter of consequences. Whereas grotesque environments are estranged and unreliable places that resist systematic analysis, *what-if* worlds are rigidly logical. Rather than make the audience sit back in wonder, *what-if* films invite us to work alongside the characters in deducing the consequences generated by the initial conceit. The result is a more engaged and analytical experience, one that occasionally places the work under greater scrutiny than it can withstand.

In the film's first half, Dukić gets good mileage and continuous laughs out of the novelty of the afterworld. Dukić strikes a nice balance in *Wristcutters*; he uses the morbid premise for dark comedy but does not allow it to overwhelm the youthful exuberance that the actors bring to the film. With a beautiful cast and a hip soundtrack, *Wristcutters* is a film that strives for mass appeal. Consequently, letting Mikal and Zia live happily ever after in the world of the dead would amount to marketing suicide. While the romantic outcome is never in doubt — Desiree doesn't stand a chance against Mikal — the film's real conflict is between the laws of romantic comedy and the ground rules of the suicide afterworld. The threat of romantic comedy looms over *Wristcutters* but its onset is averted by the film's quirkiness and ironic distance. The characters follow the roles and rules of romantic comedy but they do so with their tongues in their cheeks; the absurdity of setting a love story in a land of suicide victims is never lost on them. A romance about nihilistic hipsters with sliced veins may sound peculiar, but it is a premise that allows the director both to satirize romantic comedy and abide by its tenets.

Consider what Dukić does to the generally overwrought "you make me a better man" confession. Mikal and Zia go off to be alone and, unexpectedly, find a secluded moonlit beach. Romantic music comes on. As they get cozy, Zia reveals that with Mikal around he is not completely dead. The two fall asleep in each other's arms. When they wake up the following morning, the camera pulls away to reveal a beach covered in syringes, condoms, and beer bottles. Kneller (Tom Waits), the wise old man of the film, finds the spooning couple and explains that the beach is where "the intravenous drug users and prostitutes congregate. It was too revolting for them." This morning-after revelation that the beach is not the romantic haven it appeared is more than just a sight gag. The peculiarities of the afterworld allow Dukić to turn the romantic cliché on its head. The romance isn't completely spoiled but it is made less saccharine and better for it. Too self-aware and playful to be an earnest genre exercise, *Wristcutters* peeks out from behind the conventions to smirk along with the audience.

Dukić's playful approach to the trappings of romantic comedy reminds one of a musician who turns to acting. When rock stars attempt an unassuming role their persona — cultivated in the spotlight — tends to stick out from behind the character. The musician turned actor analogy isn't mine, it is suggested by Dukić's film. Not so much by Tom Waits' role in the film but by the shadowy presence of Eugene Hutz, the lead singer of the popular New York "gypsy punk" band Gogol Bordello. Though Hutz himself does not appear in *Wristcutters*, he is felt throughout. Zia's sidekick Eugene, with his moustache and affected Eastern European accent, is an undisguised imitation. Moreover, four Gogol Bordello tracks appear on the soundtrack with "Underground," presented as being by Eugene's former band, serving as an anthem for *Wristcutters* as a whole.

Along with contributing to the film's aesthetic, Gogol Bordello's prominence in the film sheds light on some of the decisions that an immigrant director, such as Dukić, faces in making his first feature for the US market. Generally speaking, the characters in the film can either naturalize the director or establish him as an alien. In the language of publicity this amounts to the difference between "the director Goran Dukić, originally from Croatia" and "the Croatian director Goran Dukić." In *Wristcutters*, Dukić chooses the former and the choice of Gogol Bordello fits this decision well.

Though they embrace Slavic culture, Gogol Bordello are an American success story. In song after song, Hutz gives the word "immigrant" a scrubbing, ridding it of concrete national or socio-economic traits, transforming it into a term-of-honor for the globe-trotting flaneurs of the 21st century. In *Wristcutters*, Eugene's character is, like his prototype Hutz, an Eastern European token that is fully assimilated into Dukić's American afterworld. With an affected accent and a worrisome mother, the character of Eugene identifies Dukić as being from "that part of the world" but leaves out any of the complicated backstory.

The assimilationist tendency in presenting Eugene resonates with Dukić's approach to making a quintessentially American genre film such as the road movie. Since its prototype in Frank Capra's *It Happened One Night* (1935), the road trip romance has long lured foreign directors. The most successful attempts have been unafraid to mess with the formula. Though not much of a romantic comedy, *Paris, Texas* (1984) succeeds because Wim Wenders imports to Texas a sense of timing developed in his own German road movies. Conversely, Wong Kar Wai's recent *My Blueberry Nights* (2007) is a misstep because of the director's willingness to color within the lines and settle for an occasional personal flourish.

Much like Gogol Bordello's attempt to create a 'Gypsy punk' aesthetic, Dukić's road movie tries to straddle the divide between imitation and reinvention. Though at times one feels that he capitulates too readily to conventions, the absurdist lining with which Dukić layers most scenes keeps things fresh. At first glance, *Wristcutters* is a familiar American road map; desert landscapes and power lines, payphones and diners, broken engines and crooked hillbilly cops. The dusty bygone America seems like a nostalgic collage until we realize that its lifelessness is intentional and befits the film's subject matter and the predicament of its characters.

As Zia, Eugene, and Mikal continue their trip across the American West, their interactions are interspersed with exterior transition shots. Many of these begin by panning with the moving car before settling on a piece of broken furniture or some other piece of debris littering the landscape. These embarrassed landscapes, to borrow a term from Werner Herzog, remind us that their world is a little worse than ours. Yet as the friends journey onwards, the washed-out beauty of the landscape becomes strangely therapeutic and reminds us, as well as Zia and Mikal, that death is not the end.

Wristcutters: A Love Story, USA 2006. Color 88 min.
Director: Goran Dukić
Screenplay: Goran Dukić
Based on the short story *Kneller's Happy Campers* by Etgar Keret
Cinematography: Vanja Cernjul
Original Music: Bobby Johnston
Cast: Patrick Fugit, Shannyn Sossamon, Shea Whigham, Tom Waits, Leslie Bibb
Producers: Tatiana Kelly, Chris Coen, Mikal P. Lazarev
Executive Producer: Jonathan Schwartz
Production: No Matter Pictures, Crispy Films, Adam Sherman, Halcyon Pictures

---

Hrvoje Hribar: *What is a Man Without a Moustache? (Što je muškarac bez brkova?*, 2005)
reviewed by Mima Simić

What is a movie without an audience? Croatian director Hrvoje Hribar (1962) could tell you a few things about this, as he made a couple himself (*Croatian Cathedrals / Hrvatske katedrale*, 1992; *Tranquilizer Gun / Puška za uspavljivanje*, 1997) before he finally struck a chord with filmgoers and made the biggest homemade hit of the 2000s. Indeed, next to Vinko Brešan's ultimate 1996 blockbuster (in Croatian terms) *How the War Started on My Island (Kako je počeo rat na mom otoku)*, Hribar's *What is a Man Without a Moustache?* still holds ground as the most popular Croatian feature film since the country seceded from Yugoslavia in 1991. Perhaps the number of 152,276 viewers that made this movie a hit won't sound too impressive, but for a Croatian movie-going market it most certainly is, even when it comes to Hollywood blockbusters. In fact, for Croatian audiences, always ready to get high on Hollywood celluloid carbs, Hribar's movie was more delicious than *The Da Vinci Code*, *Sex and the City*, *New Moon*, *American Pie*, *Troy*, *Shrek Forever After*, etc. As this kind of popularity of a domestic film product is nothing short of a miracle, it calls to be examined not only as a film — a piece of art, or genre — but even more so as a (pop)cultural, and social phenomenon.

Just like Brešan's *War On My Island* (which had 337,000 viewers and was in the past 20 years outdone at the Croatian box office only by Cameron's *Titanic*), *Man Without a Moustache* is a comedy. And, just like Vinko Brešan, who based his film on a script by his father Ivo, one of the most popular Yugoslav (and Croatian) playwrights, Hribar used as the textual base for his movie a bestselling novel of the same name by Ante Tomić, one of the most popular Croatian contemporary authors. Though not a guarantee of the film's success, the choice of the text denotes the director's populist tendencies as well as his desire to cater to all tastes and (as populist texts tend to do) — one ideology. When I speak about the "ideology" of Croatian society, I refer neither to its Communist past, nor its wannabe-capitalist present. The ideology that has most deeply marked Croatian society since independence is patriarchy (exemplified by/through the role of the Catholic Church, right-wing government with a strong nationalist rhetoric, socio-cultural power distribution based on gender, etc.). Yet in the pro-European society that Croatia has become following the turbulent 1990s, patriarchy is slowly retreating (and adjusting to the new, more "civilized" circumstances). This story of patriarchy with a new face

Hrvoje Hribar: *What is a Man Without a Moustache?* (*Što je muškarac bez brkova?*), 2005

(without a moustache!) is the story of Hribar's movie. So how does the author sell this old/new patriarchy to the audiences?

Croatian films have commonly drawn criticism for the "unnatural" language they use, language that doesn't reflect the (social, linguistic) reality; language that no one speaks in "real" life. It's no wonder then that a major appeal of both domestic super-successful films was the fact of their "linguistic verisimilitude." Resolutely departing from the empty/artificial linguistic "center," authors (dis)locate their narratives onto the (geographical, social, linguistic) margin: the first is situated on a small Dalmatian island, the other, the subject of this article, takes place in Dalmatian Zagora, the southern inland part of Croatia, generally viewed and represented as "backward," i.e. patriarchal, religious, traditionalist, etc. Although both narratives are built on (regional, cultural) stereotypes (which are the *lingua franca* of the symbolic system), it is the power of the linguistic performance that gives them the air of authority and legitimacy — making their conservative patriarchal values seem quaint and almost endearing — just as the rural setting makes them seem closer to nature (they are all very passionate and instinctive, especially Tatjana, the female protagonist and the driving force of Hribar's film).

Chaplin once famously observed that "Life is a *tragedy* when seen in close-up, but a *comedy* in long-shot"; and this simple sentence could well serve for the analysis of *Man Without a Moustache*. As the movie is described and formulated as a comedy, let us look at the long-shot first. It opens on a young widow Tatjana (Zrinka Cvitešić) whose husband has fallen to death while working in Germany on the construction of a building. She gets some money as compensation for the marital loss, only to (inadvertently) become seriously rich thanks to civilization coming to the village, i.e. the building of a motorway. The affluent widow falls in love with the local (Roman Catholic) priest Stipan, a recovering alcoholic (Leon Lučev). She pursues him, and when he doesn't show up for the date she gets involved with his twin brother Ivan, a Croatian Army general, the other side of the patriarchal medal. Instantaneously, she gets pregnant by him, but the general dumps her and in the end she gets together with the priest, who leaves his holy duty for his newly found(ed) family.

To be sure, the outlined plot seems like fecund ground for comic situations and treatment of the patriarchal "travesty" implied in the title.

As Croatian society is (according to the latest 2001 census) intensely religious, with 87.8% of the population declared Roman Catholic, the narrative core in which a priest is "seduced" by a woman to leave the church is quite symbolic as it implies the need for a "new" patriarchy, one that will rid itself of the barren past and the unnatural demands on both men and women. This celluloid critique of the "old" patriarchy seems even more radical for its drastic departure from the novel, in which Tatjana stays with the (moustachioed) general! But can this smooth-shaven and civilized version of patriarchy really satisfy women? To make sure it does Hribar employs all the weapons of mass seduction available to a film director.

As a strongly comedic environment, the village community is presented as a choir of charming character-stereotypes made up of a village haiku poet/environmentalist; a traditionalist father who has returned from Germany to his native village with his grown-up daughter, not having consulted her about the move; a local drunk who likes to play with hand grenades; a bishop who, as punishment for Stipan's misbehavior, sends him to "Mogambo" in Africa; Tatjana's sister, a shopkeeper who speaks Spanish with the shoppers (influenced by TV soaps), etc. In accordance to this small army of endearing weirdos, the screenplay sparkles with (populist) one-liners, idiosyncratic curses (that the Croatian movie-going audience always readily responds to), a lot of sexual innuendo (and some practice), some (ostensibly benign) nationalist songs and stands, all packaged in a "natural," rural setting where passions (be they sexual, alcoholic, patriotic, or paternalist) run free and are forgiven because it's all, presumably, human *nature*.

Before we zoom into this comedy's (already discernible) tragic close-up, perhaps we should stop to state the obvious. *Of course* populist comedies work with stereotypes, stereotypes about gender, class, ideologies, ethnicity/race, those relating to sexual orientation etc. The most influential film industry in the West, Hollywood, was built and continues to thrive on (re)producing, recycling and re-selling stereotypes. Indeed, aren't Croatian and Hollywood blockbusters, for all their differences, just like Ivan and Stipan, different sides of the same coin: one rugged, and the other close-shaven? Don't they all, by the very nature of blockbusterity, want to keep us in the long-shot, shunning close-ups or any intimation of a spectatorial tragedy?

But into the first close-up we go. Here we are first met with the problem of the "naturalizing" of traditional values (embodied by the village community existing in a bucolic patriarchal paradise). The narrative universe of the film, as mentioned, is a patriarchy undergoing a makeover. An extreme example of the patriarchy "before" would be those of the general refusing to use a condom while having sex with the widow because his "religion forbids" it. The "after" patriarchy is when Tatjana ends up with the "good" brother, who leaves the patriarchal institution, the Church. But where in the makeover process can we place this scene? The brothers are discussing Tatjana (*in her presence*). "Won't you marry her?" says priest Stipan to his womanizing brother Ivan, who had just had (unprotected) sex with her. "She is wonderful", the priest-in-love adds. "How do you know it if you haven't fucked her?" retorts the general, adding: "I've had better fucks, but I didn't marry them." All the while Tatjana listens to this brotherly debate about who's going to marry her and how good (or mediocre) a fuck she is without a single comment.

Tatjana, mind you (who in the film is indeed referred to mostly as "the widow," her identity defined by her marital status) is the richest person in the village, owns both the shop and the restaurant/pub, i.e. is economically independent, and seems to be quite headstrong when it comes to pursuing her desires. (Her stubbornness is well exemplified by her 13-month long silence following her husband's demise). Her female economic independence (facilitated by the technological development and echoing the changes that joining the EU will bring) is obviously counterbalanced by her female "nature," which is (emotional, sexual) dependence on a man. Paradoxical to her economic status, Tatjana accepts the hegemonizing discourse of the Army and the Church that want to plan out her future. Of course, the "happy" ending that is provided vouches that the woman's choice was her own as she ends up with the man she wanted in the first place, but under which conditions? Her sexual/bodily integrity was impaired by the general not using a condom (and getting her pregnant; not to mention the variety of STDs he possibly passed onto her considering his sexual life-style and "religious" beliefs), while her political integrity was compromised through her silent acceptance of the discussion between the brothers/two major patriarchal institutions. This "new" patriarchy may be looser than the old one, but the ideological change (as the title inadvertently suggests) has been — merely cosmetic.

These few examples would probably get the "civilized" "Western eye" rolling at the "Croatian guy," with or without a moustache, before or after the ideological makeover. But let's take a quick look at the ultimate Hollywood blockbuster to see how it functions on/for the American (ideological) market, whether it actually sells the same thing as does *Man Without the Moustache* only with more expensive makeup?

Our blockbuster of choice is Christopher Nolan's *Dark Knight* (2008), the movie that managed (much like Hribar's) to seduce both critics and audiences. The epitome of evil in the movie is the Joker, the essential Terrorist, who wants to prove that (American) society lies on rotten ethical foundations; that the government and individuals are equally corrupt. The Joker is, obviously, the embodiment of actual American paranoia: the "anarchist" terrorist who despises wholesome American values (their common denominator being capitalism). The ultimate ideological problem of this film, however, does not lie with/in the super-villain Joker, but with its super-hero, the billionaire Bruce Wayne aka Batman, who has teamed up with the repressive status apparatus: police and the government. In an illegal action Batman kidnaps a Chinese citizen and takes him to the US to be interrogated (and tried!), freely using the most advanced technology for surveillance of all (!) Gotham citizens in his pursuit of the enemy. The manipulative structure of American society finds ultimate redemption in the fact that the system has been preserved, regardless of the price (the breaking of inter/national laws, manipulation of the public through media, etc.). The American "superhero," tragically, is but a mentally impotent function/tool of this preservation, rather than an individual, thinking subject.

Of course, just as *A Man Without a Moustache* provides enough material for it to be read as a *subversion* of the patriarchal system (the disrobing of the priest, the economic independence of women even in the most "backward" of villages, women's political advancement in the character of the female minister of defense, etc.), we could also read the *Dark Knight* as a *critique* of American politics/society, citing all the above examples to *support* the argument. The problem with both these movies, however, is in the mainstream (critical and audience) *reception* which doesn't seem to be willing to zoom in and examine, and voice, the tragedy of their close ups, but rather consumes these films (together with their face-value dominant ideologies) as comedies, or action movies, swallowing the ideology with the denoted genre. It stops short of unmasking the creature underneath the shaven face; it stops short of unmasking Bruce Wayne.

It will come as no surprise, then, that the answer to the question — *What is a Man Without a Moustache?* is — Batman. And that is hardly a reason to celebrate, either in Croatia, or in the USA.

What is a Man Without a Moustache? (*Što je muškarac bez brkova*), Croatia, 2005. Color, 109 min.
Director: Hrvoje Hribar
Script: Hrvoje Hribar, Ante Tomić
Director of Photography: Silvije Jesenković
Music: Tamara Obrovac
Editing: Ivana Fumić
Cast: Zrinka Cvitešić, Leon Lučev, Ivo Gregurević, Jelena Lopatić, Bojan Navojec, Marija Škaričić, Jelena Miholjević, Nada Gačešić Livaković
Producers: Mirko Galić, Hrvoje Hribar
Production: Fiz Production, Croatian Radiotelevision, Vizije Sft, Croatian Film Association (Hrvatski Filmski Savez)

Zrinko Ogresta: *Fragments: Chronicle of a Vanishing* (*Krhotine — Kronika jednog nestajanja*, 1991); *Washed Out* (*Isprani*, 1995); *Red Dust* (*Crvena prašina*, 1999); *Here* (*Tu*, 2003); *Behind the Glass* (*Iza stakla*, 2008)
reviewed by Tomislav Šakić

An audiovisual inscription of the external world, film has always been understood as "moving pictures" or a real record of the world beyond the camera. Even within the illusory film realm, the fictional truth is factual since it is realizable in the material world, and the camera is always objective inasmuch as it records settings, costumes, actors... Notwithstanding its inherent immanent realism — along with its other half consisting of fantasy and the telling of stories in the traditional clash of Lumière and Méliès — it has often been interpreted as a reflection of the environment from which it originates. According to the simplistic theory of reflection, "film is seen as a 'reflection' of the dominant beliefs and values of its culture" (see Graeme Turner, *Film as Social Practice*, 1999: 152).

The film industry participates in the construction of "nation" (Turner, 156) and the concept of national culture has always been narrowly tied to the idea of national cinema — what is more, the traditions in world cinemas are customarily prefixed by national determinants — German Expressionism, the Soviet Avant-garde, French Poetic Realism, Italian Neorealism, the French New Wave, etc., a part of the cultural industry,[1] film is seen as a form of representation and as belonging to broader societal and cultural processes of creating meaning through images, sounds, and signs. Social meanings are generated through culture (Turner, 1999: 48) in a circular process (in the sense that they are produced and consumed). Film impacts the systems of meaning in a given culture, but is, at the same time, their product (Turner, 152). In other words, film is an arena of ideology.

Besides this co-relation between film, culture, and ideology, film directors themselves often do not shy away from the contexts in which they work and choose to confront their national cultures, taking on the roles of representatives, opponents, critics, or at least witnesses. In socialist Croatia Veljko Bulajić belonged to this group. In the period since Croatia's independence (1991) we should mention Krsto Papić and the more recent works by Antun Vrdoljak (*Long Dark Night / Duga mračna noć*, 2004; *Tito*, 2010). If one had to point to a director in the post-1991 period, however, who made topics of national and social interest his top priority the choice would likely fall on Zrinko Ogresta. His stories are deeply embedded in society and appear to be at the same time narratives about the nation.

1] See Richard Johnson, "What Is Cultural Studies Anyway?" 1983, in John Storey, ed. *What Is Cultural Studies? A Reader*, 1996.

Zrinko Ogresta: *Washed Out* (*Isprani*), 1995

In this sense Ogresta is perhaps the only direct successor to Krsto Papić with whose recent films — *Story from Croatia* (*Priča iz Hrvatske*, 1991); to a degree also *My Uncle's Legacy* (*Životom sa stricem*, 1988), and *When the Dead Start Singing* (*Kad mrtvi zapjevaju*, 1998)[2] — he shares both visual aesthetics and narrative patterns containing a national dimension, especially in *Fragments: Chronicle of a Vanishing* (*Krhotine*, 1991) and *Red Dust* (*Crvena prašina*, 1999).

While Papić is more direct — the author of the renowned *Handcuffs* (*Lisice*, 1969) overtly sets his films as national narratives depicting various historical traumas from the recent past, such as clashes with the followers of the communist party, the Croatian spring of 1971, economic and political emigration — Ogresta opts to pursue a seemingly more circuitous path. For instance, in Papić's *Story from Croatia* the character played by Ivo Gregurević functions as a common Croat through whom the harrowing junctures of newer Croatian history are refracted, and who stands completely disillusioned by the end of the film (he loses not only his ideals but also his family because of his imagined homeland). In this film the national narrative is turned into national trauma. By contrast, in Ogresta's *Red Dust* the character played again by Ivo Gregurević (known for his roles of the "common" Croat from the neighborhood), the local Yugoslav policeman (Kirby) first undergoes a process of transformation into a Croatian policeman — even by changing his manner of speech from Serbo-Croatian to the official version of Croatian used by authorities — only to find himself facing the failures of the new society, beating up a local petty criminal/member of the nouveau riche (the Boss, the embodiment of all the negative aspects of the Croatian war economy and privatization in the mid-90s). This scene stands as a symbolic resolution of social contradictions (see Turner, 155) i.e., of accumulated social trauma, and serves as an outlet for a cathartic purging of all the negative elements that accumulated in the body of the nation during the Tuđman era.

The characters in Papić's films are marionettes of history, politics, and the Balkans (which itself has become his almost obsessive theme); they are actors in the larger narrative about the nation that determines their fates. By contrast, characters in Ogresta's films are not so much the bear-

---

2] *Story from Croatia* (*Priča iz Hrvatske*) was distributed abroad as *Idaho Potato*. *My Uncle's Legacy* was nominated for a Golden Globe for best foreign-language film.

ers of a national narrative, as they are representatives of "ordinary people" who constitute the majority in the nation.[3] Ogresta is clearly on the one hand heir to the established traditions in Croatian cinema (note for instance his title *Fragments: Chronicle of a Vanishing* in which "chronicle," a social form *par excellence*, recalls Papić's *Story from Croatia*),[4] while on the other, he relies indirectly on Polish cinema (*Washed Out / Isprani*, 1995, is a paraphrase of Marek Hłasko's *The Eight Day of the Week*, a novel which was made into a film by Aleksander Ford in 1957) and its line of "moral concern" (Krzysztof Zanussi, Krzysztof Kieślowski). This orientation had a significant influence on Croatian cinema in general, and is visible, for instance, in the "social-essay films" of Fadil Hadžić and Bogdan Žižić of the 1970s, and films by Zoran Tadić in the 1980s.[5] Ogresta's work, focusing on ethical issues, thus continues the cycle of films by his older colleagues, i.e. it relies on the trend of social essays, created in the shadow of the political oppression which descended upon Croatia and its intellectuals after the Croatian spring. One could argue that Ogresta's films have a somewhat less blunt critical edge, as do Hadžić's and Žižić's in the 1970s. After all, *Red Dust* ends with a dramaturgical solution and fictional emptying of accumulated frustrations that was not a common occurrence in Croatian real life at that time. What Ogresta gains through such authorial choices is precisely an ethical, Catholic habitus. His moral concern is a worthy successor of a similar orientation in Kieślowski's work precisely because Catholicism is at the root of both (*The Decalogue* serves as a remote model to Ogresta here).

Moralizing with a Catholic provenance comes forth particularly forcefully in Ogresta's more recent films in which he seemingly abandons national topics — such as in *Behind the Glass* (*Iza stakla*, 2008) — only to have social issues hit back hard as a boomerang. The private soap-opera story about marital infidelity is established as a narrative about emotions burdened with upbringing, prejudice, tradition, moralizing, feelings of guilt, etc. In other words, existing societal and cultural patterns (or stereotypes) are perpetuated. Even when he chooses an intimate love story, Ogresta, for whom film is first and foremost social art, unravels it as a story about collective values rather than as a transgression of societal or religious norms. It is precisely with regard to the romantic themes that we can see how far Ogresta is from some of the standards of Croatian and (post)Yugoslav film (Rajko Grlić's 2010 film *Just between Us* is a close comparison, due to a similar story). Sexual relations are never shown overtly,[6] more-

---

[3] This picture of "ordinary people" was pushed to the grotesque in Neven Hitrec's 2009 film *The Man Under the Table* (*Čovjek ispod stola*), based on a script by Hrvoje Hitrec, which is populated by distorted creatures residing in a twisted imaginary suburb of Zagreb. Another representative of "dark Croatian realism" is Davor Žmegač's *The Golden Years* (*Zlatne godine*, 1993), the first noted feature of independent Croatia.

[4] The chronicle structure (a story following the life of a family over several decades and simultaneously refracting national history) is shared by Papić's *My Uncle's Legacy* and *Story from Croatia*, Ogresta's *Fragments*, and Žmegač's *The Golden Years*.

[5] In this sense Papić is closer to Andrzej Wajda whose films also function as narratives about the key or traumatic segments in the national history.

[6] Except in *Behind the Glass* (*Iza stakla*, 2008), but even here the sexual act is accompanied with tears, accusations, and guilt.

over, there is no "Balkan" mindset that indulges in uninhibited physical pleasures, alcohol, folk music, elements present even in Papić's work. More than anything else, Ogresta's cinematic world is full of suppressed anxiety and hopelessness.

As already pointed out, the common thread in most, if not all, of his films is the fates of ordinary people. In *Washed Out* these are a young couple who cannot find a place to make love, petty criminals, grouchy and frustrated mothers disappointed with life, a father who longs for a sunny day to go fishing… The rain pours incessantly, while the psychological states of the characters are indicated already by the film's title. Similarly, in *Red Dust* there is not a single character who is not a person from the street and events take place in an imaginary part of the city meant to represent Croatian everyday reality. The focus is on typical loci and profiles through which Ogresta gives a portrait of fallen society: a coffee shop with resident drunkards, neglected kids, a soccer club, a local brick factory (with no future), an altruist priest, a good/harsh policeman, petty criminals and a local Mafioso, a sick girl, an ex-girlfriend beaten (and eventually killed) by her new husband/criminal, a neighborhood boy who idolizes the main character, and finally the main character himself who is a fugitive from the Yugoslav Army and a hero of the Homeland war, but also a boxer with nothing to look forward to and a former prisoner (imprisoned on false charges).

The main protagonist in *Red Dust*, appropriately named Luka Crnjak (the last name means "Blacky" in Croatian) crosses the borderline of what is permissible and takes social justice into his hands when, unrelated to his other problems (although they are caused by the same person, the Boss), he is shattered by the death of his young neighbor Sonja (suffering from a heart condition) with whom he has become romantically involved. In the same spirit, when policeman/father Kirby beats the Boss at the end of the film in front of people from the neighborhood, his primary motivation is Crnjak's death, but in this moment of justified rage he also channels the society's wrath towards the Boss as a symbol of the new Croatia — an incarnation of numerous tycoons and usurers in the phase of transition.[7] Duplicity and hypocrisy prevail in this bleak picture of the nascent state and even the Boss himself dares to allude to the "common good" when he buys a local brick factory in order to build a new soccer field from which only he will profit. It is clear that a capable and genuine protector of the interests of ordinary people remains elusive, and herein lies the true tragedy. Crnjak — opposed to the Boss who serves as a pitiful symbol of a new Croatian reality — has to perish as an embodiment of an ethical line so that the neighborhood boy, Zrik, for whom Crnjak is an idol, will "no longer believe in the fairy tales." Crnjak is further contrasted to the Boss as a hero of the Homeland war who has emerged from the war untainted and is now asking himself "What did I fight for?" There is no more cigarette smuggling business for Crnjak. He goes to work honestly at the brick factory until its work is halted in the process of privatization, which sets in motion a series of events leading to the final tragedy.

7] Boss himself is in fact a ridiculous outsider on the margin of the big-ticket transactions taking place at the time this film was shot.

Zrinko Ogresta: Here (*Tu*), 2003

Unfortunately, Goran Tribuson's script remains burdened with his American models, from Martin Scorsese's New York films to the prototypes of *Rocky*-style justice seekers. The dramaturgical conflicts caused by these incompatibilities are sometimes difficult to overcome for Ogresta through directing, and the transitions from the realm of the private to that of the collective are not always adequately motivated. Still, one needs to underscore a skillful sequencing of scenes such as the opening descriptive shots which establish the chronotope for the film and introduce the character of the military deserter (i.e. Crnjak), the transitional eclipse which joins the first and the second halves of the film, and the final medium-shot in which the characters leave the site of tragedy moving diagonally across the red dust of the brick factory. All is bleak and hopeless in the fates of the ordinary protagonists choked in the dust and the atmosphere of the incessant summer drought emphasized by the prevalence of brown-reddish colors.

In his next film *Here* (*Tu*, 2003), Ogresta makes a significant shift, injecting his script with a different type of structure. This is a film in which Robert Altman's directorial concepts are recognizable: an omnibus that follows some ten characters on six parallel tracks, stringing through these vignettes a story about contemporary Croatia here and now. It is precisely this type of poetic orientation providing a vertical cut into the tissue of society that allows him a way of escaping the traps that lurked in the script of his *Red Dust*. The later film does not insist on showing a naturalistic aspect of relations in society or clashing ideological positions, rather, it provides insight into a point of time chosen seemingly by chance. This temporal juncture is then used to depict a series of individual stories (i.e. slices of life) that are related and mutually entangled, forming a collective narrative at the associative level. The introductory war segment relies on the metaphor of a wounded bird and functions as a path marker telling the spectator that the foundations for the Croatian state were forged in recent war.[8] The rest of the stories, however, are dramatically set up as "found situations" without the development of the events leading up to

---

8] The film was described along these lines also in the trailers. It is important to note that *Here* received a special jury award at the festival in Karlovy Vary, a critics' award at the festival in Montpellier, first place at the Milan festival, but also — and we should note the significance that lies in the name — the Krzysztof Kieślowski award at the Denver film festival.

them. They are populated with people typical for Ogresta's films, characters from the margins of society with no prospects who reflect the state of the entire nation. Especially memorable is the second story, a modern and powerful echo of *Trainspotting* (Danny Boyle, 1996) and *Run, Lola, Run* (Tom Tykwer, 1998), in which a girl desperately seeks a fix. The final story focuses on a family and epitomizes the culmination of traumatic experiences in Croatian society. In its final part the father, a former warrior in the Homeland war with shaky hands that intimate suppressed trauma (caused not so much by war as by a general disappointment in life) stands by a window smoking while his son stands at another window. And then just before the final darkening, as a global metaphor that puts into perspective all that has been seen up to that point, we hear the national anthem which is broadcast on the state radio every night at midnight. Perhaps unintentionally, this moment represents a sublimation of the trauma that has accumulated in the course of the film and which does not have a cathartic resolution as it does in *Red Dust*, but grows, rather, into a literal darkening that hovers over the entire nation.

In the period of Croatian cinema since independence Ogresta will be remembered for his ethically charged *Red Dust* and *Here* through which he has left a sobering statement about society in transition and the disillusionment of ordinary people. It is perhaps logical that after the ominous final scene in *Here* which summarizes the last twenty years of the country's social condition he chooses to set the topics of national narratives aside and turn his attention to personal stories such as the one in his most recent film, *Behind the Glass*, in which, however, one can still clearly recognize in the shattered personal fates the impact of a traumatized society.

Translated by Aida Vidan

Fragments: Chronicle of a Vanishing (*Krhotine — Kronika jednog nestajanja*), Croatia, 1991
Color, 100 min.
Director: Zrinko Ogresta
Script: Lada Kaštelan, Zrinko Ogresta
Director of Photography: Davorin Gecl
Editing: Josip Podvorac
Set Designer: Duško Jeričević
Costumes: Doris Kristić
Cast: Filip Šovagović (Ivan Livaja), Alma Prica (his wife), Slavko Juraga (Lovro Livaja, Ivan's father), Nada Subotić, Semka Sokolović, Đuro Utješanović, Kruno Šarić, Ivo Gregurević, Ana Karić, Lena Politeo, Božidar Orešković (Tomo Livaja, Ivan's grandfather)
Production: Jadran film, Croatian Radiotelevision

Washed Out (*Isprani*), Croatia, 1995. Color, 92 min.
Director: Zrinko Ogresta
Script: Zrinko Ogresta (based on Marek Hłasko's novel)
Director of Photography: Davorin Gecl
Music: Jasenko Houra
Editing: Josip Podvorec
Set Designer: Ivica Trpčić
Costumes: Maja Galasso
Cast: Katarina Bistrović-Darvaš (Jagoda), Josip Kučan (Zlatko), Filip Šovagović (Jagoda's brother), Mustafa Nadarević (Jagoda's father), Božidarka Frajt (Jagoda's mother), Ivo Gregurević (Ivo), Božidar Orešković
Production: Jadran film, Croatian Radiotelevision

Red Dust (*Crvena prašina*), Croatia, 1999. Color, 105 min.
Director: Zrinko Ogresta
Script: Goran Tribuson, Zrinko Ogresta (with Tarik Kulenović)
Director of Photography: Davorin Gecl
Music: Darko Hajsek
Editing: Josip Podvorac
Set Designer: Ivica Frangeš
Costumes: Vesna Pleše
Cast: Josip Kučan (Crni), Marko Matanović (Zrik), Mirta Takač (Sonja), Ivo Gregurević (Kirby), Slaven Knezović (Boss), Kristijan Ugrina (Škrga), Sandra Lončarić (Lidija), Žarko Savić (father), Ante Vican (Father Grga), Božidarka Frait (neighbor), Marica Vidušić (Lela), Jelica Vlajki (Ruža), Vanda Vujanić (Julija)
Production: Inter film

Here (*Tu*), Croatia, 2003. Color, 90 min.
Director: Zrinko Ogresta
Script: Zrinko Ogresta
Director of Photography: Davorin Gecl
Editing: Josip Podvorac
Set Designer: Goran Stepan
Costumes: Željka Franulović
Cast: Jasmin Telalović (Kavi), Marija Tadić (Duda), Zlatko Crnković (Josip), Ivo Gregurević (actor), Ivan Herceg (Karlo), Nikola Ivošević (Lala), Barbara Prpić (tourist), Filip Juričić
Production: Inter film, Croatian Radiotelevision

Behind the Glass (*Iza stakla*), Croatia, 2008. Color, 80 min.
Director: Zrinko Ogresta
Script: Lada Kaštelan, Zrinko Ogresta
Director of Photography: Davorin Gecl
Music: Bernarda Fruk-Mišković, Tomo Fogec, Zbynek Mikulik
Editing: Josip Podvorac, Vladimir Gojun
Set Designer: Tanja Lacko
Costumes: Željka Franulović
Cast: Leon Lučev, Jadranka Đokić, Daria Lorenci, Anja Šovagović-Despot, Božidarka Frait, Nina Violić, Dara Vukić, Boris Svrtan, Krešimir Mikić, Bojan Navojec, Trpimir Jurkić
Producer: Ivan Maloča
Production: Inter film in cooperation with Croatian Radiotelevision

Tomislav Radić: *What Iva Recorded* (*Što je Iva snimila 21. listopada 2003*; 2005)
reviewed by Petra Belković Taylor

By documenting the daily life of a post-communist, postwar Croatian family, Tomislav Radić's award winning film,[1] *What Iva Recorded* (2005), manages to take the pulse of the changing life of Zagreb at the start of the 21st century. His main aid in this endeavor is the technique of found footage. By putting the camera into the hands of fifteen-year-old Iva (a character played by Maša Mati Prodan), he leads us to believe that we are watching a home video made of "what Iva finds interesting." This allows the director to disappear even further behind the scenes and to conceal the fictive nature of the film, leaving the audience with the sense of observing brute reality. It also enables him to capitalize on a fortunate side effect of the documentary approach: to record more than what is intended, capturing people's lives and conversations in their original impurity, full of telling slips and symbols. The film therefore functions on two closely related levels: both as portrayal of a family trying to navigate its own dysfunction, and as an exploration of the rich milieu of verbal and nonverbal signs and symbols that reflect the struggle of a Croatian society in transition.

While Radić manages to capture a fair amount of cultural and psychological complexity, much of it can easily remain hidden to the foreign eye. The online English reviews reflect such oversights.[2] Although generally favorable towards the film and taken by its charm, acting performances and camera work, as well as the director's keen eye, American reviewers are often disappointed that the movie doesn't seem to "go anywhere," that it "falls flat" towards the end, or that it lacks some of the anticipated depth. What the same reviews fail to note, however, is the script's reliance on references embedded in verbal and non-verbal aspects of the script, i.e. the characters' mannerisms, accents, patterns of speech and seemingly unimportant minor conversations. In fact, Radić's dialogues, further improvised by the excellent acting cast, sound quite natural to the native ear and are perceived very much as a rendering of private conversations one has heard or been a part of before. In this case the English reviewers' com-

---

1] The film won The Grand Golden Arena award for best film at the Pula Film Festival in 2005. It also won the Golden Arena award for best director (Tomislav Radić) and best actress (Anja Šovagović), as well as the Croatian Film Critics' Society's Oktavijan award. The same year it also won the Fipresci Prize, awarded by the International Federation of Film Critics, at the Ljubljana International Film Festival.
2] For examples, amongst others, see: Bill Gibron's review and Trent Daniels interesting review.

Tomislav Radić: *What Iva Recorded* (*Što je Iva snimila 21. listopada 2003*), 2005

plaints are perhaps best attributed to their distance from the movie's dialogue, first by virtue of the language barrier and then by the translation subtitles. Faced with the problem of fast, improvised, and idiomatic dialogue, the translators opted to translate phrases selectively, often creating new sentences in place of partial phrasing, and producing for the English speaker a sense of the general meaning and direction of the conversation rather than of the subtle nuances found in the repetitions, hesitations, and cultural references. If we are to ascribe the lack of depth to what is lost in this particular translation, the reviewers may justifiably feel, therefore, that they are missing what for now remains between the lines.

But for those initiated into the culture, what operates between the lines in this movie is arguably that which is most poignant and uncomfortably honest. In the very opening scene of the film Radić makes sure to point out that the action takes place in one of Zagreb's wealthy neighborhoods, such as Pantovčak or Tuškanac. The view from the balcony and the architecture style of the "urban villa" betray the setting. Throughout Zagreb's 19th and 20th century, these neighborhoods have hosted the wealthy and the famous, and most of all perhaps, those favored by the various power regimes that passed through the country. Therefore, according to popular folklore, since the war in the 1990s they received yet another brand of inhabitant: those who rose to economic, political, or even underworld power during and after the war, exploiting the circumstances of a country that yet once again found itself in transition. The father's (Božo), accent betrays him as not from Zagreb, and possibly as one of "those." Božo (played by Ivo Gregurević) is most likely from a rural area, perhaps from Herzegovina, the ethnically mostly Croatian part of Bosnia and Herzegovina notorious in contemporary folklore for extreme Croat nationalism and ties to organized crime. The mother (Željka), who is played by Anja Šovagović, has a distinctly Zagrebian accent. And the resulting associations in the mind of the audience are unmistakable: the husband and wife are most likely brought together by their interest in material goods and status. He is likely looking for new status in the capital of the country, which includes a good-looking woman from a good family, and she, a single mother is aspiring to keep her life style and live up to her bourgeois reputation.

As the film progresses these stereotypes are confirmed and supported. Božo thinks mostly of his German guest, Mr. Hoffner (played by Karl

Menrad), and what he hopes will be a lucrative business contract with him, while Željka worries about her appearance and her marital unhappiness as reflected in her half-hearted efforts to prepare for Iva's birthday dinner at which Mr. Hoffner, not Iva, is to be the star. Željka's absentminded preparations further increase the tension between the couple and contribute to the escalating family discord as some guests begin to show, others cancel, Hoffner is quite late, and the food is not what Božo had asked that it be.

But as the movie progresses, these stereotypes begin to break down and the more philosophical side of Radić's project takes precedence. Before exploring this further however, we should mention one other important character, Željka's brother, Darko (played by Boris Svrtan), who is the only other invited dinner guest to attend. As a starving, free-spirited artist type, acquainted with Zagreb's bohemian counter-culture and critical of mainstream conservatism, Darko represents yet another social layer of city and family structure. Within the family he represents a more unruly, but at the same time more infantile element. And within the city, he belongs to the liberal stratum that prides itself on its critical distance from the dominant class's suspect accomplishments. Apparently relaxed and non-judgmental, he nevertheless enters the scene singing a song referring to the Ustasha military group (a Croatian faction of the WWII fascist movement that created the notorious marionette fascist Independent State of Croatia), which Božo rightly understands as being sung for his benefit. Božo later asks, "You didn't need to bring that up. Fascist! Do you really mean that?" but Darko's answer is never direct. His best answer is a type of excuse: "Well, that is what you are. You ban everything that you don't like!" Here Darko's ambivalence about the shifting political situation is revealed. Whether out of respect for his sister's family, or perhaps out of fear, apathy, lack of power or evidence, and finally out of sheer dependence on Božo from whom he frequently borrows money, Darko is unable to follow through with his criticism. The interaction between Darko and Božo therefore captures the conflicting elements of a country in transition — both feel out of place and carry a level of animosity for the other — but both also find themselves in a peculiar symbiotic relationship.

While most of the movie works to build the national stereotypes, the last brief portion, which reads very much as a fictive ending to a documentary film, unravels them. Božo is revealed not as a conniving businessman, but as fearful, naïve, and concerned about his family's financial stability. Željka is revealed as surprisingly devoted and honest, and ultimately as interested more in Božo himself than in wealth. And even Iva's fears, reflected in the long camera shots of her mother dancing with Hoffner and in her own earlier rejection of Božo as a father figure, are somewhat assuaged. Characters lost in their societal and familial roles suddenly meet their human selves, and while they do not ride off into the sunset, exhausted, embracing one another, they do make their way to the bedroom. Gently and compassionately the director puts himself on the side of these tired people, and gives them and their society a break — for now.

It could be said that this movie plays with a number of established stereotypes and boundaries: between the fictive and documentary, amateur and professional, private and public, central and peripheral. Nevertheless, it leaves one dichotomy less explored: that of foreign and domestic. From the first mention of his name, Mr. Hoffner is an elusive outsider who is to be wooed for the sake of financial gain. After he is late to the dinner, he comports himself in a superficially polite manner, condescends to Božo and his business skill, and finally proceeds to confirm his image as untrustworthy and exploitative. His humanity is never revealed and he ends up rather as the proverbial scapegoat. Hoffner's character failures bring the family together, and only against them is Božo able to act with resolve and self-confidence. Hoffner exits the film in a similarly symbolic fashion, riding away in a speeding taxi with an angry local (Božo) running after him.

While most reviews do not seem disturbed by the one-dimensionality of Mr. Hoffner's character, they do find fault with what they see as a "flat" and anticlimactic ending. Mr. Hoffner drives off, Božo tears up the contracts of the business deal he was to have with him, finally gives some of his attention to Iva, and then, followed by Iva's camera, slowly walks off into the bedroom with Željka. This presentation of the events leaves an important question unresolved: have the characters grown and taken charge of their lives, or have they merely resigned themselves to accepting what life deigns to give them? The ambivalent ending, however, is typical for Radić (see, for example, his last movie, *Three Stories About Sleeplessness* (*Tri priče o nespavanju*, 2008). Especially because we never hear the characters' inner thoughts, it is possible to interpret the events (Božo tearing up the contracts and walking into the bedroom with Željka), as either recourse to routine survival or evidence of a hopeful self-realization. The ending is a type of psychological illusion, and Radić seems to know that in order to capture reality he must leave the door open for both possibilities.

What Iva Recorded (*Što je Iva snimila 21. listopada 2003*), Croatia, 2005. Color, 92 min.
Director: Tomislav Radić
Script: Tomislav Radić and Ognjen Sviličić
Cinematography: Vedran Samanović
Art Director: Ivica Trpčić
Sound Editor: Gordan Fučkar
Production Manager: Tihomir Stivičić
Editing: Kruno Kušec
Cast: Anja Šovagović-Despot, Ivo Gregurević, Boris Svrtan, Maša Mati Prodan, Barbara Prpić, Karl Menrad
Production Company: Korus, Croatian Radiotelevision

Branko Schmidt: *The Melon Route* (*Put lubenica*, 2006); *Metastases* (*Metastaze*, 2009)
reviewed by Zhen Zhang

Those who have viewed Branko Schmidt's recent films for the first time, *The Melon Route* (*Put Lubenica*, 2006) and *Metastases* (*Metastaze*, 2009), will undoubtedly experience these two films as "depressing," "edgy," "odd," "dark" and so on. Yet, despite the bleak feelings aroused by the two films, they have not failed in attracting the audiences' attention and appreciation. *The Melon Route* won the Grand Prix at the international Slow Film Festival in Eger, Hungary, and *Metastases* won the Golden Arena of Pula, which is the Croatian equivalent of the American Academy Award (Oscar).

The story of *The Melon Route* is set in a desolate place near the river Sava, located on the border between Bosnia and Herzegovina and Croatia, where people, mostly Chinese, are smuggled to the West. At the film's opening, and with soft, somber and low-pitched background music, the main figure Mirko (Krešimir Mikić), sitting in the dark and holding a half-burned cigarette between index and middle finger, motionless and listless, keeps switching the ceiling lamp on and off rhythmically and unstoppably. Here, the shimmering light in the darkness and the flagging, dispirited Mirko set the basic tone of the film's cinematography and atmosphere — colorless and bleak. The storyline of the film is simple. During the winter, a group of Chinese is transported to the Sava river area and waiting to be smuggled to Croatia and onwards to the West. Due to the overburdened boat and the panic among the passengers, the skiff overturns as Mirko is ferrying them to the Croatian side. Consequently, only Mirko and a Chinese woman (Sun Mei) survive while all others drown in the accident. Mirko decides to hide the woman in the basement of his cabin, and gradually his life begins to change under her influence despite the linguistic barrier. When the local mafia kidnaps her (because she is a witness of the Chinese people's drowning), Mirko reverts to his past as a soldier, takes the guns out of the storage, goes to the mafia men's place and kills them all. In the end, the Chinese woman and the gypsy boy, who is Mirko's sole friend, are sent by him en route to Germany while wounded Mirko stays behind in his dwelling.

The most interesting relationship of the film, which is also particularly well portrayed, is the one between Mirko and the nameless Chinese woman. The audiences can clearly sense the gradual strengthening of the relationship between the two strangers, from initial indifference or even

 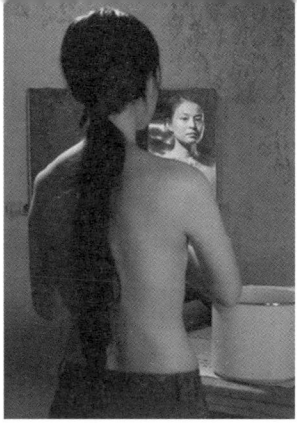

Branko Schmidt: *The Melon Route (Put lubenica)*, 2006

hatred to mutual understanding and assistance. Schmidt deals with the details very carefully. At first, when the Chinese woman and Mirko are catching their breath on the riverbank after the failed ferrying across the river, the Chinese woman grabs the mud on the ground and flings it at Mirko with animosity, seeing him as her parent's murderer. Later, she finds her father's body in the river and takes a spade from Mirko in order to bury the dead man; Mirko approaches her and snatches the spade from her despite her distrustfulness and hostility, while she even spits at him; he then begins to dig the grave for her father, without a word. At night, when he comes back to his dwelling and sees her sleeping in his bed, he indicates to her the direction of the door and forces her out, again, silently. Curling herself up in a deserted car for another night, she is so hungry and exhausted the next day that she breaks into Mirko's cabin for shelter and food, and after that a mutually peaceful and increasingly affectionate co-existence begins. Mirko even grins, for the first time in the movie, when the gypsy boy makes a bantering remark about his "wife" who said something in Chinese. This segment is not translated into any other language, but from the body language it is clear that the relationship has undergone a profound transformation. The Chinese woman actually says: "I totally understand. You don't have much money, either. But don't worry. I will return your money when I am in Germany." She has, seemingly, forgiven him. He starts to change too: he starts shaving, actively seeks a way to get her to Germany, and lets her sleep in his bed. Through the Chinese woman's eyes, the audiences get a wider scope of Mirko's earlier life: when she is randomly flipping over his personal pictures, we see Mirko's happy youth with his parents and friends, as well as his days in the army.

The director does not forget to emphasize the linguistic and cultural misunderstandings between them: Mirko bursts out laughing by the river, spurred by his own memories and experience of the place; the Chinese woman misunderstands him because he is laughing where her father died, which is a blasphemy of the dead in Chinese tradition. The climax of their relationship seems to be the moment when the Chinese woman holds Mirko's hand voluntarily and silently. Due to the complete absence of verbal understanding between the two main figures, the director focuses on the close-ups of their faces, hands, etc., and different shooting angles, to show a subtle change in their hearts, which, in my opinion, was successfully conveyed. The reason for their mutual attraction is not difficult to grasp: Mirko is a traumatized veteran who lost almost everything in the war, including passion and desire for a new life; on the contrary, the Chinese woman, despite all the misfortunes that happened to her, is passionate and determined to emigrate to Germany in search of a better life. The taciturn, poor Mirko arouses the compassion of the Chinese woman, who, as we can imagine, is equivalently poor back home. Schmidt deliberately emphasizes the silence between the two main characters, which, in the era of sound films, relocates the audiences back into the age of silent movies and forces them to refocus on body gestures, facial expressions and wordless acting, namely, on the nature of the early films.

Aside from illegal immigration and human trafficking, the film also depicts other social problems, such as organized crime in the post-war Croatia and Bosnia, prejudice against the Roma people and corruption at the border between Bosnia and Herzegovina and Croatia. Mirko's only real friend — a sympathetic and benevolent Roma boy, who steals food and trades pirate CDs for a living, is caught and badly beaten by the local gangsters. The local policeman takes bribes from the amoral traffickers. The gangsters kidnap the Chinese woman and brandish their guns. And, for a Chinese viewer such as myself, it is of course painful to see our compatriots being smuggled to the West and shown no mercy or sympathy; on the other hand, it is the undeniable truth that poor Chinese are eagerly seeking a better life in the West by illegal border-crossing.

The portrayal of a few soccer fans — hooligans captured in the film *Metastases*, might make the Croatian audiences uncomfortable just as much as the themes from Schmidt's other film do. Yet, by touching on the fringes of the society, the director successfully portrays some of the bleak realities of contemporary Croatia—and how the war and its aftermath have damaged people.

Metastases centers on four problematic young men in contemporary Zagreb, Croatia, who seem to have nothing to do except exhibit their fanatical fervor for the Zagreb's soccer club NK Dinamo, consume huge amounts of alcohol and sometimes drugs, and involve themselves in robberies, irrational fighting and domestic violence. Schmidt depicts the everyday lives of Filip (Franjo Dijak), Krpa (Rene Bitorajac), Dejo (Rakan Rushaidat), and Kizo (Robert Ugrina) sequentially; the four segments are separated by intertitles and integrated in the final scene of NK Dinamo's soccer match.

Filip has just returned to Zagreb from a Spanish drug rehabilitation commune and is urged to find a job by his father before being dragged back by his peers into the old ways of living — though he is the only person in the group who tries to deviate from the old ways. Krpa is a perpetual wife-abuser and ferociously nationalistic man often irritated by Dejo's Serbian ethnicity. Kizo is an alcoholic always in search of another drink, in a state of constant and palpable mental fog, who finally dies from his alcoholism. Yet, in a gentle moment when Kizo feeds homeless cats near his house, we may perceive a kind, fragile, vulnerable and sensitive heart that Kizo has. In order to satisfy his heroin addiction, Dejo, deluded by the

Branko Schmidt: *Metastases* (*Metastaze*), 2009

drug at all times, smuggles heroin from Bosnia, and is finally caught by the police when he is smuggling drugs over the border.

The director makes every effort to portray the real life of the people on the margins of contemporary Croatia. The narrative line is relatively simple and minimal and exhibits a certain "lack of plot" or "narrative emptiness," which results in the documentary feel of the film. It also indicates the shared characteristic of the portrayed characters — an emptiness and idleness of soul connected to irrational anger, substance abuse, and predictable behavior. The shooting technique, the hand-held camera and dialogues imbued with elliptic utterances and with vulgar talking and much swearing augment this sense of a documentary-like recording — the film's scenes seem to be shot so randomly that they appear as if taken in the genuine environment of a Zagreb neighborhood.

Both Schmidt's films are relatively short, although *Metastases* is shorter of the two. Perhaps the director understood that viewers would simply not tolerate for very long this kind of the film texture, with all the vulgar talk and unpleasant behavior. On the other hand, the director successfully depicts the reality of this environment, the intensity of its aimlessness, emptiness, and frustration. The extreme chauvinism is shown clearly, as still having its adherents in modern Croatia and as connected to this kind of an environment. People attempt to live peacefully after the war, yet, the scar of the war has never gone away — hatred, anger, violence... The post-war trauma is no less lethal than the war itself.

From the perspective of narrative and shooting techniques, *The Melon Route* is more "artistic" and stylized while *Metastases* more realistic and gritty. Some audiences might object to the "coldness" and "seriousness" of Branko Schmidt's films, but they would be missing the point. Instead of trying to entertain the viewers, Branko Schmidt pays close attention to the marginalized part of society, and makes excellent, passionate and precise films which resonate far beyond Croatian borders.

The Melon Route (*Put lubenica*), Croatia, 2006. Color, 89 min.
Director: Branko Schmidt
Script: Branko Schmidt, Ognjen Sviličić
Director of Photography: Vjekoslav Vrdoljak
Music: Miroslav Škoro
Editing: Vesna Lažeta
Set Designer: Mladen Ožbolt
Costumes: Željka Franulović
Cast: Krešimir Mikić (Mirko), Mei Sun (Chinese girl), Leon Lučev (Šeki), Armin Omerović (Meho), Emir Hadžihafizbegović (Gojko), Ivo Gregurević (Cale), Slobodan Maksimović (Edo), Zijah Sokolović (Pauk), Darijo Veličan (handicapped man), Elena Dlesk (Russian girl 1), Dora Lipovčan (Russian girl 2), Filip Šovagović (Lak), Iljo Benković Drča (Kolega), Chen Samin (the old Chinese man), Marella Oppenheim (translator)
Producer: Stanislav Babić
Production: Croatian Radiotelevision and Telefilm

Metastases (*Metastaze*), Croatia, Bosnia and Herzegovina, Serbia, 2009. Color, 85 min.
Director: Branko Schmidt
Script: Ognjen Sviličić, (based on the novel by Ivo Balenović)
Director of Photography: Dragan Ruljančić
Production designer: Mladen Ožbolt
Editing: Vesna Lažeta, Hrvoje Mršić
Costumes: Željka Franulović
Cast: Rene Bitorajac (Krpa), Franjo Dijak (Filip), Robert Ugrina (Kizo), Rakan Rushaidat (Dejo), Jadranka Djokić (Krpa's wife), Ivo Gregurević (Filip's father), Ljiljana Bogojević (Filip's mother), Daria Lorenci (Milica), Predrag Vušović (Dejo's father), Ksenija Marinković (Kizo's mother), Vera Zima (Aunt Zora), Ivan Brkić (Uncle Brane), Emir Hadžihafizbegović (Reuf), Franjo Jurčec (Krpa's neighbor)
Producer: Stanislav Babić
Production: Telefilm in association with Croatian Radiotelevision,
Refresh Production (Bosnia and Herzegovina) and Lux film (Serbia)

A Note on Contributors

Sanja Bahun: Assistant Professor at the Department of Literature, Film, and Theatre Studies, University of Essex. Her area of expertise is international modernism, and her research interests include comparative literature and film, psychoanalysis, and women's and gender studies. She has published articles and book chapters on a variety of related subjects, and she is author of *Modernism and Melancholia: History as Mourning-Work* (2011) and joint editor of *The Avant-garde and the Margin: New Territories of Modernism* (2006), *Violence and Gender in the Globalized World: The Intimate and the Extimate* (2008), *From Word to Canvas: Appropriations of Myth in Women's Aesthetic Production* (2009), and *Myth and Violence in the Contemporary Female Text: New Cassandras* (2010).

Gordana P. Crnković (editor): Associate Professor of Slavic and Comparative Literature and a member of Cinema Studies and Program for Theory and Criticism at the University of Washington, Seattle. She wrote *Imagined Dialogues: East European Literature in Conversation with American and English Literature* (Northwestern University Press, 2000), and with Sabrina P. Ramet she co-edited *Kazaaam! Splat! Ploof! American Influence on European Popular Culture, 1945 to Present* (Rowman and Littlefield, 2003). Crnković also wrote and read texts for *Zagreb Everywhere* (2001), an experimental video made in collaboration with video artist Victor Ingrassia and musician David Hahn. Her latest book, *Post-Yugoslav Literature and Film: Fires, Foundations, Flourishes,* was published by Continuum in 2012.

Marko Dumančić: Ph.D. (UNC-Chapel Hill), a visiting assistant professor of Russian and European history at Oberlin College. His special interests include media representations of gender and sexuality in Soviet and East European history. He is currently writing a monograph examining the changing portrayals of masculinity in Soviet film during the Khrushchev era and an essay on the cinematic representations of queer characters in post-Yugoslav film.

Nikica Gilić: Assistant Professor and Chair of Film Studies at the Department of Comparative Literature, School of Humanities and Social Sciences, University of Zagreb. He also teaches at the Academy of Dramatic Art in Zagreb and is editor-in-chief of *Croatian Film Chronicle* (*Hrvatski filmski* *ljetopis*). With Bruno Kragić he co-edited *Filmski leksikon* (2003) and is author of the following books on film: *Uvod u teoriju filmske priče* (2007), *Filmske vrste i rodovi* (2007), and most recently *Uvod u povijest hrvatskog igranog filma* (2010) for which he received the Vladimir Vuković award from the Croatian Association of Film Critics. He is adviser for documentary film at the Croatian Audio-Visual Center and member of Animafest's council.

Vida T. Johnson: Ph.D. in Slavic Languages and Literatures, Harvard University, with a dissertation on Ivo Andrić. Professor of Russian language, literature, and culture at Tufts University (Boston) and specialist in Soviet and post-Soviet, especially Russian and Central Asian, cinema. Consulting co-editor for film for the *Russian Review*; with Graham Petrie she co-authored a book about Andrei Tarkovsky, titled *The Films of Andrei Tarkovsky: A Visual Fugue* (1994), translated into Serbian as *Filmovi Andreja Tarkovskog: Vizuelna fuga* (2007). With Miroljub Vučković she was co-editor of the dual-language (Serbian and English) Film Center Serbia publication: *Introducing Youth: Self-Reflections on Serbian Cinema* (2008).

Hana Jušić: Graduate of the School of Humanities and Social Sciences, University of Zagreb, and at present graduate student and instructor of film directing at the Academy of Dramatic Art in Zagreb. She is currently also working as a junior researcher on the *Croatian Glossary of Film Terms*.

Mario Kozina: Finishing his M.A. in Comparative Literature at the School of Humanities and Social Sciences, University of Zagreb. He is a regular contributor to Croatian radio and television, and has been publishing reviews, essays and other film-related texts on several Internet sites as well as in the *Croatian Film Chronicle* (*Hrvatski filmski ljetopis*). He is also a regular collaborator to the 25 FPS, International Festival of Experimental Film and Video. In 2008 he was given the Diploma for Best New Critic by the Croatian Association of Film Critics.

Bruno Kragić: Film critic and historian, and co-editor of *Filmski leksikon* (2003). Adjunct lecturer in film history and film aesthetics at the Academy of Dramatic Art in Zagreb and an executive at the Miroslav Krleža Institute for Lexicography.

Tomislav Kurelec: Former editor for film, theater, and literature of the Third Program (cultural program) of Radio Zagreb, from 1968–1971 assistant professor of literary history at the Department of Comparative Literature of the School of Humanities and Social Sciences in Zagreb, and from 1986–2007 principal editor of the Film Programming Division for Croatian Radiotelevision. He directed short feature *Blue World* (*Plavi svijet*, 1969), documentaries *And Everything is Fine* (*...i sve je dobro*, 1969), *Two Years Later* (*Dvije godine poslije*, 1973), *Move Freely* (*Krećite se sasvim slobodno*, 1976), *Long Live the Little Schools* (*Živile male skule II*, 1989), the series *Short Stories for a Good Night* (*Kratke priče za laku noć*, 1978), and approximately one hundred documentary programs for Croatian Radiotelevision.

He is author of *Filmska kronika – Zapisi o hrvatskom filmu* (2004) and numerous articles published in *Kritika, Vjesnik, Prolog, Film, Studio, Vijenac, Young Cinema & Theatre, BBC, Radio France International, Canal+, Sender Freies Berlin, Hrvatski filmski ljetopis*, and *Variety's International Film Guide*. A member of several film and theater boards, since 2007 also artistic director of *Days of Croatian film* (*Dani hrvatskog filma*).

Karla Lončar: Freelance film critic. Holds a B.A. in Comparative Literature and Sociology. Contributor to the *Croatian Film Chronicle* and Third Program of Croatian Radio (film reviews and essays).

Inna Mattei: Ph.D. in Slavic Cultural Studies from Harvard University and masters in international security from Harvard Kennedy School. Her research interests focus on culture and politics in totalitarian and post-totalitarian societies around the world. Her dissertation (2009) explored the link between politics and aesthetics in Ukraine and Russia during the first post-communist decade. She has worked domestically and internationally as a strategy consultant and researcher.

Katarina Mihailović: Currently completing her Masters Thesis at Concordia University in Montreal, Canada, on the politically and aesthetically radical films of Dušan Makavejev, Jean-Luc Godard, and Pier Paolo Pasolini, entitled *The Post-1968 Political Modernisms of Godard, Makavejev and Pasolini*. Her other research interests are Yugoslav Novi Film (New Film) movement, European post-WWII Modernist cinema, and the Avant-Garde.

Nataša Milas: Ph.D. candidate at Yale University in the Department of Slavic Languages and Literatures. Her interests include Yugoslav and Post-Yugoslav film and literature, translation, and Russian and European novel. She has translated works by writers such as Marin Držić, Miljenko Jergović, and Muharem Bazdulj. She is currently writing her dissertation on Danilo Kiš and Russian Literature, and preparing the Bosnian issue of *KinoKultura*.

Lorraine Mortimer: Honorary Associate in Cinema Studies at La Trobe University, Melbourne. She introduced and translated Edgar Morin's *The Cinema, or The Imaginary Man: An Essay in Sociological Anthropology* for the University of Minnesota Press (2005). She is author of *Terror and Joy: The Films of Dušan Makavejev*, also published by University of Minnesota Press (2009). She has recently written on Robert Gardner's book about the making of his ethnographic film, *Dead Birds* (1963) for a forthcoming issue of The Australian Journal of Anthropology, and on Ilya Khrzhanovsky's film, *4* (2005) for a forthcoming special issue on disgust for *Film and Philosophy*.

Diana Nenadić: Film critic and publicist whose numerous articles and essays have appeared in newspapers, specialized arts and culture magazines, radio and TV programs, film publications, and lexicons. She has worked as an editor at the Third Program of Radio Zagreb, served as principal editor of *Croatian Film Chronicle* (*Hrvatski filmski ljetopis*) from 1997 to 2004, and since 2000 as the editor of a DVD series published by Hrvatski filmski savez (Croatian Film Club's Association). In 2008, she was appointed vice-president of the Croatian Association of Film Critics, and in 2008/2009, she started teaching film criticism as an adjunct lecturer at the Academy of Dramatic Art in Zagreb.

Jurica Pavičić: Film critic, screenwriter, and film scholar, who has published over 1700 journalist pieces on topics ranging from film, literature, language, to politics, and about twenty scholarly articles on Croatian film. He is a regular film critic and contributor to several Croatian daily newspapers. He teaches the history of cinema and the history of Croatian cinema at the University of Split. Since 2005 he has been a selector for the international film festival in Motovun and has served on several film juries, including the Berlin film festival in 2008. He has published six books of novels and short stories which have been translated into German, English, Italian, and Bulgarian. Vinko Brešan's film *Witnesses* (*Svjedoci*, 2003) was based on Pavičić's literary debut, a social thriller *Ovce od gipsa* (*Alabaster Sheep*, 1997) for which Pavičić co-authored the screenplay and received numerous awards.

Boško Picula: Graduate of the School of Political Sciences in Zagreb where he studied political science and journalism and is currently writing his Ph.D. thesis on comparative politics. He has published film reviews and essays in *Hollywood*, *Vijenac*, *Total Film*, *Globus*, *Croatian Film Chronicle* (*Hrvatski filmski ljetopis*) and in web publication www.film.hr. He is the screenwriter for the youth program, *Kokice*, at Croatian Radiotelevision where he also works as a film critic for the program *Dobro jutro, Hrvatska* as well as on the program *Licem u lice* for Croatian Radio. He is a member of several committees and film juries for various Croatian film festivals.

Maxim Pozdorovkin: Writer and director based in Brooklyn, NY. His feature film *Capital* is a modern-day city symphony about the construction of Astana, Kazakhstan's new capital city. Other recent projects include a documentary short and historical essay accompanying the Flicker-Alley DVD release of *Miss Mend*. He is currently completing production on a feature-length documentary/media archaeology database on the history of the AK-47 machine gun.

Tomislav Šakić: Managing editor of the film quarterly *Croatian Film Chronicle* (*Hrvatski filmski ljetopis*) and a board member of the Croatian Association of Film Critics. Currently completing his Ph.D. thesis in film studies and working at the Miroslav Krleža Institute for Lexicography as a member of the editorial board of the *Croatian Glossary of Film Terms*. He also edits *Ubiq*, a literary journal for science fiction, and has co-edited a critical anthology of Croatian science fiction stories. In 2007 he was given an award by the SFERA national society for science fiction. He is also a member of FIPRESCI and FEDEORA.

Mima Simić: Gender, media and film theorist. Holds degrees in comparative literature and English language and literature from the University of Zagreb and an M.A. in gender studies from the Central European University. In 2008 she received the Vladimir Vuković Award for Best Croatian Film Critic for her essays on film which were later collected in *Otporna na Hollywood: eseji iz dekonstrukcije tvornice snova* (Hrvatski filmski savez, 2009). Her short stories have been included in numerous Croatian and international anthologies.

Ivo Škrabalo: Held degrees in theatre directing from the Academy of Dramatic Art in Zagreb and an M. A. in international law from the Law School of the University of Zagreb. He was involved in Croatian film for some fifty years in various capacities ranging from support actor (as a student), to script editor, documentary director, distributor, director of the national Film Festival in Pula, president of the Croatian Association of Film Critics and lecturer of the history of Croatian film for ten years at the Academy of Dramatic Art in Zagreb. He was author of the first book on the history of Croatian film *Između publike i države* (1984) which was harshly criticized by the Yugoslav Communist Party. He also published *101 godina filma u Hrvatskoj* (1997), *Dvanaest filmskih portreta* (2006) and *Hrvatska filmska povijest ukratko* (2008). Before retirement he was a member of the Croatian Parliament.

Petra Belković Taylor: Ph.D. candidate at the Department of Comparative Literature at Harvard University. She also holds an M.A. in English from Loyola Marymount University and a M.Ed. in TESOL from Boston University. She is interested in multilingual writers and works on the 20th century American and Russian literatures, and South Slavic Oral Traditions. With her husband, James, she founded an annual international seminar on the themes of war and peace in literature and philosophy that takes place in Croatia and Bosnia and Herzegovina.

Aida Vidan (editor): Ph.D. from Harvard where she currently teaches Bosnian, Croatian, and Serbian and is a Research Fellow at the Milman Parry Collection of Oral Literature. Her publications focus on written and oral traditional literature from the South Slavic region, methodologies of teaching South Slavic languages, and film. She is author of *Embroidered with Gold, Strung with Pearls: The Traditional Ballads of Bosnian Women* and co-author of *Beginner's Croatian* and *Beginner's Serbian*. Some of her other projects concern the Yugoslav-disintegration wars of the 1990s and their influence on literature and film from the region, the application of databases in researching oral poetry, and Croatian Renaissance drama.

Zhen Zhang: Currently a graduate student at the Department of Slavic Languages and Literature, University of Washington. Educated in China as well as in Russia, Zhang got his Bachelor's Degree at the School of Russian, Beijing Foreign Studies University, in 2009, and a Certificate at the Faculty of Journalism, Moscow State University in 2008. A Chinese native speaker and a near-native speaker of Russian, Zhang is currently studying Bosnian/Croatian/Serbian and French. His research interests cover the literature and films of Russia and the countries where Bosnian, Croatian, and Serbian are spoken, including writers Fyodor Dostoevsky and Vladimir Nabokov, the early Russian films directors, the cinematography of Andrei Tarkovsky and Wong Kar-wai, as well as the literature related to the cultural dynamics between East and West.

General Bibliography

- Ajanović, Midhat. 2004. *Animacija i realizam/Animation and Realism*. Zagreb: Hrvatski filmski savez.
- Ajanović, Midhat. 2008. *Karikatura i pokret: devet eseja o crtanom filmu*. Zagreb: Hrvatski filmski savez.
- Anon. 2008. "Nova hrvatska generacija: Moćni prije četrdesete." *Nacional* (December 29).
- Bendazzi, Giannalberto. 1994. *Cartoons — One Hundred Years of Cinema Animation*. Eastleigh: John Libbey & Company Limited.
- Buden, Boris. 1999. "Europa je kurva." In *Mediji i rat*. Eds. Nena Skopljanec-Brunner, Alija Hodžić, Branimir Krištofić. Belgrade: Agencija argument.
- Crnković, Gordana P. 2001. "The Battle for Croatia: Three Films by Vinko Brešan." In *Democratic Transition in Croatia: Value Transformation, Education & Media*. Eds. Sabrina P. Ramet and Davorka Matić. Texas A & M University Press: College Station, 2007. Also in Croatian: "Bitka za Hrvatsku: tri filma Vinka Brešana." In *Demokratska tranzicija u Hrvatskoj: Transformacija vrijednosti, obrazovanje, mediji*. Eds. Sabrina P. Ramet and Davorka Matić. Zagreb: Alinea, 2006.
- Crnković, Gordana P. 2011. "Milcho Manchevski's *Before the Rain* and the Ethics of Listening," *Slavic Review* 70, no. 1.
- Crnković, Gordana P. 2012. *Post-Yugoslav Literature and Film: Fires, Foundations, Flourishes*. London and New York: Continuum.
- Čegir, Tomislav, Joško Marušić, Tomislav Šakić. 2009. *Hrvatski filmski redatelji I*. Zagreb: Hrvatsko društvo filmskih kritičara & Hrvatski filmski savez.
- Daković, Nevena. 2008. *Balkan kao (filmski) žanr — slika, tekst, nacija*. Beograd: FDU, institut za pozorište, film, radio i televiziju.
- Delcheva, Roumana. 2005. "Reliving the past in recent Eastern European cinema." In *East European Cinemas*. Ed. Anikó Imre. New York, London: Routledge.
- Ditchev, Ivaylo. 2002. "The Eros of Identity." In *Balkan as Metaphor — Between Globalization and Fragmentation*. Eds. Dušan I. Bijelić & Obrad Savić. Cambridge, Massachusetts & London: MIT Press.
- Elsaesser, Thomas. 2005. *European Cinema — Face to Face With Hollywood*. Amsterdam: Amsterdam University Press.
- Das, Veena. 1995. "National Honor and Practical Kinship: Unwanted Women and Children." In *Conceiving the New World Order*. Ed. Faye Ginsburg and Rayna Rapp. Berkley: University of California Press.

- Enloe, Cynthia H. 1990. *Bananas, Beaches, and Bases: Making Feminist Sense of International Politics*. Berkley: University of California Press.
- Franić, Severin, ed. 2002. *Svođenje računa: jugoslovenska filmska misao 1896-1996*. Belgrade: Ne / Bo, Yu Film danas.
- Freeland, Cynthia. 1996. "Feminist Frameworks for Horror Films." In *Post-Theory. Reconstructing Film Studies*. Eds. David Bordwell and Noell Carroll. Madison: University of Minnesota Press.
- Furniss, Maureen. 2007. *Art in Motion: Animation Aesthetics*. Revised edition. Eastleigh: John Libbey & Company Limited.
- Germani Grmek, S. 2010. "Let mrtve ptice." In *Subversive film festival — retrospektiva jugoslavenskog filma 1955-1990*. Zagreb: Subversive Film festival, Bijeli val.
- Gilić, Nikica and Bruno Kragić, eds. 2003. *Filmski leksikon*. Zagreb: Leksikografski zavod "Miroslav Krleža."
- Gilić, Nikica. 2007. *Filmske vrste i rodovi*. Zagreb: AGM.
- Gilić, Nikica. 2010. *Uvod u povijest hrvatskog igranog filma*. Zagreb: Leykam.
- Gilić, Nikica. 2009. "Modernizam i autorski film 1960-ih u Hrvatskoj." In *Prostor u jeziku / Književnost i kultura šezdesetih*. Eds. T. Bogdan, D. Dukić, K. Mićanović, I. Pranjković, A. Ryznar. Zagreb: Zagrebačka slavistička škola. [http://www.hrvatskiplus.org/prilozi/dokumenti/anagram/Gilic_Modernizam.pdf]
- Goulding, Daniel J. 2003. *Liberated Cinema: The Yugoslav Experience. 1945-2001*. Bloomington: Indiana University Press. Also in Croatian: *Jugoslavensko Filmsko Iskustvo, 1945–2001, Oslobođeni Film*. Zagreb: VBZ, 2004.
- Grlić, Rajko and Ante Tomić. 2006. *Karaula*: scenarij po romanu Ante Tomića "Ništa nas ne smije iznenaditi." Zaprešić: Fraktura.
- Higson, Andrew. 1989. "The Concept of National Cinema." *Screen* 30, no. 4.
- Horton, Andrew James, ed. 2000. *The Celluloid Tinderbox: Yugoslav screen reflections of a turbulent decade*. Central European Review (special issue). [http://www.kinoeye.org/03/10/celluloidtinderbox.php]
- Imre, Anikó, ed. 2005. *East European Cinemas*. New York, London: Routledge.
- Interview with Ana Hušman. 2006. Kuhinja [TV program]. Pro.ba.
- Interview with Dalibor Matanić. 2003. *Kinoeye* 3, no. 6 (May 26).
- Interview with Jurica Pavičić. 2000. *Central Europe Review* 2, no. 19 (May 15).
- Iordanova, Dina. 2001. *Cinema of Flames: Balkan Film Culture and the Media*. London: BFI.
- Iordanova, Dina. 2005. "The Cinema of Eastern Europe, Strained Loyalties, Elusive Clusters." In *Eastern European Cinemas*. Ed. Anikó Imre. New York, London: Routledge.
- Iordanova, Dina. 2006. *The Cinema of the Balkans*. London, New York: Wallflower Press.
- Jameson, Fredric. 2004. "Thoughts on Balkan Cinema." In *Subtitles*. Eds. Atom Egoyan & Ian Balfour. Massachusets Institute of Technology.
- Jergović, Miljenko. 2009. *Buick Rivera*. Sarajevo: Šahinpašić.
- Kandiyoti, Deniz, ed. 1991. *Women, Islam, and the State*. London: Macmillan.

- Kragić, Bruno. 2010. "Hrvatski film nakon 1990. — prijedlog stilske klasifikacije." *Sarajevske sveske* 19/20.
- Krasztev, Péter. 2000. "Who Will Take the Blame? — How to Make an Audience Grateful for a Family Massacre." In *The Celluloid Tinderbox: Yugoslav screen reflections of a turbulent decade*. Ed. Andrew James Horton. *Central European Review*. [http://www.kinoeye.org/03/10/celluloidtinderbox.php]
- Krelja, Petar. 1993. "Mladi hrvatski film." *Kinoteka* 40/41. Zagreb: Filmoteka 16.
- Krelja, Petar. 2006. "Žensko pismo i hrvatski film." *Zapis* (special issue). Zagreb: Hrvatski filmski savez.
- Krelja, Petar. 2006b. "Neka obilježja hrvatskog igranog filma." *Zapis* (special issue). Zagreb: Hrvatski filmski savez.
- Krelja, Petar. 2009. *Kao na filmu*. Zagreb: Hrvatski filmski savez.
- Kurelec, Tomislav. 2004. *Filmska kronika. Zapisi o hrvatskom filmu*. Zagreb: AGM, Hrvatsko društvo filmskih kritičara.
- Kurelec, Tomislav. 2008. "Hrvatski igrani film u europskom kontekstu." *Hrvatski filmski ljetopis* 53. Zagreb: Hrvatski filmski savez.
- Lamble, David. 2007. "Global Lens Festival Highlights." *Bay Area Reporter* (November 1).
- Levi, Pavle. 2007. *Disintegration in Frames. Aesthetics and Ideology in the Yugoslav and Post-Yugoslav Cinema*. Stanford: Stanford University Press. Also in Serbian: *Raspad Jugoslavije na filmu*. Beograd: XX vek, 2009.
- Levi, Pavle. 2007b. "Border Post." *Cineaste* 32, no. 3.
- Liehm, Mira and Antonín Liehm. 1977. *The Most Important Art: Soviet and Eastern European Film after 1945*. Berkeley: University of California Press.
- Longinović, Tomislav. 2005. "Playing the western eye: balkan masculinity and post-yugoslav war cinema." In *East European Cinemas*. Ed. Anikó Imre. New York, London: Routledge.
- Majcen, Vjekoslav & Hrvoje Turković. 2003. *Hrvatska kinematografija, povijesne značajke, suvremeno stanje, filmografija (1991-2002)*. Zagreb: Ministarstvo kulture RH, Hrvatski filmski savez.
- Mazierska, Ewa. 2010. "Eastern European cinema: old and new approaches." *Studies in Eastern European Cinema* 1, no. 1.
- Moss, Kevin. 2008. "Three Gay Films from Former Yugoslavia." In *American Contributions to the 14th International Congress of Slavists*, Ohrid, September 2008. Vol 2: Literature. Ed. David M. Bethea. Bloomington: Slavica.
- Munitić, Ranko. 1975. "Krotitelji divljih crteža." *Filmska kultura* 100, no. 3.
- Nenadić, Diana. 2006. "Dokumentarizam kao etički izbor. O dokumentarnim filmovima Petra Krelje." *Hrvatski filmski ljetopis*, 48. Zagreb: Hrvatski filmski savez.
- Nichols, Bill. 1991. *Representing Reality. Issues and Concepts in Documentary*. Bloomington: Indiana University Press.
- Nichols, Bill. 2001. *Introduction to Documentary*. Bloomington: Indiana University Press.
- Pavičić, Jurica. 1993. "Mladi hrvatski film." *Erasmus*. Zagreb: Erasmus Gilda (June 2).
- Pavičić, Jurica. 1993b. "Budućnost hrvatskog filma." *Erasmus*. Zagreb:

- Erasmus Gilda (November 4).
- Pavičić, Jurica. 1995. "Hrvatski film noir." *Vijenac* 43. Zagreb: Matica hrvatska (August).
- Pavičić, Jurica. 2000. "Moving into the Frame. Croatian Film in the 1990s." *Central Europe Review* 2, no. 19. [http://www.ce-review.org/00/19/kinoeye 19_pavicic.html]
- Pavičić, Jurica. 2003. "Hrvatski dokumentarac devedesetih." *Hrvatski filmski ljetopis* 33. Zagreb: Hrvatski filmski savez.
- Pavičić, Jurica. 2008. "'Lemons in Siberia': a new approach to the study of the Yugoslav cinema of the 1950s." *New Review of Film and Television Studies* 6, no. 1. Routledge: London.
- Pavičić, Jurica. 2008b. "Pregled razvoja postjugoslavenskih kinematografija." *Sarajevske sveske* 21-22.
- Pavičić, Jurica. 2010. "Cinema of normalization: changes of stylistic model in post-Yugoslav cinema after 1990s." *Studies in Eastern European Cinema* 1, no. 1.
- Pavičić, Jurica. 2011. *Postjugoslavenski film. Stil i ideologija.* Zagreb: Hrvatski filmski savez.
- Petzke, Ingo. 1996. "Četrdeset godina studija crtanog filma Zagreb filma." *Hrvatski filmski ljetopis* 7. Zagreb: Hrvatski filmski savez.
- Peterlić, Ante, ed. 1986, 1990. *Filmska enciklopedija.* Vols. 1. & 2. Zagreb: Jugoslavenski leksikografski zavod "Miroslav Krleža."
- Plantinga, Carl. 1997. *Rhetoric and Representation in Nonfiction Film.* Cambridge: Cambridge University Press.
- Polimac, Nenad, ed. 1985. *Branko Bauer — monografija.* Zagreb: Cekade.
- Polimac, Nenad. 2002. "Fine mrtve djevojke — najbolji hrvatski film od Maršala." *Nacional* (30 July).
- Polimac, Nenad. 2004. "Hrvatski blockbusteri." *Hrvatski filmski ljetopis* 40. Zagreb: Hrvatski filmski savez.
- Prica, B. 2008. "Dalibor Matanić: Od tate sam naslijedio preciznost, a od mame smisao za loš humor." *Nacional* (24 September).
- Prouse, Derek. 1959. "Yugoslav Cartoons (In the Picture)." *Sight and Sound* 28, no. 3/4.
- Puhovski, Nenad. 1999. "Tišina mržnje." In *Mediji i rat*. Eds. Nena Skopljanec-Brunner, Alija Hodžić, Branimir Krištofić. Beograd: Agencija argument.
- Rascarolli, Laura. 2009. *The Personal Camera: Subjective Cinema and the Essay Film.* London: Wallflower Press.
- Ravetto-Biagioli, Kriss. 2003. "Laughing into an Abyss: Cinema and Balkanization." *Screen* 44, no. 4.
- Ravetto-Biagioli, Kriss. 2005. "Reframing the European Double Border." In *East European Cinemas*. Ed. Anikó Imre. New York, London: Routledge.
- Renov, Michael. 2004. *Subject of Documentary*. Minneapolis, London: Minnesota University Press.
- Sailor, Dylan and Sarah Culpepper Stroup. 1999. "ΦΘΟΝΟΣ Δ ΑΠΕΣΤΩ: The Translation of Transgression in Aiskhylos' *Agamemnon*." *Classical Antiquity* 18, no. 1.
- Samardžija, Zoran. 2007. "Bal-can-can." *Cineaste* 32, no. 3.
- Simić, Mima. 2006. "Fine mrtve djevojke: Zašto su prve hrvatske celu-

- loidne lezbijke morale umrijeti?" *Cunterview: Women Art Media Space* (2 November).
- Simić, Mima. 2010. "Čuvarica granice: Celuloidna lezbijka kao dvostruka metafora u re/konstrukciji postjugoslavenskih nacionalnih identiteta." In *Na marginama: Manjine i mediji u jugoistočnoj Evropi*. Eds. Edin Hodžić and Tarik Jusić. Sarajevo: Mediacenter.
- Simić, T. 2008. "Filmska provokacija buntovnika s kamerom: Kako shvatiti ličke redikule?" *Nacional* (30 June).
- Stojanova, Christina. 2005. "Fragmented discourse: young cinema from Central and Eastern Europe." In *East European Cinemas*. Ed. Anikó Imre. New York, London: Routledge.
- Sudović, Zlatko, ed. 1978. *Zagrebački krug crtanog filma: pedeset godina crtanog filma u Hrvatskoj, almanah, 1922-1972*. (Summary: "Animated Film in Zagreb." Transl. P. Robinson). Zagreb: Grafički zavod Hrvatske.
- Sudović, Zlatko, ed. 1978b. *Zagrebački krug crtanog filma. Vol 2. Odabrani scenariji i knjige snimanja filmova zagrebačke škole*. Zagreb: Grafički zavod Hrvatske.
- Škrabalo, Ivo. 1984. *Između publike i države: povijest hrvatske kinematografije 1896-1980*. Zagreb: Znanje.
- Škrabalo, Ivo. 1996. "Hrvatski film o ratu." *Hrvatski filmski ljetopis* 8. Zagreb: Hrvatski filmski savez.
- Škrabalo, Ivo. 1997. "Apel za hrvatski film." *Hrvatski filmski ljetopis* 12. Zagreb: Hrvatski filmski savez.
- Škrabalo, Ivo. 1998. *101 godina filma u Hrvatskoj 1896-1997.: pregled povijesti hrvatske kinematografije*. Zagreb: Nakladni zavod Globus.
- Škrabalo, Ivo. 2006. *Dvanaest filmskih portreta: mali hrvatski filmski panoptikum*. Zagreb: V.B.Z.
- Škrabalo, Ivo. 2008. *Hrvatska filmska povijest ukratko (1896-2006)*. Zagreb: Hrvatski filmski savez, V.B.Z.
- Šošić, Anja. 2009. "Film i rat u Hrvatskoj — refleksija jugoslavenskih ratova u hrvatskom igranom filmu." *Zapis* 64-65. Zagreb: Hrvatski filmski savez.
- Tadić, Zoran. 2008. *Ogledi o hrvatskom dokumentarcu*. Zagreb: Hrvatski filmski savez.
- Taylor, Richard, Nancy Wood, Julian Graffy, Dina Iordanova, eds. 2000. *The BFI Companion to Eastern European and Russian Cinema*. London: BFI Publishing.
- Trajkov, Igor Pop. 2003. "I Love Actors: Dalibor Matanić Interviewed." *Kinoeye* 26.
- Turković, Hrvoje. 1999. "Kad je film nacionalan?" *Hrvatski filmski ljetopis* 16. Zagreb: Hrvatski filmski savez.
- Turković, Hrvoje. 2005. *Film: zabava, žanr, stil*. Zagreb: Hrvatski filmski savez.
- Turković, Hrvoje. 2008. "Noviji hrvatski dokumentarac (1992-2007)"/ "New Croatian Documentary Film, 1992-2007." In *Zagreb Dox. Međunarodni festival dokumentarnog filma International / Documentary Film Festival* (catalogue). Zagreb: Factum. [http://bib.irb.hr/prikazi-rad?&rad=310534]

- Turković, Hrvoje. 2010. "Esejistički dokumentarizam Ante Babaje." In *Zagreb Dox. Međunarodni festival dokumentarnog filma International / Documentary Film Festival* (catalogue). Zagreb: Factum.
- Turner, Graeme. 2006. *Film as Social Practice*. London: Routledge, First ed. 1988.
- Vidan, Aida. 2010. "A Path of No Return: Goran Rušinović's Buick Riviera." In *ARTMargins. Contemporary Central & East European Visual Culture*. (April) [http://www.artmargins.com/index.php/film-a-screen-media/569-path-no-return-goran-ruinovis-buick-riviera-film-review]
- Vidan, Aida. 2011. "Spaces of ideology in South Slavic films." *Studies in Eastern European Cinema* 2, no. 2.
- Virilio, Paul. 2000 (1984). *War and Cinema: The Logistics of Perception*. London, New York: Verso.
- Visković, Josip. 1995. "Hrvatski igrani film — prva petoljetka." *Hrvatski filmski ljetopis* 1/2. Zagreb: Hrvatski filmski savez.
- Vojković, Saša. 2006. "Subjektivnost u novom hrvatskom filmu. Kritičko-naratološki pristup." *Hrvatski filmski ljetopis* 46. Zagreb: Hrvatski filmski savez.
- Vojković, Saša. 2008. "De/re-construction of subjectivity in contemporary Croatian cinema: becoming European." *New Review of Film and Television Studies* 6, no. 1.
- Volk, Petar. 1983/1986. *Istorija jugoslovenskog filma*. Belgrade: Institut za film, Partizanska knjiga.
- Vukotić, Dušan. 1978. "Scenarij crtanog filma." In *Zagrebački krug crtanog filma. Vol 2. Odabrani scenariji i knjige snimanja filmova zagrebačke škole* [*The Zagreb School of Animated Film, Vol. 2: Selected Screenplays and Shooting Scripts*] Ed. Z. Sudović. Zagreb: Grafički zavod Hrvatske.
- Wells, Paul. 1997. "The Beautiful Village and the True Village: A Consideration of Animation and the Documentary Aesthetic." *Art and Design* 12, no. 53.
- Zvijer, Nemanja. 2009. "Ideologija i vrednosti u jugoslovenskom ratnom spektaklu." *Hrvatski filmski ljetopis* 57/58. Zagreb: Hrvatski filmski savez.
- Žižek, Slavoj. 1995. "Multiculturalism, or the Cultural Logic of Multinational Capitalism." *New Left Review* 225.
- Žižek, Slavoj. 2006. *The Parallax View*. Cambridge, Mass: The MIT Press.

Filmography

100 Minutes of Glory (*Sto minuta Slave*), Dalibor Matanić, 2005: 152

A

Above Average (*Natprosječan*), Igor Bezinović, 2008: 72
Accidental Son, An (*Slučajni sin*), Robert Zuber, 2008: 71
Acting Hamlet in the Village of Mrduša Donja (*Predstava Hamleta u selu Mrduša Donja*), Krsto Papić, 1973: 35, 118, 212, 213
Album, Krešimir Zimonić, 1983: 82
Alien, Ridley Scott, 1979: 206
All About Eve (*Sve o Evi*), Silvestar Kolbas, 2003: 74
All for Free (*Sve džaba*), Antonio Nuić, 2006: 176-182
All Men Are Good Men in Bad Society (*Svaki je čovjek dobar čovjek u rđavom svijetu*), Rajko Grlić, 1968: 109-110
All or Nothing, Mike Leigh, 2002: 173
Alone (*Sami*), Lukas Nola, 2001: 183, 185, 186, 187
And Love Has Vanished (*Dvoje*), Aleksandar Petrović, 1961: 30
Anxiety (*Tjeskoba*), Damir Čučić, 2010: 72
Armin, Ognjen Sviličić, 2007: 169, 172-174

B

Bad Blue Boys (*Panj pun olova*), Branko Schmidt, 2007: 65
Bag, Dalibor Matanić, Tomislav Rukavina, Stanislav Tomić, 1999: 66, 70
Bakonja fra Brne, Fedor Hanžeković, 1951: 26
BBB, Saša Podgorelec, 1998: 69

Before the Rain (*Pred doždot*), Milčo Mančevski, 1994: 54, 247
Behind the Glass (*Iza stakla*), Zrinko Ogresta, 2008: 225, 227, 230, 231
Battle of Neretva, The (*Bitka na Neretvi*), Veljko Bulajić, 1969: 34, 41
Battle of Sutjeska, The (*Sutjeska*), Stipe Delić, 1973: 34
Big Time, The (*Veliki provod*), Milan Trenc, 1990: 82
Blacks, The (*Crnci*), Goran Dević, Zvonimir Jurić, 2009: 14, 21, 57, 58, 70, 97, 98, 114, 183, 206-210
Blacks Have Endured (*Crnci su izdržali, a ja?*), Zvonimir Jurić, 2001: 70
Blackman Miško (*Crnac Miško*), Bogoslav Petanjek, 1949: 77
Blue 9, The (*Plavi 9*), Krešo Golik, 1950: 25-26
Blue Seagull (*Sinji galeb*), Branko Bauer, 1953: 27
Birch Tree, The (*Breza*), Ante Babaja, 1967: 32
Blue Helmet, Jelena Rajković, 1992/93: 64
Bombs (*Bombe*), Goce Vaskov, 2005: 86
Borderlines of Hunger, The (*Rubne slike gladi*), Nenad Puhovski, 1989: 139
Border Post, The (*Karaula*), Rajko Grlić, 2006: 57, 97, 101, 106, 108, 109, 110, 162-168
Boy Who Rushed, The (*Dečko kojem se žurilo*), Biljana Čakić-Veselič, 2001: 65, 70, 146
Bravo Maestro, Rajko Grlić, 1978: 100
Brcko in Zagreb (*Brcko u Zagrebu*), Arnošt Grund, 1917: 89
Bućan Triptych (*Bućan triptih*), Nenad Puhovski, 1987: 139

Buick Riviera, Goran Rušinović, 2008: 14, 21, 57, 97, 98, 114, 202-205
Butterflies (*Leptiri*), Krešimir Zimonić, 1988: 82

C

Cake, The (*Kolač*), Danijel Šuljić, 1997: 87
Captain Leshi (*Kapetan Leši*), Žika Mitrović, 1960: 51
Cash and Marry (*Plati i ženi*), Atanas Georgiev, 2008: 75
Cashier Wants to go to the Seaside, The (*Blagajnica hoće ići na more*), Dalibor Matanić, 2002: 94, 152, 153
Category: Optimist (*Klasa optimist*), Lana Šarić, 2010: 70, 146
Celestial Body (*Nebo, sateliti*), Lukas Nola, 2001: 183-187
Cesar Franck — Wolf Vostell, Tomislav Gotovac a.k.a. Antonio G. Lauer, 2005: 71, 73
Changing the World (*Mijenjam svijet*), TV-documentary series: 72
Charuga (*Čaruga*), Rajko Grlić, 1991: 100, 101, 105, 106, 108, 109
Cheerfull Event, A (*Veseli doživljaj*), Walter Neugebauer, 1951: 77
Ciguli Miguli, Branko Marjanović, 1952: 26
City Killer, Damir Čučić, 2007: 73
Concert, A (*Koncert*), Branko Belan, 1954: 27
Cormorant Scarecrow, The (*Plašitelji kormorana*), Branko Ištvančić, 1998: 67
Corn Road (*Kukuruzni put*), Petar Krelja, 1994: 63
Corridor, The (*Hodnik*), Vinko Brešan, 1994: 66, 116, 118

Countess Dora (*Kontesa Dora*), Zvonimir Berković, 1993: 40
Crazy Days (*Ludi dani*), Nikola Babić, 1977: 36
Creatures in the Pictures (*Bića sa slika*), Damir Čučić, 1999: 67
Croatian Cathedrals (*Hrvatske katedrale*), Hrvoje Hribar, 1992: 220
Curiosity (*Znatiželja*), Borivoj Dovniković, 1967: 80
Cyclops (*Kiklop*), Antun Vrdoljak, 1982: 39

Č

Činča, Nenad Puhovski, 1972: 137, 140, 149

D

Dancing in the Rain (*Ples v dežju*), Boštjan Hladnik, 1961: 30
Dark Knight, Christopher Nolan, 2008: 223
Das Lied ist aus, Ivan Faktor, 2002: 65
Date, A (*Spoj*), Darko Bakliža, 2004: 87
Da Vinci Code, The, Ron Howard, 2006: 220
Day under the Sun (*Dan pod suncem*), Vlado Zrnić, 2000: 73, 74
Days (*Dani*), Aleksandar Petrović, 1963: 30
Dead Harbour (*Mrtva luka*), Nenad Puhovski, 1976: 139, 141
Dead Man Walking, Tomislav Gotovac, 2002: 71, 73
Decalogue, The (*Dekalog*), Krzysztof Kieślowski, 1988: 227
Deliverance, John Boorman, 1972: 57
Diary (*Dnevnik*), Nedeljko Dragić, 1974: 79, 82
Direct (*Direkt*), documentary series, 2000-2010: 72
Donkey (*Kenjac*), Antonio Nuić, 2009: 176, 177, 179, 180-182
Don Quixote (Don Kihot), Vladimir Kristl, 1961: 80
Don't Lean Out the Window (*Ne naginji se van*), Bogdan Žižić, 1977: 36
Double Circle (*Dvostruki obruč*), Nikola Tanhofer, 1963: 51
Dreams from the Railway Station (*Snovi na peronu djetinjstva*), Silvio Mirošničenko, 2001: 69-70
Dreem Doll, Zlatko Grgić, Bob Godfrey, 1979: 78
Drinking Water and Freedom III (*Pitka voda i sloboda III*), Rajko Grlić, 1999: 100-101
Dubrovnik Twilight (*Dubrovački suton*), Željko Senečić, 1999: 52
Duel (*Dvoboj*), Zrinka Katarina Matijević (-Veličan), 1998: 68

E

Eighth Day of the Week, The (*Ósmy dzien tygodnia*), Aleksander Ford, 1959: 227
Elm-Chanted Forest, The (*Čudesna šuma*), Milan Blažeković, 1986: 82-83
Ersatz/Surrogate (*Surogat*), Dušan Vukotić, 1961: 31, 80
Evening Bells (*Večernja zvona*), Lordan Zafranović, 1986: 38

F

Face of Fear, The (*Lice straha*), Joško Marušić, 1986: 129
Face to Face (*Licem u lice*), Branko Bauer, 1963: 35
Facing the Day (*Što sa sobom preko dana*), Ivona Juka, 2006: 72-73
Fall of Italy, The (*Pad Italije*), Lordan Zafranović, 1982: 38
Fifth One, The (*Peti*), Zlatko Grgić, Pavao Štalter, 1964: 81
Film with a Girl, A (*Film s djevojčicom*), Danijel Šuljić, 2000: 87
Fine Dead Girls (*Fine mrtve djevojke*), Dalibor Matanić, 2002: 152-157
Fisheye (*Riblje oko*), Joško Marušić, 1980: 79, 129, 133
Flag, The (*Zastava*), Branko Marjanović, 1949: 26
Fly, The (*Muha*), Vladimir Jutriša, Aleksandar Marks, 1966: 78
Forgotten, The (*Zaboravljeni*), Damir Čučić, 2001: 73
Format, Darko Bakliža, 2010: 87, 88
Fourth Shift, The (*Četvrta smjena*), Damir Čučić, 1999: 67
Fragments: Cronicle of a Vanishing (*Krhotine: kronika jednog nestajanja*), Zrinko Ogresta, 1991: 225-227, 230
From Dawn Till Dusk (*Od jutra do mraka*), Dražen Žarković, 2005: 66

G

Girl and an Oak, A (*Djevojka i hrast*), Krešo Golik, 1955: 27
Give Them Back Their Dinamo (*Vratite im Dinamo*), Antonio Nuić, 1999: 176
Glembays, The (*Glembajevi*), Antun Vrdoljak, 1988: 39
Godfather, The, Francis Ford Coppola, 1972: 127
Gold, Frankincense and Myrrh (*Mirisi, zlato i tamjan*), Ante Babaja, 1971: 37
Golden Years, The (*Zlatne godine*), Davor Žmegač, 1993: 227
Good Luck (*Sretno*), Dalibor Matanić, Tomislav Rukavina, Stanislav Tomić, 1999: 66, 70
Good Morning (*Dobro jutro*), Ante Babaja, 2007: 71
Graham and I, a True Story (*Graham i ja, istinita priča*), Nenad Puhovski, 1998: 68, 70, 141, 143, 145
Grandpa, Batek, Granny (*Dedek, batek, bakica*), Vlatka Vorkapić, 1998: 66
Grbavica (*The Land of My Dreams*), Jasmila Žbanić, 2006: 55
Great Expectations (*Velika očekivanja*), Renata Poljak, 2005: 71
Great Relly, The (*Veliki miting*), Fadil Hadžić, 1950: 77
Groundhog Day, Harold Ramis, 1993: 216
Guardian of the Border (*Varuh meje*), Maja Weiss, 2002: 155

H

H-8, Nikola Tanhofer, 1958: 13, 28
Half-Sister (*Polusestra*), Ljiljana Šišmanović, 2006: 71
Hall (*Dvorana*), Neven Hitrec, 1993: 64
Handcuffs (*Lisice*), Krsto Papić, 1969: 170, 213, 226
Happy Child (*Sretno dijete*), Igor Mirković, 2003: 71, 74
Happy Country (*Sretna zemlja*), Goran Dević, 2009: 66
Hurt Locker, The, Kathryn Bigelow, 2008: 126
Hello, Munich (*Halo, Minhen*), Krsto Papić, 1968: 214
Here (*Tu*), Zrinko Ogresta, 2003: 225, 229, 231
Herman's Burden (*Breme*), Nicole Hewitt, 1989: 84

History of Violence, David Cronenberg, 2005: 55
Home is the Best (*Kod kuće je najbolje*), Joško Marušić, 1988: 129
Homo Volans, Dako Bakliža, 2008: 87
Hotel Sunja, Ivan Salaj, 1992: 64
House (*Kuća*), Ana Hušman, 2003: 71
How Kićo Was Born (*Kako se rodio Kićo*), Dušan Vukotić, 1951: 77
How the War Started on My Island (*Kako je počeo rat na mom otoku*), Vinko Brešan, 1996: 116, 118, 119, 120, 122, 126, 196-197, 200
Huddersfield (*Hadersfild*), Ivan Živković, 2007: 11

I

I Can Imagine It Very Well, Danijel Šuljić, 2003: 87
I Don't Remember His Name, Kristina Leko, 2001: 71
I Love You (*Volim te*), Dalibor Matanić, 2006: 152-154
I Love You Too, Joško Marušić, 1991: 129
It It Kills Me (*Kud puklo da puklo*), Rajko Grlić, 1974: 100
I Have Nothing Nice to Say to You (*Nemam ti šta reć' lijepo*), Goran Dević, 2006: 69
I Have Two Mothers and Two Fathers (*Imam 2 mame i 2 tate*), Krešo Golik, 1968: 33
I'll Kill You (*Ubil bum te*), Nikola Strašek, 2007: 72
Imported Crows (*Uvozne vrane*), Goran Dević, 2004: 66
In/Dividu, Nicole Hewitt, 1999: 84
In Quest of Šutej (*U potrazi za Šutejem*), Nenad Puhovski, 1981: 139
Inside and Out (*Iznutra i izvana*), Joško Marušić, 1978: 129, 132
In the Gypsy Style (*Ciganjska*), Davor Međurečan, Marko Meštrović, 2004: 87
In the Jaws of Life (*U raljama života*), Rajko Grlić, 1984: 38, 92-93, 100, 101, 108, 189
In the Storm (*U oluji*), Vatroslav Mimica, 1952: 27
In Time, Nicole Hewitt, 2008: 73
It Happened One Night, Frank Capra, 1935: 218
It Rains in My Village (*Biće skoro propast sveta*), Aleksandar Petrović, 1968: 122-123

J

Jasenovac, Gustav Gavrin, Kosta Hlavaty, 1945: 24
Journalist (*Novinar*), Fadil Hadžić, 1979: 36
Jurić: Fortress (*Jurić: Tvrđa*), Zvonimir Jurić, 2000: 70, 145
Just Between Us (*Neka ostane među nama*), Rajko Grlić, 2010: 17, 100, 101, 107, 111, 227

K

Kaya (*Kaja, ubit ću te!*), Vatroslav Mimica, 1967: 31, 83
Key, The (*Ključ*), omnibus, Vanča Kljaković, Krsto Papić, Antun Vrdoljak, 1965: 211
King's New Clothes, The (*Carevo novo ruho*), Ante Babaja, 1961: 32

L

Labor Days (*Praznik rada*), Damir Čučić, Antonio Lauer a.k.a. Tomislav Gotovac, Željko Radivoj, 2001: 73
Lace-Making Designs (*Pogačica, ročelica, mendulica*), Vlatka Vorkapić, 1997: 66
Lapitch, The Little Shoemaker (*Čudnovate zgode šegrta Hlapića*), Milan Blažeković, 1997: 83
Largo, Milan Blažeković, Branko Ilić, 1970: 82
Last Bay of the Pannonian Sea (*Posljednji zaljev Panonskoga mora*), Ljiljana Šišmanović, 2003: 66
Last Genuine Petrović, The (*Posljednji autohtoni Petrović*), Damir Terešak, 2006: 72
La strada, Damir Čučić, 2004: 73
Liberation of Zagreb (*Oslobođenje Zagreba*), Branko Marjanović, 1945: 23
Life in a Fresh Air, A (*Život na svježem zraku*), Danko Volarić, 2001: 69
Life is Sweet, Mike Leigh, 1990: 173
Lika Cinema (*Kino Lika*), Dalibor Matanić, 2008: 56, 152
Lisinski, Oktavijan Miletić, 1944: 23
Living and the Dead, The (*Živi i mrtvi*), Kristijan Milić, 2007: 98, 158-161
Living Truth, The (*Živa istina*), Tomislav Radić, 1972: 36, 137
Loneliness (*Samoća*), Milan Trenc, 2010: 86
Loner, The (*Samac*), Vatroslav Mimica, 1958: 31
Lone Wolf (*Vuk samotnjak*), Obrad Gluščević, 1972: 36-37
Long Dark Night (*Duga mračna noć*), Antun Vrdoljak, 2004: 225
Lora: Testimonies (*Lora: svjedočanstva*), Nenad Puhovski, 2004: 69
Lost Homeland, The (*Izgubljeni zavičaj*), Ante Babaja, 1980: 37
Lost Patrol, The, John Ford, 1934: 161
Ludar, Zdravko Mustać, 1999: 73
Lunch (*Ručak*), Ana Hušman, 2008: 86
Lunch Together (*Zajednički ručak*), Vinko Brešan, 1993: 66, 116, 118

Lj

Ljubica, Krešo Golik, 1978: 37

M

M (*M – Eine Stadt sucht einen Mörder*), Fritz Lang, 1931: 65
Madonna (*Bogorodica*), Neven Hitrec, 1999: 51
Magician's Hat, The (*Čarobnjakov šešir*), Milan Blažeković, 1989: 83
Man Under the Table, The (*Čovjek ispod stola*), Neven Hitrec, 2009: 227
Market, The (*Plac*), Ana Hušman, 2006: 85
Marshal Tito's Spirit (*Maršal*), Vinko Brešan, 1999: 116, 119, 120, 121, 123, 126, 196
Mass in A Minor (*Misa u A molu*), Goce Vaskov, 1996: 83
Master of His Own Body (*Svoga tela gospodar*), Fedor Hanžeković, 1957: 28
Mother's Name: Orange (*Ime majke: Naranča*), Jasna Zastavniković, 1995: 67
Meantime, Mike Leigh, 1981: 173
Melody Haunts My Reverie, The (*Samo jednom se ljubi*), Rajko Grlić, 1981: 38, 100, 101, 106, 107, 108, 111
Melon Route (*Put lubenica*), Branko Schmidt, 2006: 55,

95, 96, 97, 236-240
Meršpajz, Ana Hušman, 2006: 86
Metastases (*Metastaze*), Branko Schmidt, 2009: 97, 98, 177, 236-240
Metropolis (*Metropola*), Dalibor Matanić, Tomislav Rukavina, Stanislav Tomić, 1997: 67
Millions on the Island (*Milioni na otoku*), Branko Bauer, 1955: 27
Miramare, Michaele Müller, 2009: 87
Mirila, Vlado Zrnić, 1997: 66-67, 73
Miss Link, Joško Marušić, 1999: 129
Mother of Asphalt (*Majka asfalta*), Dalibor Matanić, 2010: 152, 154
Mozart 1991, Krasimir Gančev, 1992: 65
Mr. Ikl's Jubilee (*Jubilej gospodina Ikla*), Vatroslav Mimica, 1955: 27
My Blueberry Nights, Wong Kar Wai, 2007: 218
My Darling Clementine, John Ford, 1946: 51
My Neighbor Tanja (*Moja susjeda Tanja*), Petar Krelja, 2006: 73
My Son Don't Turn Round (*Ne okreći se sine*), Branko Bauer, 1956: 27-28
My Uncle's Legacy (*Život sa stricem*), Krsto Papić, 1988: 35
My Way (*Moj put*), Veljko Popović, 2010: 88

N

New Moon, Chris Weitz, 2009: 220
New, New Time, A (*Novo, novo vrijeme*), Rajko Grlić, Igor Mirković, 2001: 60, 61, 69, 74, 75, 101, 110, 146
Ninth Circle, The (*Deveti krug*), France Štiglic, 1960: 22, 30
No One's Son (*Ničiji sin*), Arsen Anton Ostojić, 2008: 192
No Sleep Won't Kill You (*Nespavanje ne ubija*), Marko Meštrović, 2010: 87, 88
Notes on Continuity (*Dnevnik trajanja*), Nicole Hewitt, 1991: 84

O

Occupation in 26 Pictures (*Okupacija u 26 slika*), Lordan Zafranović, 1978: 37-38
Of Cows and People (*O kravama i ljudima*), Zrinka Katarina Matijević-Veličan, 2000: 69
Office Window (*Šalter*), Dražen Žarković, 2001: 66
Officer with a Rose, An (*Oficir s ružom*), Dejan Šorak, 1987: 39
On a Sidetrack (*Na sporednom kolosijeku*), Petar Krelja, 1992: 63
On Site (*Na mjestu događaja*), Antonio Nuić, 1998: 176
One Song a Day Takes Mischief Away (*Tko pjeva zlo ne misli*), Krešo Golik, 1970: 188
Operation Storm (*Oluja nad Krajinom*), Božidar Knežević, 2001: 69, 144
Orbanići Unplugged, Igor Mirković, 1999: 70
Our Lady (*Gospa*), Jakov Sedlar, 1994: 90, 91
Our Stock Market (*Naša burza*), Vinko Brešan, 1988: 118
Over There (*Tamo*), Joško Marušić, 1985: 129

P

Patchwork, Tanja Miličić, 2003: 71
Pavilion 22 (*Paviljon 22*), Nenad Puhovski, 2002: 69, 143
Perpetuo, Joško Marušić, 1978: 129
Pescenopolis (*Peščenopolis*), Zrinka Katarina Matijević-Veličan, 2003: 69-70, 74
Pine Tree in the Mountain, The (*U gori raste zelen bor*), Antun Vrdoljak, 1971: 33
Plastic Jesus (*Plastični Isus*), Lazar Stojanović, 1971: 36
Poetry and the Revolution (*Poezija i revolucija*), Branko Ivanda, 1971/2000: 69, 141, 146
Predator, John McTiernan, 1987: 159, 161
Pretty Village Pretty Flame (*Lepa sela lepo gore*), Srđan Dragojević, 1996: 54
Professor Balthazar (animated series), Zlatko Grgić, 1967-1978: 81, 134
Prometheus from the Island of Viševica (*Prometej s otoka Viševice*), Vatroslav Mimica, 1964: 31
Purgatory (*Purgatorij*), Zdravko Mustać, 2005: 73

R

Radio 101 Independence Day (*Dan nezavisnosti Radija 101*), Vinko Brešan, 2007: 74, 116, 153
Radio Krapina (*Krapina, poslijepodne*), Jelena Rajković, 1997: 64, 67
Rainbow (*Duga*), Joško Marušić, 2009: 86, 129, 133-135
Rat Savior, The / *La Nuit de la Métamorphose* (*Izbavitelj*), Krsto Papić, 1976: 213, 214
Redacted, Brian De Palma, 2007: 126
Red Dust (*Crvena prašina*), Zrinko Ogresta, 1999: 225-231
Report on the Party and the Guests, A (*O slavnosti a hostech*), Jan Nemec, 1966: 156
Residency, Ksenija Turčić, 2002: 71
Return of a Dead Man (*Povratak mrtvog čovjeka*), Petar Orešković, 2006: 74
Rio Bravo, Howard Hawks, 1959: 51
Rio Bravo/Machinist (*Rio Bravar*), Tomislav Mršić, 2002: 66
Rhythm of the Crime, The (*Ritam zločina*), Zoran Tadić, 1981: 13, 39, 176
Rhythm of the Rock Tribe, The (*Ritam rock plemena*), Bernardin Modrić, 2005: 74
Rondo, Zvonimir Berković, 1966: 13, 31
Rudi's Lexicon (*Rudijev leksikon*), series, Nedeljko Dragić, 2009-: 86
Run Lola Run (*Lola rennt*), Tom Tykwer, 1998: 230
Russian Meat (*Rusko meso*), Lukas Nola, 1997: 186

S

Sand City, The (*Peščeni grad*), Boštjan Hladnik, 1962: 30
Satiemania, Zdenko Gašparović, 1978: 79-82
Scene of a Crash, The (*Putovanje na mjesto nesreće*), Zvonimir Berković, 1971: 37
Sea over Split (*More nad Splitom*), Damir Čučić, 1999: 67
Second Floor, Basement (*Drugi kat, podrum*), Ivan Salaj, 1991: 64
Secrets and Lies, Mike Leigh, 1996: 173

Sevdah, Marina Andre Škop, 2009: 75
Sewer (*Kanał*), Andrzej Wayda, 1957: 156
Sex and the City, Michael Patrick King, 2008: 220
Sex, Drink and Bloodshed (*Seks, piće i krvoprolić*e), Antonio Nuić, Boris T. Matić, Zvonimir Jurić, 2004: 176-177, 181, 182
She Who Measures (*Ona koja mjeri*), Veljko Popović, 2008: 85-86
Shop on Main Street, The (*Obchod na korze*), Elmar Klos, 1965: 104
Shrek Forever After, Mike Mitchell, 2010: 220
Sign on Kain, The (*Znak na Kajinu*), Ljiljana Šišmanović, Tihana Kopsa, 2009: 72
Silence (*Tišina*), Borivoj Dovniković, Pajo Štalter, 2009: 86
Silencium, Davor Međurečan, Marko Meštrović; 2006: 87
Single Viable Fetus, Nicole Hewitt, 1995: 84
Sky Below Osijek, The (*Nebo ispod Osijeka*), Zvonimir Jurić, 1995: 67, 70
Skyscraper, The (*Neboder*), Joško Marušić, 1981: 129
Slavica, Vjekoslav Afrić, 1947: 41
Sokol Did Not Love Him (*Sokol ga nije volio*), Branko Schmidt, 1988: 39
Sorry for Kung Fu (*Oprosti za kung fu*), Ognjen Sviličić, 2004: 17, 55, 95, 96, 169-172, 175
Southern Comfort, Walter Hill, 1981: 57
Special Guests (*Posebni gosti*), Goran Dukić, 1993: 64
Special Trains (*Specijalni vlakovi*), Krsto Papić, 1972: 214
Split Watercolor, The (*Splitski akvarel*), Boris Poljak, 2009: 73
Stone Gate (*Kamenita vrata*), Ante Babaja, 1991: 40
Stone Horizons (*Kameni horizonti*), Šime Šimatović, 1953: 27
Story from Croatia (*Priča iz Hrvatske*), Krsto Papić, 1991: 211, 214, 226, 227
Straight A's! (*Sve pet!*), Dana Budisavljević, 2004: 70, 146
Suzana's Smile (*Suzanin osmijeh*), Petar Krelja, 1994: 63

T

Take a Deep Breath (*Diši duboko*), Dragan Marinkovič, 2004: 155
There Once Was (*Bil jedon*), Hrvoje Hribar, 2002: 66
Think Pink (*Terra Roza*), Aldo Tardozzi, 1999: 70
Third Christmas, The (*Treći Božić*), Petar Krelja, 1994: 63
This Nation Will Live (*Živjeće ovaj narod*), Nikola Popović, 1947: 41
Three (*Tri*), Goran Dević, 2008: 72
Three for Happiness (*Za sreću je potrebno troje*), Rajko Grlić, 1985: 100
Three Girls Named Ana (*Tri Ane*), Branko Bauer, 1959: 28
Three Men of Melita Žganjer (*Tri muškarca Melite Žganjer*), Snježana Tribuson, 1998: 93, 188-191
Three Stories About Sleeplessness (*Tri priče o nespavanju*), Tomislav Radić, 2008: 235
Time for, A (*Vrijeme za*), Oja Kodar, 1993: 51, 90-91
Titanic, James Cameron, 1997: 119-120
Tito (TV-series), Antun Vrdoljak, 2010: 62
Together (*Zajedno*), Nenad Puhovski, 2009: 72, 74, 138, 139, 146
Train in the Snow (*Vlak u snijegu*), Mate Relja, 1976: 37
Trainspotting, Danny Boyle, 1996: 230
Train Without a Timetable (*Vlak bez voznog reda*), Veljko Bulajić, 1959: 29
Tranquilizer Gun (*Puška za uspavljivanje*), Hrvoje Hribar, 1997: 220
Troy, Wolfgang Petersen, 2004: 220
True Miracle (*Pravo čudo*), Lukas Nola, 2007: 186
Tup-tup, Nedeljko Dragić, 1972: 78
Two Sunny Days (*Dva sunčana dana*), Ognjen Sviličić, 2010: 17

U

Una storia polesana, Andrej Korovljev, 1999: 69

V

Village Without Women (*Selo bez žena*), Srđan Šarenac, 2009: 75

W

Wait, Wait... (*Čekajte, čekajte...*), Tanja Golić, 2005: 71
Waltz (*Valcer*), Nicole Hewitt, 2004: 86
Washed Out (*Isprani*), Zrinko Ogresta, 1995: 225-228, 231
What is a Man without Moustache (*Što je muškarac bez brkova*), Hrvoje Hribar, 2005: 17, 57, 92, 220-224
What Iva Recorded 21th October 2003 (*Što je Iva snimila 21. listopada 2003*), Tomislav Radić, 2005: 17, 232-235
When Miki Says He's Scared (*Kad Miki kaže da se boji*), Ines Pletikos, 2005: 74
When the Dead Start Singing (*Kad mrtvi zapjevaju*), Krsto Papić, 1998: 211-215
When You Hear the Bells (*Kad čuješ zvona*), Antun Vrdoljak, 1969: 33
Whose is This Song? (*Чия с тази песен?*), Adela Peeva, 2003: 17
Will Not End Here (*Nije kraj*), Vinko Brešan, 2008: 117, 119, 121, 122, 126, 196, 199, 200
Wish I were a Shark (*Da mi je biti morski pas*), Ognjen Sviličić, 1999: 169, 171, 175
Wish You Could Hear (*Noć za slušanje*), Jelena Rajković, 1995: 64
Witnesses (*Svjedoci*), Vinko Brešan, 2003: 15, 21, 95, 96, 117, 119, 120, 122, 123, 125, 126, 127, 183, 196-201, 244
Wolf (*Vuk*), Nikola Ivanda, 2000: 72
A Wonderful Night in Split (*Ta divna splitska noć*), Arsen Anton Ostojić, 2004: 192-195
World Heritage Site (*Spomenik nulte kategorije*), Zvonimir Rumboldt, 1999: 72
Wounds (*Rane*), Srđan Dragojević, 1998: 18
Wristcutters: A Love Story, Goran Dukić, 2006: 216-219

Y

Year-Long Road, The (*Cesta duga godinu dana*), Giuseppe de Santis, 1958: 21, 29
Years of Rust, The, Andrej Korovljev, 2000: 69

Z

Zagorje Region, Castles, The, Jelena Rajković, 1997: 67
Zlatorog, Daniel Šuljić, 2000: 87
Zoran Šipoš and His Jasna (*Zoran Šipoš i njegova Jasna*), Petar Krelja, 1992: 63

Ž

Željko Jerman – My Month (*Željko Jerman – moj mjesec*), Ivan Faktor, 2005: 71

Index

2D animation: 87, 135
3D computer animation: 83, 86, 87, 135,
4 Film (production): 72

A

Academy Award: 15, 22, 30. 34, 78, 126, 236
Academy of Dramatic Art: 8, 11, 40, 64, 68, 72, 102, 116, 118, 136, 148, 170, 176, 241, 242, 244, 245
Ajanović, Midhat: 78, 80, 82, 88
Altman, Robert: 229
Andersen, Hans Christian: 32
Andree Škop, Marina: 75
Animafest – Zagreb International Festival of Animated Film: 15, 76, 133, 242
Animation: 15, 31, 50. 73, 76-88, 129-130, 131, 133, 135; abstract a.. 84; cel-animation: 78, 83; clay a.: 86; computer a.: 82, 84; cut-out a.: 84; drawn a.: 79, 84, 85, 86; full a.: 79-81, 82; limited a.: 79-82, 83, 132, 133; model a.: 85; puppet a.: 87; stop-motion a.: 84, 85
Antifilm: 140
Anthias, Floya: 89
Antonioni, Michelangelo: 30, 104
Art-film: 21, 81, 135, 183, 185, 186
Art Film (production): 62
auteur cinema: 30-32, 33
auteurism: 32, 33, 35
Avala Film: 41

B

Babaja, Ante: 13, 32, 37, 40, 71, 73, 74, 105, 251
Babić, Nikola: 36
Bakliža, Darko: 87, 88
Bamford, Graham: 68, 143

Ban, Saša: 72
Bauer, Branko: 27, 28, 35, 112, 250
Beban, Breda: 73
Belan, Branko: 105
Benažić, Berislav: 63
Bendazzi, Giannalberto: 81, 88
Bergman, Ingmar: 30
Berković, Zvonimir: 13, 29, 31, 37, 40, 63
Berlinale (Berlin Film Festival): 52, 55, 95
Bešlagić, Enis: 175, 178, 179, 182
Bezinović, Igor: 68, 72, 146
Biagoli, Ravetto: 51, 58
Bibb, Leslie: 216, 219
Bigelow, Kathryn: 126
Bitorajac, Rene: 187, 238, 240
black wave: 12, 28, 34, 35, 58, 107, 120
Blažeković, Milan: 82-84
Bogojević Narath, Simon: 86, 240
Bondarchuk, Sergei: 34
Botica Brešan, Sandra: 15, 117, 121, 201
Bourek, Zlatko: 77
Bović, Alen: 177
Boyle, Danny: 230
Bračun, Jelena: 73
Brecht, Bertolt: 204
Bresson, Robert: 104
Brešan, Ivo: 35, 212
Brešan, Vinko: 8, 15, 16, 19, 21, 42, 52, 53, 54, 60, 65, 66, 74, 92, 94, 95, 96, 116-136, 176, 183, 196-201, 212, 220, 244, 247
Brlić-Mažuranić, Ivana: 83
Broz, Josip - Tito: 25, 49, 53, 62, 116, 119, 163
Brynner, Yul: 34, 158
Buden, Boris: 52, 58
Budisavljević, Dana: 68, 70, 71, 72, 145, 146
Buić, Jagoda: 32

Bulajić, Veljko: 41, 158, 211, 225
Buñuel, Luis: 104
Burton, Richard: 34
Butijer, Nikša: 206, 210
Butorac, Tomislav: 29

C

Cahiers du cinéma: 30
Cameron, James: 220
Cannes Film Festival: 35, 50, 87, 101, 106, 107, 114, 125
Capra, Frank: 218
Carpenter, John: 159
Censorship: 26, 36, 42, 45, 59, 94, 96, 106, 141, 152
Center for Dramatic Art (Centar za dramsku umjetnost – CDU): 142
chick flick: 92
cinema of normalization: 55, 208, 210
cinema of self-victimization: 51, 52
cinéma vérité: 73
comedy: 11, 26, 27, 33, 53, 92, 94, 96, 97, 101, 116, 119, 120, 121, 122, 123, 126, 165, 167, 169, 190, 196, 197, 199, 200, 211, 212, 213, 214, 216, 217, 218, 220-222; comedy of absurd: 123
commedia dell'arte: 121
Coppola, Francis Ford: 127
Croatia Film (production): 82, 83
Croatian Audiovisual Centre (Hrvatski audiovizualni centar – HAVC): 8, 13, 48, 60, 87, 147
Croatian Cinema Chronicle, The (Hrvatski filmski ljetopis): 67, 88, 98, 242, 243, 244, 249
Croatian Cinemateque (Hrvatska kinoteka): 8, 104, 142
Croatian Democratic Union

(Hrvatska demokratska zajednica – HDZ): 49, 94
Croatian Film Association (Hrvatski filmski savez): 8, 60, 61, 62, 73, 140, 147, 224
Croatian Homeland War (Domovinski rat): 46, 57, 58, 64, 69, 95, 116, 117, 142, 156, 196, 228, 230
Croatian Radiotelevision (Hrvatska radio televizija): 13, 43, 45, 46, 47, 126, 161, 168, 175, 182, 187, 191, 195, 201, 205, 210, 215, 224, 230, 231, 242, 244, 235, 240
Croatian Spring (Hrvatsko proljeće): 36, 37-38, 140, 143, 226, 227
Cronenberg, David: 55
Cvitešić, Zrinka: 21, 221, 224

Č

Čengić, Bata: 159
Černić, Čejen: 142
Čučić, Damir: 67, 73

D

Days of Croatian Film (Dani hrvatskog filma): 42, 61, 64, 68, 71, 142, 143, 144, 145, 148
Delić, Stipe: 34, 158
De Palma, Brian: 126
De Santis, Giuseppe: 21, 29
detective film: 39, 98, 200
Dević, Goran: 14, 16, 21, 57, 58, 66, 68, 69, 72, 97, 98, 114, 183, 206-210
Dijak, Franjo: 58, 178, 182, 207, 210, 238, 240
direct cinema: 145
Dirnbach, Zora: 30
Disney, Walt: 77
Disney-style: 82, 83, 132
documentary: 14, 15, 23, 32, 36, 56, 59-88, 108, 109, 110, 111, 118, 136-150, 164, 173, 174, 196, 211, 213, 232, 234, 242, 244, 245; ethnographic d.: 66, 67; essayistic d.: ; observational d.: 145; mockumentary: 67; para-documentary: 73, 74; political d.: 61-64, 68-69, 72; personal d.: 67, 68-71; rockumentary: 74; self-documentary: 71; and activism: 71-72; and female directors: 71
Dovniković, Borivoj: 76, 77, 80, 86
Dragić, Nedeljko: 50, 76, 77, 78, 79, 82, 86, 87, 133

Dragojević, Srđan: 16, 18, 54
Duga film: 77
Dukić, Goran: 16, 64, 216-219
Dulić, Vlatko: 21, 196
Duroviceva, Natasa: 50
Dvornik, Boris: 34, 194, 195

E

Eastern a.k.a Partisan Film: 34
Eco, Umberto: 80
Enloe, Cynthia: 90, 98, 248
Escher, M.C.: 192

F

Factum Documentary Film Project: 15, 61, 68-72, 74, 110, 111, 136, 140, 141, 142, 143, 144, 148
Fade-In (production): 72
Fairchild, Morgan: 91
Faktor, Ivan: 65, 71, 73
FAMU (Filmová a televizní fakulta akademie múzických umění v Praze / Academy of Performing Arts in Prague): 100, 103
fantastic mystery: 39
Fantasy Forest (production): 82
Fellini, Federico: 30, 104, 127
Feral Tribune: 52, 176
Film Authors' Studio (Filmski autorski studio – FAS): 140
Film News (Filmske novosti): 23
Film noir: 27, 153
Filmoteka 16: 62-63
Ford, Aleksander: 227
Ford, John: 161
Frait, Božidarka: 231
French New Wave: 30, 39, 79, 104, 225
Fugit, Patrick: 216, 219

G

Galić, Eduard: 63
Gašparović, Zdenko: 77, 78, 79, 81, 82
gender construction: 89-99, 71, 19, 220, 241
Genre Film Festival (GEFF): 30, 103
German expressionism: 87
Georgiev, Atanas: 75
Gerasimov, Aleksandar: 77
Germani Grmek, Sergio: 58
Gilić, Nikica: 8, 158, 241, 248
Girotti, Massimo: 29
Glavaš, Branimir: 207
Globočnik, Martina: 73
Gluščević, Obrad: 36

Godard, Jean-Luc: 104, 243
Godfrey, Bob: 78
Golić, Tanja: 71
Golik, Krešo: 26, 27, 33, 37, 105, 188, 190
Gomez-Delgado, Abraham: 87
Gotovac, Tomislav a.k.a. Antonio G. Lauer: 71, 73
Goulding, Daniel J.: 12, 248
Gral film (production): 68
Greenaway, Peter: 17
Gregurević, Ivo: 187, 189, 191, 206, 210, 214, 215, 224, 226, 230, 231, 233, 235, 240
Grgić, Zlatko: 76-78, 81
Grlić, Rajko: 8, 13, 15-19, 21, 38, 39, 57, 69, 92, 93, 97, 100-113, 146, 162-168, 189, 227, 248
Guilfoyle, Paul: 91

H

Hadžić, Fadil: 36, 77, 156, 227
Hadžihafizbegović, Emir: 55, 168, 173, 175, 177, 200, 240
Hanžeković, Fedor: 26, 28
Hayden, Robert M.: 90
Heidler, Kruno: 137
Herceg, Ivan: 199, 201, 231
Herzog, Werner: 219
Hewitt, Nicole: 73, 84-87
high-key technique: 32
Hitchcockians: 39
Hitrec, Hrvoje: 227
Hitrec, Neven: 51, 64, 127
Hladnik, Boštjan: 30, 113
Hłasko, Marek: 227, 231
Horton, Andrew James: 12, 58, 248, 249
Hribar, Hrvoje: 17, 21, 57, 66, 92, 220, 221-224
Hulahop, Film & Art Production: 72
Hušman, Ana: 71, 73, 84, 85, 86, 88, 248
Hutz, Eugene: 218

I

ideology: 12, 27, 31, 34, 35, 40, 46, 51, 52, 54, 78, 89, 92, 95, 98, 156, 160, 161, 220, 224, 225, 249, 252
ideological rhetoric: 33
ideological criticism: 35
Imaginary Academy (Imaginarna akademija, Grožnjan): 68, 110, 112
Independent State of Croatia (Nezavisna Država Hrvatska): 22, 39, 234
Ilić, Branko: 82

Interfilm (production): 127, 187, 201
International Short Film Festival Oberhausen (Internationale Kurzfilmtage Oberhausen): 50, 61, 118
Iordanova, Dina: 12, 50, 155, 208, 248, 251
Ištvančić, Branko: 66, 67
Ivančević, Radovan: 139
Ivanda, Branko: 39, 69, 142
Ivanda, Nikola: 72

J

Jadran film: 17, 25, 30, 41, 45, 46, 62, 77
Jameson, Fredric: 55, 58, 248
Janjić, Nataša: 176, 179, 182
Jergović, Miljenko: 57, 97, 202, 203, 204, 205, 243, 248
Joschko, Lucie: 84
Juka, Ivona: 71-72
Junaković, Svjetlan: 88
Jurić, Zvonimir: 14, 16, 21, 57, 58, 67, 68, 70, 72, 97, 98, 114, 144, 145, 176, 182, 183, 206, 207, 210
Jutriša, Vladimir: 76, 77, 78, 79
Juvančić, Joško: 137

K

Kafka, Franz: 129
Kapović, Albert: 48
Karakaš, Damir: 97
Karanović, Mirjana: 96, 198
Karanović, Srđan: 100
Kečkeš, Hrvoje: 179, 182
Kenges Studio: 86
Kerekeš, Ljubomir: 52, 191, 196, 201
Kerempuh, satirical magazine: 77, 87, 212
Khrushchev, Nikita: 30, 241
Kieślowski, Krzysztof: 227, 229
Kinoklub Zagreb (Cine-club Zagreb): 140
Kipke, Željko: 73
Klee, Paul: 78
Klos, Elmar: 104, 257
Kljaković, Vanča: 175, 211
Knežević, Božidar: 69, 144, 175, 215
Knopfler, Mark: 57
Kodar, Oja: 51, 90, 91
Kolar, Slavko: 28, 32
Kolbas, Silvestar: 70, 74
Kopsa, Tihana: 72
Korovljev, Andrej: 68, 69, 145
Koscina, Sylva: 34
Kostelac, Nikola: 77, 157
Kraljević, Nataša: 70

Krasztev, Peter: 54, 58, 249
Krelja, Petar: 11, 63, 64, 73, 249
Krvavac, Hajrudin: 158
Kristl, Vlado: 77, 80
Krleža, Miroslav: 39, 87
Krüger, Hardy: 34
Kultur-film: 63
Kurelec, Tomislav: 14, 41, 242, 249
Kusturica, Emir: 16, 54, 55, 100, 208

L

Lang, Fritz: 65
Leigh, Mike: 127, 172, 173
Leko, Kristina: 71, 73
Lentić, Branko: 63
Levi, Pavle: 12, 196, 249
Lisinski, Vatroslav: 23
London Film Festival: 82
Lonza, Tonko: 180, 182
Lorenci, Daria: 170, 171, 175, 231, 240
Lourie, Jessica: 87
Lovrak, Mato: 37
low-budget film: 39
Lučev, Leon: 21, 182, 187, 201, 202, 205, 221, 224, 231, 240
Lumière, Louis: 225
Lynch, David: 186

Lj

Ljubičić, Boris: 214

M

Maar Ton: 77
Mabić, Hrvoje: 72
Makavejev, Dušan: 35, 107, 113, 243
Malkovich, John: 49
Maloča, Ivan: 127, 201, 231
Mančevski, Milčo: 16, 54, 253
Marinković, Dragan: 155
Marinković, Ranko: 39
Marjanović, Branko: 23, 26
Marks, Aleksandar: 76-79, 90, 127, 204, 205
Marušić, Joško: 8, 15, 78, 79, 82, 86, 129, 133, 247
Matanić, Dalibor: 16, 21, 55, 56, 66, 68, 70, 94, 97, 98, 110, 145, 152, 153, 155, 156, 157, 176, 248, 250, 251
Matavulj, Simo: 26
Matić, Boris T.: 112, 117, 176, 182
Matijević-Veličan, Zrinka Katarina: 68, 69, 70, 71, 74, 145
Matišić, Mate: 119, 121, 157, 201, 211, 212, 215
Matoš, Antun Gustav: 197

McCrea, Christian: 80
McTiernan, John: 159, 161
Međurečan, Davor: 86-87
Georges Méliès: 225
melodrama: 37, 38, 39, 119
Meštrović, Marko: 86-87
Midžić, Enes: 139
Mikić, Krešimir: 57, 157, 182, 201, 206, 210, 231, 236, 240
Mikuljan, Miroslav: 63, 73
Miladinov, Angel: 109, 141
Miletić, Oktavijan: 23, 32
Miličić, Tanja: 71
Milić, Kristiijan: 14, 16, 57, 97, 98, 114, 158, 159, 160, 161, 183
Milošević, Slobodan: 109, 164, 167, 213
Milva Film & Video: 61, 73
Mimica, Vatroslav: 27, 31, 77, 159, 183
Mirković, Igor: 60, 70, 71, 74, 101, 109, 110, 145, 146
Mirošničenko, Silvio: 68, 70, 145
Mitrović, Žika: 51, 158, 182
Mlakić, Josip: 57, 97, 161
mockumentary: 67
modernism: 183, 197, 213, 241, 243
modernist film: 13, 31, 33, 38, 71, 77, 95, 159, 183, 213, 243
mosaic-like dramaturgy: 29, 55, 72, 169, 183
Modrić, Bernardin: 74
Mondschein brothers (Zvonko, Ivo and Vlado): 77
Moore, Michael: 60, 146, 149
Morgan, Michael: 84, 91
Moss, Kevin: 155, 157
Motovun Film Festival: 9, 18, 21, 61, 100, 102, 109, 110, 112, 113, 244
Mršić, Tomislav: 66, 240
Mudronja, Edi: 63
Munitić, Ranko: 78, 88, 249
musical comedy: 33
Mustać, Zdravko: 73
Müller, Michaele: 87

N

nation: 13, 47, 51, 64, 90, 94, 95, 155, 156, 164, 227, 230;
construction of nation: 11, 40, 64, 66, 90, 155, 218, 225, 226, 227, 230, 234
national culture: 22, 59, 218, 225
national cinema: 8, 12, 13, 17, 18, 28, 44-45, 47, 50, 58, 87, 89, 97, 152, 225
nationalism: 33-34, 40, 49, 51, 52, 53, 54, 58, 59, 69, 90, 94, 95, 108, 109, 155, 162, 197,

212, 220, 222, 238
Navojec, Bojan: 177, 178, 182, 187, 201, 224, 231
Navojec, Goran: 189, 191
Neorealism: 225
Nemec, Jen: 156
Nero, Franco: 34
Neugebauer, Norbert: 77
Neugebauer, Walter: 77
Nikolić, Suzana: 189, 191
Nola, Lukas: 11, 14, 16, 64, 183-187, 196
Nolan, Christopher: 223
Novak, Slobodan: 37
Nuić, Antonio: 14, 16, 17, 21, 176-182

O

Ogresta, Zrinko: 16, 17, 21, 55, 225-231
Orešković, Petar: 74
Ostalgie: 53
Ostojić, Arsen Anton: 14, 16, 192, 195

P

Pampanini, Silvana: 29
Papić, Krsto: 16, 35, 118, 127, 170, 211, 215, 225-228
Paraminski, Leona: 178, 182, 187
Participant Media: 146
Partisan film: 25, 33, 34, 39, 51
Paskaljević, Goran: 100
Pavičić, Jurica: 8, 14, 16, 17, 49, 51, 55, 58, 98, 119, 123, 198, 201, 208, 210, 244, 248, 249
Pavličić, Pavao: 142
Pavlović, Živojin: 35, 113, 127
Peeva, Adela: 17
Petanjek, Bogoslav: 77
Peterlić, Ante: 8, 13, 250
Petrović, Aleksandar: 30, 122, 123, 127
Petzke, Ingo: 76, 88, 250
Pinter, Tomislav: 31, 32
Pivčević, Mirko: 161, 176, 182, 187, 195
Pletikos, Ines: 74
Podgorelec, Saša: 68
poetic realism: 39, 225
Polanski, Roman: 127
Polimac, Nenad: 155, 157, 250
political discourse: 53, 124
Poljak, Renata: 71, 73
Popović, Nikola: 41, 85, 86, 88
Popović, Veljko: 41, 85, 86, 88
Prague spring: 109
Prague school: 37, 38, 39, 162
Prodan, Maša Mati: 232, 235
propaganda: 23, 24, 42, 46, 47, 53, 54, 59, 62, 66, 69, 90, 91, 111, 113, 152, 166, 169, 196
Puhovski, Nenad: 8, 15, 68, 69, 72, 110, 111, 136-150

Q

queer film: 155
Quien, Kruno: 141

R

Radaković, Borislav: 177
Radić, Tomislav: 16, 17, 21, 36, 137, 138, 232, 233, 234, 235
Radolfi, Davor: 190, 191
Radoš, Filip: 171, 175
Rajković, Jelena: 64, 67, 71
Ramis, Harold: 216
Ranković, Aleksandar: 32, 196
red wave: 34
Relja, Mate: 37
Restart production: 147
Robić Škarica, Vera: 8
rockumentary: 74
Rodica, Maja: 139
Roglić, Roko: 179, 182
Roklicer, Robert: 160, 161
romantic comedy: 122, 190, 216, 217, 218
Rossi Drago, Eleonora: 29
Rukavina, Tomislav: 66, 67, 68, 70
Rumboldt, Zvonimir: 72
Rushaidat, Rakan: 21, 178, 179, 182, 208, 210, 238, 240
Rušinović, Goran: 14, 16, 21, 57, 97, 98, 114, 202, 203, 205, 252

S

Sadoul, Georges: 76
Salaj, Ivan: 64, 196
Satie, Eric: 81
Satire: 52, 77, 78, 83, 197, 212, 216
Savin, Igor: 139
Schmidt, Branko: 16, 21, 39, 55, 65, 95, 97, 98, 173, 175, 177, 236-240, 253, 255, 256
Scorsese, Martin: 229
Scott, Ridley: 206
Sedlar, Jakov: 90-91
self-censorship: 36, 141
Self-managed Community Services (Samoupravna interesna zajednica – SIZ): 45, 46
Senečić, Željko: 52
Shakespeare, William: 35
Sheen, Martin: 91
Sikavica, Miroslav: 146
Simić, Mima: 15, 89, 155, 156, 157, 220, 245, 251
slapstick: 27
slow cinema: 170, 172, 174
soap opera: 115, 188
social-essay films: 227
socialist aestheticism: 31
socialist realism: 25, 31
socialist self-management: 46
Soros Open Society Institute: 68, 110, 142, 146, 147
Sossamon, Shannyn: 216, 219
Soviet avant-garde: 225
Stalin, Joseph Vissarionovich: 30
state-building cinema: 51
State Film Company (Državno filmsko preduzeće): 24, 41, 103
stereotypes: 90; stereotypes about class: 222; a. ethnicity: 90; a. gender: 90, 93, 189, 222; a. ideology: 222; a. nation: 234; a. race: 222; a. sexual orientation: 222
Stephenson, Ralph: 80
Stojanović, Lazar: 36, 107
Stoppard, Tom: 141
Strašek, Nikola: 68, 72, 145
Studio Pangolin: 85, 86
Studio ZNG: 62
Sudović, Zlatko: 63, 88, 251
Sun Mei: 236
Sviličić, Ognjen: 10, 16, 17, 21, 55, 95-98, 169-175, 235, 240
Svrtan, Boris: 231, 234, 235

Š

Šarenac, Srđan: 75
Šargin, Nada: 199, 201
Šarić, Lana: 70, 146
Šešić, Rada: 73
Šibl, Ivan: 33
Šijan, Slobodan: 122, 123, 127
Šimatović, Šime: 27, 63
Šimunović, Dinko: 129
Šišmanović, Ljiljana: 66, 71, 73
Škaričić, Marija: 21, 175, 187, 195, 224
Škorić, Irena: 71
Škrabalo, Ivo: 8, 11, 12, 14, 21, 49, 51, 58, 60, 158, 245, 251
Škrinjarić, Sunčana: 82
Šorak, Dejan: 21, 39
Šošić, Anja: 10, 16, 56, 58, 251
Šovagović, Anja: 232, 233, 235, 240
Šovagović, Filip: 160, 161, 187, 188, 191, 230, 231
Štalter, Pavao: 78, 81, 86
Štiglic, Francé: 22, 30
Štimac, Slavko: 202, 205

Šuljić, Daniel: 87
Šutej, Miroslav: 139

T

Tadej, Vladimir: 63
Tadić, Zoran: 13, 39, 73, 176, 227, 231, 251
Tagatz, Sergej: 77
Tanhofer, Nikola: 13, 29, 51
Tardozzi, Aldo: 70, 145
Terešak, Damir: 72, 145
Tarkovsky, Andrei: 186, 242, 246
thriller: 27, 57, 122, 124, 154, 159, 196, 198, 200, 205, 244
Tomić, Ante: 57, 97, 168, 220, 224, 248
Tomić, Stanislav: 66, 67, 68, 70
Tomić, Živorad: 39
tragedy: 29, 67, 96, 97, 118, 122, 166, 168, 180, 200, 205, 212, 221, 222, 224, 228, 229
transgression: 192, 193, 194, 227, 250
Trbuljak, Goran: 86
Trenc, Milan: 82, 86, 87
Tribuson, Goran: 229, 231
Tribuson, Snježana: 188-191
Trifunović, Sergej: 167, 168, 182
Truffaut, François: 30
Tuđman, Franjo: 10, 33, 46, 49, 51, 52, 54, 59, 60, 61, 69, 91, 93, 94, 109, 119, 120, 145, 146, 152, 196, 226
Tuđman, Stjepan: 52
Turčić, Ksenija: 71, 73
Turković, Hrvoje: 8, 249, 251
Turner, Graeme: 225, 226, 251
Tutić, Zrinko: 215
Tykwer, Tom: 230

U

Ugrešić, Dubravka: 38, 92, 101, 189
Ugrina, Robert: 187, 231, 238, 240
Ustasha regime: 22, 23, 24, 26, 37, 38, 39, 234

V

Van Gogh, Theo: 144
Vejnović, Sanja: 189, 191
Vejzović, Enes: 160, 161
Vidović, Ivica: 197, 201, 214, 215, 157
Volarić, Danko: 68, 69
Vorkapić, Vlatka: 66, 71
Vrdoljak, Antun: 33, 39, 49, 62, 113, 159, 211, 215, 225, 240
Vujić, Antun: 59
Vukotić, Dušan: 76, 77, 78, 80, 81, 86, 88, 252
Vušović, Predrag: 187, 199, 201, 240

W

Waits, Tom: 217, 218, 219
Wajda, Andrzej: 156, 227
war drama: 21, 39, 196
Webber, Lloyd: 142
Weiss, Maja: 155
Welles, Orson: 158, 34, 51
Wells, Paul: 83, 252, 88
Wenders, Wim: 218
Western: 29, 51, 55, 158
Weyermann, Diane: 146
Whigha, Shea: 216, 219
Wong Kar Wai: 218, 246
working communities (radne zajednice): 45

Y

York, Michael: 91
Yugoslav cinema: 12, 21, 24, 28, 31, 34, 50, 54, 55, 58, 76, 208, 210, 249
Yuval Davis, Nira: 89

Z

Zafranović, Lordan: 37, 38, 39, 73, 103, 168, 186
ZagrebDox: 15, 61, 110, 111, 136, 138, 148, 150
Zagreb School of Animated Films (Zagrebačka škola crtanog filma): 15, 31, 61, 76-82, 86, 87, 88, 116, 129, 131, 132, 133, 134, 252
Zaninović, Ante: 76
Zanussi, Krzysztof: 227
Zastavniković, Jasna: 67, 72
Zhdanov, Andrei Alexandrovich: 25
Zrnić, Vlado: 67, 73, 74
Zuber, Robert: 71

Ž

Žaja, Tomislav: 68
Žanić, Vlasta: 73
Žarković, Dražen: 66
Žbanić, Jasmila: 110
Žilnik, Želimir: 35
Živković, Ivan: 11
Živojinović, Bata: 34
Žižek, Slavoj: 16, 54, 58
Žižić, Bogdan: 36, 63, 227
Žmegač, Davor: 227